Child Maltreatment and Paternal Deprivation

Other Books by Henry B. Biller

Father, Child and Sex Role: Paternal Determinants of Personality Development (Lexington Books, 1971)

Paternal Deprivation: Family, School, Sexuality and Society (Lexington Books, 1974)

Father Power, with Dennis L. Meredith (McKay, 1974; Doubleday, paperback edition, 1975)

The Other Helpers: Paraprofessionals and Nonprofessionals in Mental Health, with Michael Gershon (Lexington Books, 1977)

La Deprivazione Paterna (Italian edition of *Paternal Deprivation*, Il Pensiero Scientifico, 1978)

Parental Death and Psychological Development, with Ellen B. Berlinsky (Lexington Books, 1982)

Child Maltreatment and Paternal Deprivation

A Manifesto for Research, Prevention, and Treatment

Henry B. Biller
Richard S. Solomon
University of Rhode Island

Lexington Books
D.C. Heath and Company/Lexington, Massachusetts/Toronto

Library of Congress Cataloging-in-Publication Data

Biller, Henry B.
    Child maltreatment and paternal deprivation.

    Bibliography: p.
    Includes indexes.
    1. Child abuse—United States. 2. Paternal deprivation. I. Solomon, Richard S. II. Title.
HV741.B49   1986   362.7«044   85-45979
ISBN 0-669-12677-2 (alk. paper)

Published simultaneously in Canada
Printed in the United States of America
Casebound International Standard Book Number: 0-669-12677-2
Library of Congress Catalog Card Number: 85-45979

The paper used in this publication meets the minimum requirements of American National Standard for Information Sciences—Permanence of Paper for Printed Library Materials, ANSI Z39.48-1984.

The last numbers on the right below indicate the number and date of printing.

10 9 8 7 6 5 4 3 2 1

95 94 93 92 91 90 89 88 87 86

*To Maggie & Karen
& The Bens Two*

Contents

Preface

The initial impetus for this book came in the spring of 1980 when we were discussing joint research ventures. I emphasized that there did not seem to be a comprehensive overview of the child maltreatment literature and that was where we should direct our primary commitment. Between 1980 and 1982 we had the opportunity to work together on child and family therapy cases, many of which involved maltreatment issues, at the Northern Rhode Island Community Mental Health Center, as well as to collaborate on research at the University of Rhode Island. During this time, we developed much of our analysis of conceptual and theoretical issues relating to child maltreatment.

Our interest in parenting and child maltreatment issues, however, began long before we began to write this book. My first professional confrontation with abused children dates back to the mid-1960s, when I was a clinical psychology intern at Emma Pendleton Bradley Hospital. I was quite skeptical about the prevailing attitude of "maternal determinism" so rampant at that time among those working in clinical settings with children. I was struck with the relative lack of attention given to paternal inadequacy in the development of various forms of child and family psychopathology.

A key experience for my coauthor, Richard Solomon, was the opportunity to consult with a local Parents Anonymous group in 1978. He also was uncomfortable with oversimplified "psychiatric deficit" explanations of child abuse and was greatly stimulated by his experiences with mothers who were trying to cope with child-rearing stress, often without partner support. We both were developing a greater awareness of the need to conceptualize child maltreatment from a multidimensional perspective, including various forms of inadequate parenting, not just focusing on extreme types of neglect and physical and sexual abuse.

In the fall of 1984, while I was on sabbatical, the complex interconnections between child maltreatment and paternal deprivation became increasingly apparent to me and we decided to expand the scope of our original project. We very much appreciate the stimulation of our colleagues at the University of Rhode Island and especially wish to thank Allan Berman, Marge Bumpus, Paul Florin, Richard Gelles, Albert Lott, Peter Merenda, Joe Rossi, Wayne Velicer, and Bill Vosburgh for their encouragement during various phases of our work. My wife, Margery Salter, a clinical psychologist working with children and families, and my sons—Jonathan, Kenneth, Cameron, Michael, and Benjamin—were very supportive during the writing of this book. Dianne Sipe provided valuable assistance, kindness, and patience in coordinating the typing of the manuscript. The publication of this book was greatly facilitated by the consistent and continuing interest of Margaret Zusky, editor, and the careful shepherding of the book through production by Susan Cummings, production editor, of Lexington Books.

H.B.B.

1
Inadequate Fathering and Socialization

Over the past decade, an increasing amount of attention has been paid to the widespread existence of child maltreatment, especially serious physical and sexual abuse. Clinicians, researchers, and the media decry the cost and suffering related to the maltreatment of children by parents and other adults. Relatively little concern, however, has been directed toward sex differences in parenting that may be related to child maltreatment; most discussions address the maternal role and inadequate mothering. Although the research on parental roles has not been focused on child maltreatment, there has also been a dramatic explosion in data relating quality of fathering to individual differences in child and adult development. Paternal deprivation (including various forms of father absence, nonparticipation, neglect, and rejection) has been linked with a wide variety of psychological difficulties in both sons and daughters (Biller, 1971a, 1974c, 1982a).

Basic Concepts

Both maltreatment *and* paternal deprivation pose serious threats to the welfare of our children, families, and society. The central thesis of this book is the existence of a complex and multilevel interconnection between paternal deprivation and child maltreatment. Certainly, factors other than paternal deprivation are involved with the occurrence of child maltreatment. Nevertheless, paternal deprivation contributes both directly and indirectly to most incidents of child maltreatment. We are considering child maltreatment to include not only severe cases of physical abuse and neglect, but also various types of insufficient, inappropriate, and inadequate parenting.

Child Maltreatment

Most researchers and clinicians employ the term *child abuse* to refer only to inappropriate physical actions on the part of a parent or caregiver. Kempe and his colleagues' (1962) pioneering investigation of the so-called battered-child syndrome initially presented physical injury as the primary indicator of abuse. Numerous subsequent researchers have limited their investigations to physical injury inflicted on the child. However, Chibucos (1980) and Steele (1976) discuss physical abuse as part of a continuum of adult-child interactions that also includes neglect and other potential interactions. Physical abuse and neglect can be viewed as components of the maltreatment environment, which may include a variety of other harmful interactions directed toward the child. From our perspective, an analysis of child maltreatment must include a multicontinuum approach, taking into account both inappropriate parental involvement and noninvolvement.

With respect to the behavior of fathers and mothers, child maltreatment pertains to those patterns of parental involvement (verbal abuse, physical abuse, sexual abuse, infantilization, overrestrictiveness, and so on) or uninvolvement (uninterest, nonresponsiveness, neglect, abandonment, and the like) that may potentially undermine adequate affective, social, sexual, intellectual, and/or physical development. Our view of the etiology of child maltreatment and paternal deprivation necessitates the consideration of biological, familial, and sociocultural factors in an interdisciplinary and longitudinal context.

Paternal Deprivation

There is a rigidity to conventional sex-role stereotypes concerning the relative importance of male and female responsibility for socializing children. Males, both in and out of the home, are noticeably uninvolved in the care of infants and young children (Biller, 1971a). In the early socialization process in the family as well as in the beginning stages of our educational process, there is often marked paternal deprivation, which—as we elaborate on in this book—is a major contributing factor to the incidence of child maltreatment. *Paternal deprivation* is a general term referring to various types of inadequacies in the child's experience with his or her father (Biller, 1974c). Most typically, it refers to the actual physical absence of the father, but it can also relate to the father's uninterest in, neglect of, or rejection of the child. The child does not necessarily have to be separated from his father; paternal deprivation can occur when the father is available but a relatively meaningful father-child attachment does not exist. The child of a verbally, physically, or sexually abusive father can also be viewed as paternally deprived because he or she is not being exposed to appropriate fathering behavior (Biller, 1971a, 1974c, 1977b, 1981a).

Child maltreatment and paternal deprivation are highly associated with each other even when the father does not directly abuse the child. In addition to child maltreatment defined in terms of paternal unavailability or neglect, a major thesis of this book is that mothers are much more likely to maltreat their children when they do not have the support of an actively involved partner. Children who are paternally deprived by having an absent father or a neglectful or noninvolved father in a two-parent family are more likely to suffer from maltreatment by their mothers than are those whose fathers and mothers have a cooperative relationship.

In the child-maltreatment literature, fathers have received some consideration as frequent initiators of physical abuse, especially sexual abuse. Relatively little consideration has been given to the incidence of paternal neglect, uninterest, and rejection, which affect many more children than actual physical and sexual maltreatment. Similarly, research concerning the role of fathers has had considerable focus on what happens to fatherless children, but not as much on the impact of insufficient and inadequate fathering in two-parent families. We certainly acknowledge the importance of such topics as paternal absence and physical and sexual abuse, but we emphasize that far more children are negatively influenced by less obvious forms of paternal maltreatment.

In fact, the most common type of child maltreatment appears to be neglect by fathers, and the quality of mothering a child receives is often adversely affected by such paternal deprivation. For example, in two-parent families, mothers seem more likely to abuse (and/or to overprotect, and so on) their children when fathers don't adequately share parenting responsibilities. Many fathers in two-parent families are only involved very narrowly, in disciplining their children, often inappropriately. The high level of maltreatment of children by single mothers can also be viewed, at least in part, as being related to a social system that tends to put too much pressure on the mother's accountability and not enough on the father's participation in child rearing. In addition to those who obviously suffer psychological difficulties, a vast number of children, though not clearly handicapped, do not realize as much of their potential as they could have if they had had a reasonably supportive and interested father (Biller, 1971a, 1974c, 1981a, 1982a; Biller & Meredith, 1974).

An understanding of the occurrence, incidence, and effects of child maltreatment requires an analysis of complex family-system and biocultural factors. In this book, we emphasize that too little consideration has been given to the father's role in child maltreatment. We do not view paternal behavior as an isolated variable, but in the overall context of biological and individual differences, marital and family relationships, and historical and sociocultural factors. Relevant data have come from contributions in many different disciplines—anthropology, child development and family relations, education, history, law, nursing, psychiatry, pediatrics, social work, sociology, and several different areas of psychology.

Preview

Chapter 2 presents an interdisciplinary analysis of the definitional-conceptual dilemma concerning child maltreatment and relevant historical-cultural issues. Child maltreatment has always existed but has only become an important public and professional issue since the 1960s (Starr, 1979). Cultural acceptance of the maltreatment of children, especially by fathers, has its roots in many earlier cultures, with the maltreatment appearing more severe the farther back in history one explores (deMause, 1973). Although it seems that our society has at least accepted the potentially deleterious effects of physical maltreatment on child development, nevertheless the phenomenon occurs all too frequently and stubbornly resists efforts to eradicate it.

From a scientific perspective, the concept of child maltreatment presents numerous problems. First, maltreatment is difficult to define, as reflected in the plethora of definitional models (Bourne, 1979). Some of these models are highly specific and therefore exclusionary, others broader and more inclusive. Also, the diverse array of definitions has hindered the research and development of valid etiological models (Belsky, 1980b). In turn, epidemiological data have had questionable generalizability because they are highly dependent on the definitional framework employed by the particular researcher and the development of reliable reporting systems (Williams, 1980a). In addition, the absence of generally valid theoretical frameworks has interfered with the establishment of intervention programs that can effectively ameliorate child maltreatment (Solomon, 1982).

In chapter 2 the definitional dilemma is discussed from the perspective of cultural and behavior-based definitions. A model of maltreatment is presented that encourages researchers to look at multiple definitional levels (cultural, legal, and behavioral) and to use a continuum perspective in assessing the nature of adult-child interactions. The current penchant for generating an all-encompassing so-called cohort-independent, acultural definitional statement is regarded as detrimental to the establishment of broad and valid definitional frameworks (Chibucos, 1980). The argument about what constitutes abuse has occupied the attention of overextended social service resources at the expense of investigating the total picture of adult-child interactions.

The continuum model of child maltreatment has several advantages. Primarily, it reinforces the need to incorporate cultural and social standards into an interpretive framework (Garbarino, 1980). This model also focuses on the complexity of parent-child interactions and recognizes the multiple levels of direct and indirect forces that impinge on the child. Alvy (1975) has indicated that parent abuse is one of several possible sources of maltreatment. Collective abuse (for example, racial and social class discrimination) and institutional abuse (such as maltreatment in juvenile detention homes) are also important aspects of maltreatment that should be taken into consideration within a definitional framework.

In chapter 3, epidemiological data are reviewed in order to estimate the extent and nature of maltreatment. Data are presented from various sources, most notably from the investigations of Gil (1970) and Straus, Gelles, and Steinmetz (1980). The difficulties involved in generating a valid definitional framework also frustrate epidemiological investigations. Despite these shortcomings, epidemiological surveys have revealed several interesting relationships.

Variables such as socioeconomic status, developmental disabilities, family structure, and sex and age of the abuser and the abused are relevant for an understanding of the incidence of child maltreatment. It is clear from such data that fathers directly and indirectly contribute in a particularly significant way to child maltreatment.

In chapter 4, theoretical models are discussed. Theoretical models of child maltreatment are as diverse as the variety of definitional frameworks (Newberger & Daniel, 1979). The current interest in child maltreatment has evolved from Kempe and his colleagues' (1962) research on the battered child. Consequently, the primary focus has been on the physical and medical aspects of child maltreatment. This has subsequently reinforced psychiatric and medical involvement in research and treatment (Ross, 1980). Theoretical foundations have typically focused on alleged psychiatric disturbances in the abuser. Numerous investigators have attempted to present a psychiatric profile of the maltreating adult, typically assessing the mother rather than the father (e.g., Steele & Pollock, 1968; Melnick & Hurley, 1969).

The *psychiatric* or *deficiency model* has been largely inconsistent and contradictory with respect to empirically derived profiles (Gelles, 1973). Reliable personality profiles of the abusing adult have not been generated, and a typical characterological pattern has not emerged from such data (Garbarino & Stocking, 1980). Consequently, other theoretical models have surfaced in the maltreatment literature. These perspectives have encouraged investigation of the cultural, sociological, and situational aspects of child maltreatment. For example, Pelton's (1978) research concerning socioeconomic factors in child maltreatment suggests a strong association between economic and cultural impoverishment and maltreatment. Warren (1980) has studied the relationship between child maltreatment and neighborhood support systems. Such perspectives address the social and cultural context of maltreatment. As we emphasize in this book, there is a great need for researchers to give more attention to considering paternal factors from a sociocultural as well as from a family perspective. The interactionist model of child maltreatment draws on the theoretical contributions of both the psychiatric and sociological perspectives (Kadushin & Martin, 1981). This model is consistent with efforts to understand the complexities of paternal influence and deprivation (Biller, 1974c; Berlinsky & Biller, 1982).

Sexual maltreatment is the focus of chapter 5. This discussion includes consideration of various types of sexual abuse in the broad context outlined by Schechter and Roberge (1976) and Kempe and Kempe (1984, p. 9): "Sexual abuse is defined as the involvement of dependent, developmentally immature children and adolescents in sexual activities they do not fully comprehend and to which they are unable to give informed consent or that violate the social taboos of family roles." We consider extrafamilial sources of sexual maltreatment also, but the emphasis is on parent-child interactions and family dynamics. There is much attention to the prevalence of direct sexual maltreatment by fathers, stepfathers, and other male family members and how this often interacts with the husband-wife and mother-child relationship. Our discussion includes different forms of incest and physical-sexual abuse but also relates to consideration of inappropriate parenting that may undermine the child's developing acceptance of his or her biological sexuality and sex-role functioning. For example, verbal derogation of the child's body inadequacy and sexuality, or active discouragement of positive sex-role development, as well as direct erotic-genital abuse, are considered to be part of a broad definition of sexual maltreatment. This chapter builds on earlier chapters in terms of dealing with definitional, epidemiological, and theoretical model issues concerning the maltreatment of children.

Chapters 2 through 5 set the stage for chapter 6, which is concerned with elaborating on the processes underlying the varied and complex interconnections between child maltreatment and paternal deprivation. Topics include the greater incidence and impact of paternal deprivation as compared to maternal deprivation, the influence of the father and the father-mother relationship on infant development, sex differences concerning different types of parental maltreatment, the interaction of biological and social factors in sex-role and parental role expectations, and marital and family-system variables. Attention is given to the significance of the father-child bonding process and the adequate preparation of men as fathers, as well as to the risks of paternal deprivation in the prenatal period and in single-parent families. The interaction of economic disadvantage with paternal deprivation and child maltreatment is also an important topic. As in other chapters, there is an emphasis on the interactionist perspective.

Developmental Implications

Chapters 7 through 10 are designed to review much significant data pertaining to the long-term consequences of child maltreatment and paternal deprivation. Most of the child-maltreatment literature is descriptive and typically alludes to behavioral consequences with respect to dramatic and relatively immediate developmental problems. Although short-term difficulties in children are important to describe and understand, we also want to emphasize the long-term developmental implications of various types of child maltreatment. We have been struck by the vast literature linking different patterns of paternal deprivation with later developmental problems in children, adolescents, and adults, as well as indicating that positively involved fathers can play an especially prominent role in fostering healthy long-term psychological adjustment in their offspring (e.g., Biller, 1971a, 1974c, 1982a; Lamb, 1976c, 1981d).

In chapters 7 and 8 there is an analysis of data dealing with the impact of the father on sex-role and personality development in the two-parent family. Findings pertaining to both paternal deprivation and adequate fathering are presented in a multidimensional context. There is emphasis on the quality of the father-mother relationship and other family-system factors. Much attention in chapters 7 and 8 is given to research relating to both the sons' and daughters' sex-role development. Sex-role functioning in young children is viewed as very important because of its initial influence on the child's basic identity and self-concept. A positive father-child relationship helps give the child a healthy start in self-acceptance, whereas paternal maltreatment makes the child especially vulnerable in later life to many different types of sex-role-related developmental difficulties. Although the degree to which an older child, adolescent, or adult conforms to sex-role expectations may tell us little about his or her adequacy and overall personality integration, the preschool child's positive acceptance of his or her sexuality and sex-role expectations is quite likely to be a function of having strong relationships with both parents.

Topics in chapters 7 and 8 include sex differences, self-concept, moral development, marital and sexual relationships, cognitive and social functioning, and family-system antecedents of psychopathology. There is a discussion of the potential consequences of different types of paternal maltreatment including neglect, rejection, emotional insensitivity, and physical and sexual abuse. In these chapters, there is again much attention given to mediating factors such as temperamental and individual differences in children, the quality of relationships with other family and nonfamily members, and sociocultural factors.

Chapters 9 and 10 include a summary of the long-term consequences of paternal deprivation and child maltreatment as they relate to development in the mother-led one-parent family. There is special emphasis on variations of postdivorce paternal involvement and also discussion of data concerning different types of father-loss. Although most children in one-parent families suffer from maltreatment in the form of paternal insufficiency or neglect, some children whose parents are divorced still have very active relationships with their fathers or with father-surrogates. There is a detailing of methodological issues pertaining to the conceptualization of father absence-availability and its highly complex interactions with other important developmental variables.

Chapters 9 and 10 include an analysis of findings relating father absence to masculine development, feminine development, intellectual functioning, social adjustment, moral development, and psychopathology. A very crucial section of chapter 10 contains an integration of data pertaining to the influences of individual differences in mothering on the paternally deprived child's development. Although ways in which paternal deprivation increases the risks of certain types of maternal maltreatment are discussed, there is also an elaboration of evidence of the ways some mothers are able to rear their children successfully in single-parent families.

In chapter 11 there is an attempt to review current intervention programs aimed at decreasing the incidence of child maltreatment. This analysis consists of a general summary of intervention strategies, conceptual models, and empirical evaluations. Treatment programs are analyzed with respect to the underlying change processes involved in particular interventions. Major sections of chapter 11 are devoted to educational, treatment, and prevention efforts concerning the link between child maltreatment and paternal deprivation. Another section of this chapter presents some practical guidelines for positive fathering. The purpose of chapter 12 is to summarize briefly and integrate some of the major points addressed in the book. We believe that the most effective way to alleviate the incidence and cost of child maltreatment is to involve men as well as women directly in various types of parenting preparation and parent training programs aimed at decreasing paternal deprivation in the family and other social institutions. Throughout the book, the goal is to provoke the reader into considering further research and practical issues concerning the complex interactions between child maltreatment and paternal deprivation.

2
Child Maltreatment: The Definitional Dilemma

A major thesis of this book is that the behavior of fathers must be considered in order to understand and prevent child maltreatment. Definitions of child maltreatment must be broad enough to encompass both the direct effects of intentionally destructive parenting and the indirect influences relating to lack of responsible adult involvement, which, as briefly outlined in chapter 1, is often linked to paternal deprivation.

At present there is no standardized definition of child maltreatment that is acceptable to all researchers in the field. Various types of assaults on children—beating, lacerating, burning, binding, suffocating, and poisoning—are clear forms of maltreatment. Harsh verbal insults and neglect of the child's emotional, nutritional, and medical needs also qualify for inclusion in a definition of maltreatment. The interpretation of what adult behaviors are considered abusive depends on the particular culture's interpretation of the role of the child and on various social and economic factors (deMause, 1980). In this chapter there is a brief evaluation of the historical and cultural context of child maltreatment and an assessment of the current state of the definitional dilemma, with particular attention to implications for research and intervention.

Cultural and Historical Background

DeMause (1973) has poignantly described the horrendous circumstances in which children tended to be reared in earlier historical periods. He claims that the farther back one delves in history, the greater the chance of evidence of severe abuse, neglect, abandonment, and sexual molestation. Chase (1976) articulately argues that child abuse and maltreatment are in no way recent historical phenomena but, rather, social problems going back to the roots of human history. Only within the past century have the concepts of child advocacy and protection gained a strong foothold in social policy (Williams, 1980b).

There is certainly some controversy about the extent and pervasiveness of child maltreatment in earlier historical epochs (Bloom-Feshbach, 1981). For example, Hunt (1970) believes that Aries (1962) put too much emphasis on the lack of active parental involvement in the well-being of children and that in most societies there has been an adequate concern for their basic welfare. In any case, there is much evidence that throughout history, fathers, as compared to mothers, have generally tended to be both more neglectful and more physically abusive (Biller, 1974a; Biller & Meredith, 1974; Chesler, 1986; Lynn, 1974, 1979).

Biblical and Ancient Times

Justice and Justice (1976) employ the term "cultural scripting" to describe the accepted patterns of interaction between individuals in a society. These spoken and unspoken scripts have provided endorsements to individuals concerning expected modes of behavior and thought. Cultural scripts have historically condoned child maltreatment as an accepted means of interpersonal behavior between children and adults. An example of this acceptance was the infanticide policy during biblical times, whereby infants who were not considered suitably strong, healthy, or useful could be murdered shortly after birth. Straus, Gelles, and Steinmetz (1980) discussed the Bible's acceptance of parental violence through Abraham's intent to murder his son as a sacrifice. Bakan (1971) recalled the biblical reference to Nimrod, the king of Babylonia, who read in the stars that a boy would be born in Mesopotamia who would eventually rule the country. Nimrod subsequently murdered 70,000 boys in his attempt to prevent the deliverance of the prophetic message.

Radbill (1980) notes that the dictum "spare the rod and spoil the child" is a biblical phrase that has become an accepted policy of child rearing. Religious ideology frequently suggests that the child is born sinful and must be severely disciplined in order to gain salvation—thus the expression "beat the devil out of a child" (Straus, Gelles, & Steinmetz, 1980). According to Bakan (1971), children are associated in the Bible with parental pain and suffering and result from so-called original sin. Biblical acceptance of violence toward children is reflected in the many instances of child sacrifice and killing of the firstborn.

Early Greek history is also filled with instances of violence toward children. The ancient Greeks tended to view children as an economic drain or a chattel for adults (Langer, 1974). Death from exposure or animal attacks was common, as infants were frequently left exposed to the elements (Fontana, 1976). Eugenics was also a rationale for infanticide. Seneca, Aristotle, and Plato accepted the notion of killing retarded or crippled babies as a means of strengthening and preserving the society (Radbill, 1980). Reviewing the history of infanticide, Sumner (1940) described this procedure as a social solution when the economic drains of caring for an infant became overwhelming. Eskimo, Chinese, Scandinavian, Polynesian, African, Native American, Australian aborigine, and Hawaiian cultures also practiced infanticide at some point in their histories.

An overview of historical research on the family does suggest that fathers as compared to mothers have more frequently committed severe acts of physical abuse toward children, as well as being more apt to neglect and/or abandon them (Lynn, 1974, 1979). On the institutional level, men who have been in positions of power have tended to demonstrate a great insensitivity to the needs and rights of infants and young children (Biller & Meredith, 1974; Chesler, 1986).

Transitional Periods

The eighteenth-century pediatrician William Burden stated that almost one-half of infants perished because of improper management and neglect (deMause, 1980). To a large extent maltreatment persisted in its most malignant forms from biblical times through the nineteenth century. Aries (1962) described how, in the sixteenth century, young children were considered to belong in adult society as soon as they progressed beyond the total dependency of infancy. During this period, children were occasionally deliberately crippled in order that they might be more effective as street beggars (Fontana, 1976).

The sixteenth century was an important period because two conflicting child-rearing philosophical camps arose—those who wanted to embrace the young within a supportive environment and those who believed in harsh discipline (Ross, 1980). This time period witnessed a shift from communal to nuclear family groups, thereby reinforcing the importance of the child to the economic survival of the family (Radbill, 1980). Slowly, the notion of the child as a protected citizen gained strength, and child-rearing practices wavered between restrictive/abusive and supportive.

Fontana (1976) depicts the nineteenth century as the nadir of child exploitation. Forced labor for children in sweat shops and mines was a prevalent and accepted practice. Nutritional, medical, educational, and emotional neglect were unfortunate and destructive by-products. However, Radbill (1980) notes that the nineteenth century also witnessed social acceptance of the need to protect children, as reflected in works like Dickens's *Oliver Twist* and Hugo's *Les Miserables*, in which the authors stirred up sentiment for children's rights.

Rousseau's statement "speak less of the duties of children and more of the rights" eventually translated itself into concrete movement toward child protection. In New York, Henry Bergh followed his establishment of the Society for the Prevention of Cruelty to Animals (SPCA) in 1866 with the establishment of the Society for the Prevention of Cruelty to Children (SPCC) in 1874. The American Humane Association was incorporated in 1877 with headquarters in Denver, Colorado. This association was also active in defining and protecting the rights of children and animals. It is rather ironic that organized concern for the welfare of animals seemed to predate a similar concern for the well-being of children.

Twentieth Century

Williams (1980b) describes the past hundred years as a period of both "cruelty and kindness to children." By the turn of the century, as Bremmer (1976) noted, there were 150 anticruelty agencies, which addressed both animal and child protection. The public community had accepted, to a minimal degree, its responsibility to venture into the home to protect children from maltreatment. Variations in cultural values among families made it extremely difficult for child protection agencies, most notably the SPCC, to differentiate abuse and neglect from so-called normative child-rearing practices, thereby hindering the courts from effectively intervening on behalf of the child (Ross, 1980).

The child protection movement dwindled in social importance with the advent of World War I and the subsequent economic depression (Williams, 1980b). Despite the public reformulation of social priorities to address immediate survival needs, the government did accept responsibility for child protection through the establishment of the Social Security Act of 1930. This legislation mandated services for "neglected, dependent children and children in danger of becoming delinquent". The delivery of protective services was delegated to child welfare departments, which generally operated at a state level. Social workers and social welfare personnel became the backbone of child protective services.

The definitional dilemma and difficulties in operationalizing incidence rates still exist. Despite over a hundred years of social acknowledgment of the need to protect children from maltreatment, the phenomenon remains very difficult to define. As Garbarino and Gilliam (1980) emphasize, however, the inability to explicate fully the parameters of child maltreatment should not preclude continued involvement in protecting children and striving to create optimal conditions for parenting.

Contemporary Father Neglect

Father-absence is a widespread occurrence in the United States. Over 20 percent of the children in this country live in fatherless homes, and in some areas the figure is over 50 percent (Biller, 1981a). These statistics indicate the scope of the problem but fail to incorporate the great prevalence of paternal deprivation found in even many so-called father-present U.S. families. Research with both intact and broken families has revealed a pervasive lack of sufficient father involvement necessary for the optimal personality development of children (Biller, 1971a, 1974a, 1981a,b).

In many situations, the father lives with his family but has little contact with his children. A review of data concerning the amount of time fathers spend at work and with their children suggests a picture of general paternal deprivation, since a large number of fathers have only minimal contact with their children (Biller & Meredith, 1974). Perhaps 50 percent of middle-class males, particularly business and professional men, work fifty-five hours or more a week. The executive or professional also often spends several hours a week commuting to work. Many men are preoccupied with work at home as well as at the office, further lessening their opportunities to interact with their children. Some research has suggested that the average family spends only about an hour a day together, most of it during mealtime (LeMasters, 1970; Lynn, 1974).

The hurried-child syndrome, so vividly described by Elkind (1981), can also be viewed as a type of unintentional maltreatment associated with father neglect. The hurried-child syndrome seems particularly prevalent in economically successful families in which both parents have demanding full-time occupations and in relatively affluent, single-parent homes. In such circumstances, parents may be able to afford an abundance of special athletic, educational, and social opportunities for their children which may help them rationalize their own lack of personal one-to-one involvement.

Middle-class families with strong expectations for achievement but with little direct father participation seem especially prone to rush their children into organized competitive activities outside the home. Often the pressure to structure their children's lives is also related to their own overscheduled existence and lack of energy to deal with family members on an emotionally supportive level. Such parents keep their children constantly busy believing that they are giving them necessary opportunities to develop social skills, but they are inadvertently putting them at risk for severe stress, excessive fear of failure, and what Elkind emphasizes is a loss of important childhood experiences. Hurrying children into a series of structured and competitive activities forces them to grow up too fast, too soon. They take on responsibilities to meet parental and social expectations, and some of the burdens of adulthood, long before they are developmentally ready.

The pattern of low participation of the husband in the family is often evident initially during the expectant-father period. Liebenberg (1967), studying first-time expectant fathers, reported that the majority were relatively unavailable to their pregnant wives because of heavy work or educational commitments. Ban and Lewis (1971) interviewed fathers of one-year-olds and found that, on average, they were with their infants only about fifteen to twenty minutes per day. Relative to the mother, the father usually spends much less time with his infant, particularly in early infancy. Biller (1974c) observed large individual differences among fathers with infants. Some fathers spent two hours a day in direct interaction with their infants by the time they were nine months old, but the majority of fathers spent little more than ten or fifteen minutes a day during the week in one-to-one interaction with them. Because of childbirth education classes and the inclusion of fathers in the delivery room, fathers tend to be much more involved with their newborns than was the case ten years ago. Even in the 1980s, however, most fathers have low levels of involvement with their children postinfancy and in the preschool years (Yogman, 1984).

Research with kindergarten-age and elementary-school children has indicated much variation in degree of father-child interaction. Again, the typical amount of father involvement appears to be relatively low. In a study of predominantly lower-middle-class and middle-class kindergarten boys, most fathers (94 of 159 families where the father was at home) were away two or three evenings a week or were away on business trips several days a month (Biller, 1968a). Other research projects have also suggested that most fathers spend relatively little time in one-to-one interactions with their children (Biller, 1974c; Lamb, 1981c). Of course, the time the father spends with his family is only one indication of his involvement, and much of the material in this book indicates that the quality of the father-child relationship is particularly important with respect to the incidence of child maltreatment.

Social and cultural factors as well as individual preferences contribute to paternal deprivation; men are not inherently less interested or less able parents than women. There is a growing trend for men to become involved with infants and young children and to be concerned with how parenting may affect their own development (Biller, 1974c, 1982a). Considerable research dealing especially with fathers and infants clearly indicates that, in general, men have just as much potential to be competent parents as women do. Although their parenting styles tend to differ, men have been found to have similar capacities to become attached and to be sensitive and responsive to the needs of infants and young children and, in fact, are generally capable, if motivated, to care adequately even for newborn babies (Biller, 1974a, 1982a; Lamb, 1981a; Parke 1981). Chapter 6 contains a summary of much relevant material concerning parent and infant development, and factors associated with the risk of child maltreatment.

Definitional Attempts

The terms *child abuse* and *neglect* have been widely employed to refer to a variety of adult-child interactions (Williams, 1980a). These labels, however, are ambiguous and amorphous and have generated considerable misunderstanding among researchers. The difficult task of establishing a conceptually sound definition is of prime importance. The definitional dilemma hinders research investigations that address incidence, etiological, and treatment issues. Child welfare departments and other concerned agencies are confronted with the task of diagnosing a problem whose structure and magnitude remains speculative. In this section there is a discussion of definitions that have been developed in the literature and an emphasis on the need for a multidimensional view of child maltreatment.

Battered-child syndrome is a term coined by Kempe and his collaborators 1962) to describe serious physical injury inflicted on children by adults. Kempe's landmark article, the result of ten years of intensive research, became the foundation for the great interest in child maltreatment during the past twenty-five years (Radbill, 1980).

The battered-child syndrome diagnosis became possible because of twentieth-century developments in pediatric radiology. Caffey (1946) and Silverman (1953) reported their observations on the frequent relationship between subdural hematoma and abnormal X-ray changes in the long bones. Advanced radiologic analysis helped to alert physicians to the probability of inflicted injury. Kempe (1962) subsequently organized a symposium entitled "The Battered Child Syndrome," sponsored by the American Academy of Pediatrics. This symposium spawned national interest, and a bandwagon effect ensued, with the distribution of many research grants through the Federal Children's Bureau.

The diagnosis of child abuse via advanced radiological analysis focused attention on the physical aspects of child maltreatment. Consequently, Kempe's battered-child syndrome and subsequent research primarily addressed physical injury to children. Most investigations were directed toward improving diagnostic techniques and treating physical trauma. But even when physical injury is used as the primary determinant of an abusive situation, confusion still exists concerning the degree of force that is acceptable. Gil (1970, p. 134) states that "no clearcut criteria exist . . . concerning the specific point beyond which the quality and quantity of physical force used against children is to be considered excessive." The determination of what is excessive force is related to cultural values and reflects varying attitudes of sensitivity toward the rights of children (Alvy, 1975).

The focus on physical maltreatment persisted throughout the 1960s, the first decade of intensive maltreatment research. This emphasis was consistent with the prevalent *medical model* used to understand the etiological basis of child maltreatment. (The medical model is discussed more fully in chapters 3 and 4.) Briefly, the medical model emphasizes the pathology of abusers and implies that abuse is committed by individuals with psychiatric deficiencies. The media focus on battered children served to increase public attention to the problem. The emphasis on physical injury made child abuse a more definable phenomenon. Statistical assessments remained questionable, however, because of inadequate reporting systems in most states (Solomon, 1982).

The battered-child syndrome concept underwent revision as researchers became more aware of other forms of child abuse and the limitations of the restricted focus on physical injury. Kempe's work, however, generated considerable research and inquiry into the existence and suffering of countless battered children. Despite the limitations in applicability, the rediscovery of child battering confirmed its existence as a pervasive problem and forced society to acknowledge its responsibility to protect children. The research and discussion that emanated from the battered-child concept eventually led to the interpretation of child abuse as a variegated and continuous phenomenon, not an all-or-nothing occurrence (Zigler, 1980).

The Abuse Continuum

Despite the inherent limitations in the battered-child syndrome model, several researchers have persisted in maintaining a primary focus on the physical aspects of the maltreatment environment, largely because they are concerned about the extreme ambiguities that exist in defining other, less quantifiable behaviors. Justice and Justice (1976) agree that physical abuse is only one component of the interaction continuum but suggest that the complete lack of consensus in other areas of maltreatment induces researchers to investigate those aspects for which there is an agreed-on definition.

Justice and Justice (1976) are accurate when they cite the confusion that exists in defining most aspects of maltreatment. Many different opinions have been offered with respect to the definitional dilemma. The physical aspects of maltreatment were discussed by Kempe et al. (1962); other researchers have investigated sexual abuse, emotional neglect, child theft, and abandonment. Taking a relatively broad perspective, Gil (1973) has defined *abuse* as acts of either omission or commission, in both cases with intentionality as the primary determinant. Acts of omission have generally been associated with the term *neglect*. Gil specifically avoids including sexual abuse within his definitional framework because he suggests that the dynamic issues are separate—a view shared by Blumberg (1974).

A basic issue is whether maltreatment consists of conceptually distinct acts of abuse or neglect or may be more accurately described on a continuum of parent-child interactions. Fontana (1974) and Gil (1973) contest the view that physical abuse and neglect are two conceptually distinct dynamic issues, whereas Gelles (1976) and Giovanni (1971) argue that acts of omission are different from acts of commission. However, there is not much consistent data to support the position on the distinctiveness of the abuse and neglect issues, and researchers have also been unable to distinguish abusive characterological profiles from nonabusive profiles (Garbarino & Stocking, 1980). A meaningful definitional framework must be broad enough to include acts of omission and commission as components of the maltreatment environment. Fontana (1974) prefers the term *maltreatment syndrome*, which may encompass physical abuse, emotional deprivation, and nutritional neglect.

Sociological Context

Some researchers define abuse in sociological rather than psychodynamic terms. Alvy (1975) interprets abuse within a comprehensive framework that primarily addresses society's attitudes toward children and the potential denial of their civil rights. He defines *abuse* within three contexts:

1. *Collective ideology:* sociological attitudes that impede children.
2. *Institutional abuse:* institutional acts of abuse perpetrated by schools, juvenile courts, correctional facilities and so on.
3. *Individual abuse:* physical and emotional abuse resulting from acts of omission or commission on the part of the caretaker.

This comprehensive definition of maltreatment indicts society for maintaining insensitive, restrictive, and abusive attitudes toward children.

Gelles (1975) focuses on child maltreatment as a "sociologically constructed" phenomenon that is defined within the cultural and sociological context of the abuser; that is, the same behavior may or may not be considered abusive in relation to the individual's social status, the intervening agency, prevailing social standards, and the like. The essential viewpoint of the sociological model is that child abuse must be defined within the cultural context of its occurrence. The implications of this definitional framework can be logically extended to etiological and intervention factors that are discussed in subsequent chapters.

Multidimensional Considerations

Numerous definitions have been invoked to conceptualize child maltreatment. The definitional model employed by researchers guides the theoretical orientation that is adopted to explain the phenomenon. For example, those researchers who define abuse in medical terms tend to focus on dynamic issues in the abuser as the primary cause of child abuse. Alvy's (1975) comprehensive framework adopts a sociological perspective in speculating about etiological factors. The time has arrived, however, to realize that a multivariate phenomenon such as child maltreatment cannot be operationalized satisfactorily by adopting a univariate focus. A definitional model must be sufficiently flexible to address the complex issues involved in specifying different forms of maltreatment.

State legislatures and child protective agencies have not been afforded the luxury that researchers have of taking an extraordinary period of time to define adequately an important social problem. Each of the fifty U.S. states and the ten Canadian provinces have enacted some form of legislation aimed at identification and intervention (U.S. Department of Health, Education and Welfare, 1979e). The Federal Child Abuse and Prevention Act of 1973 (Public Law 93-237) established the National Center of Child Abuse and Neglect (NCCAN) and charged it with the responsibility of developing research programs and disseminating information to the public. The value of this legislation also rests in the fact that this is the first occasion where child maltreatment has been addressed on a nationwide scale. The federal government definition of child maltreatment adopted in the 1973 act is:

> the physical or mental injury, sexual abuse, negligent treatment or maltreatment of a child under the age of 18, by a person who is responsible for the child's welfare, under circumstances which indicate that the child's health or welfare is harmed or threatened thereby. . . .

Giovanni and Becerra (1979) suggest that the NCCAN has been hindered in the development of its research program because of the "broadly defined and diverse phenomena" set forth by the federal government. Such terms as *negligent treatment* or *mental injury* may imply a variety of child-adult interactions. These interactions may or may not be interpreted as abusive, depending on: (1) the intentionality of the adult, (2) the effect on the child, (3) value judgment of the interaction, and (4) the cultural framework for that judgment. Garbarino and Gilliam (1980, p. 7) deal with these factors by defining maltreatment as "acts of omission or commission by a parent or guardian that are judged by a mixture of community values and professional expertise to be inappropriate and damaging."

The attribution of intentionality to aversive parental behavior is a complex issue. On the one extreme, there are parents who abuse their children in a clearly malicious and premeditated manner; on the other extreme, there are those who sincerely feel they are providing the child with constructive learning experiences. There are also many parents who are unaware that their behavior may be harmful to their children. Hypercritical and/or neglectful fathers often fit this latter category. Certainly the context of maltreatment must be considered carefully. A brief and/or accidental abusive episode should definitely be distinguished from a chronic pattern of maltreatment. However, the regular occurrence of negative parenting behavior, whether or not the perpetrator is aware that it is detrimental, or intends it to be so, clearly qualifies as child maltreatment.

Broad, circuitous definitions are being replaced in the literature with more succinct statements that draw on professional knowledge, cultural values, and common sense. Several factors must be considered in order for both public and professional groups to develop an integrated and consistent definitional framework. The growing tendency among researchers to conceptualize child maltreatment as part of the adult-child interaction continuum further facilitates the definitional process. Rather than investigating maltreatment as a distinct clustering of behaviors, the phenomenon is viewed in the context of a continuous range of interaction potentials existing on a broad continuum (Zigler, 1980). The definitional challenge may no longer rest in specifying those exact behaviors that constitute maltreatment but, rather, in deciding on the point on the continuum where intervention is necessary.

Figure 2–1 presents a multivariate framework of child maltreatment that includes three levels of relevant factors: cultural influences, legal interpretations, and a continuum of adult-child interactions. The reasoning behind such a model is that maltreatment cannot be defined without a cultural framework in which to interpret the behavior, legal applications of socially accepted norms, and a continuum depicting variations in the quality of parenting.

This model is not presented as a panacea for the current definitional dilemma. However, it does offer a reformulation and integration of important aspects of the adult-child interaction continuum and acknowledges several complex issues that are important to resolve in the definitional dilemma. Defining maltreatment within the context of a continuum leads to important implications: child abusers cannot be dismissed as a psychiatrically distinct group. A continuum definition also forces society to acknowledge maltreatment to children as a frequent phenomenon, bridges the gap between abusers and

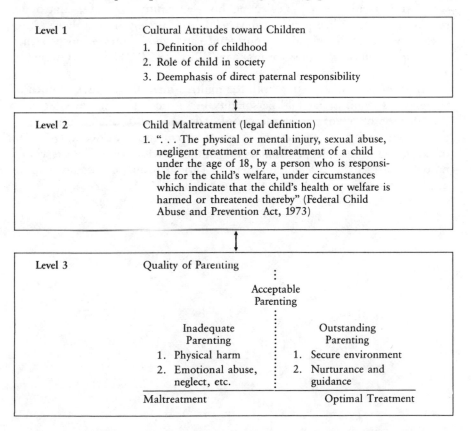

Figure 2–1. Preliminary Outline of Multivariate Definitional Framework for Child Maltreatment

nonabusers, and suggests that all mothers and fathers have to be concerned about maltreating their children.

The continuum approach to dealing with child maltreatment offers a helpful perspective toward the integration of the relevant "nonclinical" parenting and socialization literature. A major theme in this book is that evidence concerning child maltreatment and data on parental influence and personality development can be viewed as complementary. Much important research concerned with personality development in children focuses on dimensions of parenting such as acceptance–rejection, love–hostility, nurturance–neglect, and autonomy–control (Becker, 1964; Schaefer, 1965). The concepts of rejection, hostility, neglect, and over-control describe basic types of child maltreatment. Inadequately parented subjects in the personality and socialization research are not children who are clinically labelled as maltreated, although their behavior often bears a striking similarity to that of chronically abused individuals. Children whose parents are rejecting, neglecting, hostile, punitive, and over-controlling fare much worse in their personal and social development than do those whose parents are high in acceptance and nurturance and who encourage independence and responsibility in a positive manner (Biller, 1982a; Field & Widmayer, 1982).

A problem in interpreting both the maltreatment literature and much of the parent socialization–child personality literature is the lack of systematic specification of sex of parent and sex of child. A goal of this book is to emphasize the important interactions of sex-of-parent and sex-of-child factors in the processes of sex role, personality, and family development. There is a great need to consider the differential impact of various forms of adequate and inadequate parenting in a biosocial context (Biller, 1971a, 1974c).

3
Child Maltreatment: Incidence and Epidemiological Data

M uch of the detailed data relating to the incidence of child maltreatment focus only on severe physical abuse and, in some cases, severe neglect. As indicated in the first two chapters, physical abuse and neglect are just two of many forms of child maltreatment.

In intact families, available statistics indicate that fathers (or stepfathers) are responsible for about two-thirds of the incidents of child abuse associated with nonaccidental physical attack and/or injury (Gil, 1970). Such findings are particularly striking when one considers that fathers typically spend far less time with their children than do mothers. Moreover, fathers are generally reported to be the perpetrators of the more serious physical injuries to children (Gil, 1970). Some data do suggest that mothers are more likely to abuse children under the age of two physically than fathers are since in so many cases fathers are completely uninvolved in infant care (Silver, Dublin, & Lourie, 1971). In reviewing a varied population of physical-abuse cases, Paulson and Blake (1969) found that fathers were equally abusive to sons and daughters alike, but that mothers more frequently abused their daughters.

Young fathers who have several children and who have relatively low socioeconomic and educational status seem especially at risk to abuse their children physically (Kinard & Klerman, 1980). Compared to mothers, fathers are more likely to use corporal punishment in disciplining their children, and this creates more potential for them to become physically abusive (e.g., Biller, 1971b, 1974c; Lynn, 1974).

Although in two-parent families, fathers seem much more frequently to abuse children physically, more mothers are actually labeled as abusers because of the high rate of father-absence and of mother-led single families in our society. Paternal deprivation is strongly associated with child maltreatment. A major thesis of this book is that mothers are much more likely to maltreat their children when they do not have the support of an actively involved partner: neglectful fathers in two-parent families, as well as uninvolved fathers who do not live with their children, are a major factor in the incidence of mothers abusing their children.

Upwards of 25 percent of children in our society do not have a father living at home. Children in such families are overrepresented in terms of reported cases of physical abuse and other forms of child maltreatment. When statistics for physical abuse for both single-parent and two-parent families are combined, mothers are identified more often as physically abusing parents (Gil, 1970; Justice & Justice, 1976). Again as our analysis indicates, however, this is somewhat misleading. The quality of the father–mother relationship as well as the father's behavior toward the child must be taken into account in deciphering the roots of child maltreatment. From a statistical perspective, it could be hypothesized that more than 80 percent of incidents involving physical abuse toward children are associated with inadequate fathering, either with the father as the specific perpetrator, or with the father's relative noninvolvement in child rearing as a stress factor connected to the mother's abusive behavior.

In the social work and child welfare literature, there has been relatively little mention of the quality of fathering behavior as a factor in the neglect of children's nutritional, medical, and other physical needs. If she is in the home, the mother is assumed to be the exclusive caretaker of the child. As Wolins (1983) emphasizes, researchers focusing on child neglect rarely inquire as to the nature of the father-child relationship except to note whether or not the father is living in the home. However, even from such a superficial perspective, the absence of the father in the family can be viewed as a major risk factor relating to physical neglect as well as abuse of the child. Father presence is typically associated with more family financial resources than is father absence. Among poor children, those with fathers in the home are less likely to suffer from physical neglect than those whose fathers are absent; the presence of the father is positively related to the level of overall child care and the general condition of the household (Polansky, Chalmers, Butterweiser, & Williams, 1979).

Complexities in Estimation

The definitional dilemma described in chapter 2 has important implications for researchers involved in investigating the extent and nature of the maltreatment problem. The absence of an accepted definition of the phenomenon forces researchers to investigate maltreatment within their own specific definitional model. For example, those researchers who refer specifically to physical abuse estimate fewer incidents per year than do investigators who consider emotional maltreatment as part of their definition. Reporting statutes vary from state to state, and conflicting definitions further confuse the issue, rendering assessment of the problem a "guesstimate" at best (Klein, Cole, & Fox, 1981; Williams, 1980a).

Estimates of child maltreatment vary greatly among researchers, and the figures must be considered only suggestive. The American Humane Association gathered data on the number of child abuse and neglect cases reported nationally from 1976 to 1978. This organization reported 400,000 incidents during 1976, 500,000 in 1977, and 600,000 in 1978. These data include only those incidents that are reported to official state agencies. Williams (1980a) states that there is general agreement that cases of child abuse and neglect are "significantly under-reported." For example, Florida recorded only seventeen cases of child abuse and neglect in 1970. With the introduction of a state hotline in 1971, the figure rose to over 19,000 cases (Cohen & Sussman, 1975; Williams, 1980a).

Several other factors mitigate against full reporting of maltreatment incidents. Light (1974) indicates that private physicians are unlikely to report abusive behavior by their patients for fear of losing the patient or damaging their own professional reputations. In 1972, only 8 of 2,300 reported cases of child abuse in New York were referred by a physician. Many professionals lack the expertise to distinguish between accidents and intentional abuse (Williams, 1980a). Statutes also lack uniformity: most states mandate reporting by physicians, but some are inconsistent in their application to other professional groups. Avery (1973) has suggested that all professional groups that have ongoing contact with children should be subject to mandatory reporting laws. There is, indeed, a growing national trend to mandate that any adult should be subject to obligatory reporting of suspected maltreatment.

Kempe and Kempe (1978) concluded that abuse is reported approximately 320 times per 1 million population, which translates to approximately 64,000 incidents annually. Kempe and Kempe emphasize that reported cases represent only a small proportion of actual child abuse. They warn researchers to be aware that incidence rates derived from reported cases will certainly lead one to underestimate the problem.

The range of 50,000 to 60,000 incidents annually has been cited frequently in the literature (Cohen & Sussman, 1975). In testimony before subcommittee hearings on the Child Abuse Prevention Act of 1973, then Senator Mondale cited 60,000 reported cases annually. Several other reports to this subcommittee also cited 60,000 incidents, although it is not clear whether references were made to physical abuse and/or neglect.

In light of the difficulties in establishing viable definitional boundaries, the variations in reporting laws, and individual reluctance to report child maltreatment, it is not surprising that incidence estimates vary so greatly. Earlier estimates centered around 250 to 320 incidents per million, but the American Humane Association's survey suggesting much higher maltreatment rates may more accurately reflect the actual problem.

An important issue to arise out of incidence studies addresses Gil's (1973) claim that physical abuse of children is not a major issue in comparison to other more widespread social problems. The annual increase in reporting rates, however, suggests that child protective services are improving their ability to reach abusive families, and that the scope of physical and emotional abuse is much greater than perceived by most earlier researchers. The Child Abuse

Prevention Act of 1973 was passed despite inconsistent and contradictory testimony that could be characterized as inconclusive in its advice to legislators. In a survey that focused on physical violence in the family, researchers have estimated that in one of six couples one mate commits a violent act against his or her spouse annually (Straus, Gelles, & Steinmetz, 1980). Physical violence and maltreatment are established patterns of family interaction. Perhaps the major accomplishment in the past twenty-five years has been the acknowledgment, at least, of the existence of maltreatment as a pervasive phenomenon.

Gelles and Straus (1985) have recently presented evidence of a marked decrease (almost 50 percent) in the incidence of severe violence directed toward children in two-parent families. They cautiously attribute this apparent improvement to many factors, including greater public awareness concerning child abuse, more availability of planned-parenting resources, later age at marriage and at initial childbearing, better economic conditions, and increased efforts in treatment and prevention. Even if the Gelles and Straus findings are reflective of an actual decrease in severe cases of physical abuse, the incidence rate still reflects great risk to the healthy development of children. Moreover, their research does not provide findings from one-parent families, which are greatly overrepresented in the reported cases of physical maltreatment of children.

The Abused

The American Humane Association's survey of official reports of child abuse and neglect was summarized by Sears (1980). Although child-maltreatment reporting rates appeared to be increasing annually, at least until recently, the percentage distributions with respect to ages of children who are maltreated have remained virtually unchanged (Kline, Cole, & Fox, 1981). The AHA's survey suggests the great vulnerability of younger children—children who are unlikely to retaliate, unable to report the maltreatment and less able to move away. Research by Gil (1970) and Thomson (1971) also emphasizes the vulnerability of younger children to severe physical abuse. Over half of all reported incidents of physical abuse involve children under the age of seven.

Several researchers have attempted to argue that infants are the most frequently abused group. Elmer and Gregg (1967) found nineteen out of twenty physically abused children in their study were less than forty months old. Lauer, Broed, and Grossman (1974) found twenty months to be the median age for abuse in their investigation. Such data, however, may be of questionable representativeness because of relatively small sample size and because of assessment in a hospital setting.

Researchers who have used larger and more representative samples tend to be in general agreement concerning sex differences and age ranges. There appear to be no sex differences in the total number of reported incidents. Young children (under seven years) seem most vulnerable to maltreatment. Sex becomes a critical variable with respect to the age of the abused child: younger males and adolescent females appear to be at the greatest risk (Gil, 1970).

Girls tend to be viewed as more conforming than boys during childhood, so that physical force may be less necessary to control them than in the case of boys of a similar age. On the other hand, teenage boys may be likely to strike back at their abuser, thereby deterring future physical abuse. Sexual factors may also be related to increased maltreatment of older girls. Parental concerns about emerging heterosexuality, physical vulnerability, and social independence may be possible factors heightening the incidence of abuse of adolescent females.

The interaction of sex and age is noteworthy. Several factors may bias reporting rates in favor of younger males and teenage females. Abuse of older males may be a more socially acceptable behavior, as the male is encouraged to engage the world in a physical manner. Hospitals and medical personnel, the most frequent reporting agencies, may be more apt to report abused girls because of their perceived greater fragility (Gil, 1970; U.S. Department of Health, Education and Welfare, 1977).

There is a formidable literature dealing with the behavior of children who have been identified by clinicians or social agencies as the victims of parental physical abuse or neglect. Extensive data underscore the negative impact that severe abuse has on various aspects of children's psychological and social functioning. Not all physically maltreated children show basic handicaps in cognitive functioning, but even those who are very intelligent typically manifest academic performance deficits and have generally been found to be seriously hampered in self-concept and in emotional and social development (Martin, 1980). Abused or neglected children are likely to have low self-esteem, a limited capacity for experiencing pleasure, and depressive and/or hyperaggressive tendencies; researchers and clinicians have often described an insidious pattern of emotional detachment, withdrawal, and lack of a capacity to maintain a healthy reciprocity in intimate relationships among severely abused children (Martin, 1980; Polansky et al., 1981, Williams & Money, 1980).

However, it is generally impossible to disentangle the specific impact of maltreatment by parents from other experiences encountered by abused children. For example, many of the abused children described in clinical research spent part of their childhood separated from their families, living in institutions or in one or more foster homes (in which they may have also been maltreated). In addition to being maltreated by parents, most of these children can be viewed as also suffering from grave economic and social disadvantages and deprivation. In many cases, the child clinically labeled as abused has suffered multiple forms of maltreatment by various adults as well as inadequate medical care and nutrition during crucial phases in early development (Martin, 1980; Terr & Watson, 1980).

Developmental Characteristics

The notion that the child "contributes" to his or her maltreatment because of particular developmental characteristics is quite unusual in most causal explanations of its occurrence. Certainly the presence of characteristics in the child that correlate statistically with child maltreatment should not detract from investigations of psychodynamic and psychosocial variables (for example, a child's mental retardation should not become an "acceptable justification" for child maltreatment). Nevertheless, the potential correlation between developmental characteristics and child maltreatment may guide researchers in investigating relevant causes of family stress and associated social-situational variables. In many cases, it is extremely difficult to delineate cause and effect. For example, the frequent association of low birth weight and child maltreatment may reflect poor prenatal care, increased maternal anxiety during pregnancy, general parental insensitivity, or a host of other factors. Likewise, prematurity may simply be a reflection of other significant variables related to child maltreatment, such as poor economic and educational conditions.

Researchers have reported a rather consistent relationship between prematurity and child maltreatment. Elmer and Gregg (1967) presented data on twenty children who were evaluated in the Children's Hospital of Pittsburgh for physical abuse. Six of the twenty (30 percent) had birth weights between 3 pounds, 10 ounces, and 5 pounds, 4 ounces, and were considered premature. Klein and Stern (1971) studied fifty-one infants hospitalized for physical abuse at the Montreal Children's Hospital and found that twelve (23.5 percent) were low-birth-weight infants. These researchers stated that the expected rate of prematurity in the Canadian population is 7–8 percent. Martin and his colleagues (1976) found that eleven (19 percent) of their sample of fifty-eight physically abused children weighed less than 2,500 grams at birth. Sex differences were not reported in these studies.

Klein and Stern (1971) briefly reviewed the social characteristics of their subjects' families. Ten of the twelve premature infants were from deprived backgrounds. Inadequate maternal care, borderline intellectual functioning, and other negative parental characteristics were prevalent. Behavior and medical difficulties are more common with premature youngsters, which also may predispose them to maltreatment (Friedrich & Boriskin, 1976). The premature child is more likely than a full-term baby to be restless, distractable, and difficult; sleep disturbances are more common. Leiderman (1974) has found significant differences in attitudes and behavior between mothers of full-term and premature infants, indicating the latter suffer more stress and ambivalence dealing with their children.

The cause-and-effect dilemma is clear when evaluating the role of prematurity in maltreatment. Although there is correlation, the exact nature of the interaction is still unknown. Prematurity does not operate in isolation from other factors to produce maltreatment. Factors that predispose infants to be premature (inadequate prenatal care, alcoholism, and the like) are potential factors that need to be considered in research on the etiology of maltreatment.

There has also been considerable research indicating an association between physical abuse and mental retardation (e.g. Brandwein, 1974; Buchanan & Oliver, 1977). For the most part, such studies deal with the connection between severe physical abuse and resulting neurological damage and/or with extreme neglect and an intellectually deprived environment for the child. However, children who are retarded at birth or who have a learning disability and/or an attention deficit disorder may create particular stress for parents and be at increased risk of suffering from maltreatment. Obviously, if such children are maltreated, this could increase their already existing disability. Niachamin (1973) pointed out that children with neurological dysfunction tend to be anxious, tense, and more difficult to appease than other children—behavior that may heighten their vulnerability to maltreatment. Other types of exceptional or atypical childhood conditions, including various physical handicaps and chronic illness, have also been found to be associated with maltreatment of children by parents (Friedrich & Boriskin, 1976; Money, 1977; Money & Needleman, 1976).

The work of Thomas, Chess, and Birch (1968) concerning the enduring pattern of infant temperament styles appears quite relevant in identifying children who may be particularly vulnerable to maltreatment. These researchers have defined three clusters of infant temperaments:

1. The *difficult* child, characterized by irregularity in biological functions, nonadaptability, withdrawal from new stimuli, frequent negative moods, and irritability.
2. The *slow to warm up* child, characterized by inconsistent mood patterns and slow adaptation to new stimuli.
3. The *easy* child, characterized by regularity in bodily functions, quick adaptation to new stimuli, and predominantly positive mood patterns.

Children who are difficult or slow to warm up are at greater risk to be maltreated when compared to those who are socially responsive and easily adapt to new situations. The parent's own socialization experiences and temperamental style interact with the child's unique characteristics in ways that may increase or decrease the probability of child maltreatment.

The Abusers

Gil (1970) and Justice and Justice (1976) found that most parents were between the ages of twenty and forty when they were identified as child abusers.

The key variable, however, may not be the age of the abuser when the abusive act is recorded but, rather, the age of the parent when the child was born. There is evidence that younger parents, especially those couples who bear children when at least one partner is still a teenager, are more likely than older parents to abuse their children physically. Kinard and Klerman (1980) reanalyzed Gil's (1970) data using the parents' age at the birth of their first child as their definition. These researchers restricted their analysis to cases in which the abused child lived with one or both natural parents at the time of the abuse. Kinard and Klerman found that 38 percent of the mothers in Gil's sample were teenagers when their first child was born, in contrast to only 17.5 percent of the general population. Teenage fathers constituted 11.4 percent of Gil's sample using this new definition, compared to only 4.5 percent of the general population. Gil (1970) concluded from his study that teenage parenthood bore no clear relationship to child maltreatment. Kinard and Klerman, however, have taken issue with Gil and stated that an association may exist that merits further investigation.

Some reasons for the association between having a child at an early age and being an abusive parent may have been revealed in the work of researchers focusing on socioeconomic variables. Bolton, Laner, and Kane (1980) emphasized that teenage parents tend to suffer financial hardship and other related difficulties such as low educational achievement, poor housing, and unemployment. Pelton (1978) reported a strong relationship between socioeconomic factors and child maltreatment. Socioeconomic factors are also associated with the availability of social support systems that can assist a parent in child-care responsibilities (Garbarino, 1980). The relative absence of support networks such as child-care centers, medical and social services, and recreational opportunities may heighten parental stress and the related risk of child maltreatment. Pelton's and Garbarino's research is discussed more fully in chapter 4. Their approaches are helpful in evaluating the correlation between teenage parenting and child maltreatment.

It is possible that the relationship between teenage parenting and child maltreatment will become more apparent in future years. While many women are delaying child rearing until later in life, the birth rate in women under seventeen is increasing annually (Chilman, 1979). Adolescent pregnancy has a higher representation among poor families, which seems further to increase the risk of maltreatment. Bolton and his colleagues (1980) indicate that the lower-class adolescent is more apt to adopt single parenthood rather than marriage, which may also help to explain the large representation of single adolescent mothers in maltreatment cases.

Sex

Although the total number of females identified as engaging in child maltreatment is greater than the number of males, almost 30 percent of Gil's (1970) sample of physically abused children lived in homes without a father figure. In homes where a male figure was present, males perpetrated the abuse in more than 60 percent of the reported incidents. Men appear to be more abusive in families where both parents are present, as is also suggested in research by Glazier (1971), Silver, Dublin, and Lourie (1971), and Chesler (1986).

Most studies evaluating the sex of the abuser have failed to control for variations in family structure. Also, in many instances it is difficult to ascertain clearly who perpetrated the abusive act. One parent may commit the act while receiving tacit approval from the other parent. Other possibilities are that different forms of maltreatment may be committed more frequently by fathers and mothers and that the sex of the adult may interact with the age and sex of the child. Paulson and Blake (1969) have suggested that the sex of the abuser may vary with the sex of the child. They investigated ninety-six cases of physical abuse and found that biological fathers were equally abusive to both sons and daughters, whereas mothers were more likely to abuse their daughters. Silver, Dublin, and Lourie (1971) stated that although fathers were responsible for twice as many abusive incidents as mothers, mothers abused children under the age of two three times more often than fathers did. This may occur because the mother is more responsible for the daily care and discipline of infants, whereas fathers typically assume some responsibility when the child is more mobile and independent. However, *in intact families*, even though mothers typically spend much more time with children, fathers far more often physically abuse children over the age of two. In chapter 6 there is a detailed discussion of the potential reasons for fathers' direct or indirect involvement in child maltreatment to such a great extent.

Socioeconomic Factors

Steele and Pollock (1968) reported that the sixty abusive families they investigated were from various social classes. Other prominent researchers have also suggested that child maltreatment is an affliction of all social classes (Parke & Collmer, 1975). Although most researchers accept the overrepresentation of lower socioeconomic groups in maltreatment statistics, this is usually attributed to the reluctance of child protective workers to interfere in the lives of more affluent and influential individuals, and to the superior ability of middle-income individuals in preventing protective workers from hearing about the incident (U.S. Department of Health, Education and Welfare, 1977). Low-income groups also tend to employ social services and hospital emergency rooms to a greater extent than do more affluent individuals. Therefore, abusive acts are more likely to be detected and reported by public health officials, community doctors, and other personnel who are in frequent contact with low-income groups.

However, Gil (1970), Pelton (1978), and American Humane Association studies (AHA, 1979) disagree with this classlessness concept and suggest a strong relationship between economic hardship and child maltreatment. Gil (1970) reported that 60 percent of his 1967 and 1968 samples had been on welfare sometime prior to the study. Approximately 37 percent of the families were on public assistance at the time of the maltreatment. At that time close to 50 percent of the families reported incomes below $5,000 for 1967, compared with less than 25 percent of the general population. Only 3 percent of the families reported incomes above $10,000, compared to about one-third of the general population. The American Humane Association (1978) studies from 1975 and 1976 also suggested that a disproportionately large number of low-income families were included in maltreatment statistics. Over 40 percent of the families were receiving public assistance. The median income was at the 1976 poverty level (approximately $5,000) for a family of four (Pelton, 1978). It is also noteworthy that mental health professionals have frequently pointed to the loss of a job, particularly by the father, even among middle-class parents, as a contributing factor to marital stress and child maltreatment. As is emphasized in chapter 7, the way the father feels about his job can have much impact on his attitude toward his family and on their attitude toward him. Economic factors are very significant in evaluating potential family stress and the risk of child maltreatment (Steinberg, Catalano, & Dooley, 1981).

Other researchers have corroborated Gil's (1970) and the AHA's data concerning the strong relationship between child maltreatment and low family income level (e.g., Smith, Hanson, & Hoble, 1975). However, Pelton (1978) notes that the "classlessness myth" in child maltreatment persists despite a significant accumulation of data implicating lower-income families in the vast majority of incidents involving clear-cut physical abuse and neglect. The reasons for the persistence of this myth may lie in some of the theoretical models of maltreatment that are discussed in the next chapter. The psychodynamic model of child maltreatment explicitly focuses on intraindividual dynamic issues rather than on social-situational variables. Child maltreatment, within the psychodynamic context, is viewed as a disease and a function of parental psychopathology. The associated problems of poverty, such as limited social mobility, poor housing, and lack of education, are not regarded as causal agents of maltreatment in this model. Therefore, investigators can more conveniently search for a "cure" for the disease rather than address the serious social consequences of economic deprivation (Solomon, 1982).

With the more frequent involvement of lower-income families, it is to be expected that the occupational and educational status of maltreating parents is less than average (Gil, 1970). Low educational attainment is reflected in the fact that over 80 percent of the parents did not graduate from high school. Unemployment rates for the maltreating group are exceedingly high, and most jobs are in low salary ranges. Young (1964) found that in 58 percent of 300 abusive families, the wage earner had not held a job continuously for two years. Furthermore, unskilled laborers were the primary wage earners in 71 percent of the families. A U.S. Department of Health, Education and Welfare Report (1977) also concluded that unemployed, low-income, and low-education families were greatly overrepresented with respect to *reported cases* of child maltreatment.

Family Structure

Zigler (1980) found that child abuse is more likely to occur in families with four or more children. Gil (1970) also indicated that the proportion of families with four or more children in his sample was almost twice as high as the national average (37.4 percent versus 19.6 percent). Conversely, the percentage of the sample cohort that had only one child was 17.2 percent, compared to a national average of 31.7 percent. Johnson and Morse (1968) studied the families of abused children in Denver and found that one-third had four or more children. Light (1973) assessed child abusers in New Zealand, England, and the United States and found that large families (those with four or more children) were more than twice as prevalent as in the national averages for those countries.

Large family size is definitely correlated with maltreatment rates (U.S. DHEW, 1977). This relationship may exist because a greater number of children draw on the limited resources of a financially strained family. Parental strain and frustration evolving more frequently from this overcrowded situation may result in higher rates of maltreatment. It is also possible that parents who are unable to evaluate properly the number of children they can care for adequately are potentially more abusive because of a general lack of appropriate social judgment.

Even though maltreatment researchers have tended to give rather scanty attention, if any at all, to the quality of paternal behavior in the family, the consistency of findings relating father absence with child abuse is striking. Gil (1970) found that in only 46 percent of families with reported cases of child abuse was the biological father present. Over 30 percent were without a father or father-subsitute, and in 20 percent a stepfather lived with the family. In addition, the frequent deviance from nuclear family structure in maltreatment cases is suggested by the research of Zuckerman, Anbuel, and Bandman (1972) and Justice and Justice (1976). In a relatively thorough study in England, absence of the natural father from the family was the single variable found most correlated with child abuse (Hanson, McCullough, & Hartley, 1978).

Father absence, income, and ethnicity can be interrelated variables. Only one-third of Gil's (1970) sample of abused children were Caucasian, which suggests that a disproportionate number of minority-group members are represented in his study. There was no male present in 42 percent of the Puerto Rican families, 37 percent of the black families, and approximately 20 percent of the Caucasian families. The association between one-parent families and child maltreatment is in part, a function of the greater number of one-parent families in non-Caucasian and low-income groups (U.S. DHEW, 1977).

Chesler (1986) has brilliantly analyzed and documented the economic, legal, and political disadvantages of single mothers and children in our society, especially postdivorce. Mothers and children in such families are particularly vulnerable to becoming the victims of poverty, abuse, exploitation, and manipulation. Our male-dominated political and social institutions have a responsibility to demonstrate a much greater sensitivity to the needs and rights of fatherless families (e.g., Adams, Miller, & Schrepf, 1984; Biller, 1971a; Chesler, 1986).

A broad range of epidemiological factors are associated with child maltreatment. Most factors relating to child maltreatment are those that cause stress within the family. For example, the conclusion that the number of children in the family is related to abuse may suggest that any factor that contributes to the overutilization of limited family resources increases the likelihood of maltreatment. Lower income levels, single-parent families, and so-called difficult children are factors that appear to heighten stress within the family system and subsequently to affect maltreatment. In contrast, for families with average or above-average incomes, the number of children is not an important factor in the incidence of child maltreatment (Straus, Gelles, & Steinmetz, 1980) The suggestion here is that within middle- and high-income families, financial affluence permits the parents to cope more effectively with day-to-day stress and the difficulties of child rearing.

Epidemiological data become particularly relevant when considering theoretical models of child maltreatment. For example, the psychiatric model has been predicated on the notion that maltreatment occurs primarily as a function of psychopathology and is not correlated with socioeconomic status. However, much research indicates that income-related factors play an important role in the occurrence of child maltreatment. These data have motivated some researchers to develop and investigate other theoretical models that can more readily incorporate these factors. The next chapter more fully describes current theoretical models of child maltreatment.

4
Theoretical Models of Child Maltreatment

I this chapter we examine theoretical perspectives and relevant data regarding what causes parents to maltreat children. Unfortunately, theorists dealing with child maltreatment have not addressed themselves to the special characteristics of the paternal role. There has been too little attention to potential differences between fathers and mothers in the maltreating process, with relatively little emphasis on the dynamics of the father-mother relationship. The focus in theoretical models has generally been on the physical abuse of children rather than on the varied types of child maltreatment that can occur in families, the incidence and etiology of which may be much related to sex differences in parenting styles and expectations. Nevertheless, the material in this chapter is very important with respect to delineating the complexity and multifaceted nature of the maltreating environment and helps set the stage for a more in-depth analysis of the linkage between child maltreatment and paternal deprivation.

The etiology of child maltreatment has traditionally been approached from one of two theoretical perspectives: the *psychiatric* or *medical model* (Kempe & Helfer, 1972) and the *social systems model* (Belsky, 1980a). The psychiatric model emphasizes that child maltreatment arises from disturbances in the adult and is reflected in inadequate parent-child relations. Some of the deficiencies attributed to abusive parents are that they are rigid and domineering, dependent and narcissistic, impulsive and immature, with poor self-concept development and inconsistent identity formation (Blumberg, 1974).

Social systems models contend that maltreatment is the result of culturally determined values that guide adult-child interactions, and stressful environmental conditions. Essentially, social systems models can be divided into two orientations: the sociocultural and the social-situational perspectives. Both perspectives address external environmental events that impinge on the family, but the level of analysis is quite different. The sociocultural model examines how cultural values affect adult-child interactions, whereas the social-situational model focuses primarily on patterns of interaction within neighborhoods and families (Parke & Collmer, 1975).

Theoretical deficiencies of the psychiatric and social systems models have led to the establishment of a third theoretical perspective, the *transactional model*. This model suggests that child maltreatment must be investigated from the joint perspective of adult, child, and environmental characteristics. (Frodi & Lamb, 1980b; Vietze, Falsey, Sandler, O'Connor, & Altemeier, 1980.)

Psychiatric Model

Traditionally, many theorists have viewed personality as an expression of intraindividual forces, including drives, traits, impulses, and motives (Kazdin, 1975). Freud's psychoanalytic theory solidified the intraindividual or medical model by emphasizing psychological forces as primary determinants of behavior. Allport's trait theory, Jung's analytical psychology, and current interpretations of Freudian theory reflect intraindividual psychological processes that target the inner world of the individual as the cause of deviant behavior. The social environment is considered only to the extent that it provides the opportunity and impetus for intraindividual dynamic processes to take place.

The intraindividual approach is often referred to as a medical model because of its adherence to the view that psychopathological behavior reflects maladaptive psychological processes. The implications of the model are analogous to the pursuit of medical treatment when confronted with physical illness. The cure for psychological processes is assumed to be intensive dynamically oriented therapy and/or treatment with medication. The primary objective is to alter and correct the deviant internal psychological processes that are assumed to be the cause of aberrant behavior.

Many researchers have used the psychiatric model in attempting to understand the etiological structure of child maltreatment (e.g., Blumberg, 1974; Green, 1978). The majority of these researchers have been physicians focusing on the physical dangers of maltreatment and associated psychiatric disturbances in the parent. The reason for this emphasis may lie in the focus on the physical aspects of maltreatment that was prevalent in the 1960s.

Kempe et al.'s (1962) landmark article on the battered-child syndrome addressed the physical trauma of maltreatment. Although these researchers acknowledged that psychiatric information concerning abusers was meager, their conjectures about causality referred primarily to parental character defects. Deficiencies in parents that were suggested by these researchers included lack of impulse control, primary identification with an abusive parent, and inappropriate aggressive tendencies.

Green, Gaines, and Sandgrund (1974) evaluated sixty abusive mothers and mother figures in a ghetto area of New York City. Their sample was referred by the Family Court of New York. The ethnic composition was primarily black and Hispanic. Agency records were assessed, and psychiatric interviews were conducted with each of the mothers. These researchers suggest that the following personality characteristics are prevalent in physically abusive mothers: unsatisfied dependency longings, impaired impulse control because of identification with violent adult models, poor self-concept, disturbances in identity formation, and frequent use of externalization and projection including the attribution of negative parental qualities to the child.

Most medical model researchers have focused on uncovering specific personality characteristics among maltreaters rather than relying on the traditional psychiatric classifications (Parke & Collmer, 1975). The intent of most psychodynamic studies has been to generate a series of character traits that will reliably differentiate abusive and nonabusive populations. Psychotic individuals make up only a small percentage of the abusive population (Kempe, 1973). Earlier writings posited a higher incidence of severe psychotic behavior, but more recent investigations support the view that relatively few abusive parents manifest severe psychiatric pathology (Gil, 1981).

Steele (1982), from the psychiatric perspective, wrote an interesting chapter concerning abusive fathers, prepared especially for a psychoanalytically oriented book on the father-child relationship (Cath, Gurwitt, & Ross, 1982). As expected, he emphasized defects in the individual father's capacity to relate to his child and the father's own history of inadequate parenting as the major precursors of paternal physical abuse. However, Steele gives little attention to any sex-related differences in parenting styles and essentially takes the position that abuse by both mothers and fathers is a result of their own family history and defects in personal identity. Steele (1982) does not cite a single published reference relating to any research or clinical findings focusing in a special way on the father's role in child abuse or child maltreatment; it appears that the editors of the book called on his expertise to deal with an issue that has generally been ignored by psychiatrically based researchers, except with respect to the sexual maltreatment of children.

On the other hand, from our perspective, much of the provocative material discussed in the Cath, Gurwitt, and Ross (1982) book, including Steele's chapter, is relevant when we view child maltreatment as a multidimensional phenomenon. Though not sufficient in itself, a psychodynamic and psychoanaltyic perspective can be an important component to be integrated into an interactionist framework aimed at understanding the significance of the father–child relationship, and the interconnection between paternal deprivation and child maltreatment (Biller, 1971a, 1974c).

The psychiatric approach can be quite important if we are attempting to predict what types of parents may maltreat their children *in some way.* The lack of empirical support for the psychiatric approach stems from the goal of relating parental personality characteristics to a very narrow band of extremely maltreating behaviors (that is, severe physical abuse and neglect). More justification for a psychiatric (or psychological trait) approach is available when a range of child-rearing patterns is considered. For example, parents who have depressive styles are likely to have great difficulty in being emotionally responsive and supportive to their children, although they may never commit acts of physical abuse or severe neglect (Berlinsky & Biller, 1982).

Critique

A principle thesis of the psychiatric model is that socioeconomic and sociocultural stresses are neither necessary nor sufficient to account for child maltreatment. Steele (1980) acknowledges that abusive episodes can be aggravated by poverty, unemployment, marital strife, prematurity, lack of education, and other stress-inducing factors. Psychodynamic researchers, however, justifiably point out that child maltreatment occurs in some very wealthy families and, by contrast, does not always occur even in highly stressful socioeconomic conditions. Demographic variables are accorded a secondary role because the key causal agents of maltreatment are targeted within the individual (Spinetta & Rigler, 1972).

A principal problem with the psychiatric model is that despite its twenty years of theoretical supremacy, researchers have been largely unsuccessful in generating a reliable profile of abusive adults (Garbarino, 1980). Although psychiatric researchers claim that socioeconomic factors are neither necessary nor sufficient conditions for maltreatment, a valid model of internal dynamic factors remain unattained. Indeed, Helfer (1976), using available profile studies, estimated that approximately 60 percent of the adult population are at risk to abuse children. Medical model researchers have been unsuccessful in isolating a distinct set of personality attributes that are specific to the abusive population. From our perspective, it is possible that increased success in generating meaningful personality traits may emanate from considering more specific profiles concerning the interaction of such variables as sex of parent, sex of child, and the particular pattern of maltreatment. (We present much relevant research dealing with such distinctions in later chapters.)

The medical model has been contradictory and inconsistent when applied to child maltreatment. For example, Steele and Pollock (1968) emphasized individual psychopathology but also noted the wide distribution of personality characteristics among the abusive and nonabusive populations. Rosenthal and Louis (1981), in a discussion of professional testimony in maltreatment cases, concluded that psychiatric judgments are neither valid nor reliable and are greatly influenced by personal value systems. Hypotheses are usually based on clinical observations of patients, and the samples are not necessarily representative of the general population of maltreating adults.

Gelles (1973) emphasized a serious methodological flaw with most profile studies—the fact that they are ex post facto. No study has been clearly successful in predicting rates of child maltreatment simply on the basis of psychiatric profiles. Another methodological concern with profile studies is the frequent absence of control groups. With few exceptions, relevant comparison groups have been absent in psychodynamic investigations of child maltreatment. Schneider, Hoffmeister, and Helfer (1976) have developed a screening questionnaire that has met with limited success in predicting maltreatment incidents. This approach may be helpful, particularly if the questionnaire can be broadened to include a variety of dynamic, socioeconomic, and sex and style of parenting issues.

More researchers are attempting to analyze the social aspects of child maltreatment and are focusing less on individual pathology. Since medical model investigations have failed to produce the desired results, there has been an evolution of alternative research strategies. The question remains, however, whether the psychiatric focus has not been fruitful because of inadequate research methods or because of an invalid theoretical basis. Is it empirically impossible to produce a psychiatric profile because such a profile does not exist, or has research methodology been too simplistic in its approach toward generating such a profile?

McCall (1977) has criticized developmental theorists for attacking complex issues with univariate research techniques. McCall's criticisms also apply to the psychiatric study of maltreatment. A psychiatric profile of abusive adults may be valid only to the extent that situational and/or cultural variables are also considered. The interaction between these factors may be the crucial determinant in understanding child maltreatment. Thus abusive behavior may be more aptly viewed as the result of a myriad of complex interacting factors that are both external (cultural and situational factors) and internal (personality characteristics). This interactionist perspective is discussed in more detail later in this chapter, and the medical model merits further consideration when incorporated within a broader conceptual perspective.

Social Systems Model

The social systems perspective of child maltreatment has become prominent through the efforts of such researchers as Gelles (1973, 1976); Gil (1979, 1981); Pelton (1978, 1981); and Garbarino (1980, 1981). This perspective arose, at least in part, as a reaction to the inconsistent and often contradictory findings generated within medical model research. Medical model researchers have specifically discussed their belief in the irrelevancy of social variables in the causal scheme of child abuse. Steele and Pollock (1968) argued that social factors were relatively incidental and not particularly relevant to understanding the specific act of physical abuse. Social systems researchers reply that the social context is both a necessary and a sufficient factor in child maltreatment. The intent of sociological research is to explicate the potent and relevant factors in the social environment that influence individual and group behavior (Gelles, 1973).

The social systems viewpoint has evolved into two related frameworks: sociocultural and social-situational. The sociocultural model explores the cultural values that are prevalent in a society concerning expected and accepted modes of adult-child interactions. The social-situational perspective primarily addresses ecological variables such as neighborhood characteristics, family structure, and other potential stress-inducing factors. Both perspectives share a common interest—the social environment as an important medium in influencing behavior. It is the levels of analysis that differ in the two models.

Garbarino and Stocking (1980) discuss the work of Bronfenbrenner (1977) as a critical component of the theoretical justification for the sociological perspective. Bronfenbrenner's analysis of ecological factors highlights the importance of the social context in understanding social interactions. Bronfenbrenner (1975) cited the increase in family isolation as a causal agent in child maltreatment. The factors he discussed include fragmentation of the extended family, separation of residential and business areas, breakdown of neighborhoods, zoning ordinances, occupational mobility, television, working mothers, and increased use of nonfamily child care. These factors affect the social fabric of family structure and, in recent years, have further isolated child and family from each other and from extended support networks. Such factors have also contributed to the great increase in the incidence of paternally deprived children in our society (Biller, 1971a, 1974c; Biller & Meredith, 1972, 1974).

Sociocultural Perspective

The larger cultural fabric in which the individual, family, and community are immersed has been evaluated by child maltreatment researchers. This level of analysis addresses what Bronfenbrenner (1977) has labeled the *macrosystem*. According to Gelles (1976), violence is considered an accepted aspect of child-rearing practices. The use of physical force with children is one component of the high level of physical violence that characterizes U.S. society. For example, the rate (per 100,000) of assault and battery has been reported to be five times greater in the United States than in Canada. Parke and Collmer (1975) discussed reports suggesting that the murder rate is ten times higher in the United States than in England and that the incidence of violence depicted on television is also much higher than in such countries as Sweden, Israel, and England.

The basic premise of the sociocultural model of child maltreatment is that the levels of violence accepted within a culture are reflected in the levels of violence expressed toward children. For example, Steinmetz (1974) found lower levels of intrafamilial aggression in Canada, where the assault rate was less than that reported in the United States. Tietjen (1980) emphasized that Sweden's reporting rate for child abuse is approximately one-fifth that of the United States. She also indicated that Swedish culture reinforces supportive relationships between state and family and within family units. Swedish society has explicitly adopted a strong commitment to strengthening family structure through its excellent child care system and its abundance of accessible social and recreational services for parents. Physical violence directed at children is an infrequent occurrence within Swedish society (Garbarino, 1980). Physical punishment is rarely employed in China or Japan as a means of discipline, and child abuse reporting rates in both China and Japan are noticeably low (Goode, 1971; Sidel, 1972).

Alvy (1975), in a frequently cited article, evaluates child maltreatment within a comprehensive model that includes collective, institutional, and individual factors. These factors appear analogous to Bronfenbrenner's analysis of macrosystems, exosystems, and microsystems. Alvy defines collective abuse as "those attitudes held collectively by our society that impede the psychological and physical development of children" (p. 921). Examples are racial and social class discrimination and adult attitudes about the inferior status of children. Institutional abuse refers to the "acts perpetrated against children by such institutions as schools, detention centers, correctional facilities and other institutions with responsibilities for children" (p. 922). The frequent use of corporal punishment against children within schools and in other settings is a clear example of this level of abuse. Individual abuse refers to acts of physical abuse and neglect committed against children by parents and other adult caretakers.

Alvy's comprehensive model indicts all of society as intentional or unintentional contributors to child maltreatment. Abuse is evaluated as a broad-based phenomenon that permeates the fabric of each level of society and is firmly entrenched in the basic cultural values that influence public attitudes about children. More important, however, is the implication that all members of society must accept responsibility for the promulgation of abusive situations for children. U.S. society has preferred to view child maltreatment as the deviant behavior of a few disturbed parents, thereby exonerating the majority of adults from the responsibility for abusive incidents.

The sociocultural perspective derives part of its existence from the reaction in the 1970s against individual-level interpretations of child maltreatment. The convenience of assigning child abuse to the sole realm of psychiatrically disturbed adults has permitted society to ignore collective acts of maltreatment as well as its responsibility in the breakdown of social support systems. Gil (1979) concluded that preventive programs must address a broad aggregate of causal interacting factors, such as society's basic philosophy about its members; the nature of its social, economic, and political institutions; and the quality of human relations that are shaped by social forces. The macrosystem-level analysis raises serious doubts about our society's ability to eliminate child maltreatment while physical violence and corporal punishment remain accepted and condoned patterns of behavioral interaction between individuals.

An important part of the sociocultural perspective must deal with sex-role stereotypes concerning maternal and paternal behavior. A major thrust in preventive efforts should be focused on changing rigid sex-role attitudes concerning parenting responsibilities and, in particular, on helping many fathers find alternatives to physical punishment and emotional rejection when they are confronted with what they consider inappropriate child behavior. There is a tremendous need to foster, in men, the development of more accepting-affectionate styles of relating to children (Biller, 1971a, 1974c; Biller & Meredith, 1972, 1974; Chesler, 1986).

Social-Situational Model

Social-situational researchers such as Gelles (1973) and Garbarino (1976) have discussed the patterns of sociological and contextual variables that are related to child maltreatment. Garbarino (1981) characterizes his research as an ecological approach because of his attempt to delineate factors such as neighborhood characteristics and family structure that are causally related to child maltreatment. This level of analysis primarily addresses Bronfenbrenner's exosystem and microsystem levels. The exosystem level alludes mainly to social structures that do not "themselves contain the developing person but impinge upon or encompass the immediate settings in which that person is found" (Belsky, 1980a, p. 327). Microsystem-level research addresses family variables such as family size, infant temperament, spousal relationships, and behavioral interaction patterns between family members. Microsystem-level research would more readily incorporate personality traits, psychiatric disturbances, and other medical model issues.

Exosystem Factors

Economic impoverishment and neighborhood characteristics are examples of exosystem factors. Sociological investigations have identified several exosystem variables that appear to play a significant role in child maltreatment. The link between poverty and child maltreatment was introduced in chapter 3. Certainly, however, there are factors that might increase the identification of poorer parents as child abusers while underestimating the numbers of more affluent individuals who may maltreat their children. For example, Parke and Collmer (1975) note that private physicians are less apt to report abusive incidents committed by their patients than are doctors on staff at public hospitals. Middle-class housing conditions (single-family dwellings) decrease the likelihood of detection. Middle-class parents also may be more able to wield influence in order to prevent social agencies from detecting and reporting family difficulties. The implication of the lower-class discrimination argument is that a large number of undetected maltreatment incidents involving physical abuse exist among middle- and upper-class families.

It appears highly unlikely, however, that enough undetected incidents exist to distribute physical maltreatment evenly among all socioeconomic groups.

Pelton (1978) lists two factors that appear to reinforce the accuracy of current statistics. First, although reporting laws and public awareness have increased dramatically in recent years, resulting in higher recorded rates of child maltreatment, the overrepresentation of lower income groups has remained constant. Second, the most severe abuse incidents appear to occur in the poorest families, including more fatalities and serious injury. A possible implication of these data is that severe abuse may be more frequently associated with lower-class family life, whereas milder incidents on the maltreatment continuum may remain undetected. Thus the difference between socioeconomic classes may not be so much in the quantity of incidents but in the quality of incidents.

Certainly, financial impoverishment is not the sole causal agent of increased maltreatment rates (Gelles, 1980). Sociosituational researchers have investigated a number of related stress-inducing factors that may be associated with impoverishment and increase the likelihood of maltreatment. The most influential of these factors seem to be the quality of neighborhood characteristics and social support systems.

Garbarino (1981, p. 237) emphasized that the neighborhood is a key factor in child maltreatment:

> Economic factors affect the level of personal resources and therefore the importance of social resources for successful parenthood. . . . Rich people can better "afford" a weak neighborhood than can poor people, who must rely more heavily on the social resources of their ecological niche for support, encouragement and feedback.

Garbarino and Sherman (1979) investigated two neighborhoods that were similar in socioeconomic structure but evidenced different rates of child maltreatment. The high-risk neighborhood was characterized as "socially impoverished" relative to the low-risk neighborhood; mothers tended to be less communicative with one another; they were younger, less experienced, and less self-sufficient; they had fewer provisions for child care; and they were less likely to use social and professional services.

Garbarino (1981) concluded that although economic factors are the most important variable, their influence is mediated by the social structure of the community. Demographic variables that were related to high rates of maltreatment were the percentage of female-headed households, percentage of married mothers in the labor force, and percentage of residents who had lived in the community less than one year. The large number of female-headed households suggests that the families' social and financial resources would be limited compared to those of two-parent households. Families may be less able to offer support to other neighborhood residents when their own survival is a constant challenge. Similarly, the transient nature of some communities may not foster the establishment of supportive relationships among parents.

Because the poor are more dependent on local resources, "socially impoverished" neighborhoods exacerbate the already existent negative effects of poverty. The financially and socially impoverished family suffers from an irresolvable sense of isolation from potential support networks. Few opportunities exist for such families to rely on extended family and community supports to help them resolve the inevitable conflicts and difficulties that arise in child rearing. These parents, with few outlets and inadequate resources, are left to rely on themselves alone to solve serious personal and family problems (Garbarino, 1981). The intense and continuous stress that results from community isolation is considered to be an important causal variable in the chain of events leading to child maltreatment.

Microsystem Factors

Minuchin's (1974) theoretical perspective focuses on the social context of individual behavior. Minuchin considers the family environment to be one of the most important contexts of human development and an especially relevant arena for investigations of child maltreatment. The family environment, and the internal dynamic processes of family members, exist in a constantly changing system of relationships which, in turn, affect the behavior of each individual. Burgess and Conger (1978) have investigated family interaction patterns in abusive and normal families. In their observational study, abusive and neglectful families interacted less frequently and more negatively on both verbal and physical dimensions than did control families. Inconsistent communication characterized the abusive and neglectful families. Similar findings have been reported frequently in the child maltreatment literature (Parke & Collmer, 1975). Abusive households have also been found to be more disorganized than nonabusive households. Abusive parents used a broad range of disciplinary tactics, delivered in a disorganized and haphazard fashion. They were inconsistent in their disciplinary practices and often maintained conflicting behavioral expectancies for their children (Elmer, 1967; Frodi & Lamb, 1980b; Young, 1964).

Silver, Dublin, and Lourie's (1971) longitudinal study indicated that children who are maltreated often become maltreating adults. Bandura (1973) attributes this outcome to inappropriate parental modeling of violent behaviors, which are learned and subsequently performed by the child as an adult with family responsibilities. Faretra's (1981) longitudinal evaluation of sixty-six aggressive adolescents also found histories of child abuse in each case, suggesting that pathological family interaction systems have a deleterious effect on later behavior.

A shortcoming that exists in many of the family interaction studies is that conclusions tend to be descriptive rather than etiological. Although Burgess and Conger (1978) and other researchers investigating family interaction have provided valuable data concerning the nature of behavioral patterns in abusive families, they do not reveal the underlying causality for maltreatment. Multivariate studies that also consider family history and social-situational factors such as infant-parent interactions would be helpful in understanding the etiological pattern of the abusive behavior.

Infant Attachment

Parent-infant relationships have been investigated with respect to the potential effect on later abusive behavior (Ainsworth, 1980). The impetus for such research comes from the work of Spitz (1945) and Bowlby (1969), who initiated investigations into maternal-infant relationships. These researchers suggested that infant-parent relationships exert a profound effect on the infant's emotional and cognitive development and on subsequent infant-caregiver behavior. The implications of such studies are that the affectional bond between infant and parent must be encouraged from birth and that long periods of separation may lead to traumatic consequences for both infant and parent (Klaus & Kennell, 1970).

Ainsworth (1980) discussed an unpublished study by DeLozier (1979) that specifically investigated the relationship between early mother-infant attachment and later child maltreatment. DeLozier (1979) found that abusing mothers, in contrast to a control group, had histories of "severe attachment difficulties" with their own mothers during childhood, experienced frequent periods of abandonment, and were exposed to harsh disciplinary techniques. Subsequently, when these women became mothers, they were highly anxious and angry and somewhat detached from their own infants. George and Main (1979) found that abused infants exhibit frequent mother-avoidant behaviors, suggesting a circuitous pattern of parental maltreatment, infant avoidance, and impeded social development.

Klaus and Kennell (1970) suggest that affectional ties between mother and infant can be easily disturbed and altered permanently by such factors as infant illness, developmental disabilities, and prematurity. Early separation, which may be necessitated by the baby's special needs, may interfere with the maternal-infant relationship that is developing during the first hours after birth. The relationship between exceptional characteristics and subsequent child maltreatment was discussed in chapter 3. Such an exceptional child characteristic as prematurity, physical handicap, or congenital defect may interfere with the bonding process and may contribute to higher rates of child maltreatment.

The important research of Schneider-Rosen, Braunwald, Carlson, and Cicchetti (1985) highlights the attachment difficulties experienced by infants who suffer from physical abuse, neglect, and/or emotional maltreatment. In comparison to nonclinical samples, at twelve, eighteen, and twenty-four months, a much higher percentage of maltreated infants were found to have insecure parental attachments when exposed to a strange laboratory situation. The investigators were not able to detect differences among children as a function of type of maltreatment category, although they emphasized that more than half the children suffered from multiple forms of abuse. Other investigations have also clearly demonstrated deficits in attachment and in emotional and self-concept development among maltreated infants (Bretherton & Waters, 1985; Cicchetti & Rizley, 1981; Egeland & Sroufe, 1981; Gaensbauer & Harmon, 1982; Schneider-Rosen & Cicchetti, 1984).

Although research on the attachment and socioemotional retardation of maltreated infants is very important, it does not reveal the extent to which parents maltreat their children as a function of a lack of initial parent-infant bonding. For example, in such research it is not clear how much the lack of a secure parent-infant attachment is an antecedent or a consequence of maltreatment. Nevertheless, current data are consistent with the view that early bonding difficulties *can be* a factor in subsequent child maltreatment. For example, the lack of strong paternal bonding to the infant is a major factor in father neglect during childhood, and increases the likelihood of other forms of child maltreatment, as discussed in chapters 6 through 8, in particular.

Egeland and Vaughn (1981) have critiqued the attachment theory literature, specifically addressing the alleged link between problems in early maternal-infant bonding and child maltreatment. They found that most studies suffered from methodological problems and inadequate measures of the bonding process. Most studies have been retrospective analyses that have used attachment theory post hoc as a possible explanation for maltreatment. Egeland and Vaughn (1981) completed their own longitudinal analysis with 267 mothers and found no evidence to support the notion that limited contact between infant and mother after birth is in itself related to higher rates of child maltreatment. Child maltreatment appeared more attributable to maternal attitudes toward the infant and other complex factors, such as situational experiences with the infant.

The particular strength of Egeland and Vaughn's (1981) investigation is that it uses a prospective design and therefore does not fall prey to the assumed linearity of cause and effect often proposed in retrospective studies. However, Egeland and Vaughn also had difficulty in generating a valid definitional framework for the maternal-infant bonding process. In addition, there may be benefits to the child of early infant-parent contact that are not considered in Egeland and Vaughn's analysis, such as stimulation of certain aspects of emotional and cognitive development. It is more prudent to evaluate very early infant-parent contact as only one component of the total ecological system that affects the reciprocal attachment of infant and parent. A broader approach, one that incorporates the many levels of environmental factors that affect the family, may offer a more accurate model of child maltreatment.

A major problem with much of the work on infant-parent bonding is that more diverse family-system factors have not been considered. The quality of the father-mother as well as the father-infant relationship must be taken into account (Biller, 1971a, 1982a). The work of Lamb (1976b, 1981a), Parke (1981); Pedersen (1980); and Yogman (1982) seems especially relevant in attempting to understand the early attachment process, because these investigators are concerned with infant bonding to both fathers and mothers. As is discussed in greater detail in chapter 6, lack of appropriate father involvement greatly increases the risk of child maltreatment. From a social systems perspective, it is clear that the more fathers can be helped to become involved positively with their children by means of cultural, educational, institutional, and neighborhood supports as well as by intrafamily encouragement, the less likely child maltreatment will be to occur. At the most general level, there must be a much stronger expectation for fathers, and men in general, to take constructive responsibility for the welfare of children, actively cooperating with females rather than abdicating responsibility to them for child rearing.

Theoretical Limitations

The foundation of the social systems model is sound to the extent that it effectively connects sociocultural and social-situational variables to child maltreatment. Researchers such as Garbarino (1980) and Pelton (1981) have related social system variables including financial stress and neighborhood characteristics to abusive parental behavior. The social systems model tends to address concrete variables such as family structure, education, income, and neighborhood characteristics that can be directly associated with abuse. On the contrary, psychodynamic researchers tend to become immersed in a vast array of alternative conceptual models and questionable assessment procedures. Progress in developing a meaningful psychiatric model may have to wait until better validated assessment methods of associating characterological profiles with abusive behavior are available.

Because the social systems model is still a relatively recent development in the maltreatment literature, the initial conclusions have yet to be verified experimentally to the extent that they can be clearly translated into effective social programming. According to Albee (1980), this may be due to three factors. Prevention and intervention techniques are still primarily based on the *defect* or *medical model,* with minimal generalizability to a social systems approach. Second, the science of prevention is still in its initial stages of development and is not yet easily channeled into program development. Third, epidemiological data may tend to identify a large number of false positives, particularly among the poor, with the consequence of negative social labeling. Albee indicates that prediction techniques, including those applied to incidence rates of child abuse, are not sufficiently accurate for effective social programming. The implications of Albee's criticism address the need for continued research with prediction models such as Garbarino's (1980) investigations of neighborhood characteristics and Pelton's (1981) work relating poverty to child maltreatment.

In the areas of prediction and prevention, the social systems model exhibits a conceptual advantage over the psychiatric perspective. The psychiatric approach, attributing maltreatment to internal psychopathology, places the causes of abuse in a largely unreachable and unchangeable internal realm. From this perspective, the most effective intervention is dynamically oriented psychotherapy. A social systems model offers greater promise for intervention because the alleged etiological system exists within the social environment. Prevention and intervention can be targeted at observable and measurable social variables. For example, Garbarino's data suggest that certain types of neighborhoods could benefit from programs that emphasize social support programs such as home intervention or community day care. Pelton's (1981) studies linking economic disadvantagement and child maltreatment offer a strong rationale to those social leaders who want to eradicate poverty and develop a more efficient system of child and family financial support.

A difficulty inherent in the social systems perspective is the inability to integrate intraindividual factors within its structure. This may be due, in part, to the limitations of the psychiatric perspective and the unreliability of characterological profiles. It would seem, however, that the focus in the social systems model on conceptual analysis of the external environment leaves little room for internal factors, even if the science of character assessment should advance. Researchers who take into account the manner in which environmental and social factors interact with internal psychological processes may help us to understand better the complex etiological structure of child maltreatment. Mischel's (1979) analysis of the impact of situational affects on behavior includes a detailed discussion of cognitive variables such as self-regulatory rules, encoding strategies (the interaction between a person's actual competencies and the self-perception of those competencies), and metacognitive factors (exploring the individual's own understanding of developing strategies for self regulation). Bandura (1973) also addresses cognitive variables through his discussion of memory representations and internal anticipatory factors in mediating environmental contingencies. Research that specifically considers the mediative effect of cognitive processes and the manner in which they are related to child maltreatment may assist investigators to conceptualize the relative contributions of both internal and social factors (Solomon, 1982).

The inclusion of cognitive factors appears to fall between the theoretical premises of the psychiatric and social systems perspectives. The former primarily investigates psychopathological factors; the latter addresses situational determinants of abuse. Cognitive factors may be more readily incorporated within an interactionist perspective that includes psychiatric, environmental, and cognitive mediative variables.

Transactional Model

Chibucos (1980) has suggested that child maltreatment is the result of a number of interacting influences and represents one developmental outcome from a continuum of potential outcomes. This continuum model of parent-child interactions lends itself to the notion that many potential factors, which have been identified from different fields of investigation, can affect parental behavior.

The transactional or interactionist perspective incorporates the notion of multivariate causation and the need for more individualized and specific assessment procedures. For example, Frodi and Lamb (1980b) discussed the contribution of child, adult, and situational characteristics as joint determinants of maltreatment. Vietze et al. (1980) used an interactionist perspective in an attempt to predict child maltreatment. The principal contribution of the interactionist perspective is the recognition of multiple causation.

Child maltreatment may be more validly conceptualized with an interactionist perspective taking into account the contributions of several different theoretical models. The interactionist focus appears to maintain more potential for researchers to integrate successfully the various causal factors (situational stress, developmental history, parental traits, and so on) into a comprehensive theoretical framework. The primary objective of such research is to encourage the development of multivariate models that investigate multiple causation rather than focusing on a single set of variables.

However, methodological and theoretical shortcomings restrict the potential contribution of a multiple regression prediction model. It may be premature for researchers to attempt prediction models based on the data currently available. Retrospective multivariate analyses that investigate relevant factors may add to the knowledge base and eventually contribute to the construction of valid, reliable prediction models. Vietze et al. (1980) suggest that the analysis of interactional variables will provide new ideas concerning methods of targeting and integrating relevant factors into a comprehensive theoretical framework. The inclusion of specific social-ecological variables, such as neighborhood characteristics or extended family support systems, may also increase the predictable variance in a longitudinal study of child maltreatment.

It is relevant to construct an integrative model of child maltreatment that draws on the hypotheses suggested by current theoretical perspectives. This model should incorporate potential causal variables that have been suggested by psychiatric and social system models to be directly or indirectly related to child maltreatment. The major implication to be derived from such a model is that multiple levels of causation are potentially involved in the maltreatment situation.

Figure 4–1 presents a preliminary outline for a transactional model of child maltreatment and paternal deprivation. Several important implications may be

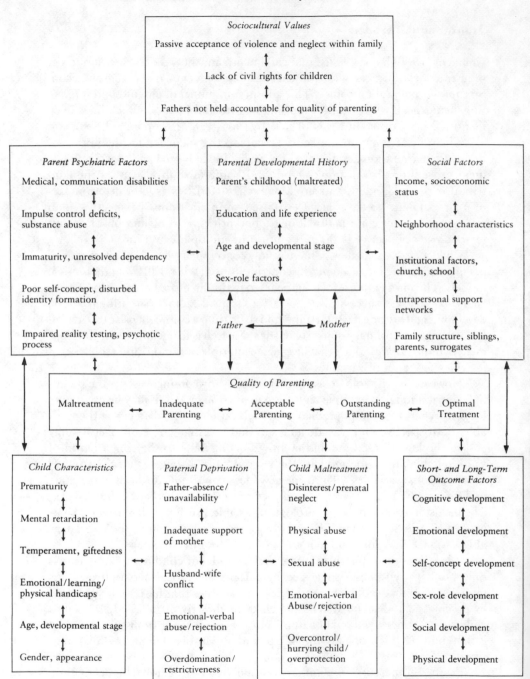

Figure 4–1. Preliminary Outline of Transactional Model of Child Maltreatment and Paternal Deprivation

derived from the model. The initial point is that child maltreatment does not reflect unitary disturbances in the parents but results from the interaction of several potential factors, including paternal deprivation. Second, causal variables do not exist in isolation but are components of constantly changing dynamic processes. For example, psychiatric factors related to child maltreatment and paternal deprivation may only gain expression in the presence of specific social situational factors. This point is consistent with the interactionist models of Bem and Allen (1974) and Mischel (1979). Causal variables are not static structures. They reflect reciprocal relationships that exert mutual influences and may eventually translate into maltreatment. A third implication of this model is that variables that are related to child maltreatment also reflect the dominant sociocultural perspective of child rearing, which, as we have emphasized, includes an unbalanced distribution of expected child-rearing responsibilities between mothers and fathers. The social acceptance of both intrapersonal violence and paternal neglect is an important factor in the frequent occurrence of child maltreatment.

The interactionist perspective is a crucial component of the continued development of theoretical models. The unitary perspective of the psychiatric and social systems models has served to hinder the integration of key elements of each model into a larger conceptual framework. Zigler (1980) has discussed the "alienation" of child maltreatment research from the socialization literature. Using an interactionist perspective, we have made an initial attempt to begin to integrate relevant socialization research, focusing on the complex interrelationships between paternal deprivation and child maltreatment.

5
Sexual Maltreatment

S exual abuse is one of the most common forms of child maltreatment. Most epidemiological estimates are somewhat suspect and indicate widely varying incidence rates. Some retrospective research findings, however, suggest that during childhood, sexual abuse rates may be as high as 19 percent for females and 8 percent for males (Finkelhor, 1979). Female children appear more likely than male children to be victims of sexual abuse. Data from interviews with adult females indicate that 12 percent were victims of intrafamilial sexual abuse before the age of fourteen and 16 percent before the age of eighteen. It is important to emphasize, however, that for only 2 percent of the sexually abused children was there actually a report made to the police (Russell, 1983).

Approximately two-thirds of all reported cases of sexual maltreatment of children involve either fathers or potential father substitutes, including stepfathers or mothers' boyfriends (Kempe & Kempe, 1984). The fact that a very large proportion of incidents occur in families in which the biological father is not living in the home reinforces the notion that sexual abuse must frequently be considered as a correlate of paternal deprivation. In the reconstituted family, the quandary the child encounters is clear. Should the child take the risk of revealing the abuse and subsequently being blamed for possibly inducing an additional family separation or trauma? This conflict helps to maintain the shroud of secrecy that surrounds most sexually abusive relationships within families. The sexually maltreated child usually attempts to remain silent in order to support the fragile structure of the family.

Nevertheless, reporting rates for the sexual abuse of children are increasing dramatically, as is indicated by the American Humane Association's annual data: 1,975 cases in 1976, 4,327 in 1977, 22,918 in 1982. The statistics for 1984 revealed a 54 percent increase in reported incidence over 1983—far and away the most dramatic increase of any form of child maltreatment. The increase is hauntingly similar to the pattern evident in other areas of child maltreatment where improvements in local, state, and federal reporting systems have started to present a more accurate picture of the scope of the problem (Finkelhor, 1984).

Much previous research has suggested that female children are more likely to be victims of sexual abuse than are male children. However, recent data underscore the interconnection between inadequate fathering and the sexual maltreatment of male children as well as female children. A high proportion of child victims, both boys and girls, come from single-parent, female-headed households or from families where there is a stepfather or live-in boyfriend. It is common for children who are victims of sexual abuse to also suffer from other types of physical and emotional maltreatment. As with most other forms of maltreatment, children who are sexually abused are especially likely to come from economically impoverished single-parent families and/or from families in which the father is cold, rejecting, or otherwise inadequate (Biller, 1974c; Finkelhor, 1984; Finkelhor & Browne, 1985).

Paternally deprived children are more susceptible to both intrafamilial and extrafamilial sexual abuse. Children who do not receive adequate nurturance from adult males within their family are more vulnerable to inappropriate advances by older children and adults, whether they be family members, neighbors, teachers, or strangers. Paternally deprived children are likely to feel "starved" for male attention and to be overly receptive to men who want to sexually, or otherwise, manipulate them. As is elaborated in chapters 7 through 10, inadequately fathered children often have special difficulty setting their own limits and behaving in an independent manner.

This chapter is not an attempt to explicate all the varied aspects of sexual maltreatment but, rather, will focus on family context variables that have an impact on the child. The goals are twofold: to offer a biocultural and historical framework, and to address the most salient clinical factors involved in families experiencing sexual maltreatment. There is an exploration of definitional difficulties that have also plagued the areas of physical and emotional abuse. With regard to the definitional dilemma, data on incidence rates and types of sexual maltreatment are discussed. The latter sections of the chapter center on family system factors associated with the sexual maltreatment of children.

Historical Background

The cultural perspective of a particular society guides the way in which children are viewed and protected within the family and other social institutions. As emphasized in chapter 2, economic pressures, religious views concerning violence, and the roles of mothers and fathers are among the many factors influencing a society's treatment of its children. Unfortunately, very few societies throughout history have viewed children as individuals in need of special sensitivity, protection, and guidance. DeMause (1974) has graphically depicted the horrors inflicted on children in many societies, particularly in earlier epochs, including extremely severe physical and sexual abuse. The history of violence and terror perpetrated on children is not unlike or less severe than other mass forms of torture or genocide directed toward other relatively powerless groups of individuals throughout history. The regrettable legacy of continual subordination of children to adult whims and needs is an all too recurrent theme in human history. Sexual maltreatment represents an especially destructive aspect of the denial of human rights to children.

Historians of childhood have documented a variety of sexually abusive practices that, viewed from a modern perspective, are among the cruelest transgressions that adults can commmit against children. In the early Roman era, the use of children as sexual partners was socially sanctioned, as was castration of children to maintain their later sexual attractiveness as male prostitutes (deMause, 1974). The intricate relationships among social health standards, moral concerns, and scientific knowledge about development intertwine to form the network of values that a society establishes to guide its treatment of children. For example, early Roman times were characterized by a shorter life span; clouded boundaries between childhood, adolescence, and adulthood; ignorance concerning the emotional needs of children; and rigid social class divisions. Such factors left children totally dependent on the individual scruples of caretakers, who in many cases were not the biological parents.

Aside from the use of children to serve the sexual desires of adults, other cultures believed that sexual behavior was needed in childhood in order to ensure appropriate growth and development. Members of the court of little Louis XIII in eighteenth-century France sexually aroused him through penile and nipple stimulation on a regular basis. His basic sexuality was not viewed as being different from that of his caretakers, and they believed that he would mature faster if he were to experience active erotic stimulation as a young child (deMause, 1974).

Without strong moral and religious prohibitions, children would continue to be viewed as potential sexual partners for more powerful adults. This situation is analagous to the depersonalization process that occurs in most circumstances where there is victimization of a large segment of the population. False characteristics attributed to the victimized group justify the offensive act in the mind of the perpetrator. Rapists often describe their victims as having "asked for it" through behavior and dress, thereby entitling the perpetrator to commit the deed. Totalitarian leaders such as Hitler have been able to convince others of the "inferior" qualities of particular groups of people, thereby justifying the mass extermination of the "deserving" victims. The victimization of a group, however, betrays the psychological inadequacies of the perpetrators. The victim plays a role—a role whose boundaries are prescribed by the perpetrator, thereby revealing the psychological and social structure of the latter while revealing little about the victim. "In sexual abuse, as in physical abuse, the child was only an incidental victim, a measure of the part it played in the defense system of the adult" (deMause, 1974, p. 545).

Strong religious, moral, and legal sanctions are important in lowering the incidence of sexual and physical abuse of vulnerable children. Gil (1979) has emphasized that research and treatment dollars are misspent when they do not include procedures to decrease the social sanctioning of violence toward children by dealing with our cultural value system. Secondary prevention aimed at high-risk groups and tertiary programs focused on offenders may serve as little more than Band-Aids in the absence of a broader model of societal intervention that has the backing of major political and religious leaders.

Children's Rights

Recent child advocacy efforts, while alerting the public to the rights and needs of children, appear to have enjoyed mixed results with respect to actual changes in adult behavior. Although public condonement and support of child-staffed prostitution houses like those found in ancient Rome is no longer in vogue, few can dispute the widespread existence of child pornographic rings, the use of runaways for prostitution, and the sexual maltreatment of children in their own homes and communities. The principal difference between the twentieth-century United States and ancient Rome is that present-day leaders of society would condemn sexual maltreatment and lobby for legislation to outlaw it, while their ancient counterparts would likely be active participants themselves and fail to understand its malignant course in a child's development. But at least our ancient counterparts were acting in a manner consistent with their theoretical understanding of children, a primitive understanding at best. Current legislators can draw on the knowledge of countless professionals from a number of child health fields to find justification for discouraging sexual maltreatment. Yet few legislative efforts are directed toward establishing the type of social change advocated by Gil (1979).

Sexual maltreatment and other forms of child abuse are no less common than a decade ago and, unfortunately, may actually have increased, at least in part as a function of a rise is family instability and paternal deprivation during the 1970s. An unending stream of research, much of it badly needed, flows into the professional journals each year with apparently little resultant change in social behavior. Although we appear to be becoming more proficient at tertiary prevention—that is, at understanding the dynamics involved in sexual maltreatment and becoming effective in helping afflicted families—we seem to be relatively inept at attacking the etiological foundation of the problem. On the other hand, changes in social values may take considerable time to be reflected in basic family and institutional processes. As is discussed in chapter 11, it is hoped that a growing concern for the father's involvement in the family, and the increasing commitment of many young people to preventing paternal deprivation associated with divorce, will do much to lessen the incidence of child maltreatment in the next decade (Biller, 1981a, 1984a, 1984b, 1984c). Certain types of child maltreatment, such as severe physical abuse, may already be declining. There has been definite progress in the reporting of cases of physical and sexual maltreatment, and an apparent rise in the incidence rate may actually be an artifact of better assessment procedures.

Definitional Problems

A major reason for conceptualizing sexual maltreatment within a cultural framework is that our understanding of the phenomenon is based on a socially mediated value structure. Conflicting opinions exist concerning whether the twentieth-century United States represents a new wave of interest in child-related advocacy. Greene (1979, p. 9) asserts that "there has been a new willingness, in various quarters, to confront the oppressiveness and inequities in our society, particularly as these find expression through our caretaking and our training institutions." In contrast, Burgess (1979, p. 99) states:

> In the United States today the needs of children have been submerged under a wave of adult indifference. The causes are complex. Adults live not in a child-oriented but a youth-culture. . . . Many adults, including several leaders of the current women's liberation movement, are so preoccupied with individual self-fulfillment that the needs of children have been forgotten.

The reality of contemporary sensitivity to the needs of children lies somewhere between these two positions. Certainly, with the discovery in the late 1950s and early 1960s of child abuse as a serious threat to our children, and the later emergence of increased awareness of sexual abuse, more attention is being paid to child maltreatment than ever before. With this vivid surge of concern, as evidenced by the public media and the availability of treatment programs, comes the need to define with greater clarity the behaviors constituting various types of child maltreatment. As discussed in chapter 2, arriving at uniform frameworks acceptable to all interested parties has proved a most difficult task.

The definitional model offered in chapter 2 (figure 2–1) is based on a continuum of family functioning. Child maltreatment can occur in a variety of forms, some overtly very destructive and some more subtle, difficult to detect, and debatable. This dilemma is particularly prevalent with respect to emotional abuse, where different cultures and even different professionals will heatedly debate whether or not various behaviors and/or environments are abusive. We contend that this is the case with sexual maltreatment, although in general researchers and clinicians have found consensus definitions somewhat easier to attain than have those focusing on physical or emotional abuse.

Most researchers define sexual maltreatment as inappropriate physical contact between an adult and child for the purposes of the sexual gratification of the adult (Faller, 1981). A recent amendment to the Federal Child Abuse Prevention and Treatment Act of 1974 defines sexual maltreatment as

> the obscene or pornographic photographing, filming or depiction of children for commercial purposes, or the rape, molestation, incest, prostitution or other

such forms of sexual exploitation of children under circumstances which indicate that the child's health or welfare is harmed or threatened thereby.

The National Center on Child Abuse and Neglect (NCCAN), which is the federal agency designated to research and fund child maltreatment research, has proposed the following definition (NCCAN, 1981, p. 2):

contacts or interactions between a child and an adult when the child is being used for the sexual stimulation of the perpetrator or another person. Sexual abuse may also be committed by a person under the age of 18 when that person is either significantly older than the victim or when the perpetrator is in a position of power or control over another child.

Types of Sexual Maltreatment

Few individuals contest the malignant effects of sexual molestation on the child. The explicit aspects of sexual maltreatment, and those forms that constitute the majority of reported sexually abusive incidents, are agreed on by most professionals. We suggest, however, that other, more subtle forms of parental abuse also need to be understood and defined, although certainly such adult-child interactions will draw much less consensus when labeled as acts of sexual maltreatment. For example, the father who, while not physically accosting his daughter, states that she is inferior and much less capable than her brother because she is only a female is, in our view, sexually maltreating her. The little boy who is constantly berated by his parent because he is not athletic or aggressive (or "masculine") enough would be another victim of such verbal sexual maltreatment. Certainly these situations do not fall within the definitional boudaries offered by the NCCAN or the Federal Child Abuse Prevention and Treatment Act of 1974. Nor are they likely to be malignant to the child to the explicit extent of causing serious physical harm or necessitating some form of family separation. As is discussed in chapters 7 and 8, however, the psychological consequences may be just as devastating.

The boundaries between sexual maltreatment and emotional abuse for this type of verbal assault are definitely blurred. The need to place this form of maltreatment within any particular category could be viewed as an irrelevant concern. The principal issue here is that healthy self-concept development may be seriously impeded through continuous verbal assaults on the constitutional inclinations of the particular child.

Continuum Model

We offer a continuum definition in order to establish a broader conceptual framework of sexual maltreatment. This type of framework does not obviate the need for more specific definitions such as those offered in state statutes or the Federal Child Abuse Prevention and Treatment Act (1974). The rationale for such highly specific definitions relating to adult-child physical interactions is made clear by the need for legislators to establish guidelines that are readily interpretable by social workers, law enforcement personnel, and child care workers. For example, day care workers need to be aware of mandatory reporting statutes relating to highly explicit acts of sexual and physical abuse. In the broader context of child development, however, we suggest that sexual maltreatment has many forms, some that are clearly overt and directly harmful to the child and others that are more subtle and nested within parent-child communication patterns.

The continuum model is likely to be more palatable to clinicians who have undoubtedly experienced the difficult task of helping a patient work out significant personal difficulties related to parental responses to his or her sexual development. A particularly common example is that of the young woman who is experiencing interpersonal difficulties because of parental feedback that her sexuality is unacceptable. Because of parental reactions, this young woman may have been made to feel horribly guilty at the time of initial menstruation and may have experienced the need to repress any good feelings about her sexual development. Although most researchers would agree that such a form of sexual maltreatment is not likely to necessitate investigation from the child protective department, this form of abuse may be quite deleterious in the long run and does require that some action at the primary prevention educational level be directed at potential parents and those with younger children. Failure to acknowledge these more subtle forms of sexual abuse offers passive condonement of parental, institutional, and other forms of caretaking abuse that, though not physical, continue to interfere with the positive sexual and emotional development of males and females. In chapter 11 there is a discussion of various types of prevention strategies that may be applicable to decreasing the incidence of different forms of sexual maltreatment as well as other aspects of child abuse.

Statistical Data

At this point it is impossible to offer exact figures concerning the frequency of sexual abuse, for several reasons. First, statistical estimates reflect reported cases, and it is widely accepted among researchers that a very small percentage of actual cases are brought to the attention of local authorities (Kempe, 1980). Hence the American Humane Association (AHA, 1978) documented only 6,087 cases in 1978 based on the number of officially reported incidents. Faller (1981, p. 144) notes, however, that "We can be well assured that this is only the 'tip of the iceberg' and that the real incidence is much higher." Second, the conceptual or definitional basis that researchers use to determine the statistics varies across different studies. Although this concern does not present as precipitous a dilemma as exists in other areas of child maltreatment, the number of cases will be dependent on a particular researcher's conceptual biases. An example of this difficulty would be sexual abuse studies that focus on reported cases of incest but fail to include other forms of sexual abuse such as child pornography and child prostitution. Most estimates of sexual abuse, unless otherwise indicated, do not include the latter two categories. Other forms of sexual abuse, such as fondling or forcing the victim to fondle, may also not be included within a particular study.

Finkelhor (1979) reported findings from a university-based study in which students were asked about their sexual experiences as children. Among the women, 19.2 percent, and among the men, 8.2 percent, reported having been sexually victimized during childhood. Another retrospective study of 1,800 college students revealed that almost a third of the respondents from both sexes reported some form of sexual victimization (Landis, 1956). Perhaps an even more noteworthy statistic concerning the latter study is the fact that only half the females and one-tenth of the males told their parents about the sexual abuse.

Other studies offer widely varying statistics. DeFrancis (1969) and the American Humane Association estimated that sexual maltreatment occurs approximately at the rate of 40 per million. The Santa Clara County (California) Child Sexual Abuse Treatment Programs suggest an incidence rate of 800–1,000 per million. Giaretto's (1982) estimate (the Santa Clara County Program) would prorate a national incest rate of 250,000 cases annually. Contrasted to this is the National Center on Child Abuse and Neglect's (1981) estimate of 100,000 cases per year. This wide variation between statistical estimates is related in part to different conceptual frameworks. The smaller estimate likely refers to the prorated amount of currently reported cases. Kempe and Kempe (1984) suggest that the larger figures reflect the prorated percentage obtained in most questionnaire studies and that this number is generally significantly greater than the number of officially reported cases.

Researchers also differ with respect to reports of the age ranges of the victims. Kempe and Kempe's (1984) research suggested that male victims were distributed evenly from six to sixteen years of age, whereas 50 percent of all female victims were under the age of eleven. Finkelhor (1979) reported in his assessment that the average age of female victims is ten and that of males approximately eleven. Female victims outnumber male victims by a 4 to 1 ratio in many studies. Mother-son incest appears to be relatively infrequent, or at least rarely reported. Father-daughter incest and female sexual molestation by other males appear to be the more predominant forms of victimization. When the victim is female, the perpetrator tends to be male. The male victim, however, usually is accosted by another male. This may also relate at least in part to why the reporting rates for the sexual abuse of males tend to be low. Socially, males are expected to remain strong and silent, and sexual victimization may be interpreted as an especially serious affront to their masculinity. Though certainly often very difficult, it would seem at least more socially acceptable for a female victim to report her victimization without serious challenge to her sex-role identity.

Most studies suggest that the perpetrator is usually well known to the victim (Groth, Hobson, & Gary, 1982). The American Humane Association's (1978) review of 9,000 cases revealed that 75 percent of the incidents were perpetrated by a member of the victim's household, a relative, a neighbor, or an acquaintance. Other studies have suggested that from 30 to 80 percent of other sexually abusive incidents are committed by parents, parent substitutes, or relatives charged with care of the child. DeFrancis (1969) noted that sexual abuse by a stranger is usually a singular occurrence outside the home, whereas intrafamilial abuse is typically repetitive and homebound. Kempe and Kempe (1984) found that the duration of sexual abuse tends to be approximately five years, with one-third of reported cases involving natural fathers or mothers, one-third nonrelated parental substitutes, and one-third nonparental perpetrators. Biological mothers were discovered to be accomplices to the sexual abuse in at least 43 percent of reported cases. Cantwell (1981) reviewed all reported cases of sexual abuse in Denver in 1979 and found that 45 percent of the victims were under twelve and 16 percent under six. Over 50 percent of the perpetrators lived with the family (fathers, stepfathers, mothers' boyfriends, and so on). Some children were victimized by babysitters, distant relatives, and family friends. Most sexual abuse is committed by individuals familiar with the child.

The reporting rate for sexual maltreatment has risen dramatically within the past decade, but this is much more a reflection of better record keeping than of a change in the actual incidence. This situation is directly connected to the general difficulty in deriving accurate statistics concerning family violence. Reporting rates are a function of the validity and depth of the assessment systems available to produce such data. A dramatic example of this difficulty is the number of reported cases of child abuse in the state of Florida in 1970 and 1971 (Kempe & Kempe, 1984). In 1970, before the introduction of a statewide child abuse reporting hotline, seventeen reports of child abuse were recorded for the entire state. With the onset of a well-publicized reporting hotline the next year, the number of reported cases exceeded nineteen thousand. An analogous dilemma exists for researchers in sexual abuse. The current reporting systems are inadequate for two reasons. First, most sexual victimization is invisible, leaving few physical stigmata and remaining undetected by authorities. Second, the reporting systems that are in place are frequently incomplete, with data remaining unavailable to local agencies.

Inappropriate Parenting

Extensive research has been generated, particularly within the past fifteen years, on the psychological factors associated with sexual victimization. Although there are some conflicting findings, many common threads emerge that present a substantial knowledge base for researchers and clinicians. This section focuses on data concerning both intrafamilial and extrafamilial sexual maltreatment. As emphasized earlier in this chapter, within our societal value structure, all forms of overt sexual activity between children and adults are forbidden both morally and legally. Legal statutes are exemplified by the Child Abuse Prevention and Treatment Act of 1974, which includes the targeting of sexual abuse perpetrated by adults. Moreover, our scientific knowledge about developmental needs permits us to understand that sexual behavior between an adult and a child is not in the child's best interests. The abuse is clearly committed to meet the sexual and emotional needs of the abuser. Perhaps it is this latter fact that most differentiates other forms of child maltreatment from sexual abuse.

As noted in chapters 3 and 4, physical abuse and neglect, for example, seem frequently to be related to parental stress and appear often to be linked with the inability of the family to cope with socioeconomic and community pressures (Pelton, 1981). Vastly different rates of child abuse are evident within different neighborhoods with varying socioeconomic conditions and support services for parents (Garbarino & Stocking, 1980). This relationship, however, has appeared much less linear with respect to sexual abuse (Groth, Hobson, & Gary, 1982). According to Kempe and Kempe (1984), sexually abusive families within a particular community are relatively representative of the population distribution, and there is no clear correlation with low socioeconomic status. Nevertheless, there has been an increase in recent research exploring the relationship among socioeconomic factors, social isolation, and sexual abuse. As with research on other forms of child abuse, there is beginning to be a conceptual shift away from a narrow psychiatric deviancy focus to a broader one that includes social and cultural influences. Children from economically impoverished single-parent families and those who suffer from paternal inadequacy are overrepresented in sexual abuse statistics (Biller, 1974c; Finkelhor, 1984; Finkelhor & Browne, 1985).

Throughout this book it is maintained that the single most detrimental factor damaging family functioning is the lack of sufficient positive involvement of fathers. Inappropriate fathering and paternal deprivation are major variables contributing strongly to the incidence of sexual abuse and to other forms of child maltreatment. Available evidence suggests that the psychodynamic, personality, and relationship characteristics of fathers and mothers may be especially revealing with respect to understanding sexual maltreatment.

Context of Abuse

Conte (1982, 1984) has noted that most researchers and practitioners divide sexual abuse into two conceptually distinct contexts. The first involves incestuous relations, typically between father and daughter, and is clinically presumed to exist with the explicit or implicit collusion of the mother (Justice & Justice, 1979). The second context involves the nonrelated adult, typically male, who acts on his or her sexual interest in children. By far, the majority of the sexual abuse literature has been directed toward the incestuous family, even though it represents only about half of the reported cases when contrasted to other sexually abusive situations involving children. Conte and Berliner (1984) reviewed data concerning 583 sexually abused children and found that 16 percent involved fathers, 15 percent stepfathers, and 15 percent other male relatives such as uncles or grandfathers. This data is consistent with Cantwell's (1981) review of reported cases in Denver. In his study, 54 percent of sexual abusers were "family members" (fathers, stepfathers, mothers' boyfriends), leaving almost half the remaining incidents accounted for by adults not connected with the family. Burgess and Holmstrom (1975) also found about half of their sexually abused population to be victims of incest.

The tendency for researchers to direct their efforts toward incestuous situations is associated with several factors, including the clinical accessibility of incestuous families and the presumption that incest is a family system dysfunction rather than a reflection of severe individual psychopathology. Incest would seem to be more amenable to psychotherapeutic interventions because of its role within the family system, whereas the nonrelated adult sexual offender is labeled as having characterological psychopathology, which is generally viewed as more resistant to change (Groth, 1979).

Conte (1982, 1984) strongly contests the assumptions made by most clinicians that intrafamilial and extrafamilial sexual abusers have little in common. Traditionally, most researchers have viewed the incestuous father or stepfather as expressing nonsexual frustrations such as a need for intimacy, comfort, or security that is relatively unavailable elsewhere in his family. Conversely, the nonrelated sexual abuser is presumed to be expressing maladaptive sexual behavior reflective of individual psychopathology.

However, the presumptions that have typically guided clinical intervention concerning intra- and extrafamilial sexual abuse have not been subjected to rigorous scientific scrutiny. Researchers have begun to question the assumption that incestuous fathers are usually sexually abusive only within the confines of their home. Hence, incestual and pedophile offenders may attain their diagnosis on the basis of where their dysfunction is identified (that is, whether they are detected outside or inside the family) rather than on the basis of their particular personality functioning. As long as there are relatively few studies comparing them on measures of personality dynamics, it does seem more appropriate to reserve judgment on the degree of similarity or difference between males who are related to their sexually maltreated child victims and those who are not (Chandler, 1982). There is further discussion of the overlapping issues between intrafamilial and extrafamilial sexual abuse later in this chapter.

Sexual and Sex-Role Issues

Incest usually refers to father-daughter relationships but may also include other intrafamilial relationships such as mother-son, grandfather-granddaughter, and sibling incest. Weissberg (1983) reports that intercourse occurs in about half the reported cases, father-daughter fondling and oral-genital sex in about 20 percent. In his study, Finkelhor (1979) found that only 4 percent of the victims reported intercourse, whereas masturbation and fondling appeared to be the most common forms of sexual abuse. Although incestuous sexual abuse may occur only once, more typically the behavior pattern lasts for approximately three or four years, is directed toward the eldest daughter, and endures until the adolescent terminates the behavior or it is discovered. Father-daughter (and stepfather-daughter) incest accounts for approximately three-quarters of the reported cases (Kempe, 1980). The remaining cases involve mother-son, mother-daughter, father-son, and sibling incest. Few studies have investigated these rarer forms of incest. The impression among researchers is that other types of incest are grossly underreported in comparison to father-daughter incest. In general, father-daughter incest becomes intolerable to the daughter as she matures and seeks out peer relationships, which often leads to a crisis within the dysfunctional family (Kempe & Kempe, 1984).

Family Typologies

Several different family typologies have been suggested to describe incestuous families. A common thread through most of these models is the adult's use of emotional manipulation rather than violent power in order to violate the child (Chandler, 1982). Certainly violence and/or alcohol may be present, but most researchers believe the power of the adult is exercised through a variety of complex manipulative and dysfunctional strategies. An example of this would be the father who gives his daughter a special role, usually involving a preferred attentional status within the family structure, a role more typically occupied by a mother but forced on the child.

Faller (1981) places incestuous families into one of four categories:

1. Families in which most if not all relationships are sexual in nature.
2. Families in which either the victim or the perpetrator is mentally retarded.
3. Families in which the perpetrator is psychopathic, bearing little feeling of responsibilities for what has happened.

4. Families in which there has been a role exchange between mother and daughter. Incest involving role exchange, where the mother has usually abdicated many of her maternal and spousal responsibilities, is certainly much more prevalent than the first three types.

Justice and Justice (1979) suggest that a nonparticipating mother has one or more of the following characteristics:

1. She seeks a role reversal with the daughter.
2. She keeps herself tired and worn out.
3. She is frigid and wants no sex with her husband.
4. She is weak and submissive.
5. She becomes "Mom" to her husband, assumes control of most responsibilities, and is no longer viewed as a spouse.
6. She is indifferent, absent, or promiscuous, and particularly uncaring about the daughter participating in the incest.

Justice and Justice (1979) also present three personality typologies for sexually abusing fathers. Symbiotic fathers are described as those who have overwhelming unmet needs for love, intimacy, and acceptance and cannot attain these objectives outside a sexual relationship. The other two categories include those fathers with basic psychopathic personalities (an underlying lack of development of an adequate conscience and sense of interpersonal responsibility) and those with pedophilic personalities, who are obsessed with what they perceive is the sexual attractiveness of children, their own as well as those unrelated to them. In addition, Justice and Justice describe cases of so-called cultural incest involving fathers who grew up in a social milieu in which incest was an accepted practice and who therefore feel that such behavior is an appropriate part of their paternal responsibilities.

According to Justice and Justice, symbiotic men, who are essentially starved for affection and unable to attain this affection within their marital or adult relationships, represent the largest category of sexual abusers. For such a man, the sexually abusive relationship with a child may become one where sex in itself is a relatively unimportant part of the agenda. It is the use of sexuality to attain intimacy with another person that is most significant.

Clinical research suggests that the structure of incestuous families becomes one in which the individuals are bound within a system of dysfunctional and dependent relationships. Most typically, an emotionally starving father, involved in a relationship with an indifferent, rejecting, or unavailable wife, displaces his needs onto a child, usually his eldest daughter. The abuse most often remains undetected. If it is exposed, however, it is usually through a crisis precipitated by the daughter because of her maturing needs for independence and separation from the family.

It appears ironic that, although fathers and father substitutes are typically the perpetrators of intrafamilial sexual abuse, so much emphasis has been placed on the mother's responsibility. Some of the literature casts the father as a victim along with his child while blaming the mother for not providing an adequate affectional and parental structure within the family. We do not question that in most cases both parents contribute to the incestuous situation, but we do wonder whether some of the focus on the mother's culpability is also, in part, a function of our social values deemphasizing paternal responsibility and accountability for children. Though acknowledging the impact of both parents in intrafamilial sexual maltreatment, some explanations suggest the mother has the basic control of the situation and is in some way setting up the father.

Extrafamilial Abuse

Despite the possibility that extrafamilial sexual abuse accounts for the majority of sexually abusive incidents involving children, there are relatively few data available on this vital subject (Conte, 1982). The reason for this situation appears to be related to the clincal biases and theoretical orientations of researchers, the more limited accessibility to nonfamilial offenders, and the seemingly smaller detection rate for extrafamilial sexual abuse. Extrafamilial sexual abuse must be considered within the broader context of social neglect, thereby mandating theoretical frameworks that extend beyond the familial boundaries of incestuous situations. The detection and support system vitally necessary for the completion of research on extrafamilial sexual abusers is almost nonexistent. This is alarming in light of the fact that some studies suggest that as much as 70 percent of child maltreatment involving sexual abuse is committed outside the nuclear family (Conte & Berliner, 1984).

It is important to emphasize that many children suffer from both intrafamilial and extrafamilial sexual abuse. Unfortunately, some children learn to respond to inappropriate sexual advances from adults because this is the only way they can receive attention within the family system. When they seek relationships with others outside the family, they may even come to expect that being maltreated is a necessary contingency of intimacy with another person. Paternally deprived individuals, even if they have not previously been directly sexually abused by family members, seem particularly vulnerable to sexual seduction by nonrelated older males, adolescents as well as adults (Biller, 1971a, 1974c) This desperate need for attention and recognition from older males, often manifested by young paternally deprived children, can make them especially easy targets for child molesters. Children who run away from home frequently do so in response to physical and/or sexual maltreatment by family members. It is not surprising that so many runaways become victims of child pornography, prostitution, and other forms of sexual maltreatment.

The insidious consequences of sexual maltreatment can spread across intrafamilial as well as extrafamilial boundaries. Within a highly disordered and disturbed family system, marital violence and spousal sexual maltreatment may coexist with incest. Some children, for example, are sexually molested by both their father and an older brother, who themselves may have an incestuous relationship. Male children who are incest victims may in turn sexually abuse their peers—in particular, defenseless younger children. With the passage of time, victims of incest, especially males, often shift roles; having internalized destructive interpersonal styles, they initiate sexual maltreatment toward others. Many individuals fluctuate in their development between being a victim and being a victimizer. In chapters 7 through 10, there is a summary of findings relating early paternal deprivation and maltreamtent to later social and emotional deficits, including inadequate patterns of sexual functioning.

The presumption that nonincestual and incestual child molesters represent different populations has been challenged by the results of recent research. Groth, Hobson, and Gary (1982) describe two general types of child molester, fixated and regressive, who share many personality characteristics. These men sexually abuse children in an attempt to resolve their unmet needs and unresolved developmental issues; they search for acceptance and caring in their sexual contact with children; and they are basically immature individuals who obtain a sense of power, control, and competence by involving themselves with younger children whom they can interpersonally dominate. Such data indicate that fathers who sexually maltreat their children may not be too different from those men who sexually abuse children to whom they are unrelated and, furthermore, underscore the fact that many men are involved in both intrafamilial and extrafamilial sexual abuse.

Sex Differences

Men are reported to commit the vast majority of both intrafamilial and extrafamilial sexual maltreatment incidents against children. Certainly there are also many women who sexually maltreat children, and our culturally related sex-role biases probably lead to the underestimation of direct physical and sexual abuse by females even more than for males. Nevertheless, it seems clear that men, in contrast to women, are much more likely to initiate acts of physical and sexual intrusiveness and violence toward those who are less powerful than themselves. There is a greater tendency of males to react in a physically aggressive manner, coupled with the fact that more males than females suffer from biologically related deficits in impulse control (Nash, 1978; Rutter, 1979).

In addition to males' biological disposition to be more prone to physical acting out and impulsiveness, there is the reality that males are less apt than females to have an adequate same-sex parental model of self-control during childhood. In general, mothers are much more available and accessible to their daughters than are fathers to their sons (Biller, 1971a, 1974c; Lynn, 1974). The prevalence of paternal deprivation in our society denies many boys access to a consistent and reliable adult male role model with whom they can identify and learn to channel their aggressive and sexual impulses in an interpersonally constructive manner. Certainly females also suffer when deprived of positive fathering; compared to males, however, they are less likely to express their frustrations in direct physical and sexual attacks on others (Biller, 1971a, 1982a).

Sexual abuse and various other forms of emotional and physical maltreatment tend to have an intragenerational family-system quality. It is very common for men who themselves were victims of incest to maltreat their own children sexually. There also are many cases of women who were incest victims marrying men who in turn sexually abuse their children. For every case of clear-cut sexual abuse, there are probably at least two cases of more subtle gender abuse. The individual who has been incestuously maltreated may not directly repeat his victimization on his own offspring, but his conflicts concerning sex-role development may more subtly damage his ability to be an adequate parent. Children of both sexes are greatly influenced by the quality of the father-mother relationship, and much of what they internalize about male-female interactions centers around observations of their parents interacting with one another.

In chapter 6 there is some discussion of ways in which paternal deprivation negatively affects the socialization of males, and of how parental roles and sex roles may interact to increase the incidence of various forms of child maltreatment, including sexual abuse. In chapters 7 through 10 there are many examples of data linking paternal deprivation and the sexual maltreatment of young children with deficits in their later stages of development. As already mentioned, the legacy of early sexual maltreatment is often most poignantly and destructively manifested when children who have been incest victims become adults who in turn sexually abuse their own sons and daughters and/or children who are not related to them.

6
Parent and Infant Development

T his chapter can be viewed as an integrative attempt to elaborate some of the basic family processes that can underlie the complex connections between child maltreatment and paternal deprivation. There is a discussion of data concerning father-infant attachment and the effect of paternal influence and the father-mother relationship on the quality of family functioning and early cognitive and social development. Much of the chapter deals with sociocultural and biological factors that interact and affect parental and sex-role expectations to create the context for family influence. Emphasis is placed on the lack of social support for father participation in child rearing and how this increases the incidence of child maltreatment.

Parental Roles

A major assumption in linking paternal deprivation and child maltreatment is that children develop best when they have relationships with a positively involved father as well as a positively involved mother. Both men and women have something special to offer children. For various important cognitive, emotional, and social learning experiences, the presence of two parents is advantageous for the child. Boys and girls need to learn how to interact effectively with both males and females, and the two-parent family situation should provide a competent model of parental communication (Biller, 1974c, 1981b). Although we advocate the advantages to the child of living with two parents, we do not automatically depreciate alternative family forms. For example, some children develop very well even though one parent is frequently absent from the home as a result of occupational demands; others thrive in so-called joint or shared custody situations after divorce or in the presence of a highly effective single parent (see chapter 10).

Positive father involvement is a great advantage for both sons and daughters. Effective fathering can help protect the child from maltreatment and from inadequate mothering both by contributing directly to the mother's emotional well-being and by lessening her stress level through cooperative sharing of parental responsibilities. Mothers in families with high levels of father involvement are less likely to be rigidly punitive, restrictive, or overprotective. The well-fathered child is very likely to have the security and assertiveness to resist inappropriate manipulation and maltreatment from other family members.

Effective fathering can also lessen the probability of the child being maltreated by nonfamily members. The child with two effective parents is less likely to be vulnerable to manipulation and abuse by neighbors, teachers, or strangers. Compared to those who are paternally deprived, such a child is likely to have a more well-developed sense of assertiveness and independence and to be able to resist inappropriate relationships with other adults. Moreover, such a child is likely to be emotionally secure and able to communicate potential problems to parents. Because of their thirst for love and acceptance, children who do not have involved fathers are more likely to be vulnerable to inappropriate overtures by nonfamily members. On the other hand, for example, the well-fathered child is not as likely to be sexually seduced by the affectionate and generous but manipulative male stranger (Biller, 1971a, 1974c).

Because of a complex of sex role, socialization, and social support system factors, paternal deprivation is a much greater problem than maternal deprivation in the frequency and intensity of its impact on children. When a child is fatherless or is grossly neglected or rejected by the father, it is unlikely that there will be any consistent compensatory influence from other adult males. Historical and subcultural factors conspire to relieve most men of any feeling of responsibliity for other parents' children. If a child has no mother present (or has a mother who is grossly handicapped in her ability to provide parental care), other females—relatives, family friends, neighbors, and/or teachers— are likely at least to take some special interest in trying to meet his or her needs. Thus the social support system for the mother-deprived child is generally greater than that for the father-deprived child (Biller, 1971a, 1974c; Biller & Meredith, 1972, 1974).

Fathers and Infants

In this section we emphasize the importance of early father-infant bonding. There is great variability in the quality of the reciprocal attachment process between fathers and infants. Individual differences for fathers are much greater than for mothers with respect to the amount of responsibility they take in interaction with infants. In families where fathers and newborn infants are involved with each other, the probability of later child maltreatment is greatly reduced.

It is rare for a father to maltreat a child with whom a close attachment has developed in early infancy. On the other hand, a father who has not formed a strong parental bond is much more likely to maltreat his child or passively allow others to abuse the child (Biller, 1971a, 1974c). Investigators have found that infants can form strong attachments to their fathers even during the first year of life (e.g., Biller, 1971a, 1974c). These attachments are clearly reflected in the infant's responses to the father's behavior. For example, infants who are attached to their fathers spend much time looking at their fathers, react animatedly when their fathers enter or leave the room, and often make movements indicating a desire to be close to their fathers. The extent of such father attachment is highly related to the quality of the father's involvement with the infant.

Fathers usually look, feel, and sound different to infants than mothers do, and their way of holding and relating to infants is also likely to be somewhat different even when they are engaged in the same activity. Such physical and behavioral variations between mothers and fathers can play an important part in stimulating infants to respond differentially to their environments and can foster their perceptual and cognitive development (Biller, 1974c, 1982a). Such differentiation by infants is often expressed in the specific quality of their attachments with their mothers and fathers. When both parents are present, an infant may spend more time looking at his father or may be more interested in playing with his father after he has eaten; he may particularly seek out contact with his mother for cuddling when he is hungry or tired. The important point, however, is that the infant may, overall, have as strong or even a stronger attachment to his father (Biller, 1974c, 1982a).

Most infants form stronger initial attachments to their mothers; unfortunately, a large proportion of infants react to their fathers as if they were strangers. But the crucial point is that a weak father-infant bond is a reflection of lack of father involvement rather than of any inherent preference for the mother or any natural disinclination on the infant's part to develop an attachment to the father (Biller, 1974a, 1977a, 1982a).

Yogman (1982) has found differences in father and mother relationships with the infant by the time the infant is six weeks to three months old. Fathers and infants are involved in more arousal of idiosyncratic physical interaction than are mothers and infants, who are more likely to interact in smoothly modulated, soothing, quieting patterns, often in a verbal and visual context. The father-infant mode of interaction may particularly help the infant develop a basic sense of competence and assertiveness in exploring and controlling its increasingly complex environment. It can have a facilitating effect on the infant's curiosity, autonomy, and independence. The infant's progression through sensory-motor stages of development seems to progress more rapidly when the father as well as the mother is involved on a day-to-day basis (Biller, 1974c, 1982a). The father, even in early infancy, can be a source of stimulation and differentiation, effectively complementing the mother's style of intervention. The infant learns to adapt to differential patterns of adult behavior.

Exploratory Behavior

Some research has suggested that well-fathered infants are more curious in exploring their environment than are paternally deprived infants. They seem to relate more maturely to strangers and to react more positively to complex and novel stimuli (Biller, 1974c). Well-fathered infants seem more secure and trusting in branching out in their explorations; there are also indications that their motor development, in terms of crawling, climbing, and manipulating objects, is more advanced. Involved fathers tend to initiate more active play and to be more tolerant of physical exploration by infants than are mothers. It is common to observe involved fathers encouraging their infants to crawl a little further or reach a little higher. Fathers are usually less concerned than mothers if a child gets tired or dirty. This generally allows them to tolerate the temporary discomforts that the child may experience in exploring the environment (Biller, 1974c). Of course, at the extreme a father can maltreat his infant through insensitivity to the child's limitations and lack of awareness of pain he may be inflicting. Fathers who play too roughly with their infants may indeed physically damage them (Biller & Meredith, 1974).

Unfortunately, fathers are more likely than mothers to institute a clear-cut double standard in terms of the infant's sex. Even with infants, fathers appear to be more influenced by the sex of the child than are mothers. Fathers are more likely to cuddle infant daughters gently and to engage in rough-and-tumble activities with sons (Biller, 1974c; Lamb, 1976b). Some data suggest that fathers are more likely to accept a temperamentally difficult male infant but to withdraw from a female infant who presents similar problems (Rendina & Dickerscheid, 1976). Some fathers consistently encourage their infant sons to achieve competence in the physical environment but inhibit their infant daughters out of fear for their supposed fragility. Ironically in many such cases the daughter was even more robust than the son was at a similar age (Biller & Meredith, 1974; Biller & Weiss, 1970). Certainly an inhibiting sexist attitude toward a daughter can be viewed as maltreatment by the father.

Another factor in facilitating the child's exploration of his environment is that the father provides an additional attachment figure. In many families the paternally deprived child becomes excessively and exclusively attached to the mother, often in a clinging, dependent fashion. In such families, mothers may unintentionally maltreat their children by overprotecting them. Infants who develop an attachment to their fathers as well as their mothers appear to have an easier time relating to other people. A child who has frequent interactions with both parents has access to a wider variety of experiences and may be more adaptive to changes in the environment. Less separation and stranger anxiety are found among well-fathered infants. The infant's positive reaction to the returning father may be a prototype for his or her reaction to the entry of other people into the enviornment (Biller, 1974c; Biller & Meredith, 1974; Biller & Salter, 1985).

Cognitive-Social Growth

We have underscored the reality that fathers and mothers present somewhat different patterns of behavior in their interactions with their infants, and that infants and fathers can be just as attached to each other as can infants and mothers. In addition, it is important to describe briefly some of the research indicating that variations in the quality of the father-infant relationship can have positive or negative implications for child development. Evidence concerning the ways in which the quality of the father's interaction with the infant can influence the degree of his child's attachment to him has already been reviewed. Here we are concentrating our attention on studies indicating the impact of the father-infant relationship on the child's cognitive and social development. (Much more research dealing with the long-term effects on older children of adequate and inadequate fathering is reviewed in chapters 7 through 10.)

Pedersen, Rubinstein, and Yarrow (1979) found that among five- to six-month-old black boys, measures of cognitive functioning were correlated with the degree to which the babies were involved with their fathers. Frequent interaction with fathers (maternal report) was associated with high Bayley scores on mental and psychomotor functioning for sons. Although girls did not seem to be influenced by family structure, Pedersen et al. also presented evidence that father-absent infant boys were less cognitively competent than boys from father-present homes. Father-present boys demonstrated more social responsiveness, secondary circular behavior, and novelty-seeking behavior than did father-absent boys. Having found no discernible differences in the behavior of married and husbandless mothers, Pedersen et al. attributed variations in the infant boys' behavior to the degree of interaction with fathers, who, as we have described, tend to behave in a qualitatively different way toward infants than do mothers. Wachs, Uzgiris, and Hunt (1971) also reported an association between high paternal involvement and infant intellectual development. Biller (1974c), Lamb (1981a), and Radin (1981) reviewed other data suggesting a linkage among high-quality father-participation, the infant's comfort with novel situations, and facilitation of cognitive development. There is consistent evidence that high paternal involvement relates to lessened separation protest behavior in infants when they are left by a parent or are confronted by a stranger (Main & Weston, 1981; Spelke, Zelazo, Kagan, & Kotelchuck, 1973). Such data can be viewed as suggesting that a high level of paternal participation is conducive to the development of social curiosity and exploratory competence (Biller, 1974c; Biller & Meredith, 1974).

Clarke-Stewart (1978) performed an observational study on a small sample of fifteen- to thirty-month-olds and uncovered a strong association between intellectual competence in children, father's engagement of the child in play, and paternal expectations of independence. Clarke-Stewart, however, interpreted her correlational pattern in a way that indicated that maternal influence was a major factor and that paternal behavior was a consequent rather than an antecedent factor in the children's intellectual functioning. We would suggest that Clarke-Stewart's findings could be viewed as supporting the importance of both parents.

Belsky's (1980b) research contained indications that both maternal and paternal influence were important factors in the degree of development of exploratory competence. The most competent infants tended to have fathers who were very active in interacting with them. Such fathers expressed high levels of verbal responsiveness and affection and initiated vigorous motion play when with their infants, as well as participating in their physical care. Belsky stressed similarities as well as differences in the paternal and maternal factors that influenced infant competence. In their efforts to encourage infant competence, mothers are generally more concerned with verbal-intellectual teaching, whereas fathers are more oriented toward active, arousing play and fostering autonomy and independence (e.g., Lewis, Feiring & Weinraub, 1981; Yogman, 1982).

In a fascinating and pioneering intervention study, Zelazo, Kotelchuck, Barber, and David (1977) trained (using a social-learning strategy) low-interacting fathers to interact more with their year-old firstborn sons. Zelazo et al. reported evidence that this training not only helped the fathers become more active but also influenced the infant sons to take more social initiative with their fathers in free play sessions. In another intervention study, Dickie and Carnahan (1979) trained parents to become more effective with their four-to twelve-month-old infants. Like Zelazo et al., (1977) they found that infants of fathers who received training initiated social interactions with their fathers more often than did the infants in the control group. Interestingly, the results of this study also suggest that the mothers were allowing and encouraging fathers to interact more with their infants while at the same time decreasing the amount of their own interaction with their infants.

Parke and Tinsely's (1981) interpretation of the Dickie and Carnahan (1979) findings supports a view that shared, competent child rearing by both parents is particularly facilitative of a healthy mother-father relationship and family process. Parke and Tinsely (1981) noted that in nonhuman primate groupings, maternal possessiveness-restrictiveness tends to be inversely correlated with degree of father participation with infants (e.g., Redican, 1981). Historical and cross-cultural data can also be viewed as indicating that infants benefit from paternal participation in societies that do not expect exclusive mother-child relationships for young children (Biller, 1974c; Biller & Meredith, 1974). A major theme of this book is that shared parenting greatly decreases the probability of child maltreatment.

Yogman (1984) summarized data from his research suggesting the facilitative effect that early father participation may have on the developmental competence of infants. He reported significant relationships between a combined measure of paternal involvement in the prenatal and postnatal periods and the infants' developmental functioning at nine months. In addition, he mentioned a collaborative study done in Ireland that revealed a positive correlation between level of father involvement and the cognitive functioning of year-old infants.

Easterbrooks and Goldberg (1984) also have conducted research that clearly supports the importance of positive paternal influence in the young child's development. Their study with twenty-month-old firstborns and their parents indicated a strong association between fathers' behavior and toddler instrumental and affective development, especially for boys. Paternal participation in caregiving was not a factor in itself, but the overall level of father involvement was a significant variable. Even more important was paternal sensitivity to and acceptance of the child. Fathers who encouraged autonomy but also intervened with age-appropriate cues when necessary had toddlers who were particularly competent in problem solving. Positive paternal influence was linked to the child's persistence in completing tasks and secure parental attachment when the child was with the father, and to an even greater extent when the child was with the mother. The researchers emphasized that there were stronger associations between the child's functioning and paternal behavior than between functioning and maternal behavior. Other facets of this research program have also underscored the impact of the father and total family system on toddler development (Easterbrooks & Goldberg, 1985; Goldberg & Easterbrooks, 1984).

Psychoanalytic Perspective

No group of clinicians or scientists have stimulated more research on parent-infant relationships than the psychoanalysts. Yet psychoanalysts have been slow to turn their attention to the remarkable explosion in data linking variations in paternal behavior with infant and family functioning (Cath, Gurwitt, & Ross, 1982). With few exceptions, not until the mid-1970s did analysts begin to acknowledge the preoedipal role of the father.

Even in the landmark psychoanalytic volume *Father and Child* (Cath, Gurwitt, & Ross, 1982), the acceptance of the father's potential importance in early infant development is still marked by ambivalence (see especially chapters by Galinson and Roiphe, Greenspan, Kestenberg et al., Ross, and Tyson). Unquestionably, in the majority of families, mothers are the primary parents for infants and toddlers; but in increasing numbers fathers play an equally significant role, and in some families the father is indeed the primary parent. It is important to emphasize that the father's having a crucial role from the child's birth does not necessarily mean that the mother is absent, severely depressed, or otherwise handicapped. In many families, an infant is more attached to a father in early infancy but also has a very strong, healthy attachment to the mother. In such families, mothers are certainly important, but fathers are at least equally significant.

Throughout much of *Father and Child,* there is still reference to the universality of an initial and primary "feminine" identification with the mother, which must be shifted and/or modified in the separation-individuation process. Our point is not to deny the general prevalence of an initial maternal identification, but to acknowledge that this is neither biologically imperative nor necessary for healthy infant and child development. No doubt, as some of the provocative clinical examples presented in the Cath, Gurwitt, and Ross (1982) book so clearly demonstrate, many fathers become highly involved early in the infant's life as a function of some type of maternal inadequacy or abdication of parenting; but it is also clear from the parent-infant research of the 1970s and 1980s that the father may play a primary or equal role right from birth within the context of healthy marital and family functioning (Biller, 1974c, 1982a; Greenberg & Morris, 1974; Lamb, 1976c, 1981d).

Another, perhaps more subtle, indication of the resistance of many psychoanalysts to seeing the potential impact of the father on infant development is the emphasis on the mother as the interpreter and conveyor of her feelings about the father, without a similar acknowledgment of how the father's communications about the mother can affect the child's development. An additional way that the primacy of the mother seems to be emphasized relates to descriptions of how fatherly tendencies supposedly evolve in males (e.g., Ross, 1982b; Tyson, 1982). To most analysts, fathering an infant is an expression of the underlying feminine identification that boys make with their mothers. It could also be suggested that mothers "father" their children to the extent that they have been exposed to an active father in their own infancy and early childhood. The view of a male parent as generally a *mothering* individual for the infant seems to exclude the fact that a man's parenting style may be basically masculine (active, playful, stimulating, and so forth) and that it can be based on a primary attachment/identification as much with his own father as with his mother (e.g., Biller, 1971a, 1974a, 1982; Lamb, 1981d).

The preceding comments should not be construed as minimizing or depreciating the valuable psychoanalytic contributions to our understanding of the father's role in development as presented in *Father and Child* (Cath, Gurwitt, & Ross, 1982). We are merely pointing out that there is some distance to transverse before there is a full integration of psychoanalytic theory and existing data on family development.

Family-System Influences

Some of the most important research relating to the father's role in the family system concerns ways in which the father's presence, and the quality of the father-mother relationship, can influence and mediate the mother-child relationship. There is much evidence that when fathers are supportive and encouraging, mothers are more competent and responsive to their infants and young children. In fact, even before the birth of the child, the presence of an emotionally supportive husband can contribute to the expectant mother's sense of well-being and is likely to be associated with a relatively problem-free pregnancy, delivery process, and success in parenting (Biller & Meredith, 1974; Lamb, 1981c; Lewis, Feiring, and Weintraub, 1981; Parke & Tinsley, 1981; Pedersen, 1980, 1981).

Support

A provocative data anlaysis by Pedersen, Anderson, and Cain (1980) revealed that mothers were more interested in caring for their newborn infants, including nursing them, when they received a high level of emotional support from their husbands. In a longitudinal investigation, Barnard (1980) found an association between maternal reports of husband-related emotional and physical support during pregnancy and the mother's level of responsibility and involvement with her child from infancy through four years of age. As Pedersen (1981) points out, the results of several investigations, including Barnard's (1980), suggest that the quality of the husband-wife relationship is more predictive of the mother's success in dealing with her child than is the degree to which the father actually participates in child care.

Pedersen (1981) also cites data indicating that fathers are more comfortable parenting their infants when they receive encouragement and emotional support from their wives. Studying fifteen-month-old babies and their parents, Belsky (1979a, 1980b) reported that the extent of husband-wife communication about their infants was positively associated with the amount of father's interaction with the child, though not seeming to be clearly connected with the rate of mother-infant interaction. Belsky interpreted this finding as an indication of the mediating role of the husband-wife relationship on the father's behavior with the infant.

Pedersen (1975, 1976) discovered a strong association between the amount of tension and conflict in the marriage, the father's perception of the mother, and the degree to which the father played with his infant son. Fathers with good marital relationships and a positive view of their wives were more likely to be actively involved in playing with their infant sons, whereas those who experienced stressful interactions with their wives and perceived them negatively were more apt to engage in a low level of playful activity with their infant sons. It is clear that dyadic subsystems within the family can interact with one another. For example, in Heath's (1976) research, there was a significant correlation between a wife's view of her husband's competence as a father and her satisfaction with him as a husband. Women tended to define good husbands as those who were able to be supportive of them in their roles as both wives and mothers. There is considerable data suggesting that the father's affection and warmth toward the mother buttresses her competence to parent. On the other hand, when husbands are aloof and uninvolved in child rearing, or are absent from the home, mothers are apt to have much more difficulty in dealing positively with their children (e.g., Biller, 1974c, Biller & Meredith, 1974).

Lamb and Elster (1985) found a strong interrelationship among measures of father-infant interaction and dimensions of the mother-father relationship. In contrast, there was little connection in their study between measures of mother-infant interaction and the mother-father relationship. Fathering behavior appears to be both more variable than quality of mothering behavior and more influenced by the marital relationship. Mothers are expected to be highly involved with their infants, but social values allow fathers much more latitude. An unsupportive mother-father relationship was related to a relative lack of paternal involvement with the infant, whereas positive marital interactions were associated with a high level of father-infant engagement and social interaction. The quality of father-infant interactions was much facilitated by marital and social support factors.

Lytton's (1979) analysis revealed that mothers were much more successful and comfortable in setting limits and controlling their two- and three-year-old children when fathers were present in the situation. Children were more likely to comply with their mothers requests for appropriate behavior, even if the father was not directly involved in the situation, than if he was not there at all. When fathers explicitly supported the mothers' requests, children were especially likely to comply. Mothers seemed much more able to carry through in setting reasonable limits for their young children when fathers were present. In fact, paternal presence decreased the number of maternal demands for control while at the same time increasing the success of maternal discipline and the positive quality of maternal response to compliance by children. When the father is present, the mother's limit-setting behavior appears to be more appropriate and realistic.

Lytton's (1979) research is important in providing some very provocative data on the indirect effects that the father can have on the mother's behavior. From the perspective of our anlaysis of the relationship between paternal deprivation and child maltreatment, Lytton's data appear especially significant. We have been arguing that mothers who lack adequate support from their children's fathers are likely to have considerable conflict and difficulty in dealing with parenting issues and are more at risk to engage in maltreating behaviors than are those whose partner is positively involved in the family system.

Conflict

Mothers whose children do not comply with their demands are likely to feel stress and to act irrationally in a verbally or physically abusive manner, especially if they do not have active co-parents. Patterns of overprotection or even neglect seem more common when mothers feel isolated in their responsibility for childrearing (Biller, 1974c, 1981a). Mothers who have custody of their children after divorce typically report a great deal of difficulty in disciplining and controlling their children, especially sons (Hetherington, Cox, & Cox, 1978b; Hoffman, 1981). On the other hand, there is much evidence that a high level of involvement by the father in child rearing after divorce, even as the non-custodial parent, and a relatively positive father-mother relationship, make the custodial mother's parenting responsibilities much more manageable (e.g., Biller, 1974a, 1981a; Hetherington, Cox, & Cox, 1978; Wallerstein & Kelly, 1980b).

Much evidence is reviewed in the next two chapters that emphasizes the disruptive impact that father-mother conflict can have on parent-child interactions. According to some researchers, the negative implications for the child's development of a hostile and conflict-ridden marital relationship are typically more severe than are the effects of divorce and parent-child separation. When spouses are hostile and insensitive toward one another, and where conflict between them is rampant, children appear especially vulnerable to serious emotional and social adjustment problems (e.g., Biller, 1971a, 1974c, 1982; Biller & Davids, 1973; Hetherington, Cox, & Cox, 1978b; Lamb, 1981d; Rutter, 1971, 1979).

Frustrations in the marital relationship, as well as the individual characteristics of the child, can result in the scapegoating of a particular child. A longitudinal perspective, which takes into acocunt the parent's history as well as the child's, is needed. Feelings of neglect, abuse, or powerlessness that a parent perceives with respect to the other parent can easily be redirected in a destructive manner toward a defenseless infant or young child. For example, child abuse often occurs simultaneously in families where there is wife abuse. A general atmosphere of family violence is all too common (Gelles, 1972). Spouse abuse and child maltreatement are frequently associated with the alcohol-related problems of the father. Men with substance abuse problems seem particularly likely to inflict physical and/or emotional maltreatment on other family members (Willoughby, 1979).

In many intact families in which child maltreatment occurs, there are inequities in the balancing of responsibilities for children. Both mothers and fathers should be involved in sharing in the marriage and in child rearing. A severe imbalance in the family system, typically with the mother being overinvolved and the father underinvolved, can result in problems for the parents as well as the children (Biller, 1974c, 1981b). Both parents may abuse their children but maltreatment often seems to be expressed in different styles and forms by fathers and by mothers. Forms of maltreatment that appear more common for fathers include emotional neglect, rejection, and physical and sexual abuse. On the other hand, mothers seem more apt to participate in overprotection and excessive restrictiveness. Despite such parental sex differences, there is much overlap in the types of child maltreatment committed by mothers and fathers, and many parents participate in multiple forms of abuse (Kempe & Kempe, 1984).

In the successful family system, a balance needs to be achieved between the needs of the parents and those of the children. In families where there is not a functional husband-wife relationship and/or all the energy of a particular parent, typically the mother, is devoted to child care, there is a great increase in the likelihood of child maltreatment. Parents who can be supportive to one another in child-rearing functions are also generally enriching the quality of their marital relationship as well as presenting a positive model of male-female interaction, which bodes well for the development of their children (Biller, 1974a; Biller & Meredith, 1974, 1982; Biller & Salter, 1986).

It is important to reemphasize that the infant is not a passive participant in the family system. How the infant responds to parental overtures has much influence on how a father or mother perceives the child. For example, it may not simply be just a sexist attitude on the part of most fathers to pay more attention to sons than to daughters. The child's reaction can be a major factor; in general, infant sons may actually display more positive affect than do daughters when fathers engage in physically stimulating rough-and-tumble play with them. In any case, there are vast individual differences in infant temperament and responsiveness to various parental interactions, and those infants who react in a way that helps their mothers and fathers feel adequate and competent can have a positive impact on their parents' development and marital relationship (Galinsky, 1982). Throughout this book we emphasize the reciprocal influences that children and parents have on one another.

Sociocultural Variables

Much of child maltreatment is a function of the lack of preparation and social support men have as parents (and, relatedly, as responsible husbands). This is often a vicious cycle in the sense that many men themselves have been inadequately fathered and/or abused. In other words, fathers tend to be the weak links in families. This is particularly true in poor families but is also often the case among the affluent (Biller & Meredith, 1974).

Men and women do not have equal opportunities in terms of accessibility to same-sex parents during childhood. Boys generally spend much less time with their fathers than girls do with their mothers. (Both boys and girls are usually with their mothers far more than with their fathers.) Not only the quantity of adequate modeling opportunities, but also the quality, is at issue. Children can certainly learn a great deal from both fathers and mothers, but there is much evidence that a particularly significant dimension of their basic gender identity, and attitudes toward parenting, stems from their experiences with the same-sex parent. In this sense, compared to women, men as a group are less likely to be secure in their basic sex-role orientation or in their competence as parents because so many of them had a very limited, fragile relationship with an elusive and often emotionally inaccessible father (Biller, 1971a, 1974c; Biller & Meredith, 1974).

We are not suggesting that men who engage in child maltreatment fit any definite psychological pattern. As summarized in chapters 4 and 5, there are wide individual differences in personality styles and in occupational and interest patterns. Although great variability in abusive parents of both sexes has been reported, fathers who physically maltreat their children, even if financially successful, are likely to be described as having basic insecurity and personal identity problems (Steele, 1982). Most of these men do not fit neatly into the psychiatric nomenclature. Their handicap may be most clearly manifested in their relationships with their children, even though they may be functioning adequately in their extrafamilial endeavors and careers. Their deficit in parenting is generally a reflection of the poor relationships they had with their own fathers, for which they may be able to compensate except when confronting the emotional demands of their children.

Sex-role stereotypes can confound the accurate reporting of the incidence of abuse with respect to sex of parent. As in other areas of attributing parental responsibilities, there are double standards. Many men are never labeled abusers by others because their derogatory communications toward their children are perceived as simply "blowing off steam" from work pressures. Other men remain defensively aloof from their families, a trait that in males is not as quickly defined as serious child neglect as it is in women. The more successful such men are financially and professionally, the more they may be able to hide their basic identity and parenting defects from nonfamily members. Paternal neglect, aloofness, and rejection are as much forms of child maltreatment as are various types of physical and sexual abuse.

Fathers often maltreat children when their only consistent contact with them is as disciplinarians. A common scenario in many families is the pattern of the harassed mother beseeching the father, who has just returned from work, to discipline out-of-control children or to punish those who have misbehaved earlier in the day. For some fathers, contact with their children seems to revolve around being physical and emotional intimidators at the behest of mothers. Unfortunately, such fathers and children lack the opportunity to bond adequately with each other, and a frustrating cycle of mistrust develops. Discipline by parents is much more effective when it is built on a warm, affectionate relationship (Biller & Meredith, 1974).

When analyzing the impact of physical punishment, it is important to consider the overall parent-child relationship. We in no way advocate physical punishment as an effective form of parent-child communication, but the context of physical or otherwise potentially harsh punishment needs to be taken into account. For example, the father who has a generally warm and affectionate relationship but, in a consistent way, uses spanking to reprimand a child should certainly be differentiated from the father whose primary interactions with the child center on the administration of physical punishment when the child is viewed as misbehaving. The latter can be characterized as a maltreating father not only because of potential physical abuse but also because of a pervasive style of paternal neglect (except for disciplinary action), whereas the former, though not practicing optimal child rearing, is likely to be a relatively involved and successful parent (Biller & Meredith, 1974).

Unfulfilled Expectations

Fathers often act in a rejecting and punitive manner at least in part because of unrealistic expectations about the actual capabilities of their children. Mothers, too, can overestimate a child's capacity for self-control and maturity, but fathers as a group seem more unrealistic, especially concerning their high expectations for their sons. This in part may be a function of their relative inexperience with caring for children before becoming parents, but many are also beset by unfulfilled fantasies of achievement and progress for themselves, which they may project onto their children. One consequence of such attitudes may be an overly-punitive style toward the child who does not respond in the way the father expects. For example, in some families, a nonathletic (or nonscholarly) child may be maltreated by the father because he has not responded to the father's coaching for a higher level of performance. An attitude of rejection is likely to generalize beyond the specific activity in which the father expects more competent performance. Fathers, as a group, appear to base their acceptance of the child more on performance than do mothers; when the child cannot deliver the desired level of accomplishment, they are more likely to respond in an uninterested, punitive, or rejecting manner. There may be special risks to a boy who is unresponsive to what the father perceives as his helpful commitment to greater competence. Paternal hostility may be especially intense because the father may more readily identify with and be threatened by the boy's failure (Biller, 1971a, 1974c).

On the other hand, as emphasized earlier, fathers may maltreat daughters by expecting too little of them. They may not take their daughters' accomplishments seriously and may convey an uncaring attitude unless the daughters' interests are in traditional feminine areas. It is noteworthy that women who achieve in science, business, and athletics are very likely to have had fathers who encouraged their competence as well as accepting their femininity (Biller, 1974a; Biller & Meredith, 1974).

Single Parents

One-parent families present a special risk for child maltreatment. The everyday pressures and stress on the single parent increase the probability of child maltreatment (and of parent maltreatment by the child). Without the emotional support and sharing of responsibility with a partner, the single parent is at risk, if not to practice blatant physical child abuse, then at least to develop an inappropriate relationship with the child, whether it be in the form of neglect or of emotional overinvestment. Almost 90 percent of one-parent families are mother-only families, and the father's lack of commitment can put a particularly heavy burden on the mother, who is unlikely to receive other male support for child rearing from her social system (Biller, 1971a, 1973a, 1981a).

In the case of divorced parents where the mother has custody, the degree and quality of the father's involvement with the child is a key factor in decreasing the probability of child maltreatment. When the father is unavailable and uncommitted, the child will suffer from maltreatment at least in the sense of paternal neglect unless there is an adequate male surrogate figure. The child whose father shows no consistent interest in him or her is likely to feel a deep sense of rejection. Most children without an active father do not have an alternative source of adult male support (Biller, 1974c, 1981a).

There is much evidence that father-absence during the first few years of life makes children more vulnerable for developmental and psychological problems than does father-absence after the age of five (Biller, 1971a, 1974c, 1981a). On the other hand, the number of studies revealing a linkage between the quality of fathering during infancy and positive social, emotional, and cognitive development in children has dramatically increased in the last decade (Biller, 1974c, 1981a, 1982a). During infancy, father-absence and other forms of paternal deprivation can have detrimental effects on the child's functioning, whereas the presence of an active and involved father can do much to stimulate positive development. Infants are particularly susceptible to the negative impact of both child maltreatment and paternal deprivation.

Although paternal deprivation and child maltreatment occur to some extent in all socioeconomic levels and sociocultural settings, it is clear from data reviewed in chapters 3 and 4 that the risk is heightened in the context of poverty. Economic deprivation, with such associated dangers as inadequate prenatal and medical care and insufficient educational and occupational opportunity, tends to exacerbate the impact of paternal deprivation, although most low-income mothers remain committed to their children (Berlinsky & Biller, 1982; Biller, 1981a). But the stress connected to overcrowding and to having several closely spaced young children makes even the well-intentioned and motivated mother, who lacks family and social support as well as an active partner, particularly vulnerable to periods of grossly inappropriate parenting ranging from serious neglect to harsh physical abuse. On the other hand, two parents working and growing together are far more likely to cope adequately with the stresses of economic deprivation and to provide a relatively healthy psychological and social environment for their children (Biller, 1981a; Biller & Meredith, 1974).

Biosocial Factors

In addition to family and social systems variables, individual and sex differences in constitutional predispositions need to be considered if we are to understand the complex links between paternal deprivation and child maltreatment. Certain forms of severe physical abuse are especially likely to be targeted at male children, who are more apt to have attention deficit and/or impulse control problems than are female children. The grossly handicapped child, more often a son than a daughter, is especially likely to be neglected by the father and overprotected by the mother. Similarly, we speculate that male adults, in many situations, often respond more harshly to children than do their female counterparts not only because they are socialized differently but also because they themselves are more likely to suffer from biologically based impulse disorders (Biller, 1974c; Rutter, 1979).

Prenatal Risk

Research on the prenatal period suggests some interactions between biological and sociocultural factors that may in turn contribute to child maltreatment and paternal deprivation. Problems in infancy and childhood are often connected to inadequate prenatal care. Economic and subcultural factors certainly are involved in the availability of quality prenatal care, but as a group, expectant mothers with supportive husbands or committed boyfriends are more likely than those without a partner to accept their pregnancy, to go for regularly scheduled obstetrical visits, and to be appropriately concerned about how their well-being and health may affect the fetus. In some cases a major factor may simply be having an interested person available to transport the pregnant mother to her medical appointment and/or to help maintain an appropriate diet (Holmes, Reich, & Pasternak, 1983).

We have already noted the particularly negative influence of paternal deprivation and child maltreatment during infancy, but it could be argued that lack of adequate medical care and concern for the physical and emotional well-being of the expectant mother represents the most serious type of potential child maltreatment in terms of the numbers of children affected with relatively permanent and serious disabilities. In fact, lack of concern for her health and well-being by the expectant mother herself and/or by her partner should be considered extremely severe child abuse. More and more evidence is accumulating about the significance of the prenatal period for later development. Expectant mothers without partners are more at risk than those with partners not only to have difficulties during the prenatal period but also to deliver premature infants and to have children who suffer from developmental disabilities (Holmes, Reich, & Pasternak, 1983).

In this context it is also relevant to cite research suggesting an association between death of the father during the last trimester of pregnancy and serious behavioral problems of offspring when they were assessed in adulthood (Huttunen & Niskanen, 1978). Certainly, it is impossible retrospectively to untangle the multiplicity of factors that could contribute to such a finding: early paternal deprivation for the child may have been a major variable, the risk of child neglect may have increased because of the mother's depression and sense of loss, and the stress of husband absence may have been related to depression as well as to physiological changes in the expectant mother that directly and negatively influenced fetal development (Berlinsky & Biller, 1982). A general point here is that whatever the exact process involved, it is less likely that a child will suffer from negative prenatal factors if the expectant father is supportively involved with the expectant mother. Even during the prenatal period, it is vital to be concerned with paternal deprivation and child maltreatment.

7

Developmental Implications for Males in Two-Parent Families

C hapters 7 through 10 present some relevant research findings linking maltreatment by fathers to short- and long-term developmental problems for children. Many different styles of fathering and forms of paternal deprivation are discussed, along with their implications for the child's functioning. Much of the data concern the impact of paternal rejection, neglect, and absence on child and adult development. This presentation is not a complete review of the literature but, rather, highlights possible connections between various forms of maltreatment by fathers and problems in the psychological adaptation of their children. There is also a selective consideration of findings relating positive fathering to the successful adjustment of children; this material is included to provide a frame of reference for paternal deprivation, to emphasize individual differences in the quality of fathering, and to reiterate the importance of a multicontinuum approach in evaluating adequacy of parenting.

All forms of paternal deprivation and child maltreatment do not present the same risk for children. Generally speaking, severe consistent physical and/or sexual abuse has more negative impact than does neglect, overprotection, or restrictiveness. For example, the child who is fatherless, though at risk, may attempt to search for some sort of father-surrogate, whereas the child with a grossly inappropriate or abusive father may be rigidly trapped with a view of all adult males as destructive (Biller, 1971a, 1974c). Similarly, a very negative relationship with a family member with whom a child lives on a day-to-day basis may be much more insidious than intermittent contact with a maltreating extended family member. The child who is occasionally physically abused but has at least one generally adequate parent and some family warmth does not seem as much at risk for a severe psychological handicap as does the child who is consistently the recipient of hostile verbal and emotional rejection by both parents.

We have already emphasized the importance of a biofamilial perspective in chapter 6; individual differences in both children and adults must be considered. On the one hand, we see cases where a child's characteristics increase the likelihood of maltreatment (for example, when the child has an attention deficit disorder, is mentally retarded, or is otherwise cognitively impaired). On the other hand, some children either are less likely to be targets of maltreatment or are more resilient in the face of typically negative experiences. Some children, even as infants and toddlers, are very adaptable and have the capacity to relate quickly in a positive way to nonfamily members. Such children, because they are especially attractive, sociable, bright, and/or perceptive, may be able to decrease their susceptibility to abuse within their own family. Even when they are subjected to very inadequate parenting, some children may have the personal resources and abilities somehow to still achieve a relatively positive personality adaptation.

Fathers and Sons

Much of the focus in this chapter is on how fathers can either promote healthy personality functioning in their sons through positive involvement or can undermine their children's sense of competence and well-being by maltreating them. A central theme in the study of paternal influence in the family has been the father's impact on children's sex-role development and gender identity. Data are reviewed that indicate that nurturant, competent, and available fathers are important contributors to their sons' sex-role and personality functioning at various stages of development, whereas maltreating (including abusive and neglectful) fathers put their children at great risk for both short- and long-term psychological and social problems.

The first section of this chapter reviews research concerning the father-child relationship and the boy's sex-role development. Other sections deal with a variety of findings linking individual differences in the father-son relationship to emotional, cognitive, and social functioning in children and adults.

Some controversial issues are associated with the study of sex-role development (Biller, 1974c, 1977c, 1980b, 1981b). Many researchers would prefer that definitions of sex-role behavior be radically transformed or translated into so-called nonsexist terms and/or that sex-role concepts be eliminated as relevant topics to investigate. Some perceive that sex-role research, in itself, reinforces outmoded and dysfunctional patterns of behavior. Certainly, traditional definitions of sex role have tended to be limited, restrictive, and rigid. Perhaps because of the increasing realization that certain sex-role expectations can be handicapping, there appeared, beginning in the mid-1970s, to be a marked decline in the number of investigations directed at understanding parental influence in the sex-role development process, although there were numerous attempts to construct less biased sex-role measures and to demonstrate the negative implications of traditional conceptions of sex-role behavior (e.g., Bem, 1979; Kelly & Worrell, 1977; Lott, 1981; Pleck, 1981; Spence & Helmreich, 1979).

Despite our agreement with most criticisms of the bias and inadequacy inherent in both the conceptual and methodological underpinnings of much of the previous research on sex-role functioning, we believe much can be learned about major dimensions of personality formation by attempting to understand how family interactions influence children's sex-role development. For better or worse, sex roles will continue to influence personality development. The father can, of course, have a positive or negative impact on his child's sex-role development. The quality of the father-child relationship can be a factor in learning either socially desirable or socially undesirable sex-role patterns, which can affect many areas of the child's emotional, cognitive, and interpersonal functioning.

Throughout this chapter it is emphasized that variations in paternal influence do not occur in a vacuum. Other factors include the child's constitutional characteristics and developmental status, the quality of the mother-child and father-mother relationships, the family's sociocultural background, and the availability of surrogate models. Unfortunately, most investigators have not systematically evaluated the potential interactions of paternal influence with factors such as the quality of the mother-child relationship or the child's constitutionally based individuality, and frequent comments concerning the methodological shortcomings of previous research are necessary (Biller, 1971a, 1974c, 1981b).

Masculine Development

This section provides an analysis of ways in which family factors and, in particular, the quality of fathering can affect the young boy's masculine development. There is an emphasis on how effective fathering facilitates the child's positive acceptance of his maleness, whereas paternal indifference and maltreatment may undermine his basic sex-role security. The quality of the father-child relationship can greatly influence the learning of either socially functional or dysfunctional sex-role patterns. The boy's self-definition including his underlying sex-role orientation and gender identity is often much linked to the type of fathering he receives and, in turn, can be a major factor in other facets of his cognitive, emotional, and social development.

Masculinity is treated as a complex and multidimensional concept. The degree of overt masculinity, as expressed in interests, activities, and interpersonal style, in and of itself is not assumed to reflect level of psychological adjustment. That is, high masculinity is not necessarily associated with adequate psychological functioning, nor is low masculinity always connected with poor adjustment or psychopathology. For example, adolescent or adult males who are labeled highly masculine may in fact be aloof and insensitive and may also have much underlying insecurity concerning self-acceptance. Nevertheless, the young boy's happy embrace of what he perceives as masculine endeavors is often an expression of a healthy self-identity and a strong feeling of positive similarity to his father. The ability to pursue masculine activities competently and to be assertive and independent is related to constructive personality functioning, whereas a rigid and insensitive interpersonal style, combined with fearful avoidance of any endeavor that could be construed as feminine, is indicative of serious maladjustment (Biller, 1971a; 1974c). In this and other chapters, there is an attempt to differentiate sex-role patterns that are related to self-acceptance and competence from those associated with constricted, defensive, or inadequate personality adaptations.

Identification Theories

Most of the studies referred to in this section were stimulated by hypotheses derived from so-called theories of identification. These hypotheses center on the significance of the father acting in a certain manner and being perceived by the boy in a particular way, if the boy is to identify with his father and become masculine (Biller, 1974c). Freudian theory emphasizes the importance of the father being perceived as punitive and threatening (Fenichel, 1945). Status-envy theory emphasizes that the father needs to be perceived as the primary and envied consumer of resources (Burton & Whiting, 1961). Learning theory underscores the importance of the father being affectionate and rewarding (Sears, 1957). Role theory stresses that the father should be a primary dispenser of both rewards and punishments (Parsons, 1955). Social power theory also suggests that the model who is most likely to be imitated is the one who most controls valued resources (Mussen & Distler, 1959).

The Freudian view of the father's role in masculine development is described first, since many other identification theory hypotheses are, at least in part, derivatives of this perspective (Bronfenbrenner, 1960). Freud postulated that during the oedipal period, when he is three to five years of age, the boy desires to have an exclusive relationship with his mother. Freud believed that the boy, initially identified with his mother, comes to see his father as a very aggressive competitor for his mother's affection and to fear that the father will castrate him. According to Freud, the normal resolution of the Oedipus complex takes place when, in order to cope with his fear of castration, the boy identifies with his father, the aggressor, and represses his desire for his mother. The boy's subsequent strong masculine strivings and desire to be like his father were seen as a by-product of his identification with his father.

In an interesting account of Freud's consideration of the father's role, Burlingham (1973) noted that Freud occasionally alluded to affectionate father-child attachments in preoedipal development. Despite this, in Freudian theory, the perception of the father as punitive and threatening, as the "source of decisive frustrations" during the oedipal period, is seen as a major prerequisite for the boy's masculine development (Fenichel, 1945). As emphasized in chapter 6, there has been a tremendous expansion of psychoanalytic thinking concerning the significance of early fathering in the last decade (Cath, Gurwitt, & Ross, 1982; Machtlinger, 1981).

Whiting's status-envy theory of identification is an extension of the Freudian hypothesis of identification with the aggressor (Burton & Whiting, 1961). Whereas the Freudian hypothesis stresses the boy's desire to possess his mother, Whiting emphasized that the child wants to engage in many of the activities of the envied parent. Whiting argued that the boy will achieve a masculine identification if he perceives his father as having access to more privileges and attractive objects and activities than his mother does (Burton & Whiting, 1961). It is assumed that the child is motivated to imitate the behavior of the primary recipient of valued resources and that his identification with that person is much strengthened by fantasy rehearsal of the envied behavior. According to this conception, a young boy will develop a masculine identification only if his father (or father-surrogate) is the primary consumer of valued resources.

Mowrer (1950) attempted to reformulate Freudian theory in terms of learning theory concepts. He distinguished between defensive and developmental identification. *Defensive identification* is synonmous with identification with the aggressor; *developmental identification* with anaclitic identification. *Anaclitic identification,* a concept used at times in Freudian theory to explain how girls identify with their mothers and become feminine, is based on the fear of loss of love.

Although Mowrer acknowledged that identification with the aggressor may be involved in masculine development, he emphasized the importance of developmental identification in the sex-role development of both boys and girls. The basis for developmental identification is an affectional-emotional link with the parent that motivates the child to reproduce "bits of the beloved parent" in order to avoid the feeling of loss of love when the parent withholds rewards or is absent. The identification is supposed to develop out of a nurturant parent-child relationship in which the child becomes dependent on the parent for nurturance and affection. As in Freudian theory, the boy's initial identification is viewed as a non-sex typed one with the mother. As the father becomes more a source of reinforcement (supposedly around the age of four), the boy imitates the father and gradually becomes masculine. Other learning theorists have expressed similar viewpoints (e.g., Sears, 1970).

A view of identification that in certain respects combines the Freudian and learning theory hypotheses has been advanced by some sociologists (e.g., Parsons, 1955). According to role theory, the boy identifies with the person who is most able to dispense both rewards and punishments to him. Bronfenbrenner (1960, p. 32) pointed out that the novel conception of role theory, as elaborated by Parsons, is that "the child identifies not with the parent as a total person, but with the reciprocal role relationship that is functioning for the child at a particular time."

Johnson (1963) stressed the importance of fathering in her elaboration of Parsons's theory of identification. According to Johnson, the mother has a primarily expressive relationship with both boys and girls; in contrast, the father rewards his male and female children differentially, encouraging instrumental behavior in his son and expressive behavior in his daughter. The identification with the father leads to the internalization of a reciprocal role relationship that is crucial for the sex-role development of both boys and girls. For example, with his son the father plays roughly and invites aggressive and assertive responses, whereas with his daughter, he is flirtatious and pampering, thereby encouraging her to be affectionate and nurturant.

Like role theorists, social learning (or social power) theorists emphasize that the model who is most likely to be imitated is the one who most controls valued resources (e.g., Bandura, 1973; Mussen, 1961). These theorists vary somewhat in their specifics, but they all emphasize basic learning principles. The degree to which the father is observed to be a recipient of high status and attractive privileges within the family will increase the probability that children will imitate him.

A general disadvantage of identification theory hypotheses is that they do not differentiate among different aspects of sex role (Biller, 1974c). In fact, masculinity is generally treated as a unidimensional concept. To the extent that these hypotheses consider that the boy begins to become masculine around the age of three or four, when he supposedly begins to make a shift from a maternal to a paternal identification, they are inconsistent with data indicating masculine sex typing even in two-year-old and younger boys and, more important, strong father-infant attachments in families (e.g., Biller, 1971a, 1974c). From material presented in chapter 6, it is clear that father-infant interactions can have an impact on the child's sex-role functioning. In chapters 9 and 10 focusing on father-absence and personality development, we have also summarized many studies that suggest that a lack of fathering during infancy can be disruptive to the child's sex-role development.

Paternal Masculinity

The quality of the father-son relationship is a more important influence on the boy's masculine development than the amount of time the father spends at home (Biller, 1968a, 1971a). A crucial factor in this development is the degree to which the father exhibits masculine behavior in family interactions. Imitation of the father *directly* strengthens the boy's masculine development only if the father displays masculine behavior in the presence of his son.

When the father consistently adopts a motherlike role, it is likely that his son will be relatively low in masculinity. Bronfenbrenner (1958), reanalyzing data originally collected by Lansky (1956), found that adolescent boys low in masculinity of interests often came from homes in which the father played a traditionally feminine role. The fathers of these boys took over activities such as cooking and household chores *and* generally did not participate in family decision making or limit setting. Bronfenbrenner also described the findings of a study by Altucher (1975, p. 120) in which adolescent boys with low masculine interests "were likely to come from families in which there was little role differentiation in household activities, and in which the mother, rather than the father, tended to dominate in the setting of limits for the child." What seemed to inhibit the boy's masculine development was not the father's participation in some traditionally feminine activities in the home in itself, but the father's passivity in family interactions and decision making.

Biller (1969b) found a strong relationship between kindergarten-age boys' masculinity and the degree to which they perceived their fathers as making family decisions. On measures of sex-role orientation (masculinity-femininity of self-concept), sex-role preference (masculinity-femininity of interests and attitudes), and sex-role adoption (masculinity-femininity of social and environmental interactions), a high level of perceived decision making by the father was associated with strongly masculine behavior. Perception of the father's status in decision making was particularly correlated with sex-role orientation, although it was also significantly related to preference and adoption. Other studies have also suggested a positive association between the son's masculinity and his perception of his father's masculinity (Heilbrun, 1965b, 1974; Kagan, 1958a; Rychlak & Legerski, 1967).

Even though they consistently show a relationship between father's and son's masculinity, the studies cited here share a common methodological shortcoming. Measurement of father's and son's masculinity was generally not independent, since both assessments were usually deduced from the son's responses. Such evidence is not a sufficient basis on which to conclude that father's and son's masculinity are related. An alternative explanation is that masculine sons tend to see their fathers as highly masculine, regardless of their father's actual masculinity. A boy may appear similar to his father and yet may have learned his masculine behavior not from the father, but from his peer group. As Bronfenbrenner (1958) pointed out, the boy's perceived similarity to his father is not necessarily a measure of his identification with his father. Father-son similarity may be simply a reflection of exposure to a common social environment.

In a methodologically impressive study, Hetherington (1965) evaluated the relative dominance of parents by placing them in an actual decision-making stituation. She found that masculinity of preschool-age and preadolescent boys' projective sex-role behavior (IT Scale) was positively related to paternal dominance. She discovered, moreover, a general tendency for both similarity between father and son and the extent of filial imitation of fathers to be higher in father-dominant than in mother-dominant homes (Hetherington, 1965; Hetherington & Brackbill, 1963; Hetherington & Frankie, 1967).

Using essentially the same parental interaction procedure as Hetherington, Biller (1969b) found that father dominance in father-mother interaction was positively related to the masculinity of kindergarten-age boys' sex-role orientations, preferences, and adoptions. Father dominance in parental interaction, however, showed weaker relationships with sex-role development than did the boy's perception of father dominance. The boy's behavior seems to be much determined by his particular perception of family interactions, and it may be that his view of the father is the most relevant measure. The boy's perception of his father can also be much influenced by his mother's behavior. In father-mother interactions, some mothers encouraged their husbands to make decisions, whereas others appeared to prevent their husbands from serving as adequate models by constantly competing with them for the decision-making role.

Other analyses of the data suggested the complex influences of family interactions on the boy's sex-role development. Several of the boys low in masculinity had fathers who were dominant in interactions with their wives and generally seemed masculine. These fathers, however, also appeared to be controlling and restrictive of their son's behavior. For instance, this type of dominant father punished his son for disagreeing with him. Such fathers were clearly maltreating their sons.

Masculine development is facilitated when the father is a competent masculine model and allows and encourages the boy to be dominant. This type of paternal behavior is particularly important in the development of sex-role adoption. In families in which the mother and father were competing for the decision-making function, boys were often very restricted. In some families, where the mother does not allow her husband to share in family decisions, he is more apt to attempt to dominate his son in a restrictive and controlling manner.

It is the father's sex-role adoption in family interactions that is important, not the degree of masculine behavior he exhibits outside the home. Many fathers have masculine interests and are masculine in their peer and work relationships but are very ineffectual in their interactions with their wives and children. The stereotype of the masculine, hard-working father whose primary activity at home is lying on the couch, watching television, or sleeping is an all too accurate description of many fathers. If the father is not consistently involved in family functioning, it is much harder for his child to learn to be appropriately assertive, active, independent, and competent. Lack of father involvement can be a particularly insidious form of child maltreatment. On the other hand, active parenting can have much constructive influence on the father's own sex-role development and sense of personal maturity (Biller & Meredith, 1974; Heath, 1978; Russell, 1978).

Paternal Nurturance

In general, paternal nurturance refers to the father's affectionate, attentive encouragement of his child. Such behavior may or may not be manifested in caretaking activities, which appear more common in descriptions of maternal nurturance. From a learning theory perspective, it could be predicted that masculine development is positively related to the degree of warmth and affection the father gives to his son; or, to put it another way, the more love and respect the boy has for his father, the more reinforcing his father's approval will be for him.

In a study of elementary-school-age children, Bronson (1959) reported findings indicating that both the father's masculinity and the quality of the father-son relationship must be taken into account. The father's behavior and the father-child relationship were assessed from interviews of the fathers and family history data. The masculinity of toy preferences of boys who had chronically stressful relationships with their fathers was negatively associated with the fathers' masculinity. Maltreatment by fathers appeared to impede severely the sex-role development process in sons. Boys who had undemonstrative, frustrating, and critical fathers seemed to reject them as models. In contrast, where the father-son relationship was nonstressful (that is, where fathers were warm, affectionate, and supportive), the masculinity of boys' toys preferences was positively correlated with fathers' masculinity. Masculine development is facilitated when the father is both masculine and nurturant.

A warm, affectionate father-son relationship can do much to strengthen the boy's masculine development constructively. Pauline Sears (1953) found that preschool boys who assumed the father role in doll play activities (used the father doll with high frequency) tended to have warm, affectionate fathers. Mussen and Distler (1959) studied the structured doll play of kindergarten boys. Boys who scored high in masculinity of projective sex-role responses perceived their fathers as warmer and more nurturant than did boys with low masculinity scores. Using the same methodology, Mussen and Rutherford (1963) reported similar findings for first-grade boys. Studying kindergarten-age boys, Biller (1969b) found that perceived paternal nurturance was related to a fantasy game measure of sex-role orientation.

According to maternal interview data collected by Mussen and Distler (1960), the high-masculine boys described in their earlier (1959) article had more affectionate relationships with their fathers than did the low-masculine boys. Interviews with the boys' mothers suggested a trend for the fathers of high-masculine boys to take care of their sons more often and to have more responsibility for family child-rearing practices. Many researchers have found that paternal nurturance is related to older boys' masculinity and/or similarity to their fathers (e.g., Bandura & Walters, 1959; Bronson, 1959; Distler, 1964; Mussen, 1961; Payne & Mussen, 1956).

Paternal nurturance is positively linked to boys' success in peer relationships; they can model their fathers' positive behaviors in their interactions with other children. For boys, the presence of a masculine and nurturant father, generally sex-appropriate behavior, and popularity with peers are strongly related (Biller, 1974c, 1976a). Paternal nurturance can also be a facilitating factor in many other facets of the individual's development, including various cognitive abilities and vocational adjustment (Biller, 1974c, 1976a, 1982a).

Paternal Limit Setting

A relationship between paternal limit setting and masculine development has been found by several researchers. Lefkowitz's (1962) analyses revealed that third- and fourth-grade boys who made at least some feminine toy choices had fathers who took less part in setting limits for them than did fathers of boys who made completely masculine toy choices. In Altucher's (1957) study, more adolescent boys who scored high in masculinity of interests than boys who scored low said their fathers set limits for them. Moulton, Burnstein, Liberty, and Altucher (1966) reported a similar association among male college students, but Distler (1964) did not. Other investigators have reported results connecting paternal discipline with various forms of aggressive behavior in boys (e.g., Eron, Walder, Toigo, & Lefkowitz, 1963; Kagan, 1958b; Levin & Sears, 1956).

An implication of such data is that boys often learn to be aggressive and masculine by modeling themselves after their fathers, with the disciplinary situation being particularly relevant. Other factors may be operating to produce a relationship between paternal limit setting and boys' aggressive behavior. Boys may be negatively aggressive and abusive as a function of the frustration engendered by severe paternal punitiveness. Furthermore, global ratings of aggression and other complex personality traits should be viewed with some degree of caution. For example, not all forms of aggression are culturally accepted as appropriate for boys; assertiveness in play and an active physical stance in interactions with peers seem appropriate, but tattling on other children and fighting with younger children seem inappropriate (e.g., Biller & Borstelmann, 1967; Shortell & Biller, 1970).

In any case, findings about the influence of paternal limit setting are inconsistent (Biller, 1976a, 1982a). In Mussen and Distler's (1959) study, the kindergarten boys who manifested highly masculine projective responses perceived their fathers as somewhat more punitive and threatening in structured doll play situations than did boys low in masculinity. Mussen and Rutherford (1963) found a similar trend for first-grade boys. In both studies, however, perceived nurturance of the father was found to be much more related to high masculine preferences. In addition, Mussen and Distler (1960) ascertained nothing to indicate that the fathers of the high-masculine boys actually punished them more than the fathers of the low-masculine boys punished their sons. In Biller's (1969b) study with kindergarten-age boys, perceived paternal limit setting was slightly related to a measure of sex-role orientation but not to measures of sex-role preference or adoption. Sears, Rau, and Alpert (1965) did not find a consistent relationship between interview measures of paternal limit setting and preschool boys' masculinity.

The adolescent boys with high masculine interests in Mussen's study (1961) described fathers (in their TAT stories) as nonpunitive and nonrestrictive. Some of the discrepancy between this study and the Mussen and Distler (1959) and Mussen and Rutherford (1963) studies may be due to age differences. For example, a father who earlier was perceived as threatening because of his "awesome size" may be less threatening in adolescence, when his son becomes similar in size and strength. During adolescence the father is also less likely to use physical means of punishment and more likely to set limits verbally. A related point is that limit setting is not necessarily performed in a punitive context.

When the father plays a significant part in setting limits, the boy's attachment to his father and his masculine development are facilitated only if there is an already established affectionate father-son relationship. If the father is not nurturant and also is punitive, the boy is likely to display a low level of father imitation. Bandura and Walters (1959) found that adolescent boys who had highly punitive and generally nonnurturant and nonrewarding fathers exhibited relatively low father preference and little perception of themselves as acting and thinking like their fathers. Consistent maltreatment by the father can greatly damage the child's capacity to identify positively with him.

The emphasis in future research should be on gathering data on paternal participation in setting limits and expectations rather than simply on the relative amount of time the father acts as a punishing agent. Firmness and consistency of setting limits relate to clear-cut expectations for the child by the parent and to what Baumrind (1967) terms authoritative child rearing. In this context, it is interesting to note that Coopersmith (1967) reported that fathers of elementary-school boys with high self-esteem were more active in setting limits than were fathers of boys with low self-esteem.

Paternal Power

Mussen and Distler (1959) found that boys with highly masculine projective sex-role behavior perceived their fathers as more "powerful" than did boys low in masculinity. When perceived nurturance and perceived punitiveness scores were combined, the difference between the masculine and nonmasculine boys was particularly clear-cut. Mussen and Rutherford (1963) reported similar results for first-grade boys, but the relationship was not as strong. The father's total salience to the child and overall involvement in family decision making is the best predictor of the elementary-school boy's masculinity (Freedheim & Borstelmann, 1963). In Biller's (1969b) study with kindergarten-age boys, the overall amount of perceived father influence was much more important than the perception of the father as dominant in a particular area of family or parent-child functioning.

Hetherington, Cox, and Cox (1978; 1982) carried out an especially impressive study that included an analysis of factors related to the sex-role development of preschool-age children. Their use of measures dealing with different aspects of sex-role functioning is noteworthy. In general, they found that fathers were more important than mothers in sex typing. For boys, masculinity on measures of sex-role orientation, sex-role preference, and sex-role adoption was related to paternal warmth, paternal demands for maturity, and paternal dominance and participation in decision making. Boys who seemed able to combine a positive masculinity with more generally androgynous patterns of social interaction had fathers who were warm, active in decision making and child care, emotionally expressive, and supportive of the mother-child relationship. Maternal behaviors generally were more influential for sex-role functioning in families where the parents were divorced and the boys were living with their mothers. The Hetherington, Cox, and Cox data concerning children in divorced families are discussed in chapters 9 and 10.

Parent perception and sex-role research with college students has also yielded results that are in line with formulations emphasizing the importance of the total father-son relationship. Distler (1964) found that college males who described themselves as strongly masculine on an adjective checklist viewed their fathers as high in nurturance, limit setting, and competence—in other words, as very powerful. In a study by Moulton et al. (1966), college males with the most masculine sex-role preferences (modified version of Gough's Femininity Scale) reported that their fathers were high in affection and were the dominant disciplinarians in their families.

Bronfenbrenner (1961) found that the development of leadership, responsibility, and social maturity in adolescent males is closely associated with a father-son relationship that not only is nurturant but also includes a strong component of paternal limit setting. A study by Reuter and Biller (1973) has underscored the importance of both the quality and the quantity of paternal behavior. The combination of at least moderate paternal availability with at least moderate paternal nurturance was associated with positive personal adjustment among male college students.

In general, knowledge of the child's overall relationship with the father, including the degree of paternal availability, nurturance, limit setting, competence, and masculinity, is much more predictive of the child's sex-role and personality functioning than is information pertaining to only a limited dimension of the father-child relationship.

Methodological Limitations

Some caution must be offered about most of the studies reviewed in this chapter. Many of the researchers used only a very restricted and sometimes vague measure of sex role, yet generalized about the effects of a particular variable on overall sex-role development. Much more attention needs to be given to carefully defining and measuring various aspects and patterns of sex-role functioning. In the great majority of studies, no account was taken of certain variables other than parent-child relations that might influence sex role development. For example, there was no consideration of individual differences among children in intelligence, temperament, or physical appearance.

The bulk of research on father-child relationships and sex role development can be criticized because of methodological deficiencies and/or limited generality (Biller, 1974c, 1981b). In most investigations the father's behavior is not assessed directly; instead, maternal or child reports of paternal behavior are used. In many of the studies the sources of evidence about paternal behavior and the child's behavior are not independent, leading to problems of interpretation. In many studies children are asked to describe both their own and their parents' behavior.

Most of the studies on the father-child relationship and personality development have been correlational. Often the child's perception of his father or some report of the father's behavior is linked to a measure of the child's personality development. For instance, when significant correlations are found between the degree to which a boy perceives his father as nurturant and the boy's masculinity, it is usually assumed that paternal nurturance has been an antecedent of masculine development. But fathers may become nurturing and accepting when their sons are masculine, and rejecting and maltreating when their sons are unmasculine. Longitudinal research would be particularly helpful in determining the extent to which certain paternal behaviors precede or determine particular dimensions of children's behavior. Careful observations of families in various sociocultural settings could be especially revealing.

A Multidimensional Perspective

There have been some first steps toward formulating a multidimensional and interactionist perspective of the father's influence on sex-role development (Biller, 1971a, 1974c; Biller & Borstelmann, 1967). This approach emphasizes the complexity of factors involved in sex-role development. The quality of the father's interactions with his child are seen as very important, but the father and child seldom live in isolation from other family members. The quality of the mother-child relationship, the parental relationship, and the entire family system (father-mother-child-sibling(s) interactions), as well as various biological and sociocultural factors, all contribute to the father's and son's influences on each other. The following is a brief summary of some of the major points of this multidimensional perspective as they relate to the sex-role development of the young boy.

Self-Perception

The father can play a significant role in the development of sex-role orientation, a basic facet of self-concept, even during infancy. Infants and fathers can become very attached to each other, and the boy's perception of himself as a male, and thus as more similar to his father than to his mother, is an impetus for him to imitate his father. Parents can, of course, facilitate their son's perception of greater similarity to his father than to his mother by their verbal and behavioral cues. Children generally imitate the behaviors of both parents, and the degree of actual similarity between father and son can be influenced by genetic and/or constitutional factors. A child's particular resemblance to one parent in terms of temperament and physical characteristics can be an impetus to being viewed as similar to that parent. However, the quality of fathering the boy receives is generally the most crucial factor in the positive development of his view of himself as a male. Consistent maltreatment by the father can greatly damage the child's capacity to identify positively with him.

There are many commonalities between Kohlberg's (1966) cognitive-developmental conception of sex-role development and this formulation; the early learning of orientation, the importance of cognitive factors, the predisposing influence of orientation on later sex-role development, and the influence of self-concept and competency motivation. The multidimensional formulation is much more inclusive, however. Kohlberg gave a somewhat circumscribed description of sex-role development and generally downplayed the importance of parental factors. He seemed to assume that knowledge of sex-role norms is relatively isomorphic with sex-role development. Although the ability to discriminate masculine and feminine roles, symbols, and activities is an important factor, it does not encompass all of sex-role development. Many individuals know the sex-role norms but prefer to behave in a manner more characteristic of the other sex. For example, a boy can be aware that he is a male and know about sex-typed toys, yet choose to play exclusively with girls and to engage in feminine sex-typed activities.

The development of an individual's sex-role preference, along with his or her relative desire to adhere to culturally defined sex-role guidelines, is usually influenced by sex-role orientation. But whereas *orientation* is very much related to discrimination between the specific sex-role models of mother and father, *preference* pertains to discrimination between more general, socially defined symbols and representations of sex role. Sex-role orientation is involved with the individual's self-evaluation; sex-role preference is related to the individual's evaluation of environmental activities and opportunities. In developing a masculine sex-role preference, the boy learns to value certain toys, activities, and interests. Learning experiences are based on more than family interactions; peers and the mass media become increasingly influential.

Sex-role adoption refers to the masculinity and/or femininity of the individual's social and environmental interactions. Whereas sex-role orientation is related to individuals' views of themselves, sex-role adoption pertains in part to the way in which individuals are perceived by other members of their society. Correlates of sex-role adoption are present even in infancy, and sex-role adoption continues to evolve in adolescence and adulthood. During this time interpersonal skill development in heterosexual relationships is particularly important. The formation of a masculine sex-role adoption, especially in the preschool years, is often related to imitation of the father. A young boy's masculinity is positively related to the degree to which his father is available and behaves in a masculine manner in his interaction with his family. Siblings and peers can, of course, also influence the development of the child's sex-role adoption.

Paternal masculinity is much related to what White (1960) has subsumed under the heading of *competency*. The boy's desire to imitate his father and become masculine can be associated with a desire to master his environment. For example, the boy's ability to solve problems and to build and repair various objects can be greatly increased by frequent opportunities to observe and imitate his father. Child maltreatment in the form of paternal neglect and rejection can be especially detrimental to positive sex-role adoption.

Assuming the father is relatively masculine, paternal nurturance facilitates the boy's development of a masculine sex-role adoption. A nurturant father more frequently rewards his son's approach responses than does a nonnurturant father, and thus provides more opportunities for his son to observe and imitate his behavior. In other words, a nurturant father is a more available model than a nonnurturant father. The nurturant father's behavior is more often associated with affection and praise, and it acquires more reward value. Thus a boy with a nurturant father has more incentive to imitate his father than does a boy with a nonnurturant father. Moreover, a nurturant father seems more likely to reinforce his son for imitating him.

If the father is a frequent participant in setting limits for his son, other opportunities for imitation are provided. If the father is much more abusive, punitive, and frustrating than he is rewarding, however, then his behavior will not have a high incentive value and will be less reproduced. A positive relationship between paternal limit setting and the masculinity of the boy's sex-role adoption is predicted only if the father is relatively nurturant. The father's masculinity, nurturance, and limit setting add up to his total salience for his son. The boy's perception of his father influences his perception of the incentive value of the masculine role and affects all aspects of his sex-role development.

Physical Status

A boy can have a masculine orientation and preference but be limited in the development of a masculine adoption by an inadequate or inappropriate physical status. For example, a boy who is very short or thin may be at a disadvantage in a subculture that strongly associates physical prowess and masculinity. Height and muscle mass seem positively related to masculinity of sex-role adoption.

Although a particular type of physique is not sufficient to produce masculine behavior, a boy who is tall and broad, or broad though short, is better suited for success in many masculine activities than a boy who is tall and thin or short and thin. Parents and others seems to expect more masculine behavior from tall, broad, and/or mesomorphic boys (Biller, 1968a).

The boy's physical status can influence his sex-role orientation and sex-role preference as well as his sex-role adoption. For example, during adolescence boys with especially unmasculine physiques are apt to have insecure self-concepts. Even though they are also likely to be low in masculinity of sex-role adoption, they may express very masculine sex-role preferences in an effort to convince themselves and others that they are masculine (Biller & Liebman, 1971; Martel & Biller, 1986).

Children's constitutional predispositions have much to do with their personality development and with the way others respond to them. The boy who has a sensory-motor handicap or is intellectually limited can be extremely frustrating to his father. For example, a sports-minded father might find it very difficult to interact with a poorly coordinated son. Similarly, an intellectually striving father may be unintererested in spending his time with a son who possesses little verbal or cognitive ability. On the other hand, a boy with a mesomorphic physique, high activity level, superior intelligence, and good coordination is likely to be perceived as masculine and to attain much success in many traditionally male activities even if he has been exposed to paternal deprivation and child maltreatment (Biller, 1974c, 1981b).

Cognitive Functioning

In this section, we present data that underscore the potential significance for cognitive functioning of variations in fathering and paternal maltreatment. In chapter 10 there is a discussion of much more research linking father-absence and paternal deprivation with children's deficits in intellectual adjustment.

Intellectual Attainment

Kimball (1952) studied highly intelligent boys enrolled in a residential preparatory school. She compared twenty boys who were failing in school with a group of boys who were selected at random from the total school population. Interview and psychological test material consistently revealed that the underachieving boys had very inadequate relationships with their fathers. Many of the fathers were reported to work long hours and to be home infrequently, or to attempt to dominate and control their sons by means of excessive discipline. Physical abuse by the father was quite common among the underachievers. Other research reviewed by Biller (1974c) also suggested a connection between academic underachievement and poor father-son relationships.

In contrast, both Katz (1967) and Solomon (1969) reported data indicating a strong positive association between paternal interest and encouragement and academic achievement among lower-class black elementary-school boys. Katz's findings were based on the boys' perception of their parents, whereas Solomon rated parent-child interactions while the boys performed a series of intellectual tasks. In both studies, the father's behavior appeared to be a much more important factor than did the mother's behavior.

The studies so far discussed have dealt with paternal factors and their association with academic achievement. In addition, there is much evidence that the quality of fathering is related to the child's performance on intelligence and aptitude tests.

Radin (1972) found both the quality and quantity of father-son interactions strongly associated with four-year-old boys' intellectual functioning. Father-son interactions during an interview with the father were recorded and later coded for frequency of paternal nurturance and restrictiveness. The overall number of father-son interactions were positively correlated to both Stanford-Binet and Peabody Picture Vocabulary Test Intelligence Test scores. However, the strongest relationship was observed between paternal nurturance (seeking out the child in a positive manner, asking information of the child, meeting the child's needs, and so on) and the intelligence test measures. On the other hand, paternal restrictiveness (demands for obedience and the like) was negatively correlated with level of intellectual functioning. Verbal abuse by the father seemed to inhibit the child's intellectual competence. The quality of the father's behavior, particularly paternal nurturance, appeared to be more important than the total number of father-son interactions.

In a subsequent study, Radin (1973) reported evidence indicating that the amount of paternal nurturance at the time of the initial study was also positively related to the boys' intellectual functioning one year later. In addition, a questionnaire measure of degree of paternal involvement in direct teaching activities (for example, teaching the boy to count and read) at the time of the initial study was positively associated with the boy's intellectual functioning both at that time and one year later.

In their reviews of the literature relating to the father's impact on cognitive development, Biller (1974a, 1974b, 1974c, 1982a). Lynn (1974); Radin (1976, 1981); and Shinn (1978) cite much other research that can be construed as indicating that paternal deprivation and maltreatment can negatively influence the child's intellectual functioning, whereas positive father-son involvement is quite advantageous. For example, Blanchard and Biller (1971) discovered that among third-grade boys in two-parent families, those with highly available fathers performed significantly better on achievement tests and with respect to grades than did those whose fathers were relatively inaccessible to them. (The Blanchard and Biller research is discussed in more detail in chapter 10.) Reis and Gold's (1977) study suggested that highly involved fathers are especially likely to have young sons who are strong in problem-solving competence. Among adolescent males, Gold and Andrés (1978a) found data supporting a link between paternal involvement and grade point average. Biller (1974a, 1974b, 1974c) and Radin (1976, 1981) summarized several studies suggesting that mutual father-son identification is conducive to the development of cognitive competence in male children.

Many investigations have yielded relatively strong positive correlations between various indexes of children's intellectual functioning and such variables as father's education, father's occupational status, and father's job satisfaction (see especially reviews by Lynn, 1974, and Radin, 1981). Such findings are consistent with the view that educationally and occupationally successful fathers can be particularly salient models for their children's cognitive development. As emphasized by Biller (1971a, 1974c) and Radin (1976, 1981), however, it is crucial to consider the quality of the father-child relationship, not just the father's behavior outside of the home.

On the other hand, paternal hostility, punitiveness, and rigidity appear to undermine cognitive functioning among adolescent males (e.g., Baumrind, 1971; Heilbrun, 1973). In a research project with a longitudinal perspective, Harrington, Block, and Block (1978) reported evidence indicating a connection between paternal emotional rigidity and impatience during their sons' preschool years, and difficulties in the children's cognitive functioning and problem solving in second grade. Of course, as the investigators and Radin (1981) pointed out, fathers may be greatly influenced by the level of intellectual ability their sons display, and paternal rigidity and impatience may, at least in some cases, be a reaction to actual incompetence in particular children. Nevertheless, overly intrusive and restrictive fathers who attempt to impose their solutions on problems confronting their children can certainly inhibit their sons' achievement motivation, cognitive competence, and creativity (Biller, 1974a, 1974b, 1974c, 1982a; Lynn, 1974; Radin, 1976, 1981).

Individuality

Correlational data do not prove that a positive father-son relationship directly facilitates the boys' intellectual functioning. For example, a father may be much more available, accepting, and nurturant to a son who is bright and performs well in school. On the other hand, disappointment with a son's abilities may lead the father to reject or abuse him, and/or the son's performance may further weaken an already flimsy father-son relationship. Individual differences in the child's constitutional predispositions and behavior can greatly influence the quality of interactions between father and child (Biller, 1971a, 1974c, 1982a).

Fathers are reported to be much less tolerant of severely intellectually handicapped children than are mothers (Farber, 1962a). The father who highly values intellectual endeavors is especially likely to reject a retarded child (Downey, 1963). Paternal deprivation lessens the probability that the retarded child will maximize his intellectual potential or have adequate sex-role development (Biller, 1971a; Biller & Borstelmann, 1965).

In addition to being the antecedents of some forms of mental retardation, constitutional predispositions and genetic factors may be related to other types of influences affecting the father-child relationship (Biller, 1971a, 1974c). Father and son can manifest cognitive abilities in the same area primarily as a function of a similar genetic inheritance. Poffenberger and Norton (1959) found that the attitudes toward mathematics of fathers and their college-freshman sons were similar, yet were not related to the closeness of the father-son relationship. These investigators speculated that genetic factors are involved in degree of success in mathematics and can predispose similar father-son attitudes toward mathematics. Hill's (1967) findings, however, suggest that more than genetic factors are connected to the child's attitude toward mathematics. In studying the relationship between paternal expectations and upper-middle-class seventh-grade boys' attitudes toward mathematics, Hill found that positive attitudes toward mathematics were more common among boys whose fathers viewed mathematics as a masculine endeavor and expected their sons to behave in a masculine manner.

Self-Esteem and Personal Adjustment

There is a strong association between self-esteem in children and constructive paternal involvement. Children's self-acceptance is negatively related to various forms of maltreatment by the father, whereas paternal nurturance facilitates healthy self-esteem. The father's interest and consistent participation strongly contribute to the development of the child's self-confidence and self-concept. Sears (1970) found a relationship between mother-reported paternal warmth and a questionnaire measure of sixth-grade boys' self-esteem. Medinnus (1965a) reported that college students' self-esteem was positively related to paternal love and negatively related to paternal rejection and neglect. Mussen, Bouterline-Young, Gaddini, and Morante's (1963) data revealed that adolescent boys with unaffectionate relationships with their fathers were particularly likely to feel rejected and unhappy.

In Coopersmith's (1967) study with elementary-school boys, paternal involvement in limit setting was associated with high self-esteem. In contrast, boys with low self-esteem were much more likely to be disciplined exclusively by their mothers. Boys who were able to confide in their fathers were also likely to have high self-esteem. Rosenberg (1965) discovered that the early father-child relationship is particularly important for the development of the child's self-esteem. Father-absent adolescents had lower self-esteem than father-present ones, particularly when father-absence had begun in early childhood.

Reuter and Biller (1973) studied the relationship between various combinations of perceived paternal nurturance-availability and college males' personal adjustment. A family background questionnaire was designed to assess perceptions of father-child relationships and the amount of time the father spent at home when the subjects were children. The personal adjustment scale of Gough and Heilbrun's Adjective Checklist and the socialization scale of the California Psychological Inventory were employed as measures of personality adjustment. High paternal nurturance combined with at least moderate paternal availability, and high paternal availability combined with at least moderate paternal nurturance, both were related to high scores on the personality adjustment measures. A male who has adequate opportunities to observe a nurturant father can imitate his behavior and develop positive personality characteristics. The father who is both relatively nurturant and relatively available may have a more adequate personality adjustment than other types of fathers.

In contrast, high paternal nurturance combined with low paternal availability, and high paternal availability combined with low paternal nurturance, were associated with relatively poor scores on the personality adjustment measures. The boy with a highly nurturant but seldom-home father may feel frustrated that his father is not home more often and/or may find it difficult to imitate such an elusive figure. Males who reported that their fathers had been home much of the time but gave them little attention seemed to be especially handicapped in their psychological functioning. The unnurturant father is an inadequate model, and his consistent presence appears to be a detriment to the boy's personality functioning. In other words, the boy with an unnurturant father may be better off if his father is *not* very available. This is consistent with evidence suggesting that father-absent boys often have better personality adjustments than do boys with passive, ineffectual fathers (Biller, 1974c, 1982a).

There are some very extensive longitudinal data that underscore the importance of both the father's behavior and the father-mother relationship in the personality adjustment of the child. Block (1971) found that males who achieved a successful emotional and interpersonal adjustment in adulthood had both fathers and mothers who were highly involved and responsible in their upbringing. Those adult males who were poorly adjusted, however, had fathers who were typically neglectful and uninvolved in child rearing, and mothers who tended to have a neurotic adjustment.

In a related investigation, Block, von der Lippe, and Block (1973) reported that well-socialized and successful adult males were likely to have had highly involved fathers and to come from homes where their parents had compatible relationships. In contrast, adult males who were relatively low in socialization skills and personal adjustment were likely to have grown up in homes in which the parents were incompatible and in which the fathers were either uninvolved or weak and neurotic.

Moral Development and Antisocial Behavior

Paternal involvement in discipline, when combined with a high level of paternal affection, is strongly associated with male children's sensitivity to their transgressions (Moulton et al., 1966). The father who can set limits firmly but who can also be affectionate and responsive to his child's needs seems to be a particularly good model for interpersonal sensitivity and moral development. Holstein (1972) found that adolescents who were morally mature were likely to have warm, nurturant, and highly moral fathers.

Hoffman (1971a, 1971b) found that weak father-identification was related to less adequate conscience development than was strong father-identification. Father-identification was determined by response to questions involving the person to whom the boy felt most similar, whom he most admired, and whom he most wanted to resemble when he grew up. Among the seventh-graders that Hoffman studied, boys with strong father-identifications scored higher on measures of internal moral judgment, moral values, and conformity to rules than did boys with low father-identifications.

Hoffman (1981) reveiwed data supporting the father's role as an identification figure in the moral development process for both sons and daughters. Hoffman (1975) reported an association between the degree to which fathers manifested prosocial moral values and ratings of their children's prosocial behavior by peers. Haan, Langer, and Kohlberg (1976) found moral judgment scores of sons to be positively correlated with those of their fathers. Hoffman (1981), in his provocative comments about the complexity and multidimensionality of the moral development process, points out that parents may also learn from their children about moral reasoning. The reciprocal nature of parent-child learning with respect to moral development was also discussed by Biller and Meredith (1974). They emphasized that involved fathers may need to reanalyze their own values if they are to be more adequate models for their children.

Hoffman (1981) speculated that identification with the father may contribute to the acquisition of observable moral attributes, but that the internalization of moral standards and values is a complex process, in which the mother may play a more primary role. Hoffman also discusses evidence suggesting that for fathers and their sons, achievement may become a moral imperative that obscures the learning of important values dealing with sensitivity to others' feelings and interpersonal commitment. Hoffman does emphasize, however, that father-absence may make it particularly difficult for the male child to internalize moral values appropriately (see chapter 10 for further discussion of father-absence and moral development).

The quality of the father-child relationship has particular influence on whether the child takes responsibility for his own actions or operates as if his behavior is controlled by external forces. A father who is actively committed to his children facilitates their development of responsible behavior. Radin (1982) and Sagi (1982) reported that high father participation in child rearing was associated with an internal locus of control and taking responsibility for one's actions for both boys and girls. Fathers who actively choose to be regularly involved with their children may be presenting them with an especially salient model of responsible behavior (Radin & Russell, 1983). Children who have a warm relationship with a competent father who can set limits for them constructively are much more likely to develop a realistic internal locus of control (Biller, 1974c, 1982a).

Delinquency

Antisocial behavior among children and adolescents can have many different etiologies, but paternal deprivation and various forms of child maltreatment by fathers are frequent contributing factors. Research findings relating to the fact that father-absence is much more common among delinquent boys than among nondelinquent boys are reviewed in chapter 10. Father-present juvenile delinquents generally appear to have very unsatisfactory relationships with their fathers; a history of emotional and physical abuse by their fathers seems common. Bach and Bremmer (1947) reported that preadolescent delinquent boys produced significantly fewer father fantasies on projective tests than did a nondelinquent control group. The delinquents portrayed fathers as lacking in affection and empathy. Similarly, Andry (1962) found that delinquents characterized their fathers as glum and uncommunicative and as employing unreasonable punishment and little praise. Father-son communication was particularly poor.

Andry's (1962) findings are consistent with those of Bandura and Walters (1959), who reported that in intact families, the relationship between delinquent sons and fathers is marked by rejection, hostility, and antagonism. McCord, McCord, and Howard (1963) found that a deviant, aggressive father in the context of general parental neglect and punitiveness was strongly related to juvenile delinquency. Medinnus (1965b) obtained data suggesting a very high frequency of poor father-child relationships among delinquent boys. The subjects in his study perceived their fathers as much more rejecting and neglecting than they did their mothers.

Schaefer's (1965) results also revealed the particularly negative way delinquent boys often perceive their fathers. Compared to nondelinquent boys, delinquent boys viewed their fathers as more lax in discipline, more neglecting, and generally less involved. Surprisingly, the delinquents described their mothers as more positive and loving than did the nondelinquents. Gregory (1965a) found a higher rate of delinquency among boys living with their mothers following father-loss than among boys living with fathers following mother-loss. Paternal deprivation is more of a factor in the development of delinquency than is maternal deprivation.

Father-present delinquents are likely to have inadequate fathers who themselves have difficulties in impulse control and who maltreat their children. Jenkins (1969) found that the fathers of delinquent children seen at a child guidance clinic were frequently described as rigid, controlling, and prone to alcoholism. McCord, McCord, and Howard (1963) reported that criminal behavior in adulthood was often found among men whose fathers had been criminals, alcoholics, and/or extremely abusive to their families. Other researchers also have presented data suggesting a link between paternal inadequacy and delinquent behavior (e.g., Bennett, 1959; Cath, Gurwitt, & Ross, 1982; Gardner, 1959; Glueck & Glueck, 1950; Rosenthal, Ni, Finkelstein, & Berkwitz, 1962).

As with other types of developmental outcomes, it is again important to caution against a simple "poor father–troubled child" hypothesis. Adolescent and adult males who commit criminal acts, especially of an aggressive nature, often have some biologically based impulse control disorder. Retrospective data suggest that a great many of these males had undiagnosed, untreated learning disabilities, including attention deficit problems, even as very young children (Berman & Siegal, 1976a, 1976b). The extent to which the father is able to be positively involved and supportive very much influences the development of the learning disabled child. If the father perceives the child in a negative way (as stubborn, lazy, and the like) and maltreats him, the child is likely to act out in a delinquent manner.

Interpersonal Relationships

The father-infant relationship can have a strong impact on the child's subsequent relationships with others. In chapter 6 we reviewed evidence indicating that fathers can greatly influence their infants' interpersonal competence. For example, infants who have little contact with their fathers, as compared to those who have much, are more likely to experience greater separation anxiety from their mothers and to have more negative reactions to strangers (Biller, 1974c; Spelke et al., 1973). The way the father interacts with the child presents a particularly potent modeling situation, which the child is apt to generalize to his relationships with others.

A positive father-son relationship gives the boy a basis for successful peer interactions. Rutherford and Mussen (1968) reported evidence indicating that nursery-school boys who perceive their fathers as warm and nurturant are generous with other children. Payne and Mussen (1956) found that adolescent boys who were similar to their fathers in terms of responses to the California Psychological Inventory were rated as more friendly by their teachers than were boys who had responses markedly different from their fathers'. In Lois Hoffman's (1961) study, boys from mother-dominant homes had much more difficulty in their peer relationships than did boys from father-dominant homes. Maternal dominance was associated with impulsiveness and an inability to influence peers. On the other hand, self-confidence, assertiveness, and overall competence in peer group interactions were related to a warm father-son relationship.

As we emphasized in chapter 5, sexual abuse is an especially insidious form of child maltreatment. More and more attention is being focused on males (as well as females) who are sexually abused during childhood (Kempe & Kempe, 1984). Boys who are sexually abused by fathers and stepfathers or other male family members seem to have special difficulty attaining a healthy masculine self-esteem, a comfortable attitude toward their bodies, and successful romantic relationships with females. Sexual abuse by a father or stepfather is very often linked with severe acting out, serious sexual maladjustment, and psychopathology in children.

Sexual Relationships

A positive father-child relationship can greatly facilitate the boy's security in interacting with females. The boy who has developed a positive masculine self-image has much more confidence in heterosexual interactions (Biller, 1974c). There are longitudinal data suggesting that the male who develops a strong sense of masculinity in childhood is likely to be successful in his heterosexual relationships in adulthood (Kagan & Moss, 1962). There is considerable evidence indicating that the male's adjustment to marriage is related to his relationship with his father and to the quality of his parents' marital relationship (Barry, 1970; Cross & Aron, 1971). Much research documenting difficulties in forming successful heterosexual relationships that are linked with paternal deprivation is reviewed in chapters 9 and 10 focusing on father absence and divorce.

An inadequate father-child relationship often appears to be a major factor in the development of homosexuality among males. West (1967) presented an excellent review of data pertaining to the antecedents of male homosexuality. Males who as children have ineffectual fathers (or are father-absent) and are involved in an intense, close-binding mother-son relationship seem particularly prone to develop a homosexual pattern of behavior. A close-binding mother-son relationship seems more common in families in which the father is relatively uninvolved and may, along with related factors, lessen the probability of the boy's entering into meaningful heterosexual relationships. It is common to find that homosexuals were discouraged by their mothers during childhood from participating in masculine activities and were often reinforced for feminine behavior (e.g., Bieber et al., 1962; Gundlach, 1969).

Male homosexuals do not usually develop strong attachments to their fathers. Chang and Block (1960) compared a group of relatively well adjusted male homosexuals with a heterosexual control group. They found that the homosexuals reported stronger identification with their mothers and weaker identifications with their fathers. Nash and Hayes (1965) discovered that male homosexuals who take a passive, feminine role in sexual affairs have a particularly weak identification with their fathers, in contrast to a very strong one with their mothers.

Both Bieber et al. (1962) and Evans (1969) found that more fathers of homosexuals than fathers of heterosexuals were described as detached and hostile. Mothers of homosexuals were depicted as closely bound with their sons and relatively uninvolved with their husbands. Bené (1965) reported that more male homosexuals than heterosexuals perceived their fathers as weak and were hostile toward them. Similar studies by Apperson and McAdoo (1968) and Saghir and Robbins (1973) suggested a pattern of very negative father-child relations during the childhoods of male homosexuals.

A particularly extensive study of the developmental histories of homosexuals was conducted by Thompson, Schwartz, McCandless, and Edwards (1973). College-age, well-educated homosexuals were recruited through their friends, and their family backgrounds and childhood activities were compared with those of a control group. Homosexual men described very little interaction with their fathers and a relative lack of acceptance by their fathers during their childhoods. The homosexuals generally viewed their fathers as weak, hostile, and rejecting. In general, Thompson et al. found the classic male homosexual pattern of paternal deprivation coupled with an overintense mother-child relationship and early expression of avoidance of masculine activities.

Heterosexuals, as well as homosexuals, who avoided masculine activities in childhood reported more distance from both their fathers and from men in general. It may be that a major difference between these homosexuals and heterosexuals was their adolescent sexual experience. For example, opportunities for positive heterosexual relationships may have been more readily available for some of the boys. More homosexuals than heterosexuals also described themselves as frail or clumsy during childhood; again, there may be mediating constitutional factors in the development of many cases of homosexuality. The data fit well with a hypothesis suggesting that early paternal deprivation makes certain individuals particularly susceptible to negative influences in later development. Paternally deprived males are quite vulnerable to seek out older males, some of whom may maltreat them and/or be homosexual (Biller, 1974c, 1981b).

A picture of an emotionally maltreating father is quite common in the family histories of homosexuals. In at least some cases, however, the father may be especially abusive toward a particular child (while treating his other children in a relatively adequate manner) because he feels intensely threatened by that child's lack of conformity to sex-role expectations and/or what he may perceive as homosexual tendencies. This in no way absolves such fathers from responsibility for their behavior, but it underscores the need to examine how child-related characteristics influence parental behavior in a longitudinal context.

Sexual abuse by fathers and other family members is also quite common in the background of male homosexuals. As we discussed in chapter 5, flagrant sexual abuse is only one form of sexual maltreatment. Parents and other family members can much impair a child's sexuality by inappropriate physical interactions and comments. For example, a father who touches and speaks to a male infant as if the child were a daughter is maltreating him even if there is no directly inappropriate genital contact. The father who is so anxious about his own sexuality that he does not dare touch his infant, or who derogates the infant for touching himself in genital areas, is very likely to produce a negative impact on the child's body image and sexuality. Such parental behavior is counterproductive to the development of a healthy sexuality, although in and of itself it does not necessarily produce homosexual children. Sexual-identity problems can be manifested in a myriad of patterns. The particular form of adjustment the paternally maltreated or deprived child makes is determined by a complex interaction of factors (Biller, 1974c, 1981a, 1981b).

Transsexual Behavior

Stoller (1968) described the case histories of several boys who felt that they were really females. These boys represented an extreme in terms of the pervasiveness of their femininity. Stoller referred to them as *transsexual.* These boys had unusually close physical relationships with their mothers. Mutual mother-child body contact during infancy was especially intense, and there was much evidence that the mothers reinforced many forms of feminine behavior. In none of these cases was the father assertive or involved with his child. Stoller's book is replete with references to case studies suggesting that disturbed sex-role development in males is associated with an overly intense, relatively exclusive mother-son relationship.

Green (1974) reported a high rate of early paternal deprivation among extremely feminine boys who wished they were girls and preferred to dress as females. These boys had exceedingly strong identifications with their mothers and were very feminine in their sex-role orientations, preferences, and adoptions, generally manifesting a transsexual behavior pattern. Of the thirty-eight boys that Green intensively studied, thirteen became father-absent prior to age four. Among the other boys, who were father-present, father-son relationships seem to have been very limited or distant. In contrast, the mothers were excessively attached to their sons and had difficulty in perceiving that there was anything deviant in the boys' behavior. Although many of the fathers were quite upset that their sons continued to behave in a feminine manner once the boys reached four or five years of age, they had been generally tolerant and probably at least indirectly reinforcing of feminine behavior during the infancy and toddler periods. Such data suggest that these fathers were very different from most men, who are extremely unfomfortable when their young children, especially their sons, deviate from culturally expected sex-role behavior (Biller, 1971a).

Further analysis of data from Green's provocative research program revealed that fathers spent less time with "feminine" sons during the first years than did fathers of conventionally masculine sons. There was a tendency for less father-son interaction even in the first year, and significant differences emerged beginning in the child's second year. In intact families, parental role differentiation in household management did not appear to be related to the boys' sex-role development. Among divorced parents, those with feminine sons separated earlier than those with masculine sons. In general, early paternal deprivation, whether in the context of two-parent or one-parent families, was much more common for the feminine boys than it was for the comparison group (Green, Williams, & Goodman, 1985).

Green's work is particularly valuable because he traces the complex interaction of various factors in the development of unusually feminine boys. He discusses how, in some cases, sibling and peer group reactions as well as parental behavior can strongly reinforce inappropriate sex role behavior. Perhaps most significantly, his research suggests ways in which the child's characteristics may influence parental behavior. For example, in at least several of his cases, paternal deprivation was increased because of the young boy's disinclination to participate in masculine activities and seeming inability to relate to his father (Biller, 1975b).

Constitutional predispositions as well as direct parental influence are often involved in the child's developing a transsexual behavior pattern. Boys who become transsexual are frequently rather "pretty," delicate, and nonmesomorphic, and they resemble their mothers more than their fathers in outward appearance. This is not to say that biological factors caused the children to become transsexual but that constitutional predispositions may increase the likelihood that certain children will develop "feminine" behavior patterns. Parents' expectations are very much influenced by their children's appearance and behavior (Biller, 1974c). There are some cases where biological factors such as genetic anomalies have a relatively more direct impact on the development of transsexualism or other forms of atypical sex role development (Money & Erhardt, 1972). There are also accumulating data indicating that prenatal androgenic hormone balance is connected to the degree to which young children engage in rough and tumble play, are assertive or timid, and express interest in babies and doll play (Maccoby & Jacklin, 1974; Money & Ehrhardt, 1972; Jacklin, Maccoby, & Doering, 1983).

Psychopathology

Much data relating inadequate fathering to maladjustment in children have already been reviewed. The investigations described here generally focus on clinically diagnosed individuals. In most of the studies discussed previously, the subjects were grouped according to their test responses, their behavior in specific situations, and/or ratings made by others; they were not clinically diagnosed as having some form of psychopathology or being treated at a clinic or hospital. It is important to emphasize that individuals who are clinically labeled are not necessarily more psychologically impaired than individuals who have not been clinically diagnosed. Much of the time, the major difference is that so-called mentally disturbed individuals have simply come into formal contact with a mental health professional.

The Becker and Peterson research group conducted extensive studies designed to ascertain the association between parental behaviors and specific types of clinically diagnosed psychological disturbance among six to twelve-year-old children (Becker et al., 1959, 1962; Peterson et al., 1959, 1961). Maltreatment by fathers was very common among emotionally disturbed children. Children who had conduct problems (problems in impulse control and/or aggressiveness) frequently had fathers who were dictatorial and controlling. Children who had personality problems (shyness, hypersensitivity, low self-concept) frequently had fathers who were insensitive and dictatorial.

Block (1969) also attempted to distinguish between the parental characteristics of children in different diagnostic groupings. Although the findings from Block's study were not specifically consistent with the Becker and Peterson studies, a picture of paternal inadequacy as a major factor in childhood psychopathology again emerged. Liverant (1959) found that fathers of disturbed children responded in a much more negative fashion on the MMPI than did fathers of nondisturbed children. The responses of the fathers of disturbed children indicated that they were impulsive, anxious, depressed, and concerned with bodily complaints—certainly the kind of adults who may be at risk to maltreat family members. Of course, such data can also be interpreted as suggesting that disturbed children can have a negative effect on the personality functioning of their parents (Biller, 1974c, 1982a).

Family Interaction Patterns

Some of the most intriguing and methodologically soundest studies have provided observations of family functioning in standardized problem-solving situations. For example, Mishler and Waxler (1968) and Schuham (1970) learned that high paternal involvement in decision making is uncommon in families in which there is a severely disturbed son. In families with nondisturbed sons, the fathers were most often the ascendant figures, and mutually acceptable decisions were much more common (Schuham, 1970).

In his observational study, Alkire (1969) noted that fathers usually dominated in families with normal adolescents, but mothers dominated in families with disturbed adolescents. Other research on interactions among disturbed families has pointed out several subtypes of inappropriate fathering (McPherson, 1970). Paternal hostility and emotional abuse toward the child and mother and lack of open communication among families were very common. Leighton, Stollak, and Ferguson (1971) found that paternal dominance was more likely and more accepted in families with well-functioning children, whereas an ambivalent maternal dominance was common in families with disturbed children.

Maternal dominance has been associated with a varied array of psychopathological problems, especially among males (Biller, 1974c). Many investigators have, however, found evidence indicating that overly dominant fathers can have just as negative an effect on their child's development as overly dominant mothers can. Researchers have reported much data relating arbitrary paternal power assertion and overcontrol to poor adjustment and psychopathology among children (Biller, 1974c).

The degree of husband-wife dominance may not be a particularly good indication of degree of paternal deprivation, except where there is extreme maternal dominance. Extreme paternal dominance, which is indicative of inadequate fathering, squelches the development of independence and competence in the child as much as does extreme maternal dominance. The excessively dominant father is typically verbally abusive and sometimes also physically abusive with his spouse as well as with his children.

Adequate personality development is facilitated in families in which the father clearly represents a positive masculine role and the mother a positive feminine role. Kayton and Biller (1971) studied the parent perceptions of matched groups of nondisturbed, neurotic, paranoid schizophrenic, and nonparanoid schizophrenic adult males. Nondisturbed subjects perceived their parents as exhibiting sex-appropriate behaviors to a greater extent than the disturbed subjects did. A smaller proportion of individuals in the disturbed groups viewed their fathers as possessing masculine-instrumental traits and, particularly among the schizophrenic groups, their mothers as having feminine-expressive characteristics. Severely disturbed behavior is often associated with difficulties and/or abnormalities in sex-role development (e.g., Biller, 1973b; Biller & Poey, 1969; Heilbrun, 1974; Kayton & Biller, 1972; McClelland & Watt, 1968).

The Kayton and Biller (1971, 1972) research suggests that sex-appropriate parenting may increase the probability of (though not ensure) adequate personality adjustment in children. But individual differences in vulnerability to stress, and other biologically related factors, may be much more important in determining the extent of psychopathology among those children who do not achieve a basic sex-role security and healthy personality adjustment. Kayton and Biller did not find any clear-cut differences among their disturbed subjects with respect to parent perceptions. The degree of psychopathology among the disturbed subjects was probably more a function of constitutional predispositions than the quality of parenting that was available to them as children.

Block, von der Lippe, and Block (1973) reported longitudinal data indicating the complexity of the associations between parental behavior and the child's later personality functioning. They assessed a sample of adult males and a sample of adult females from the Berkeley Longitudinal Study. The sex-role and socialization status of the subjects was determined by their scores on the Femininity and Socialization Scales of the California Psychological Inventory. The males and females were separately grouped according to their sex role and socialization patterns. (Data concerning the female groups are discussed in chapter 8.)

Comparisons of the personality characteristics of different groups were done with respect to Q-sort analyses of extensive interview data. The various groups were also compared in terms of observational and interview ratings of the subjects' family backgrounds, based on data collected during childhood, and there were also contemporaneous interviewer judgments based on the subjects' retrospective reports of their home environments.

The high-masculine, high-socialized males were perceived as being self-confident, competent, optimistic, and buoyant in affect. Analyses of their family background suggested that their parents had a compatible relationship and that the father was the most important person in their personality development. The fathers of such men granted their sons autonomy and were highly available as models as well as accepting of their sons.

The low-masculine, high-socialized males were seen as overcontrolled, conventional, conscientious, and productive. They were viewed as markedly unaggressive yet appeared quite responsible and successful. Their fathers were depicted as very positive models in terms of success, ambition, adjustment, and interpersonal relations. The researchers emphasize that the father's capacity for delay of gratification and long-term commitment seems most evident in this group. This group also appeared to have particularly admirable mothers and to have been exposed to highly compatible father-mother interactions.

The high-masculine, low-socialized males were perceived as hypermasculine in a compensatory manner. They represented a constellation of traits including egotism and lack of impulse control. Family background data clearly indicated that these men had weak, neurotic, and somewhat rejecting fathers. The mother-father relationship was described as very poor, and the mothers seemed resentful and dissatisfied with their husbands. In general, the fathers seemed to be very poor models.

The low-masculine, low-socialized males communicated an attitude of submissiveness, self-doubt, vulnerability, and defensive blame of others. Their fathers appeared to have been relatively uninvolved with their families and yet at the same time conflict-producing. The mothers also appeared very inadequate and were described as neurotic, lacking in energy, and rejecting of the maternal role. There was also some evidence indicating that both parents, particularly the fathers, had difficulties in maintaining marriage relationships. In chapter 6, we reviewed research that highlighted the impact of family dynamics and the reciprocal influence of marital interactions and child development.

8
Developmental Implications for Females in Two-Parent Families

Most of the research concerning paternal influence and the child's personality development and cognitive functioning has focused on the father-son relationship. The quantity and quality of fathering, however, can affect girls as well as boys. Nurturant, competent, and available fathers are important contributors to both their sons' and daughters' sex-role and personality functioning at various stages of development, whereas maltreating (including abusive and neglectful) fathers put their children at great risk for both short- and long-term psychological problems. Maltreatment by the father can have an especially profound impact on the way a daughter views herself as a female and how she feels about her femininity.

Theoretical Perspectives

Unfortunately, much of the theorizing about the father-daughter relationship is marred by negative conceptions of feminine behavior. Freud's theory of feminine identification for girls centers around the Oedipal complex: when the girl discovers that she lacks a penis after being exposed to her brother or male peer, she supposedly blames her mother. She then seeks out her father in an attempt to retaliate against her mother. Because of her wish to replace her mother, the girl supposedly becomes fearful that she will suffer maternal rejection. To ward off this fear of loss of love, the girl then identifies with her mother. According to Freud, however, the fear of the loss of love is not as strong as the fear of castration, and the girl does not identify completely enough with her mother to resolve the Oedipal complex fully (Fenichel, 1945).

Deutsch (1944) described the traditional psychoanalytic viewpoint in her discussion of Freud's conception of the process of feminine development. According to Deutsch (1944), the father plays an important function in leading the girl to adopt an erotic-passive mode of interacting with males. He showers her with love and tenderness when she acts passive, helpless, and/or femininely seductive, but discourages her masculine and/or aggressive strivings.

The importance of successfully resolving the feminine Oedipal complex was emphasized in a somewhat more positive way by Leonard (1966), who suggested the need for a girl to "establish a desexualized object relationship to her father" in order to be able "later to accept the feminine role without guilt or anxiety and to give love to a young man in her peer group" (p. 332). Adequate fathering is assumed to be an essential requirement for the success of this phase of psychosexual development. Without paternal participation, the girl may idealize her father and later, as an adolescent, seek a love object similar to this ideal or maintain a pre-Oedipal narcissistic attitude. Leonard (1966, p. 332) described such an adolescent as being "unable to give love but rather seeks narcissistic gratification in being loved." Leonard suggested that a father who ignores or rejects his daughter may contribute to her remaining at a phallic, masculine-identified phase of development because in this way the daughter hopes to receive the love of both parents: the mother's love because the daughter is like the father, whom the mother loves, and the father's love because the daughter has become the boy he once was or the son he wished for.

Some psychoanalytic theorists have emphasized that sex-role development begins before the Oedipal period and have pointed to the emergence of the girl's feminine behavior patterns by the time she is two or three years old (Horney, 1933; Machtlinger, 1981). In fact, Kleeman (1971a, 1971b) and Green (1974) emphasized that the dynamics of the father-daughter relationship can stimulate or disrupt the girl's feminine development even during her first year of life. Much relevant psychoanalytically oriented research is presented in the important book edited by Cath, Gurwitt, and Ross (1982).

Such learning theorists as Mowrer (1950) and Sears (1957) focused on the importance of parental nurturance in rewarding the child's sex-appropriate behaviors. They hypothesized that the child becomes strongly dependent on the parents for supplying nurturance and learns to perform those behaviors that the parents reward. Learning theorists do not generally attach special significance to the father-daughter relationship. To the extent that the father has the ability to reward particular behaviors, however, it can be argued that he is a significant influence on his daughter's personality development. Paternal reinforcement of the girl's attempts to emulate her mother's behavior, and the father's general approval of the mother's behavior, seem particularly important (Biller, 1971a,b; 1981a).

From his sociological perspective, Parsons (1955) emphasized the role of the father in feminine as well as masculine development. He viewed the mother as very influential in the child's general personality development, but not as significant as the father in a child's sex-role differentiation. The mother does not vary her role as a function of the sex of the child as much as the father does. The father is seen as the principal transmitter of culturally based conceptions of masculinity and femininity. Johnson (1963) emphasized that the mother has a primarily expressive relationship with both boys and girls, whereas the father rewards his male and female children differently, encouraging instrumental behavior in his son and expressive behavior in his daughter. For example, the father's flirtatious and pampering behavior is expected to elicit affection and docility in his daughter.

Sex-Role Definitions

There has been a marked tendency to define femininity in negative terms and/or as the opposite of masculinity, with an emphasis on such traits as passivity and dependency. Traditional femininity has often been found to be negatively associated with adjustment (Bardwick, 1971; Johnson, 1963). But since this discussion is focused on ways in which the father can facilitate his daughter's sex-role competence, it is relevant to analyze elements of femininity that are related to psychological adjustment rather than to maladjustment. It is meaningful to define feminine behavior in positive terms; for example, femininity in social interaction can be related to skill in interpersonal communication, expressiveness, warmth, and sensitivity to the needs of others (Biller, 1971a; Biller & Weiss, 1970).

Femininity, according to the present definition, is based on a positive feeling about being a female and a particular patterning of interpersonal behavior. Whether or not a women enjoys housework or chooses a career should not be the ultimate criterion in assessing her femininity. Women who possess both positive feminine and positive masculine characteristics and have secure sex-role orientations are most able to actualize their potential. Women who have pride in their femininity and are independent and assertive as well as nurturant and sensitive are likely to achieve interpersonal and creative fulfillment (Biller, 1971a, 1971b, 1974c; Biller & Meredith, 1974; Lott, 1981).

The child is not merely a passive recipient of familial and sociocultural influences. As has been emphasized throughout this book, the child's constitutional predispositions can play an important part in influencing parent-child and environmental interactions. For example, the young girl who is temperamentally responsive to social interactions and is very attractive may make it especially easy for her father to encourage her positive feminine development. If a girl facially and physically resembles a highly feminine mother, the father is likely to treat her as a female. On the other hand, the girl who is physically large and unattractive may be perceived as unfeminine by her father. The father may reject his daughter if she does not fit his conception of the physical characteristics of femininity. If the father has no son and his daughter is particularly vigorous and well-coordinated, he may tend to treat her as if she were a boy (Biller, 1971a, 1974c, 1981b).

Paternal Differentiation

The daughter can suffer greatly in her feminine development if her father does not participate in the family and neglects her. The girl's feminine development is much influenced by how the father differentiates his masculine role from her feminine role. Mussen and Rutherford (1963) found that fathers of highly feminine girls encouraged their daughters more in sex-typed activities than did fathers of unfeminine girls. Masculine fathers who actively encourage and appreciate femininity in girls are particularly able to facilitate their daughter's sex-role development. In their study with nursery-school children, Sears, Rau, and Alpert (1965) reported a significant correlation between girls' femininity and their fathers' expectations of their participation in feminine activities.

In an examination of the familial antecedents of sex-role behavior, Heilbrun (1965b) concluded that fathers are more proficient than mothers in differentiating between their male and female children. He emphasized that "fathers are more capable of responding expressively than mothers are of acting instrumentally . . . that fathers systematically vary their sex role as they relate to male and female offspring" (p. 796). Heilbrun found that daughters who perceive themselves as feminine, as well as sons who perceive themselves as masculine, are likely to view their fathers as masculine.

Goodenough's (1957) results support the view that fathers are more concerned with their children's sex-role development than are mothers. Focusing on the impact of the parents in determining the social preferences of nursery-school children, she learned that "the father has a greater interest in sex differences than the mother and hence exerts stronger influence in general sex-typing" (p. 321); for example, there was much more paternal encouragement for girls, as compared to boys, to develop skills in social interactions. Strong paternal emphasis on sex-role differentiation was also noted in a study by Aberle and Naegele (1952). Differences in parent-child interactions are a function of the sex of the child as well as of the sex of the parent (e.g., Bronfenbrenner, 1961; Rothbart & Maccoby, 1966).

Tasch (1955) interviewed fathers of boys and girls in order to learn about their conceptions of the paternal role. Like other researchers, she found much evidence of paternal differentiation in terms of the child's sex. Her results indicated that fathers viewed their daughters as more delicate than their sons. Fathers were found to use physical punishment more frequently with their sons than with their daughters. Fathers tended to define household tasks in terms of their sex-appropriateness. For example, they expected girls to iron and wash clothes and to babysit for siblings, whereas boys were expected to be responsible for taking out the garbage and helping their fathers in activities involving mechanical and physical competence. Unfortunately, fathers often have rigid sex-role stereotypes and, in their zeal to "feminize" their daughters, actively discourage the development of intellectual and physical competence (Biller, 1974b, 1981b; Biller & Meredith, 1974).

Even with infants, fathers appear to be more influenced by the sex of the child than are mothers (see chapter 6). They tend to play more with infant sons than with infant daughters. Among fathers, gentle cuddling is more frequent with infant daughters, whereas rough-and-tumble activities are more common with sons (Biller, 1974c; Lamb, 1976b). Some data suggest that fathers are more likely to accept a temperamentally difficult male infant but will withdraw from a female infant who presents similar problems (Rendina & Dickerscheid, 1976).

Hetherington, Cox, and Cox's (1978, 1982) data indicate that in intact families fathers play a more important role in the development of femininity in young girls than do mothers. For example, the fathers of extremely feminine four- to six-year-old girls were generally highly masculine in their sex-role preferences, liked women, and reinforced feminine behaviors in their daughters. These fathers were nurturant and actively involved with their daughters but also somewhat restrictive and controlling. In contrast, only maternal warmth was related to the girls' femininity, and other maternal variables appeared to have no direct impact on the sex-typing of daughters. Girls who displayed a positive androgyny in their sex-typed behavior seemed to be influenced by the behavior of both parents: their fathers were warm, had positive views toward females, and consistently encouraged independence and achievement; their mothers were likely to be working and also to encourage independence. Parental encouragement of independence and achievement and a lack of rigid restrictiveness does seem especially important if young girls are to develop competence in intellectual endeavors (Biller, 1974c, 1982a; Biller & Meredith, 1974).

Cognitive Competence

Current evidence supports the view that paternal deprivation has a more negative effect on the cognitive abilities of boys than it does on girls (Radin, 1981; Shinn, 1978). However, there is also much data indicating that fathers can greatly stimulate or inhibit their daughter's cognitive functioning and intellectual attainment. Plank and Plank (1954) discovered that outstanding female mathematicians were particularly attached to and identified with their fathers. Bieri (1960) also reported that high analytical ability in college women was associated with father identification. Crandall, Dewey, Katkovsky, and Preston (1964) found that elementary-school girls who did well in both reading and mathematics had fathers who consistently praised and rewarded their intellectual efforts. High paternal expectations for competence in the context of a moderately warm father-daughter relationship seem conducive to the development of autonomy, independence, achievement, and creativity among females (e.g., Crandall et al., 1964; Honzik, 1967; Lynn, 1979; Nakamura & Rogers, 1969; Radin, 1981).

On the other hand, paternal maltreatment and abuse can inhibit the daughter's intellectual development. Paternal rejection seems related to deficits in female performance in certain types of cognitive tasks (Heilbrun, Harrell, & Gillard, 1967). Findings from a study by Hurley (1967) suggested that paternal hostility can be particularly detrimental to a girl's scholastic functioning.

Other less extreme types of paternal behavior often interfere with the cognitive development of females. The highly nurturant father who reinforces the feminine stereotype of passivity, timidity, and dependency can also greatly inhibit his daughter's intellectual potential (Biller, 1974c).

In her insightful review, Radin (1981) articulated the highly complex interrelationships between paternal factors and female intellectual functioning. Overall, it is clear that fathers can greatly influence their daughter's cognitive development; but, as Radin emphasized, the findings are generally less straightforward than those reported for fathers and sons. A major reason for this appears to be that traditional fathers often communicate ambivalent and mixed messages about their expectations to their daughters; in some ways they may encourage competence, but in others they may appear uncomfortable about their daughters doing too well in intellectual tasks (or in those areas that they consider relatively masculine endeavors).

Radin (1981) cited some of her findings suggesting that daughters' cognitive functioning is likely to be enriched by fathers who are highly committed to basic child rearing and who have flexible views regarding sex roles for themselves and their children. Interest, involvement, and encouragement by such fathers may do much to stimulate intellectual competence among daughters, whereas the traditional father may be most nurturant when his daughter is conforming to his rigid sex-role expectations. In fact, Radin reviewed some data suggesting that girls with traditional fathers do better in their intellectual functioning when there is some distance in their relationship.

Radin (1981) commented on some of her data indicating that too much nurturance in the father-daughter relationship may inhibit intellectual development: fathers who are overly affectionate and solicitous with their daughters may be especially likely to foster dependence rather than competence. Having an accessible and interested father, but one who allows autonomy and the space to develop mastery, appears quite important in the daughter's as well as the son's intellectual development. Fathers who are too intrusive in solving problems for their children seem to inhibit the growth of self-sufficiency (Biller, 1971a, 1974c; Biller & Meredith, 1974).

Personal and Social Adjustment

An investigation by Fish and Biller (1973) suggested that the father plays a particularly important role in the girl's personality adjustment. College females' perceptions of their relationships with their fathers during childhood were assessed by means of an extensive family background questionnaire. Subjects who perceived their fathers as having been very nurturant and positively interested in them scored high on the Adjective Checklist personal adjustment scale. In contrast, subjects who perceived their fathers as having been rejecting scored very low on personal adjustment. Findings from other investigations have also pointed to the influence of positive paternal involvement on the girl's interpersonal competence (e.g., Baumrind & Black, 1967; Torgoff & Dreyer, 1961).

Block's (1971) analysis of data collected from the Berkely Longitudinal Study highlighted the importance of both the father-daughter and father-mother relationships in the quality of the female's personality functioning. Females who were best adjusted as adults grew up in homes with two positively involved parents. Their mothers were described as affectionate, personable, and resourceful and their fathers as warm, competent, and firm. A second group of relatively well-adjusted females came from homes with extremely bright, capable, and ambitious mothers but rather passive yet warm fathers. In contrast, poorly adjusted females were likely to have been reared in homes where either one or both parents were very inadequate. Even though they represented a wide range of personality adaptations, the poorly adjusted women were likely to come from homes where there was little opportunity to view a positive father-mother relationship.

Block, von der Lippe, and Block's (1973) study also helps to convey some of the complexity of the associations between parental behavior and later personality functioning. As mentioned when their results concerning male personality development were discussed in chapter 7, these investigators studied groups of subjects who differed in terms of their femininity and socialization scores on the California Psychological Inventory.

Highly feminine, highly socialized women were described as fitting comfortably into the culturally expected role for females. They were described as conservative, conventional, dependable, and docile. This picture was not completely tranquil, however, since interviewers frequently perceived vulnerability, indecision, and personal dissatisfaction among this group. They came from a family-centered environment and had particularly close, warm, and sharing relationships with their mothers. Their mothers seemed to also typify a positive adjustment to the stereotypic feminine role. Interestingly, no distinctive picture of the father emerged for this group. (We would speculate that a relatively passive father who reinforced stereotyped feminine behavior could easily contribute to such overly conforming behavior.)

The high-feminine, low-socialized females in many ways resembled the high-masculine, low-socialized males. They seemed quite narcissistic and hedonistic. These women appeared to have very inadequate and rejecting mothers and, like them, had unstable marriages. Their relationships with their fathers seemed stronger but appeared to have been overly seductive and may have prematurely stimulated these females into early sexual experiences. (The investigators noted that members of this group were particularly attractive. We would emphasize that their appearance may have had a strong impact on their parents. For example, a very attractive daughter may exacerbate an insecure mother's anxiety about herself while increasing the probability of seductive behavior on the father's part.)

The low-feminine, high-socialized women conveyed a relaxed, poised, and outgoing appearance and generally seemed to be the most well adjusted group. They were viewed as conservative and not at all introspective. Their family backgrounds seemed stable, affectionate, and comfortable. Their fathers were warm and accepting and their mothers oriented toward rationality, achievement, and intellectual attainment.

The low-feminine, low-socialized women appeared to be assertive, critical, and rebellious. (As with the high-feminine, low-socialized group, they seemed to be unhappy with life but expressed their displeasure in a very different manner.) They were aggressively insistent on their autonomy and independence and communicated decisiveness and competence. These women came from conflict-ridden and inadequate backgrounds. Their mothers appeared to be neurotic, vulnerable, unhappy, and generally interpersonally incompetent. Their fathers were hard-driving and status-oriented. The fathers were uninvolved with their families and tended to reject their daughters.

The most well adjusted females in the longitudinal study by Block, von der Lippe, and Block (1973) tended to come from families in which both parents had been positively involved with them. Their fathers were described as warm and accepting, and their mothers appeared to be excellent role models with respect to intellectual competence. A variety of complex family patterns emerged among the less well adjusted females, but it was clear that few if any had family backgrounds marked by a combination of a compatible father-mother relationship and a positively involved father.

A retrospective study by Huckel (1984) generally revealed findings very consistent with the longitudinal data provided by Block (1971) and Block, von der Lippe, and Block (1973), underscoring the contribution of the father-mother team in the personality development of the child. Huckel's provocative findings were based on an ambitious self-report study with a nonclinical university population consisting primarily of upper-middle-class young adult females. The subjects were volunteers and were administered a broad range of assessment devices, which included a variety of questions on family background and measures of current psychological functioning. Although very complex and variegated relationships were revealed, in general, the data indicated that maltreatment by parents during childhood was associated with vulnerability to psychological and interpersonal difficulties in early adulthood. Individuals who reported being exposed to a pattern of childhood neglect, rejection, and aggressive-punitive power assertion by parents were likely to manifest personal insecurity, poor self-concept, and emotional instability. A style of interpersonal avoidance and emotional unresponsiveness was particularly characteristic of those individuals who reported multiple forms of maltreatment by parents. On the other hand, those whose parents were nurturant and accepting, expressing low levels of verbal and physical aggression toward them, scored high on measures of self-assurance, emotional stability, and interpersonal competence.

The manner in which Huckel (1984) presented her data suggests that both fathers and mothers are significant contributors to the relative adequacy of parenting that the child experiences, and that both parents are usually responsible when there is child maltreatment. She reported strong correlations between such variables as perceived paternal and maternal acceptance, and perceived paternal and maternal nurturance. Furthermore, the degree to which paternal and maternal factors are related to various parental maltreatment and child personality variables was generally quite similar. Of course, the self-report format may have contributed to the strength of such relationships.

Huckel (1984) had the students respond to separate items relating to their mothers and fathers, but in her description of data analyses, parents were generally treated as a unit and she made no distinction between children from one- and two-parent families. Nevertheless, some of her results suggested that paternal verbal aggression was more likely to lead to difficulties for children than was maternal verbal aggression. Because fathers tend to spend much less time with their children than do mothers, they may have relatively little opportunity to compensate for their abusive tendencies. Given the same amount of verbal abuse, a mother is still apt to be perceived in a somewhat more favorable light because she typically has a broader range of contact with the child.

Huckel emphasized the similarity between her findings of poor personal and social adjustment among previously maltreated college students and descriptions of children who have suffered severe emotional neglect (Polansky et al., 1981). Symptoms of emotional inaccessibility and emotional detachment seem quite evident in both groups.

The most psychologically handicapped individuals in Huckel's study were those who were maltreated in a multifaceted manner, including emotional neglect, rejection, *and* physical maltreatment. (Among women, incest and father-to-mother violence also tended to be associated with a pervasive pattern of maltreatment.) Individuals who suffered from general maltreatment were likely to show an interpersonal style of emotional detachment and/or hostile aggressiveness. Although having problems, individuals who were either emotionally maltreated (rejection, neglect) *or* physically maltreated did not appear as vulnerable to psychological difficulties as did those who received both types of parental abuse.

Individuals who were the recipients of parental abuse but also received a moderate amount of parental affection expressed much ambivalence toward other people, some apparently alternating dependent and hostile response patterns. However, these individuals did not appear as vulnerable to psychological difficulties as did those who both received little physical affection and were physically abused.

Individuals who were emotionally maltreated, but not physically maltreated, tended to have a depressive, passive-dependent interpersonal style. Those who were physically maltreated but not emotionally maltreated tended to have suspicious, dominant, and/or dependent interpersonal styles and lack of empathy toward children. In contrast to those who were more globally maltreated, those who were either emotionally *or* physically maltreated attempted to involve themselves with others, even though they seemed to experience considerable interpersonal difficulty and frustration (especially when compared to other individuals who reported a generally positive parenting history). In any case, given their personal and interpersonal limitations, it is clear that individuals who have been maltreated are at risk themselves of becoming very inadequate parents.

There were other findings from Huckel's research which also support the importance of a multidimensional view of child maltreatment. Neglect and rejection seemed to have particularly negative consequences in undermining self-confidence in interpersonal relationships, especially for females. Individuals who experienced neglect and rejection were generally nonassertive, dependent, depressive, and anxious about the potential loss of interpersonal support. This pattern of adaptation bears some similarity to the passive-dependent feminine personality style found for many individuals who have experienced the death of a parent in early childhood (Berlinsky & Biller, 1982; see chapter 10).

Marital and Sexual Relationships

Many women choose to pursue a full-time career rather than marriage because of realistic factors such as self-fulfillment and economic need. Sometimes, however, the choice of a career is motivated by a fearful avoidance of family intimacy and marriage. Unmarried career women often have much underlying sex-role conflict (Levin, 1966). In Rushing's (1964) study with adolescents, girls who reported satisfactory relationships with their fathers were less likely to give priority to a career than were those who had unsatisfactory relationships with their fathers.

A girl who is continually frustrated in her interactions with her father may develop a negative attitude toward marriage and close relationships with men. White (1959) compared the self-concepts and familial backgrounds of women whose interests focused on marriage and child rearing with those whose interests revolved around a career. More of the women interested in careers came from homes in which the father had died or in which there was inadequate parent-child communication. Of course, one problem with such studies is that they do not include a group of women interested both in careers and in marriage and child rearing. Women who can comfortably pursue their occupational interests and develop their intellectual competence while also being successful wives and mothers are more likely to have come from homes in which both parents were positively involved.

Lozoff's (1974) findings from a study with upper-middle-class individuals strongly suggest that father-daughter relationships are crucial in the development of women who are able to be successful in both their heterosexual relationships and their creative and professional endeavors. Such women had brilliant fathers who were personally secure, vital, and achievement-oriented. The fathers treated their children with respect. They valued their daughters' basic femininity but at the same time encouraged and expected them to develop their competencies without any infringement of sex-role stereotypes. There was great compatibility between their fathers and mothers and the women developed positive identifications with both parents, and comfortable and feminine sex-role orientations. Women who have achieved a high level of success in various intellectual and occupational endeavors are very likely to have had a strong relationship with a father who accepted their femininity but expected them to be persistent and competent (Biller, 1974c).

A second group of women that Lozoff (1974) described also were very autonomous but were involved in much personal conflict. Their fathers tended to be aloof, perfectionistic, and self-disciplined. They had very high expectations for their daughters but did not provide enough emotional support for them to develop a solid self-confidence. A third group of women who were very low in autonomy came from economically privileged but highly sex-typed family situations. The father in such a family seemed to offer his daughter little encouragement for intellectual competence, leaving her socialization mainly up to his wife.

Findings from the Block, von der Lippe, and Block study (1973) suggested how difficult it is for a female to get the necessary family support to develop into a well-rounded, secure, and competent adult. It is striking how few fathers tended to be adequately involved with their daughters and to encourage both a strong feminine self-concept and instrumental competence. Again, many of these problems seem associated with an overly rigid sex typing and negative definition of feminine behavior. Gradually increasing flexibility in sex roles should lead to more and more women having a positive feminine self-concept as well as a wide range of competencies and fulfilling careers (Biller & Meredith, 1974).

Other data reveal the lasting consequences that the father-daughter relationship can have on the women's marital adjustment. In Winch's (1949, 1950) questionnaire study of college students, females who had long-term romantic attachments reported closer relationships with their fathers than did females who did not have serious heterosexual involvements. Luckey (1960) discovered that women who were satisfied with their marriages perceived their husbands as more similar to their fathers than did women who were not satisfied in their marriages. The female's ability to have a successful marriage is increased when she has experienced a warm, affectionate relationship with a father who has encouraged her positive feminine development. Divorce, separation, and unhappy marriages are much higher among women who grew up in families with an absent or inadequate father (Biller, 1974c, 1981b).

Fisher (1973) presented evidence that paternal deprivation in early childhood is associated with infrequent orgasms among married women. He and his co-workers studied the sexual feelings and fantasies of almost three hundred middle-class married women. The women were well-educated volunteers, most of them married to graduate students and in their early and middle twenties. An extensive array of assessment procedures, including interviews, questionnaires, and projective techniques, was used. The representativeness of Fisher's sample could be questioned, but his results do seem very consistent with other data about the father's general impact on the female's sexual development.

A central theme emerging from the low-orgasmic women was their poor relationships with their fathers. There was a high incidence of early loss and of frequent separation from the father during childhood among the low-orgasmic group. These women were more preoccupied with fear of not having control than high-orgasmic women were, and this was associated with their lack of security and lack of trust in their fathers during childhood. They more often saw themselves as lacking dependable relationships with their fathers.

Questionnaire data revealed that the lower a woman's orgasmic capacity, the more likely she was to report that her father treated her in a laissez-faire manner. Low-orgasmic women decribed uninvolved fathers who did not have well-defined expectations or rules for their daughters. They also recalled much physical and psychological father-absence during early childhood. In contrast, high-orgasmic women were more likely to perceive their fathers as having had definite and demanding expectations and a concern for their enforcement. Fisher (1973) continually emphasized that his findings revealed that the father is much more important in the development of orgasmic adequacy in females than is the mother.

There has been a great increase of evidence in the last decade that links father—and stepfather—sexual abuse and incest with interpersonal problems and severe maladjustment in females (e.g., Forward & Buck, 1978; Kempe & Kempe, 1984). In addition to direct genital maltreatment, however, fathers as well as mothers who have serious sexual conflicts can convey, verbally and nonverbally, a damaging attitude toward the body. For example, many parents who would never commit incest nevertheless maltreat their children sexually in the sense that they express negative gestures, facial grimaces, and unkind verbalizations when they view their children naked or when the child touches herself in genital areas (see also chapter 5).

Homosexuality

Inappropriate and/or inadequate fathering seems to be a major factor in the development of homosexuality in females as well as in males. Bené (1965) reported that female homosexuals felt their fathers were weak and incompetent. The homosexual women were more hostile toward and afraid of their fathers than the heterosexual women were. Kaye et al., (1967), analyzing background data on homosexual women in psychoanalysis, discovered that the fathers of the homosexual women (as compared to the fathers of the women in the heterosexual control group) tended to be puritanical, exploitative, and feared by their daughters, as well as possessive and infantilizing. They also presented evidence that female homosexuality is associated with rejection of femininity early in life. In another study, lesbians described their fathers as less involved and affectionate than heterosexual women did (Gundlach & Reiss, 1968). In general the lesbians portrayed their fathers as acting like strangers toward them. Other researchers have also found that females who feel devalued and rejected by their fathers are more likely to become homosexual than are females whose fathers are warm and accepting (e.g., Hamilton, 1929; West, 1967).

College-age, well-educated female homosexuals were recruited by their friends in a study by Thompson et al. (1973). Compared to a control group of female heterosexuals, the female homosexuals indicated that they were less accepting of their fathers and their femininity during early childhood. There was also some evidence that they perceived their fathers as more detached, weak, and hostile toward them. In general, available research has suggested that inadequate fathering is more of a factor in the development of female homosexuality than is inadequate mothering. Note also the general similarity in negative father-child relations among female and male homosexuals (see chapter 7).

Inadequate fathering makes the child more vulnerable to difficulties in sex-role and sexual development, but again it is only one of many factors that determines the quality of the individual's adjustment. Other facets of family functioning, and the child's constitutional and sociocultural background, must be considered if there is to be a better understanding of the influence of the father-child relationship on the sex-role development process.

Some preliminary data presented by Green (1978) do not support the notion that homosexual and/or transsexual parents are likely to have children who develop similar sexual adaptations. For instance, a child who has a homosexual parent does not seem especially likely to become a homosexual; however, longitudinal data may indicate that children with homosexual parents are more at risk than children with heterosexual parents to develop other serious difficulties in sex-role and sexual functioning. In any case, it is certainly relevant to note that most homosexuals have heterosexual parents and that, moreover, the sexual inclination and sexual functioning of the parents in itself does not appear to be as important in the child's sex-role development as the quality of parent-parent and parent-child relationships does.

Family Pathology

Inadequate fathering or mothering is frequently a reflection of difficulties in the husband-wife relationship. Such difficulties may be particularly apparent in the husband's and wife's inability to provide one another adequately with affection and sexual satisfaction. The parents' interpersonal problems are usually reflected in their interactions with their children and in their children's adjustment. For example, clinical studies have revealed that difficulties in parental sexual adjustment, combined with overly restrictive parental attitudes, are often associated with incestuous and acting-out behavior among adolescent females (Kaufman, 1982). Mothers who dominate fathers and are cold and controlling are especially likely to undermine their daughters' interpersonal competence (Biller, 1969c; Biller & Zung, 1972; Hoffman, 1961).

Paternal inadequacy can clearly be a factor in the development of severe psychopathology in the female child as well as in the male child. Unfortunately, many of the studies examining the influence of paternal deprivation on childhood psychopathology did not include female children or did not take the sex of the child into account in the data analyses. There is, however, some research that focuses on—or specifically includes—females.

In their extensive studies, Lidz, Parker, and Cornelison (1956) reported a high incidence of inadequate fathering for female as well as male schizophrenics. The fathers of the schzophrenic females were frequently observed to be in severe conflict with their wives' decisions, and to degrade their wives in front of their daughters. These fathers made rigid and unrealistic demands on their wives. Similarly, such fathers were insensitive to their daughter's needs to develop an independent self-concept. The fathers of the schizophrenic females made attempts to manipulate and mold their daughters in terms of their own unrealistic needs. Females who formed an allegiance to a disturbed father, frequently in reaction to rejection by an unloving mother, seemed most likely to become psychotic.

Hamilton and Wahl (1948) found that almost 75 percent of the hospitalized schizophrenic women they studied had experienced some inadequacy of fathering in childhood. Prolonged father-absence, paternal rejection, and paternal abuse of daughters were very common. Baker and Holzworth (1961) compared a group of male and female adolescents who were hospitalized because of psychological disturbances with a control group who were successful in their interpersonal and school adjustments. The fathers of the hospitalized group were more likely to have had social histories involving court convictions and excessive drinking than were the fathers of the successful adolescents. The implication that such fathers physically and psychologically abused their daughters seems clear.

It is important, however, to emphasize that variations in sociocultural background may be a primary factor contributing to such findings. For example, both criminal convictions and commitment to state hospitals are more frequent for lower-class individuals than for middle-class individuals. The general economic and social deprivation that lower-class children experience seems to exacerbate the effects of inadequate fathering (Biller, 1971a, 1974c).

Severe psychopathology also is often related to the child's constitutional predispositions and usually does not develop simply as a function of disturbed parent-child relationships. For example, the girl who is temperamentally unresponsive to affection may negatively reinforce her father's attempts to form a relationship with her. Similarly, if she is extremely hyperactive and aggressive, it may be very difficult for her father to relate to her (Biller, 1971a, 1974c).

Incest

An extremely devastating form of maltreatment by the father is sexual abuse and incest. In a certain way, the daughter may suffer from father-loss as a result of incest far more than she does if her father is absent because of death or divorce. The manipulation and the loss of protection and trust may be far more incapacitating for the daughter than any physical violation in itself. When the father-daughter relationship is sexualized in inappropriate ways, the girl loses boundaries necessary in developing a healthy sexual identity, and her capacity to trust men is greatly damaged. Incest with the father puts a daughter at risk for severe depression, suicidal behavior, and alcohol and other drug problems, as well as for conflicts centered around sexual relationships such as promiscuity and prostitution. The particular impact of sexual maltreatment on the daughter seems very much a function of how close she was to the abuser, how old she was, how much she perceives herself as responsible, and how much understanding and support she receives from other family members—especially her mother (Forward & Buck, 1978; Kempe & Kempe, 1984; Meiselman, 1978).

Long-term negative consequences for female development of father-daughter incest have often been suggested in the literature. Rosenfeld (1979a) found that one-third of the adult female psychiatric inpatients in his sample had a history of father-daughter incest. A myriad of problem behaviors in daughters have been associated with paternal sexual abuse. In terms of the perpetuation of child maltreatment, a particularly devastating outcome appears to relate to the tendency of women who have been incest victims themselves to marry (or live with) men who in turn sexually abuse their children (Cooper & Cormier, 1982; Finkelhor & Browne, 1985; Forward & Buck, 1978; Meiselman, 1978).

In a self-report/questionnaire study, Huckel (1984) found that females who were physically abused by their fathers and witnessed much father-to-mother physical violence, also were likely to have been sexually abused, particularly by other male family members. Paternal physical abuse even when it is not associated with incest seems to put the female at particular risk for maltreatment, including sexual abuse by other males.

Many of the behavior patterns of incest victims can be viewed as masochistic and self-abusive: women who have had sexual relationships with their fathers are particularly prone to have depressive tendencies, low self-esteem, and a proclivity to be vulnerable to harsh manipulation by men. Drug addiction, sexual acting out, prostitution, and generally inadequate interpersonal relations have frequently been linked with a history of father-daughter incest (Benward & Densen-Gerber, 1975; deYoung, 1982; Forward & Buck, 1978; Herman, 1981; James & Meyerding, 1977; Kaufman, Peck, & Tagiuri, 1954; Meiselman, 1978).

As discussed in chapter 5, there is no distinct personality profile for the father who engages in an incestuous relationship with his daughter. Such fathers, however, often have alcohol and/or other drug problems and difficulties in impulse control. In addition to their sexual abuse of at least one of their children, their overall interactions within the family clearly indicate the presence of other forms of child maltreatment; they may be emotionally abusive, ineffectual, and neglectful. In such families the mother is also usually described as neglectful and distant with respect to the daughter; she herself may have been a victim of incest as a child. There is much evidence that the mother's behavior is a contributing factor to the incestuous relationship, which in many families is the bond that holds the family together while victimizing the daughter (Anderson & Shafer, 1979; Cohen, 1983; Finkelhor, 1979; Forward & Buck, 1978; Rosenfeld, 1979b).

Supportive Parenting

Fathers, more than mothers, vary their behavior as a function of the sex of the child, and fathers appear to play an especially significant role in encouraging their daughters' feminine development. The father's acceptance and reinforcement of his daughter's positive femininity greatly facilitates the development of her self-concept, but a negative or overly rigid view of femininity can hamper her social and sexual development (Biller, 1974c; Biller & Meredith, 1974).

Interaction with a masculine and competent father provides a girl with basic experiences that she can generalize to her relationships with other males. Girls who have positive relationships with their fathers are more likely to be able to obtain satisfaction in their heterosexual experiences and to achieve happiness in social and sexual commitments as well as in occupational and career endeavors.

Other facets of family functioning, however, in addition to the child's temperament and sociocultural background, must also be considered if a thorough understanding of the influence of the father-child relationship is to be achieved. The father-mother relationship has great impact on the child's personality development. Chronic marital conflict and inappropriate husband-wife interaction can greatly distort the child's view of heterosexual interactions. The girl may learn very unsatisfactory patterns of interacting with males or may wish to avoid close relationships with males. On the other hand, if the father and mother mutually satisfy and value each other, the child is much better able to learn effective interpersonal skills.

In the optimal situation, the child has both an involved mother and an involved father and is thus exposed to a wider degree of adaptive characteristics. Children who are both well mothered and well fathered are likely to have positive self-concepts and feel comfortable with their biological sexuality. They are content with their gender and have security in their basic sex-role orientation. They are comfortable with themselves and their sexuality, but yet are able to be relatively flexible in their interests and responsivity to others. Security in sex-role orientation gives the child more opportunity for self-actualization. On the other hand, children who are paternally deprived are more likely either to take a defensive posture of rigid adherence to cultural sex-role standards or to attempt to avoid expected gender-related behaviors.

Perhaps the most crucial factor for the child in the intact home is the overall impact of the father-mother model of interaction. The quality of communication, respect, and cooperation between father and mother has a strong effect on the child's developing conceptions of male-female relationships and the overall quality of his or her sex-role functioning. To understand parent-child influences, we must consider the relative qualities of the parents vis-à-vis one another; we have to grapple with the gestalt of father-mother functioning as it appears to the child. Studying father-child and mother-child relationships in a vacuum may give us only a restricted and distorted view of the influence of different parenting styles.

9
Developmental Implications in One-Parent Families: Sex-Role Functioning

One-parent families present a special risk for child maltreatment. The everyday pressures and stress on the single parent increase the probability of child maltreatment (and also parent maltreatment by the child). Without the emotional support and sharing of responsibility with a partner, the single parent is at greater risk, if not to practice blatant physical child abuse, then at least to develop an inappropriate relationship with the child whether in the form of neglect or emotional overinvestment in the child. Almost 90 percent of one-parent families are mother-led families, and the father's lack of commitment can place a particularly heavy burden on the mother, who is unlikely to get other male support for child rearing from her social system (Biller, 1971a, 1971c, 1981a).

In the case of divorced parents where the mother has custody, the degree and quality of the father's involvement with the child is a key factor in decreasing the probability of child maltreatment. When the father is unavailable and uncommitted, the child will suffer from maltreatment at least in the sense of paternal neglect unless there is an adequate male surrogate figure. The child whose father shows no consistent interest in him or her is likely to feel a deep sense of rejection. Most children without an active father do not have an alternative source of adult male support (Biller, 1974a, 1981a).

Much of the current interest in the father's role has been intensified by the growing awareness of the prevalence of fatherless families and the social, economic, and psychological problems that such families often encounter. The fatherless family is a source of increasing concern in many industrialized countries. More than 20 percent of the children in the United States, a total in excess of 15 million, live in fatherless families. Father-absent families are especially common among lower-class black families, surpassing 50 percent in some areas (Biller, 1974c; Moynihan, 1965). Although there are many different contexts in which father-absence occurs, divorce is frequently an associated factor. Because of the currently high divorce rate, it is estimated that 40–50 percent of children born in the 1970s will spend at least a significant portion of their childhoods in a single-parent family. At present only about 10 percent of the children in single-parent homes live with their fathers, although this percentage is increasing (Glick & Norton, 1978; Hetherington, 1979).

Father-absence, or at least decreased father availability, is a typical concomitant of divorce. There has been a great deal of controversy about the consequences of both divorce and father-absence on child development. On one extreme are those who seem to attribute all undesirable effects in fatherless homes simply to father-absence; on the other hand, there are those who believe that adequate financial and emotional support of single mothers will alleviate any of the so-called detrimental effects of father-absence and divorce on children. Research reviewed in this and the next chapter will make it clear that an understanding of the influence of father-absence and divorce on development demands the consideration of many different and complex factors.

Chapters 9 and 10 are an attempt to review a surprisingly vast literature on the alleged effects of father-absence. These chapters are an effort to give the reader an overview of a seemingly disparate and fragmented literature. It is not a completely exhaustive review, but it does highlight the most methodologically sound and/or provocative research endeavors. There are frequent reminders of potentially confounding factors and the need for more systematic research.

The first section of chapter 9 is an initial brief summary of the many methodological issues that need to be addressed in evaluating findings concerning the impact of father-absence and its highly complex interactions with other important developmental variables. The second and third sections contain a summary of studies dealing with father-absence and masculine development. The relevance of developmental stages, different aspects of sex-role development, and surrogate models are also discussed in these sections. The fourth and fifth sections of chapter 9 focus on father-absence and feminine development, with a particular emphasis on social factors and heterosexual functioning.

Father Absence

It is important to emphasize that father-absence in itself does not necessarily lead to developmental deficits and/or render the father-absent child inferior in psychological functioning to the father-present child. Fatherless children are far from a homogeneous group; an almost infinite variety of patterns of father-absence can be specified. Many factors need to be considered in evaluating the father-absent situation: length of separation from the father; type of separation (constant, intermittent, temporary); cause of separation (divorce, death, and so on); the child's age and sex, the child's constitutional characteristics; the mother's reaction to her husband's absence; the quality of mother-child interactions; the family's socioeconomic status; and the availability of surrogate models. The father-absent child may not be paternally deprived because he has a very adequate father-surrogate, or he may be less paternally deprived than are many father-present children.

The child who has an involved and competent mother *and* father is more likely to have generally adequate psychological functioning and is less likely to suffer from developmental deficits and psychopathology, than is the child who is reared in a one-parent family. This generalization, however, does not presume that all father-absent children will have more difficulties in their development than will all father-present children. For example, there is evidence that father-absent children with competent mothers are less likely to have certain types of developmental deficits than are children who have a dominating mother and a passive or ineffectual father. The father-absent child may develop a more flexible image of adult men, and at least may seek out some type of father surrogate, whereas the child with a passive, ineffectual and/or rejecting father may have a very negative image of adult males and avoid interacting with them (Biller, 1971a, 1974c).

In addition to the obvious theoretical and practical relevance of studying the effects of father-absence, a possible methodological justification is that father-absence is a "naturalistic manipulation" (a naturally occurring variation in family structure that can be helpful to researchers). It can be argued that father-absence must be an antecedent rather than a consequence of certain behaviors in children. (Of course, in some instances, a child's handicaps or "abnormalities" may actually be a factor in divorce and the child's subsequent father absence.) A general problem with studies comparing father-absent and father-present children is that investigators have usually treated both father-absent children and father-present children as if they represented homogeneous groups. There has been a lack of concern for the meaning of father-absence and father-presence. For example, there have been few attempts to ensure that a group of consistently father-absent children is compared with a group who have a high level and quality of father availability (Biller, 1971a, 1974c).

Most researchers have treated father-absence too simplistically. Many studies do not specify such variables as type, length, and age of onset of father-absence. Potentially important variables such as the child's sex, IQ, constitutional characteristics, birth order, relationship with his or her mother, and sociocultural background, as well as the availability of father-surrogates, are often not taken into account, either in subject matching or data analysis. When careful matching procedures are followed, more clear-cut findings seem to emerge (e.g., Biller, 1968b, 1971a; Blanchard & Biller, 1971; Hetherington, 1966, 1972; Hetherington, Cox & Cox, 1978, 1982).

Although children living with their mothers subsequent to a divorce may technically be considered father-absent, there is tremendous variability in the amount of contact they have with their fathers (Biller & Meredith, 1974; Keshet & Rosenthal, 1978). In some families children whose parents are divorced may never again see their fathers; in other families, they may have contact with them on a daily basis and may even spend more time with them than they did before the divorce. Many children whose fathers do not live with them spend more time with their fathers than do children in so-called father-present families. Research has clearly supported the advantages for children of a high level of father-child interaction, even when the parents are divorced (Abarbanel, 1979; Biller & Meredith, 1974; Greif, 1979; Hetherington, Cox, & Cox, 1982; Wallerstein & Kelly, 1980a).

It is not surprising that some researchers have reported few, if any, differences between so-called father-absent and father-present children. There is a high proportion (more than 50 percent) of seriously paternally deprived children whose fathers live with them. Unless there is a careful analysis of the degree of adequate fathering that children in two-parent families receive (as well as consideration of the existence of continued fathering and/or father-surrogates for children in one-parent, female-led families), comparisons of father-absent and father-present children can be extremely misleading. On the other hand, comparison of children who have from an early age been consistently deprived of paternal influence with those who have had actively and positively involved fathers clearly reveals that the former are generally less adequate in their functioning and development.

Many of the methodological issues considered in this section have been dealt with in Biller's earlier publications (e.g., Biller, 1970, 1971a, 1974c, 1976a, 1978, 1981a). Some other analyses of methodological issues relating to divorce and father-absence are particularly worthy of the reader's consideration, including Hetherington (1979), Lamb (1979), Pedersen (1976) and Shinn (1978).

Following Berlinsky and Biller's (1982) analysis focusing on research dealing with parental death, we would emphasize that evaluation of studies concerning father-absence should include the following considerations:

1. Was the type of parental loss specified (divorce, death, employment, and so on)?

2. Was a comparison group specified? (Was the quality and quantity of father involvement in the father-present group *specified*?)

3. Were subjects and controls matched on age, sex, and socioeconomics status?

4. Were the comparison groups homogeneous on variables such as age and socioeconomic status, or, if not, were these variables accounted for in the interpretation of results?

5. Were characteristics of the "absent" parent specified (and was there consideration of the dimensions of the continuing relationship between parent and child)?

6. What measurement instruments were used? Have these tools been documented as valid and reliable?

7. Were the data statistically analyzed? If so, were the techniques used appropriate to the data?

8. Were characteristics of family structure and living situations prior to and subsequent to the parent loss detailed?

9. Was information provided regarding the time at which subjects were assessed for research purposes relative to the time of the parent's absence? Was this information considered in the analysis of data?

Masculine Development

Many researchers have speculated that the primary effects of father-absence are manifested in terms of deficits and/or abnormalities in boys' sex-role development. However, differences between the sex-role functioning of young father-absent and father-present boys do not, in themselves, have to be construed in the framework of psychopathology or deviance. Father-absent boys, especially in the preschool years, may be slower in developing certain aspects of sex-role behavior than are father-present boys, but this does not necessarily mean they are severely handicapped. In fact, some data suggest that father-absent boys when compared to those with rigid paternal influence are likely to be more flexible and adaptive in some facets of their interpersonal and intellectual functioning (Biller, 1974c; Parke, 1981; Russell, 1983).

In this section, research findings concerning the relationship between father-absence and the boy's sex-role development are discussed. A comparison of the sex-role development of father-absent and father-present boys suggests some of the ways that paternal deprivation can influence personality development.

Sears and Sears conducted a pioneering investigation of the effects of father-absence on three- to five-year-old children who were given an opportunity to play with a standardized set of doll play equipment. Compared to the father-present boys, the father-absent boys were less aggressive and also had less sex-role differentiation in their doll play activity. For example, their play contained less emphasis on the maleness of the father and boy dolls (Sears, 1951; Sears, Pintler, & Sears, 1946).

Bach (1946) used a similar procedure to study the effects of father-absence on six- to ten-year-old children. As in the Sears study, father-absent boys were less aggressive in doll play than were father-present boys. Bach observed that "the father-separated children produced an idealistic and feminine fantasy picture of the father when compared to the control children who elaborated the father's aggressive tendencies" (p. 79).

In Santrock's (1970a) study of four- and five-year-old disadvantaged black children, father-absent boys exhibited less masculine and more dependent behavior in standardized doll play situations than did father-present boys, although the two groups of boys did not differ in amount of aggressive behavior. In addition, maternal interviews suggested that the father-absent boys were less aggressive as well as less masculine and more dependent in their interpersonal relations than were the father-present boys.

In a very thorough investigation, Stolz et al. (1954) gathered data concerning four- to eight-year-old children who for approximately the first two years of their lives had been separated from their fathers. Interview results revealed that the previously father-separated boys were generally perceived by their fathers as being "sissies." Careful observation of these boys supported this view. The previously father-separated boys were less assertively aggressive and independent in their peer relations than the boys who had not been separated from their fathers. They were more often observed to be very submissive or to react with immature hostility. The boys who had been father-absent were actually more aggressive in doll play than boys who had not been separated from their fathers. However, the fact that the fathers were present in the home at the time of this study, and that the father-child relationships were stressful, makes it difficult to speculate about what influence father-absence in itself had on the children's personality development (Biller, 1978).

There is additional evidence that the effects of early father-absence on boys persist even after their fathers return. Carlsmith (1964) studied middle-class and upper-middle-class high school males who had experienced early father-absence because of their father's military service during World War II. Father-absence before the age of five was related to the patterning of College Board Aptitude Scores. Compared to the usual male pattern of math scores higher than verbal scores, the pattern of the father-absent subjects was more frequently the same as the female pattern, with verbal score higher than math score. Moreover, "the relative superiority of verbal to math aptitudes increases steadily the longer the father is absent and the younger the child when the father left" (p. 10). Other researchers have also found that early father-absence is related to a feminine patterning of aptitude test scores (e.g., Altus, 1958; Nelsen & Maccoby, 1966),

Identification

Leichty (1960) compared the projective test responses of male college students who were father-absent between the ages of three and five to those of a matched group who had not been father-absent. In terms of responses to the Blacky Pictures, fewer of the father-absent students said "Blacky" would like to pattern himself after his father, more often choosing "Mother" or "Tippy," a sibling. Such a response can be conceived of as a projective indication of underlying sex-role orientation, with the father-absent males being less masculine. However, it is not clear from Leichty's data how many of the father-absent group chose Tippy. This response might also indicate a masculine sex-role orientation if the respondent depicted Tippy as a male sibling.

Paternal occupation can be related to frequent father-absence. In a very extensive investigation, Tiller (1958) and Lynn and Sawrey (1959) studied Norweigian children aged eight to nine and a half whose fathers were sailors absent at least nine months a year. They compared these father-separated children with a matched group of children whose fathers had jobs that did not require them to be separated from their families. The boys' responses to projective tests and interviews with their mothers indicated that separation from their fathers was associated with compensatory masculinity (with the boys at times behaving in an exaggerated masculine manner, at other times behaving in a highly feminine manner). The father-separated boys appeared to be much less secure in their masculinity than did the control group boys. Consistent with the findings of Bach (1946) and Sears (1951), the father-separated boys were less aggressive in doll play than the control group.

Rogers and Long's (1968) data also suggest that boys whose fathers are away for long periods of time have difficulties in their masculine development. These investigators studied children from two communities in the Out islands, Bahamas. In one community, Crossing Rocks, there was a high level of paternal deprivation because men were involved in long fishing trips that took them away for weeks at a time, for a total of at least six months a year. In the other community, Murphy Town, men were primarily wage laborers, sometimes unemployed but generally not away from home for any long period. A preference-for-shapes procedure was administered to six- to fifteen-year-old children. Among the boys, a much lower percentage (25 percent versus 61 percent) of those from the paternally deprived community made masculine responses (chose the angular shape rather than the curved shape). Interestingly, the majority (80 percent) of the adult males in the paternally deprived community who were tested made masculine responses on the preference-for-shapes procedure. Rogers and Long speculated that there was often a shift from a feminine to a masculine sex-role identification as a result of informal initiation rites during the adolescent male's first year of going on fishing trips.

Several investigators have attempted to assess differences between father-absent and father-present boys in terms of their human figure drawings. Phelan (1964) assumed that boys who draw a female when asked to draw a person had failed to make a shift from an initial identification with the mother to an identification with the father. In her study, there was a higher rate of father-absence among elementary-school-age boys who drew a female first than among those who draw a male first. An additional analysis of some of Biller's (1968a) data with kindergarten-age children revealed that father-absent, as compared to father-present, boys were less likely to draw a male first or to differentiate clearly their male and female drawings, particularly if they became father-absent before the age of four.

Burton (1972) asked eight- to fifteen-year-old Caribbean children to draw human figures. His evidence suggested that father-absence during the first two years of life was associated with relatively unmasculine self-concepts for boys. Compared to father-present boys, boys who had been father-absent during their first two years of life (and did not subsequently have a permanent father figure) less often drew a male first and drew males shorter in stature. Also, the father-absent boys generally drew males shorter in stature than they drew females.

No clear-cut correlations between father-absence and figure drawings have been found consistently with older children. By adolescence, the reasons for drawing a particular sex figure first, or in a relatively differentiated manner, became more complex, especially with respect to increased interest in heterosexual activity. A problem with many of the studies involving figure drawings is that there is no presentation of specific information regarding length and age of onset of father-absence (e.g., Donini, 1967; Lawton & Sechrest, 1962).

Sexual Conflict

Difficulty in forming lasting heterosexual relationships often appears to be linked to father-absence during childhood. Andrews and Christensen's (1951) data suggested that college students whose parents had been divorced were likely to have frequent but unstable courtship relationships. Winch (1949, 1950) found that father-absence among college males was negatively related to degree of courtship behavior (defined as closeness to marriage). He also reported that a high level of emotional attachment to the mother was negatively related to the degree of courtship behavior. In their interview study, Hilgard, Neuman, and Fisk (1960) detected that many men whose fathers died when they were children continued to be very dependent on their mothers, if their mothers did not remarry. For example, only one of the ten men whose mothers did not remarry seemed to manifest a fair degree of independence in his marital relationship.

Jacobson and Ryder (1969) did an exploratory interview study with young marrieds who suffered the death of a parent prior to marriage. Death of the husband's father before the son was twelve was associated with a high rate of marital difficulty. Husbands who had been father-absent early in life were described as immature and as lacking interpersonal competence. Participation in "feminine" domestic endeavors and low sexual activity were commonly reported for this group. In general, their marriages were relatively devoid of closeness and imtimacy. In contrast, husbands who had lost their fathers after the age of twelve were more likely to be involved in positive marriage relationships.

Other researchers have reported evidence that individuals who have experienced father-absence because of a broken home in childhood are more likley to have their own marriages end in divorce or separation (Landis, 1965; Rohrer & Edmonson, 1960). In many of these situations there is probably a strong modeling effect; children see parents attempting to solve their marital conflicts by ending a marriage and are more likely to behave in a similar fashion themselves. Research by Pettigrew (1964) with lower-class blacks is consistent with the supposition that father-absent males frequently have difficulty in their heterosexual relationships. Compared to father-present males, father-absent males were "more likely to be single or divorced—another manifestation of their disturbed sexual identification" (p. 420).

Because of frequent paternal deprivation and maternal disparagement of maleness, lower-class black males often suffer in terms of their sex-role orientations, even though they may be quite masculine in other facets of their behavior. Some researchers have found both father availability and sociocultural background to be related to indicators of sex-role orientation (Barclay & Cusumano, 1967; Biller, 1968b). Studying lower-class black and lower-class white boys, Biller (1968b) did not find any clear-cut differences in sex-role preference or sex-role adoption. In terms of projective sex-role orientation responses (ITSC), however, black, father-absent boys were the least masculine; there was no significant difference between white, father-absent and black, father-present boys; and white, father-present boys were the most masculine.

A great deal of the heterosexual difficulty that many paternally deprived, lower-class males experience is associated with their compulsive rejection of anything they perceive as related to femininity. Proving that they are not homosexual and/or effeminate is a major preoccupation of many lower-class males. They frequently engage in a Don Juan pattern of behavior, making one conquest after another, and may not form a stable emotional relationship with a female even during marriage. The fear of again being dominated by a female, as they were in childhood, contributes to their continual need to exhibit their masculinity by new conquests. The perception of child rearing as an exclusively feminine endeavor also interferes with their interaction with their children and helps perpetuate the depressing cycle of paternal deprivation in lower-class families. Although such a pattern of behavior seems particularly prevalent among lower-class black males, it is by no means limited to this group.

Developmental Stages

The quality of the early father-child attachment is an important factor in the child's sex-role and personality development. The degree and quality of the father's involvement, even in the first year of life, has much influence on the child's behavior (Biller, 1974c). Research by Money and his co-workers has also pointed to the first two to three years of life as being of crucial importance in the formation of an individual's sex-role orientation (Money & Ehrhardt, 1972). On the basis of their clinical observations of individuals with physical-sexual incongruencies, these investigators have concluded that self-conceptions relating to sex role appear particularly difficult to change after the second or third year of life. This suggests the possibility of crucial periods in sex-role development, and early father-absence particularly seems to interfere with the development of a secure sex-role orientation.

Father-absence before the age of four or five typically retards masculine development. Hetherington (1966) reported that nine- to twelve-year-old father-absent boys manifested less masculine projective sex-role behavior and were rated by male recreation directors as more dependent on their peers, as less aggressive, and as engaging in fewer physical contact games than were father-present boys. However, there were no consistent differences on the sex-role measures when the father-present boys were compared with boys who had become father-absent after the age of four.

Biller (1969a) found father-absent, five-year-old boys had less masculine sex-role orientations (fantasy game measure) and sex-role preferences (game choice) than did father-present boys. Moreover, the boys who became father-absent before the age of four had significantly less masculine sex-role orientations than did those who became father-absent in their fifth year. In an investigation Biller and Bahm (1971) conducted with junior high school boys, those who became father-absent before the age of five scored less masculine on an adjective checklist measure of masculinity of self-concept than did those who were father-present. Research by Burton (1972) with Caribbean children also indicates the disruptive effect of early father-absence on masculinity of self-concept.

In a study that included a longitudinal format and an impressive array of sex-role measures, Hetherington, Cox, and Cox (1978b; 1982) found relatively clear-cut differences in sex-role functioning between young boys (five and six years old) from intact families and those who were father-absent for two years because of divorce. The father-absent boys had lower masculine sex-role preference scores but higher feminine sex-role preference scores than did the father-present boys. On the Draw-A-Person Test, the father-absent boys more often drew a female first and also demonstrated less differentiation between their drawings of males and females than did the father-present boys. In addition, father-absent boys spent more time playing with females, younger peers, and in activities generally regarded as feminine.

Almost one-half (seventeen out of thirty-eight) of the extremely feminine boys in Green's (1974) investigation experienced at least three consecutive months of father-absence prior to the age of four. The separations were temporary in only three of the cases, and most if not all of the remaining twenty-one feminine boys who were not father-absent appeared to suffer from some other form of paternal deprivation during their first few years of life. However, Green's research reveals that many factors in addition to early paternal deprivation are involved in the development of extremely feminine behavior patterns among boys.

From their cross-cultural perspective, Burton and Whiting (1961) discussed the possible differential impact of father-absence at different stages of the sex-role development process. Burton and Whiting pointed out that many societies have a "discontinuous identification process." The father is virtually excluded from contact with his young children, who are cared for exclusively by women. Supposedly, a discontinuity in identification is produced when the boy is pushed into masculine behavior sometime in preadolescence or adolescence, particularly through his experiences during initiation rites. In contrast to earlier female domination, the boy is suddenly under the direct control of adult males, and feminine behavior is actively discouraged. It is assumed that the boy must learn to repress his earlier feminine identification. Whiting, Kluckhohn, and Anthony (1958) discovered that societies with exclusive mother-son sleeping arrangements and long post partum sex taboos were likely to have elaborate male initiation rites; Burton and Whiting (1961, p. 90) hypothesized "that the initiation rites serve psychologically to brainwash the primary feminine identity and establish firmly the secondary male identity."

In support of their "sex-role identification conflict hypothesis" Burton and Whiting (1961) reported some rather dramatic cross-cultural evidence. In societies in which the infant sleeps and interacts almost exclusively with females during the first few years of his life, a custom called the *couvade* was likely to occur. This custom stipulates that the husband retire to his bed upon the birth of his offspring and act as though he had just gone through childbirth. This custom can be interpreted as symbolic of an underlying feminine identification.

The effects of early father-absence are not restricted to sex-role functioning, and many other personality characteristics can be influenced. A study of lower-class fifth-grade boys by Santrock (1970a) revealed that boys who became father-absent before the age of two were more handicapped in terms of several dimensions of personality development than were boys who became father-absent at a later age. For example, boys who became father-absent before age two were found to be less trusting and less industrious and to have more feelings of inferiority than boys who became father-absent between the ages of three to five. Other evidence is consistent with the supposition that early father-absence is associated with a heightened susceptibility to a variety of psychological problems (Biller 1971a, 1974c). Research by Wallerstein and Kelly (1980a, 1980b) has clearly shown that developmental stage is a crucial factor in determining the type of reaction children have to divorce and separation from the father. Studies relating to the effects of the timing of father-absence on various other dimensions of psychological development are reviewed in chapter 10.

Different Aspects of Sex-Role Development

As the findings relating to developmental stages have suggested, different aspects of sex-role may not be affected in the same way by father-absence. It is common for young father-absent children to seek intensely the attention of older males. Because of deprivation effects, father-absent children often have a strong motivation to imitate and please potential father-figures, which makes them especially susceptible to extrafamilial maltreatment. Father-absent boys may strive to act masculine in some facets of their behavior while continuing to behave in an unmasculine or feminine manner in others. For example, a paternally deprived boy may interact only with females who encourage passivity and dependency in the first four or five years of his life, but later will face much peer and societal pressure to behave in a masculine manner. Demands for masculine behavior may not become apparent to the boy until he reaches school age or even adolescence, but in any case under such conditions his sex-role preference and/or sex-role adoption may differ from his basic sex-role orientation (Biller & Borstelmann, 1967).

Barclay and Cusumano (1967) did not find any differences between father-present and father-absent adolescent males on a measure of sex-role preference (Gough Femininity Scale). However, the father-absent males, as compared to the father-present males, were more field-dependent in terms of Witkin's rod-and-frame test. Barclay and Cusumano conceptualize the field dependence–field independence dimension as reflecting underlying sex-role orientation. In a study with lower-class, six-year-old children, Biller (1968b) found that father-absent boys were significantly less masculine than father-present boys on a measure of projective behavior that was used to assess sex-role orientation, but the two groups were not consistently different in terms of their direct sex-role preferences (the toys and games they said they liked) or teachers' ratings of sex-role adoption. Results from a study with five-year-old boys also suggested that sex-role orientation is more affected by father-absence than are sex-role preference or sex-role adoption (Biller, 1969a). Even though the father-absent boys had significantly less masculine game preferences than the father-present boys, differences between the groups were most clear-cut in terms of responses to the sex-role orientation procedure. No consistent differences were apparent with respect to the sex-role adoption measure.

Although many father-absent males remain quite insecure in their basic sex-role orientations, most are able to learn to act in a relatively masculine manner in their choice of activities and in their day-to-day peer interactions. An examination of data from several other studies suggests the hypothesis that, particularly by adolescence, there is relatively little difference between lower-class father-present and father-absent boys with respect to many facets of sex-role awareness, preference, and adoption (e.g., Barclay & Cusumano, 1967; Greenstein, 1966; Mitchell & Wilson, 1967; McCord, McCord, & Thurber, 1962; Santrock, 1977; Tiller, 1961).

Surrogate Models

Paternal absence or inadequacy does not rule out the possible presence of other male models. A brother, uncle, grandfather, or male boarder may provide the boy with much competent adult male contact. An important role can be played by peers, neighbors, and teachers. Male teachers seem to have much potential for influencing father-absent boys (Biller, 1974a, 1974b, 1974c; Lee & Wolinsky, 1973).

The child may even learn some masculine behaviors by patterning himself after a movie or television star, an athlete, or a fictional hero. Freud and Burlingham (1944) described how a fatherless two-year-old boy developed a fantansy role model. Bob's mother had told him about a nine-year-old boy whom he referred to as "Big Bobby," and thereafter Bob actively used Big Bobby as a masculine model, attempting physical feats that he thought Big Bobby could perform. Bob perceived Big Bobby as physically superior to everyone else.

Some investigators have found that masculinity is related to the general amount of contact boys have with adult males. Nash (1965) studied a group of Scottish orphans who went to live in cottages run by married couples, the husbands thus offering them a masculine model. Though less masculine (on a variety of sex-role measures) than boys who were raised in a typical family setting, they were more masculine than a group of orphans brought up entirely by women.

Stepfathers can have a facilitating effect on the father-absent child's development, particularly if the stepfather-child relationship begins before the age of four or five. Research relating to cognitive functioning has indicated that previously father-absent children who gain a stepfather in early childhood are not usually handicapped in their cognitive functioning, whereas children who remain without a father substitute are likely to suffer in at least some facets of their cognitive functioning, often in areas that are considered masculine-related skills (Lessing, Zagorin, & Nelson; 1970, Santrock, 1972). However, there has been little systematic consideration of the role of the stepfather in the child's personality development. Some investigators have found evidence suggesting that the presence of a stepfather can negatively affect the child's psychological functioning (e.g., Benson, 1968; Langner & Michael, 1963). On the other hand, Anderson (1968) reported evidence that the early presence of a stepfather can lessen the chance of the father-absent boy becoming delinquent.

It is, of course, the quality of the stepfather-child relationship and not the presence of a stepfather in itself that affects the child's personality development. The child's age at the time the mother remarries seems to be a critical variable. The young child who feels paternally deprived may find it much easier to accept a stepfather than the adolescent who may have established a strong sense of independence. The stepfather may react more favorably to an affectionate young child than to an older child who refuses to accept his authority. The quality of the mother-child relationship and the mother's attitude toward the stepfather are also very important factors (Biller & Meredith, 1974).

Siblings

Older brothers can be very important masculine models for children. Paternal deprivation may have a much different effect on a five-year-old boy who is an only child than on a five-year-old boy who has, say, two older brothers who themselves were not paternally deprived in early childhood. Obviously, there are many other variables, including the frequency and quality of interactions among siblings. Unfortunately, most of the sibling studies consider only the presence or absence of a particular type of sibling. This is somewhat analogous to studies that take into account only whether a child is father-present or father-absent (Biller, 1974c).

Interestingly, in two-child, father-absent families there is some evidence that boys with brothers suffer less of a deficit in academic aptitudes than do boys with sisters (Sutton-Smith, Rosenberg, & Landy, 1968). In Santrock's (1970b) study, father-absent boys with only older male siblings scored more masculine (on a maternal interview measure of sex-role behavior) than did father-absent boys with only female siblings. In an extension of Santrock's investigation, Wohlford, Santrock, Berger, and Liberman (1971) found that father-absent children with older brothers were less dependent than those with older sisters in terms of both doll play and maternal interview measures. The presence or absence of older female siblings was not related to the sex-role measures and did not affect the older brothers' influence.

Although the presence of male siblings may mitigate the effects of father-absence, data from one of Biller's (1968a) investigations was consistent with the conclusion that the presence of a father is generally a much more important factor in masculine development than is the presence of an older brother.

Peers

The masculine role models provided by the peer group can be particularly influential for the paternally deprived boy. In a subculture in which instrumental aggression and physical prowess are very important as a means of achieving peer acceptance, many father-absent boys are likely to emulate their masculine peers. Peer models seem especially important in lower-class neighborhoods. Miller (1958) emphasized the centrality of such traits as toughness and independence in the value system of lower-class adolescents. Lower-class boys honor aggressiveness more than middle-class boys do; one of the types of boys they most admire is the aggressive, belligerent youngster who earns their respect because of his toughness and strength (Pope, 1953). The paternally deprived boy is particularly vulnerable to being overly influenced and abused by dominant peers.

The boy who is physically well equipped may find it relatively easy to gain acceptance from his peers. Many paternally deprived boys behave in a generally effective and masculine manner. For example, an additional case study analysis of some of the five-year-old boys in Biller's (1968a, 1969a) studies indicated that father-absent boys who are relatively mesomorphic are less likely to be retarded in their sex-role development than are father-absent boys with unmasculine physiques. A boy's physique has important stimulus value in terms of the expectations and reinforcements it elicits from others; it may, along with correlated constitutional factors, predispose him toward success or failure in particular types of activities. The influence of the child's anatomical, temperamental, and cognitive predispositions on parental and peer behavior must be taken into account (Biller, 1974c).

Feminine Development

Females are less affected during early childhood by father-absence than are males (Hetherington, Cox, & Cox, 1978a, 1982). There is some research that supports the conclusion that by adolescence girls are at least as much influenced in their social and heterosexual development by father-absence as are boys (e.g., Biller & Weiss, 1970; Hetherington, 1972). The extent and direction of the differential impact of father-absence on males and females varies depending on which dimensions of personality are considered.

Father-absence can interfere with the girl's feminine development and her overall heterosexual adjustment. In Seward's (1945) and White's (1959) studies, women who rejected the feminine role of wife and mother were more likely to come from broken homes than were women who accepted these roles. Landy, Rosenberg, and Sutton-Smith's (1969) results suggest that among college females, father-absence during adolescence is sometimes associated with a rejection of feminine interests. Although she studied father-present females, Fish's (1969) data also seem relevant. College females who reported that their fathers spent little time with them during their childhoods had less feminine self-concepts than did those who reported moderate or high father-availability. There is anthropological evidence suggesting that low father availability in early childhood is associated with later sex-role conflicts for girls as well as for boys (Brown, 1963; Stephens, 1962).

In Jacobson and Ryder's (1969) interview study, many women who had been father-absent as young children complained of difficulties in achieving satisfactory sexual relationships with their husbands. Lack of opportunity to observe meaningful male-female relationships in childhood can make it much more difficult for the father-absent female to develop the interpersonal skills necessary for adequate heterosexual adjustment. Case studies of father-absent girls are often filled with details of problems concerning interactions with males, particularly in sexual relationships (e.g., Cath, Gurwitt, & Ross, 1982; Leonard, 1966; Neubauer, 1960).

Other findings, however, suggest that father-absent girls usually are not inhibited in terms of their development of sex-typed interests or perceptions of the incentive value of the feminine role. In Baggett's (1967) research, college women whose fathers had died before they were eight were more traditionally feminine in terms of sex-role preference than were women who had grown up with their fathers in the home and women who had lost their fathers for other reasons before the age of eight. In a study with disadvantaged black children, Santrock (1970b) found a tendency for father-absent girls to be more feminine on a doll play sex-role measure than were father-present girls; a very high level of femininity may be associated with a rigid sex-role development that devalues males and masculine activities. In any case, father-absence seems to have more effect on the girls' ability to function in interpersonal and heterosexual relationships than on her sex-role preference in itself.

The father-absent girl often has difficulty in dealing with her aggressive impulses. In their study of doll play behavior, Sears, Pintler and Sears (1946, p. 240) found "no indication that the girls are more frustrated when the father is present; on the contrary, his absence is associated with greater aggression, especially self-aggression." These investigators speculated that a high degree of aggressive doll play behavior may be a function of the father-absent girl's conflict with her mother. In a clinical study, Heckel (1963) observed frequent school maladjustment, excessive sexual interest, and social acting-out behavior in five fatherless preadolescent girls. Other investigators have also found a high incidence of delinquent behavior among lower-class father-absent girls (Monahan, 1957; Toby, 1957). Such acting-out behavior may be a manifestation of frustration associated with the girl's unsuccessful attempts to find a meaningful relationship with an adult male. Father-absence generally increases the probability that a girl will experience difficulties in interpersonal adjustment.

The devaluation of maleness and masculinity so prevalent in paternally deprived, matrifocal families adversely affects many girls as well as boys. Children in lower-class families often lack opportunities to interact with adequate adult males. Even in two-parent lower-class families, father-daughter relationships are frequently not very adequate. The father may be very punitive, physically abusive, and unaffectionate toward his daughter (Elder & Bowerman, 1963). Many investigators have observed that lower-class black girls in families in which the father is absent or ineffectual quickly develop derogatory attitudes toward males (e.g., Pettigrew, 1964; Rohrer & Edmonson, 1960).

The downgrading of males in terms of their apparent social and economic irresponsibility is common in many lower-class families. Negative attitudes toward males are transmitted by mothers, grandmothers, and other significant females, and unfortuantely are often strengthened by the child's observation or involvement in destructive male-female relationships. Paternal deprivation, in the rubric of the devaluation of the male role, is a major factor in the lower-class females' frequent difficulties in interacting with their male relatives, boyfriends, husbands, and children. Maternally based households seem to be like family heirlooms—passed from generation to generation (Rohrer & Edmonson, 1960).

Male-Female Interactions

The most comprehensive and well-controlled study concerning father-absence and the girl's development was conducted by Hetherington (1972). Her subjects were white, adolescent, lower-middle-class girls (ages thirteen to seventeen) who regularly attended a community recreation center. Hetherington was particularly interested in the possible differential effects of father-absence due to divorce or death of the father. She compared three groups of girls: girls whose fathers were absent because of divorce and who had no contact with their fathers since the divorce, girls whose fathers were absent because of death, and girls with both parents living at home. She was careful to control for sibling variables (all the girls were firstborns without brothers), and none of the father-absent children had any adult males living in their homes following separation from the father.

The most striking finding was that both groups of father-absent girls had great difficulty in interacting comfortably with men and male peers. Hetherington discovered that the difficulties were manifested differently for the daughters of divorcées than for the daughters of widows. The daughters of divorcées tended to be quite aggressive and forward with males, whereas daughters of widows tended to be extremely shy and timid in interacting with males. In contrast, all three groups of girls generally appeared to have appropriate interactions with their mothers and with female adults and peers. One exception was that the father-absent girls seemed more dependent on women, which is consistent with Lynn and Sawrey's (1959) findings of increased mother dependency among father-separated girls.

Observations at the recreation center revealed that, compared with the other girls, daughters of divorcées sought more attention from men and tried to be near and have physical contacts with male peers. On the other hand, the daughters of widows avoided male areas and much preferred to be with females. Compared to other girls, the daughters of widows reported less heterosexual activity; the daughters of divorcées reported more heterosexual activity.

With male interviewers, the daughters of widows sat as far away as possible, whereas the daughters of divorcées tended to sit as close as possible. (The girls from intact families generally sat at an intermediate distance.) Daughters of widows also showed avoidance behavior in their postures during interactions with male interviewers; they often sat stiffly upright, leaned backward, kept their legs together, and made little eye contact. In contrast, the daughters of divorcées tended to sprawl in their chairs, have an open leg posture, lean slightly forward, and exhibit eye contact and smiling. Nelsen and Vangen (1971) also found that among lower-class eighth-grade black girls, those who were father-absent because of divorce or separation were more precocious in their dating behavior and in their knowledge of sex than were father-present girls. Nelsen and Vangen emphasized that when the father is in the home he is an important limit-setter for the girl's sexual behavior, and that when he is absent there is a great decrease in parental control.

Hetherington generally found that girls had the most difficulties in their heterosexual interactions when their father-absence began before the age of five. Early father separation was usually more associated with inappropriate behavior with males than was father-absence after the age of five, although differences were not significant for every measure. Early father absence was also associated with more maternal overprotection than was father-absence after the age of five. There is other evidence indicating that early father-absence is more associated with maternal overprotection than is father-absence beginning later in the child's life (e.g., Biller & Bahm, 1971). Another study has not replicated Hetherington's (1972) findings, but the subjects were college students and differed in sociocultural background from those in her research (Hainline & Feig, 1978).

Additional findings of Hetherington's study indicated the importance of taking into account the context of and reason for father-absence. Daughters of widows recalled more positive relationships with their fathers and described them as warmer and more competent than did daughters of divorcées. The divorced mothers also painted a very negative picture of their marriages and ex-husbands. Daughters of divorcées were quite low in self-esteem, but daughters of widows did not differ significantly in their self-image from daughters from father-present homes. Nevertheless, both groups of father-absent girls had less feeling of control over their lives and more anxiety than did father-present girls.

Hetherington found evidence that suggests the continuing influence of father-absence on adult female development (Hetherington & Parke, 1986). She followed the development of daughters of divorcées, daughters of widows, and daughters from intact families for several years. The daughters of divorcées seemed to have especially troubled heterosexual relationships. They were likely to marry at an earlier age than the other groups and also to be pregnant at the time of marriage. After a brief period of time, some of these women were separated or divorced from their husbands. A variety of data from interview, observational, and test measures indicated that the daughters of divorcées married less adequate men than did the women from the other groups. The husbands of the daughters of divorcées appeared to have a lower level of educational and vocational accomplishments, and more often had been involved in difficulties with the law. These men also had more negative feelings toward their wives and infants and had more difficulty in controlling their impulses and behaving in an emotionally mature manner than did the husbands of the women in the other groups.

In contrast, there were findings that revealed that daughters of widows tended to marry vocationally successful and ambitious men who were overly controlled and inhibited in their social interactions. In general, the results of Hetherington's follow-up study suggested that women from intact families tended to make the most realistic and successful marital choices. These women also reported more orgasmic satisfaction in their sexual relationships with their husbands than did the two groups of women who grew up in father-absent homes (Hetherington & Parke, 1986).

10
Developmental Implications in One-Parent Families: Cognitive and Social Functioning

This chapter is divided into six major sections, which explore and integrate a wide array of research findings linking father-absence to various facets of psychological functioning. As in chapter 9, there is an emphasis on the importance of viewing the impact of paternal deprivation in the context of the complex interaction of biological, family, and social variables. In particular, there is a focus on variations in mothering and the sociocultural situation of the female-led single-parent family. The first section of the chapter analyzes data relating to cognitive functioning, including academic performance and specific facets of intellectual ability. The second section reviews research pertaining to personal and social adjustment and such topics as self-control, anxiety level, moral development, and delinquency. The third section deals with various forms of psychopathology that have been linked with different types of paternal deprivation. The fourth section summarizes longitudinal evidence concerning the consequences of divorce on short- and long-term development. The fifth section integrates data pertaining to the influence of individual differences in mothering on the paternally deprived child's development. The final section of the chapter highlights important issues that need to be addressed in future father-absence research.

Cognitive Functioning

Much of the evidence supporting the father's importance in cognitive development has come indirectly from studies comparing father-absent and father-present children. The first investigator to present data suggesting an intellectual disadvantage among father-absent children was Sutherland (1930). In an ambitious study involving Scottish children, he discovered that those who were father-absent scored significantly lower than did those who were father-present. Unfortunately, specific analyses concerning such variables as length of father-absence, sex of child, and socioeconomic status are not included in his report. A number of more recent and better controlled studies are also generally consistent with the supposition that father-absent children, at least from lower-class backgrounds, are less likely to function well on intelligence and aptitude tests than are father-present children (e.g., Blanchard & Biller, 1971; Deutsch & Brown, 1964; Lessing, Zagorin, & Nelson, 1970; Santrock, 1972).

Maxwell (1961) reported some evidence indicating that father-absence after the age of five negatively influences children's functioning on certain cognitive tasks. He analyzed the Wechsler Intelligence Test scores of a large group of eight- to thirteen-year-old children who had been referred to a British psychiatric clinic. He found that children whose fathers had been absent since the children were five performed below the norms for their age on a number of subtests. Children who had become father-absent after the age of five had lower scores on tasks tapping social knowledge, perception of details, and verbal skills. Father-absence since the age of five was the only family background variable which was consistently related to subtest scores; it seems surprising that there were no findings related to father-absence before the age of five.

Sutton-Smith, Rosenberg, and Landy (1968) explored the relationship between father-absence and college sophomores' aptitude test scores (American College Entrance Examination). These investigators defined *father-absence* as an absence of the father from the home for at least two consecutive years. Compared to father-present students, those who were father-absent performed at a lower level in terms of verbal, language, and total aptitude test scores. Although father-absence appeared to affect both males and females, it seemed to have more influence on males. Some interesting variations in the effects of father-absence as a function of sex of subject and sex of sibling are also reported; for example, in two-child father-absent families, boys with brothers appeared to be less deficient in academic aptitude than did boys with sisters. On the other hand, the father-present girl who was an only child seemed to be at a particular advantage in terms of her aptitude test scores.

In a related investigation, Landy, Rosenberg, and Sutton-Smith (1969) found that father-absence had a particularly disruptive effect on the quantitative aptitudes of college females. Total father-absence before the age of ten was highly associated with a deficit in quantitative aptitude. Their findings also suggested that father-absence during the age period from three to seven may have an especially negative effect on academic aptitude.

Lessing, Zagorin, and Nelson (1970) conducted one of the most extensive investigations concerning father-absence and cognitive functioning. They studied a group of nearly 500 children (ages nine to fifteen) who had been seen at a child guidance clinic, and explored the relationship between father-absence and functioning on the Wechsler Intelligence Test for Children. They defined father-absence as separation from the father for two or more years, not necessarily consecutive.

For both boys and girls, father-absence was associated with relatively low ability in perceptual-motor and manipulative-spatial tasks (block design and object assembly). Father-absent boys also scored lower than did father-present boys on the arithmetic subtest. In terms of our society's standards, such tasks are often considered to require typically male aptitudes. In a study with black elementary-school boys, Cortés and Fleming (1968) also reported an association between father-absence and poor mathematical functioning.

The results of the Lessing, Zagorin, and Nelson (1970) investigation revealed some complex interactions between father-absence and social class. Among working-class children, those who were father-absent performed at a generally lower level than those who were father-present. They were less able in their verbal functioning as well as on perceptual-motor and manipulative-spatial tasks. In comparison, middle-class children did not appear to be as handicapped by father-absence. They earned lower performance scores (particularly in block design and object assembly) but actually scored higher in verbal intelligence than did father present children.

Lessing, Zagorin, and Nelson also found that previously father-absent children who had a father-surrogate in their home (such as a stepfather) did not have intelligence test scores that differed significantly from those of father-present children. (In general, children with no father figure in the home accounted for most of the differences between father-absent and father-present children.) These findings can be interpreted in terms of a stepfather presenting a masculine model and/or increasing stability in the home.

The Lessing, Zagorin, and Nelson study is interesting and impressive, representing a vast improvement over earlier research attempting to link father-absence and intellectual deficits. There is more detail in the analysis of sex differences, social class, and specific areas of intellectual functioning. In general, the investigators showed awareness of potential variables that may interact with father-absence. Nevertheless, a number of serious questions can be raised concerning the methodology of the research. The investigation can be criticized because it was based solely on the findings from a clinic population. Even more directly relevant, the study has a weakness similar to almost all its predecessors in that the variables of father-absence and father-presence are not defined clearly enough. Two years of not necessarily consecutive separation from the father was used as the criterion for father- absence. An obvious question is whether age at onset of father-absence is related to intellectual functioning. There is also no consideration of the amount of availability of present fathers or the quality of father-child interactions in the intact home. Similar inadequacies may account for the lack of clear-cut findings concerning father-absence and academic functioning in some studies (Biller, 1974c; Herzog & Sudia, 1973).

Early Paternal Deprivation

Blanchard and Biller (1971) attempted to specify different levels of father availability and to ascertain their relationship to the academic functioning of third-grade boys. They examined both the timing of father-absence and the degree of father-son interaction in the father-present home. The boys were of average intelligence and were from working-class and lower-middle-class backgrounds. Four groups of boys were studied: early father-absent (beginning before age three), late father-absent (beginning after age five), low father-present (less than six hours per week), and high father-present (more than two hours per day). To control for variables (other than father availability) that might affect academic performance, there was individual subject matching so that each boy in the early father-absent group was matched with a boy from each of the other three groups in terms of essentially identical characteristics of age, IQ, socioeconomic status, and presence or absence of male siblings.

Academic performance was assessed by means of Stanford Achievement Test Scores and classroom grades. (The teachers did not have access to the children's achievement test scores until after they had assigned final classroom grades.) The high father-present group was very superior to the other three groups. With respect to both grades and achievement test scores, the early father-absent boys were generally underachievers, the late father-absent boys and low father-present boys usually functioned somewhat below grade level, and the high father-present group performed above grade level.

The early father-absent boys were consistently handicapped in their academic performance. They scored significantly lower on every achievement test index as well as in their grades. The early father-absent group functioned below grade level in both language and mathematical skills. When compared to the high father-present group, the early father-absent group appeared to be quite inferior in skills relating to reading comprehension.

Santrock (1972) presented additional evidence indicating that early father-absence can have a significant debilitating effect on cognitive functioning. Among lower-class junior high and high school children, those who became father-absent before the age of five, and particularly before the age of two, generally scored significantly lower on measures of IQ (Otis Quick Test) and achievement (Stanford Achievement Test) that had been administered when they were in the third and sixth grades than did those from intact homes. The most detrimental effects occurred when father-absence was due to divorce, desertion, or separation, rather than to death. The findings of this study provided support for the positive remedial effects of a stepfather for boys, especially when the stepfather joined the family before the child was five years of age.

Hetherington, Cox, and Cox (1978b, 1982) also reported data indicating that early father-absence can impede cognitive development. They found differences between the cognitive functioning of young boys (five- and six-year-olds) who had been father-absent for two years because of divorce and that of boys from intact families. Boys from intact families scored significantly higher on the block design, mazes, and arithmetic subtests of the WIPSI as well as achieving higher Performance Scale Intelligence scores and marginally higher Full-Scale Intelligence scores. Other data from this study clearly suggest that the decreasing availability of the divorced fathers for their sons during the two years following the divorce was a major factor in these boys lower level of performance compared with boys from intact families. In contrast, no clear-cut differences in cognitive functioning were found between father-absent girls and girls from intact homes.

In chapter 8 we noted that, with respect to cognitive functioning, fathers seemed to have more of an influence on sons than on daughters. Consistent with such findings, father-absence has less impact on the cognitive functioning of girls than that of boys (Biller, 1974c). Although some research indicates that the cognitive performance of girls is hampered by various forms of paternal deprivation, boys are more likely to manifest obvious decrements in intellectual and/or academic functioning associated with father-absence (Chapman, 1977; Hetherington, Cox, & Cox, 1982; Lessing, Zagorin, & Nelson, 1970; Pedersen, Rubinstein, & Yarrow, 1979; Santrock, 1972; Shelton, 1969).

Developmental Level

The studies just reviewed do indicate that early paternal deprivation, especially before the age of five, can negatively influence certain aspects of cognitive functioning. However, cognitive functioning is complex and multidimensional, and the quality of father involvement at various stages of development—not just in the first few years of life—can be very important to the child. As Radin (1981) has emphasized, there is not consistent data indicating that a particular stage of development is especially critical in terms of the general relationship between father-absence and cognitive functioning. On the other hand, several researchers have also stressed that many intellectual abilities are difficult to assess in young children, even by kindergarten or first grade, and that may contribute to the apparently delayed effects of paternal deprivation found in older children (Deutsch, 1960; Radin, 1981; Shinn, 1978).

There is evidence that early paternal deprivation has a cumulative impact as the child grows older. In her excellent review, Radin (1981) noted several studies that indicated few if any cognitive differences associated with father-absence for black children entering first grade, but evidence of clear-cut superiority of father-present children by the later elementary-school years. Differences in academic performance as a function of variations in the quality of early father involvement seem to become more apparent as children grow older (Deutsch, 1960; Deutsch & Brown, 1964; Hess, Shipman, Brophy, Bear, & Adelberger, 1969; Sciara, 1975).

The young child has a quite limited intellectual capacity with which to respond to paternal deprivation. In their analysis of the impact of parental death on psychological functioning, Berlinsky and Biller (1982) emphasize the ability of the child to understand and cope with the loss. Children below the age of seven or eight typically have not reached the stage of concrete operations at which they can realistically confront the loss (Piaget, 1958). On the other hand, the older child who has attained the capacity to think abstractly may have a great advantage compared to his younger counterpart in dealing with the loss of a parent or a radical change in family living circumstances. Younger children are less likely to have attained a full understanding of death and may adjust less adequately after bereavement. Death of a parent before the child is seven, as well as early father-absence for other reasons, has been found to be especially associated with later developmental problems (Berlinsky & Biller, 1982).

Individual differences among children of the same age are very important. A child who is intellectually very precocious may have the cognitive capacity to deal with severe family difficulties at an earlier age. Under some circumstances, family stress factors may actually stimulate certain areas of cognitive functioning. Kane (1979) found that, among children younger than six, those who had experienced death were relatively sophisticated in understanding the concept of loss. Early comprehension of death has also been reported to be associated with anxiety about death (Melear, 1973). There are additional data suggesting that early father-loss may be a variable stimulating, in some individuals, unusual cognitive accomplishments at a relatively early age (Berlinsky & Biller, 1982; Eisenstadt, 1978).

Cognitive Style

Carlsmith (1964) made an interesting discovery concerning the relationship between father-absence and intellectual abilities. She examined the College Board Aptitude Test scores of middle-class and upper-middle-class high school males who had experienced early father-absence because of their fathers' military service during World War II. Boys who were father-absent in early childhood were more likely to have a feminine patterning of aptitude test scores. Compared to the typical male pattern—math score higher than verbal score—males who had experienced early separation from their fathers more frequently had a higher verbal score than math score. She found that the earlier the onset of father-absence, the more likely was the male to have a higher verbal than math score. The effect was strongest for students whose fathers were absent at birth and/or were away for over thirty months. Higher verbal than math functioning is the usual pattern among females, and Carlsmith speculated that it reflects a feminine global style of cognitive functioning. Results from other studies have also indicated a relationship between father-absence and a feminine patterning of aptitude test scores among males (e.g., Altus, 1958; Maccoby & Rau, 1962; Nelsen & Maccoby, 1966).

A study with adolescent boys by Barclay and Cusumano (1967) supports the supposition that difficulties in analytical functioning are often related to father-absence. Using Witkin's rod-and-frame procedure, Barclay and Cusumano found that father-absent males were more field-dependent than those who were father-present. Wohlford and Liberman (1970) reported that father separation (after the age of six) was related to field dependency among elementary-school children from an urban section of Miami. Their procedure involved an embedded figures test. Field-dependent individuals have difficulties in ignoring irrelevant environmental cues in the analysis of certain types of problems.

Louden (1973), in a very extensive study with college students, presented evidence indicating that both males and females who had been father-absent during childhood were more field-dependent than were those who were father-present. Father-absence was defined as the continuous absence of the father or father-surrogate for at least three years during one of three age periods: zero to five years, six to twelve years, or thirteen to eighteen years. Field dependence-independence was measured by a group-administered embedded figures procedure. Father-absence during each age period was associated with greater field dependence than was father-presence; but, as in Wohlford and Liberman's research, father-absence during the six- to twelve-year age period seemed to be most linked with field-dependent behavior. Louden argued that this period is especially important for the development of an ability to adapt to changing environments. Such data suggest that the father may serve different functions at different stages of the child's development.

Lifshitz (1976) compared nine- to fourteen-year-old children whose fathers had been killed in an Israeli war three to six years prior to testing to children from intact families. The subjects and controls were matched on relevant variables and were assessed with structured observations, teacher ratings, and the Bieri test of cognitive complexity. Father-absent children were relatively deficient in cognitive skills related to awareness and differentiation of environmental variables. Children who had lost a father before the age of seven scored lower on measures of cognitive complexity than did subjects who were older when their father died.

Though not specifying the child's age at time of father-loss, Parish and Copeland (1980) found that male college students whose fathers had died were more externally oriented in terms of locus of control than were males and females from divorced families, males and females from intact families, and females who had lost a parent through death. The bereaved males perceived themselves as having relatively little control over their lives. An external locus of control is associated with instrumental dependency, a lack of initiative in making decisions, and the passive-depressive personality style often found among paternally bereaved children (Berlinsky & Biller, 1982).

Sociocultural Variables

Paternal deprivation is a major factor contributing to a disadvantaged environment (Bronfenbrenner, 1967). Father-absence appears to hamper lower-class children in particular. Some investigators have reported that among lower-class black children, those who are father-absent score considerably lower on intelligence and achievement tests than do those who are father-present (e.g., Cortés & Fleming, 1968; Deutsch, 1960; Deutsch & Brown, 1964).

In her review of relevant research, Radin (1976) emphasized that several studies did not reveal any cognitive deficits associated with father-absence for black children. Shinn (1978) also noted that there appeared to be more consistency in the effects of father-absence on white children than on black children. Shinn did point out, however, that almost half of the methodologically adequate studies involving black children did produce results suggesting detrimental effects of father-absence on cognitive functioning. For example, Pedersen, Rubinstein, and Yarrow (1979) reported that among the black infants they studied, those who were father-present generally scored higher on a variety of cognitive-development measures than did those who were father-absent.

Radin (1976) cited Coleman et al.'s (1966) data indicating that father-absence may be more detrimental in societies in which the father generally has a strong role, the implication being that children are more likely to miss out on a particularly important source of cognitive stimulation. For example, Coleman et al. (1966) found that Asian-American and Mexican-American children were negatively influenced by father-absence, although lower-class black children were not. Other investigators have reported that father-absence may have less detrimental effect in societies where the mother is expected to play a particularly influential role in family and economic functioning (Ancona, Cesa-Bianchi, & Bocquet, 1964).

There is ample documentation of the association between socioeconomic status and various aspects of children's cognitive and social functioning. Many researchers have argued that the impact of father-absence and divorce on children's development is, for the most part, an artifact of lowered socioeconomic status. Some research, however, suggests that, in fact, single-parent status may actually be a more powerful predictor of the academic and social functioning of young children at school entry than is socioeconomic status or any other family background, developmental history, or health variable. Guidubaldi and Perry (1984) reported striking evidence that single-parent status accounts for much statistically independent variance, and is highly predictive of performance on various indexes of academic and social competence, even when socioeconomic status is controlled through regression analyses. Although family structure in itself was not associated with intellectual ability measures, children from single-parent homes were found to be much more at risk for poor academic performance and sociobehavioral difficulties upon entering school than were children from two-parent families (Guidubaldi, 1983; Guidubaldi & Perry, 1984).

Socioeconomic and sociocultural variables must be considered more carefully if there is to be a greater understanding of the effects of paternal deprivation on cognitive development. A problem in some research is the absence of specific comparisons among individuals from different social backgrounds. In particular, culturally disadvantaged groups and members of stable blue-collar occupations (such as teamsters and skilled factory workers) are often grouped together as "lower-class." Such generalizations seem to obscure possible relationships (Biller, 1971a). The incidence of continual father-absence is much higher among culturally disadvantaged families than among working-class families (Zill, 1985).

The classification becomes very difficult to untangle because a family that has been working-class may be redefined as disadvantaged or lower-class if it becomes father-absent. Herzog and Sudia (1973) pointed out the lack of adequate controls for income levels in research with disadvantaged children. They emphasized that differences in income level between father-absent and father-present families may be more closely related to intellectual disadvantagement than is father absence in itself.

In any case, paternal deprivation generally seems to be associated with much more serious consequences among lower-class children than among middle-class children (Biller, 1971a). Some research already discussed in this chapter has suggested that among father-absent children, those from working-class backgrounds are consistently more handicapped in their cognitive functioning than are those from middle-class backgrounds (Lessing, Zagorin, & Nelson, 1970). A general depression in academic achievement associated with father-absence has usually been found with working-class or lower-class children (Blanchard & Biller, 1971; Santrock, 1972).

On the other hand, middle-class father-absent children often do well in situations requiring verbal skills. In Lessing et al.'s (1970) study, middle-class father-absent children had higher verbal scores, though lower performance (for example, perceptual-manipulative) scores, than did father-present children. Dyl and Biller (1973) found that, although lower-class father-absent boys were particularly handicapped in their reading skills, middle-class father-absent boys functioned quite adequately in reading. Because academic achievement, particularly in elementary school, is so heavily dependent on verbal and reading ability, father-absent middle-class children do not seem to be very much handicapped. There is also evidence that loss of a father may be a stimulus for unusual achievement in certain individuals. In some cases a child's abilities may be strengehened in the attempt to cope with the loss of a parent (Biller, 1974c).

Eisenstadt (1978) presented some provocative data suggesting that the death of a parent, particularly a father, during childhood could be a stimulating factor in the achievement of occupational eminence, and even genius, as well as in serious psychopathology. He compared the family histories of individuals who were eminent in their professions with demographic data from various populations. He consistently found that a greater proportion of those with unusual accomplishment appeared to have had experienced the death of their fathers during childhood. He also cited some other research, including the work of Albert (1973) that supported the notion that death of a father may, in some cases, spur an individual on to great creative accomplishment, even though the majority of studies he reviewed focused on the link between parent loss and psychopathology.

In general, Eisenstadt put forth the argument that the bereavement process can be worked through in a very constructive manner by some children so that they become particularly motivated and energized toward creative accomplishment. We would emphasize that such factors as the quality of mothering that the child receives and the child's own constitutional predispositions are particularly important in determining whether the bereavement process might help stimulate an individual toward the pathway to eminence and genius (Berlinsky & Biller, 1982; Biller, 1974c).

Maternal Influence

The middle-class mother seems to have a strong influence on her father-absent son's intellectual development. In an interview study in a university town, Hilgard, Neuman, and Fisk (1960) found that men who lost their fathers during childhood tended to be highly successful in their academic pursuits despite, or maybe because of, a conspicuous overdependence on their mothers. Clinical findings presented by Gregory (1965) also suggest that many upper-middle-class students who have been father-absent do well in college. Evidence reviewed by Nelsen and Maccoby (1966) reveals that high verbal ability in boys is often associated with a close and restrictive mother-son relationship. Levy (1943) reported that middle-class maternally overprotected boys did superior work in school, particularly in subjects requiring verbal facility. Their performance in mathematics, however, was not at such a high level, which seems consistent with Carlsmith's (1964) results.

Middle-class mothers are much more likely to place strong emphasis on academic success than are lower-class mothers (Kohn, 1959). Some findings suggest that among lower-class mothers, those without husbands are preoccupied with day-to-day activities and less frequently think of future goals for themselves or for their children (Hecksher, 1967; Parker & Kleiner, 1956). Compared to the middle-class mother, the lower-class mother usually puts much less emphasis on long-term academic goals and is also generally a much less adequate model for coping with the demands of the middle-class school.

In homes in which the father is absent or relatively unavailable, the mother assumes a more primary role in terms of dispensing reinforcements and emphasizing certain values. A father-absent child who is strongly identified with an intellectually oriented mother may be at an advantage in many facets of school adjustment. He may find the transition from home to the typically feminine-oriented classroom quite comfortable. Such father-absent children might be expected to do particularly well in tasks where verbal skills and conformity are rewarded.

Although they may stimulate the paternally deprived child's acquisition of verbal skills and adaptation to the typical school environment, middle-class, overprotecting mothers often inhibit the development of an active, problem-solving attitude toward the environment. A mother who is excessively over-protective and dominating may interfere with the development of the child's assertiveness and independence (Biller, 1971c). The mother's own psychological adjustment is crucial; a mother who is emotionally disturbed and/or interper-sonally handicapped can have a very negative effect on the father-absent child's self-concept and ability to relate to others. On the other hand, mothers who are self-accepting, have high ego strength, and are interpersonally mature can do much to facilitate positive personality development among their paternally deprived children (Biller, 1971a, 1971c).

Variations in fathering can influence the child's cognitive development, but father-absence is only one of many factors that have an impact on the child's intellectual functioning. Sociocultural, maternal, and peer group values are especially important. For example, among lower-class children, paternal depriva-tion usually intensifies lack of exposure to experiences linking intellectual ac-tivities with masculine interests. Many boys, in their desperate attempts to view themsleves as totally masculine, become excessively dependent on their peer group and perceive intellectual tasks as feminine. The school setting, which presents women as authority figures and makes strong demands for obedience and conformity, is particularly antithetical to such boys' fervent desire to feel masculine (Biller, 1974c; Sexton, 1969; Zill, 1985).

Underlying Processes

An especially impressive analysis of research concerning father-absence and cognitive functioning was conducted by Shinn (1978). She focused her discus-sion on twenty-eight studies that met some minimal methodological criteria: data were collected from nonclincial populations, there was some sort of father-present control group, and there was some effort to control for socioeconomic status. The majority of these studies indicated that father-absence was associated with detrimental effects in cognitive functioning. Her survey indicated that father-absence due to divorce may be particularly detrimental, and there was some evidence that early, long-term, and complete father absence was especially likely to be negatively associated with intellectual competence. She also found some data indicating negative effects from later, short-term, and partial father absence. More clear-cut results were reported from studies involving lower-class individuals and among males, although Shinn emphasized that there is much evidence that females' cognitive functioning generally appears also to be af-fected by father-absence.

There have been several interpretations of the process by which father-absence may influence the child's cognitive functioning and also other facets of personality development (Biller, 1974c). In her review, Shinn (1978) tried to differentiate systematically between the relevance of various hypotheses con-cerning underlying factors that may be responsible for an association between father-absence and cognitive functioning. Some children may be predisposed to father-absence as a result of divorce because of the parents' family backgrounds. The child's development may be negatively affected even before the divorce takes place. For example, high levels of father-mother conflict, financial stress, and paternal deprivation seem to be characteristic for some children in the years preceding the divorce.

The father's absence may, in turn, be linked to a variety of factors that may be more directly associated with deficits in the child's cognitive functioning. Shinn (1978) concluded that data linking disruption of sex-role identification with impaired cognitive functioning are relatively meager, but Biller's (1974c) review has indicated that sex-role functioning may interact with the cognitive development of the paternally deprived child in a variety of complex ways. The family instability and financial difficulty often associated with father absence may be primary factors interfering with the child's cognitive functioning. Shinn (1978) agreed, however, that the major influence of father absence appears to be lessened parental interaction and attention, which in turn often seem to result in a decrease in the child's level of cognitive stimulation and the opportunity to model more mature types of information processing and problem solving.

Personal and Social Adjustment

Although it did not focus on father-absent children, a study by Reuter and Biller (1973) appears to have some interesting implications concerning father-absence and availability. This research explored the relationship between various combinations of perceived paternal nurturance-availability and college males' personality adjustment. A family background questionnaire was designed to assess perceptions of father-child relationships and the amount of time the father spent at home when the subjects were children. The personal adjustment scale of Gough and Heilbrun's Adjective Check List, and the socialization scale of the California Psychological Inventory, were employed as measures of personality adjustment. High paternal nurturance combined with at least moderate paternal availability, and high paternal availability combined with at least moderate paternal nurturance, were related to positive scores on the personality adjustment measures. A male who has adequate opportunities to observe a nurturant father can imitate his behavior and develop favorable personality characteristics. The father who is both relatively nurturant and relatively available may also have a more adequate personality adjustment than other types of fathers.

In contrast, high paternal nurturance combined with low paternal availability, and high paternal availability combined with low paternal nurturance, were associated with relatively poor scores on the personality adjustment measures. Males who reported that their fathers had been home much of the time but gave them little attention seemed to be especially handicapped in their psychological functioning. The unnurturant father is an inadequate model, and his consistent presence appears to be a detriment to the child's personality functioning. In other words, the child with an unnurturant father may be better off if his father is not very available. This is consistent with evidence suggesting that father-absent children often have better personalitiy adjustments than children with passive, ineffectual fathers (Biller, 1971a, 1974c). The child with a highly nurturant father who is seldom available may feel quite frustrated that his father is not home more often and/or may find it difficult to imitate such an elusive figure. Children whose parents are divorced often fit this pattern; they see their fathers infrequently and/or unpredictably, but their fathers are often extremely nurturant during such interactions.

Anxiety

Inadequate fathering is often associated with a high level of anxiety in children. The paternally deprived child's insecurity in interpersonal relationships can contribute to feelings of anxiety and low self-esteem. In addition, the paternally deprived child may experience much anxiety because of an overly intense relationship with the mother. The father-absent child, in particular, is likely to encounter economic insecurity, and, depending on the reason for paternal absence, may be concerned with his father's well-being. Feelings of being different from other children may also increase his anxiety and perception of being inadequate. A principal role of the father is to help the family deal with environmental problems, and the paternally deprived child may encounter more than his share of apparently irresolvable crises. Children with adequate and available fathers are exposed to a model who can deal realistically and creatively with some of the problems that a mother may not have experience or time to solve (Biller, 1971a, 1981a).

Stolz et al. (1954) reported that four- to eight-year-old children, paternally deprived the first few years of life while their fathers were away in military service, were more anxious than children whose fathers had been consistently present. Previously father-separated children were observed to be more anxious with peers and adults, and in story completion sessions when the situation involved the father, as well as in terms of maternal reports of seriousness and number of fears. It is important to note that the fathers were not absent at the time of the study and were having stressful relationships with their children. In a study of nursery school children, Koch (1961) found that father-absent children (eight boys and three girls) exhibited more anxiety on a projective test than did a matched group from intact families. The father-absent children more often selected unhappy faces for the central child depicted in various situations.

McCord, McCord, and Thurber (1962) analyzed social workers' observations of ten- to fifteen-year-old lower-class boys. They concluded that father-absent boys manifested more anxiety about sex than did a matched group of father-present boys, although the difference concerning amount of general fearfulness was insignificant. In a retrospective study, in which Stephens (1961) asked social workers about their experiences with father-absent boys, such boys were described as being more effeminate and anxious about sex than were father-present boys. Leichty (1960) did not find any evidence that father-absence during early chidhood was associated with castration anxiety in college males, although some of her findings did suggest that father-absence was related to anxiety concerning mother-father sexual interaction. There is at least some initial increase in anxiety level for all children whose parents divorce, although many are able to cope very well because of their developmental stage or other factors (Hetherington, Cox, & Cox, 1978; Wallerstein & Kelly, 1980a).

Self-Control and Moral Development

Mischel (1961c) conducted a series of studies concerning the antecedents and correlates of impulse control in Caribbean children. In an earlier phase of his research, Mischel (1958) reported that seven- to nine-year-old black West Indian children chose immediate gratification significantly more frequently than did white West Indian children. The difference between the black and white children appeared to be related to the greater incidence of father-absence among the black children. Studying eight- and nine-year-olds, Mischel (1961b) found that father-absent children showed a stronger preference for immediate gratification than did father-present children. Father-absent children, for instance, more often chose a small candy bar for immediate consumption over waiting a week for a large candy bar.

Santrock and Wohlford (1970) studied delay of gratification among fifth-grade boys. They found that boys who were father-absent because of divorce, as compared to those who were father-absent because of death, had more difficulty in delaying gratification. Boys who were father-absent because of divorce more often chose an immediately available small candy bar rather than waiting until the next day for a much larger one. Boys who became father-separated before the age of two or between the ages of six and nine were more likely to choose the immediate reward than were those who were separated from their fathers between the ages of three and five.

There is also some evidence that individuals who have been father-absent during childhood are likely to have difficulties making long-term commitments. Studying Peace Corps volunteers, Suedfield (1967) discovered that those who were father-absent during childhood were much more likley not to complete their scheduled overseas tours than were those who had not been father-absent. Premature terminations were associated with problems of adjustment and conduct, and included some psychiatrically based decisions. Other research suggests a relationship between father-absence in childhood and unemployment in adulthood (Gay & Tonge, 1967; Hall & Tonge, 1963).

Hoffman (1971a) analyzed data concerning conscience development in seventh-grade children. Father-absent boys consistently scored lower than father-present boys on a variety of moral indexes. They scored lower on measures of internal moral judgment, guilt following transgressions, acceptance of blame, moral values, and rule-conformity. In addition, they were rated as higher in aggression by their teachers, which may also reflect difficulties in self-control. Although the influence was less clear-cut, weak father identification among father-present boys was also related to less adequate conscience development. Father identification was determined by responses to questions involving the person to whom the boy felt most similar, whom he most admired and most wanted to resemble when he grew up. Boys with strong father identifications scored higher on the measures of internal moral judgments, moral values, and conformity to rules than did boys with low father identifications (Hoffman, 1971a, 1971b).

Whiting (1959) hypothesized that paternal deprivation is negatively related to the strength of the child's conscience development. In a cross-cultural analysis, he assumed that self-blame for illness is an indication of strong conscience development. In societies in which fathers have little control over their younger children, there is more of a tendency to blame others and/or supernatural beings for one's illness. Blaming oneself for illness was stronger in nuclear households and least common in polygynous mother-child households. Such evidence is also consistent with the view that paternal deprivation can inhibit the development of trust in others.

A number of clinicians, including Aichorn (1935) and Lederer (1964), have speculated about inadequacies in the self-control and conscience development of the father-absent boy. In his experience as a psychotherapist, Meerloo (1956) found that a lack of accurate time perception, often associated with difficulties in self-control, is common among father-absent individuals. In a study of elementary-school children in a Cuban section of Miami, Wohlford and Liberman (1970) reported that father-absent children had less well developed future time perspective than did father-present children.

Meerloo (1956) assumed that the father represents social order and that his adherence to time schedules gives the child an important lesson in social functioning. The paternally deprived child may find it very difficult to follow the rules of society. Antisocial acts are often impulsive as well as aggressive, and there is evidence that inability to delay gratification is associated with inaccurate time perception, lack of social responsibility, low achievement motivation, and juvenile delinquency (Mischel, 1961a, 1961b). Compared with those from intact two-parent families, father-absent adolescent males are more likley to have difficulties in impulse control associated with a high level of alcohol and marijuana use and with sexual activity (Stern, Northman, & Van Slyk, 1984).

The father-absent child often lacks a model from whom to learn to delay gratification and to control his aggressive and destructive impulses. A child who has experienced paternal deprivation may have particular difficulty in respecting and communicating with adult males in positions of authority. Douvan and Adelson (1966) observed much rebelliousness against adult authority figures and particularly a rejection of men among father-absent adolescent boys. (It is interesting to contrast such a reaction to the continual seeking of male adults among many young father-absent children; perhaps there has been a disillusionment process.)

Delinquency

Antisocial behavior among children and adolescents can have many different etiologies, but paternal deprivation and various forms of child maltreatment by fathers are frequent contributing factors. Many researchers have noted that father-absence is more common among delinquent children than among nondelinquent children. Studying adolescents, Glueck and Glueck (1950) reported that more than two-fifths of the delinquent boys were father-absent, compared with less than one-quarter of a matched nondelinquent group. McCord, McCord, and Thurber (1962) found that the lower-class, father-absent boys in their study committed more felonies than did the father-present group, although the rates of gang delinquency were not different. Gregory (1965a) listed a large number of investigations linking father-absence with delinquent behavior and also detected a strong association between these variables in his study of high school students. Brown and Eppos (1966) found father-absence to be characteristic of the backgrounds of both male and female prison inmates.

Early father-absence has a particularly strong association with acting-out behavior among males. Siegman (1966) analyzed medical students' responses to an anonymous questionnaire concerning their childhood experiences. He compared the responses of students who had been without a father for at least one year during their first few years of life with those of students who had been continuously father-present. The father-absent group admitted to a greater degree of antisocial behavior during childhood. Anderson (1968) found that a history of early father-absence was much more frequent among boys committed to a training school. He also discovered that father-absent nondelinquents had a much higher rate of father substitution (stepfather, father-surrogate, and so on) between the ages of four and seven than did father-absent delinquents. Kelly and Baer (1969) studied the recidivism rate among male delinquents. Compared to a 12 percent rate among father-present males, they found a 39 percent recidivism rate among males who had become father-absent before the age of six. However, boys who became father-absent after the age of six had only a 10 percent recidivism rate.

Miller (1958) argued that most lower-class boys suffer from paternal deprivation and that their antisocial behavior is often an attempt to prove their masculinity. Bacon, Child, and Barry (1963), in a cross-cultural study, found that father availability was negatively related to the amount of theft and personal crime. Degree of father availability was defined in terms of family structure. Societies with a predominantly monogamous nuclear family structure tended to be rated low in the amount of theft and personal crime, whereas societies with a polygynous mother-child family structure tended to be rated high in both theft and personal crime. Following Miller's hypothesis, Bacon, Child, and Barry suggested that such antisocial behavior was a reaction against a female-based household and an attempted assertion of masculinity. A large number of psychiatric referrals with the complaint of aggressive acting out are made by mothers of preadolescent and adolescent father-absent boys, and clinical data suggest that sex-role conflicts are very common in such boys (Biller, 1974c).

Herzog and Sudia (1973) carefully analyzed the methodological defects of studies linking father-absence and delinquency. They pointed out that socioeconomic and sociocultural factors often are not taken into account in comparisons of father-absent and father-present children. Furthermore, Herzog and Sudia emphasized that law enforcement officials and other community agents may react differently when a father-absent child, rather than a father-present child, behaves in an antisocial manner, especially when the child comes from an economically disadvantaged family. They may expect the father-absent child to commit increasingly serious offenses, and he may be dealt with more severely. It is also noteworthy that Santrock and Tracy's (1978) data clearly indicate that teachers are likely to stereotype boys from father-absent and divorced families. Such treatment may negatively influence the father-absent child's self-concept and strengthen the probability that he will become involved in more antisocial acts.

The difficulty that boys from father-absent homes often have in relating to male authority figures can also contribute to the reactions of law enforcement officials. The father-absent boy's supposed lack of respect can lead to negative interactions with male authority figures, and some data suggest that father-absent boys are more prone to commit offenses against authority than against property (Herzog & Sudia, 1973; Nye, 1957; Zill, 1985).

Much evidence is cited by Herzog and Sudia (1973) indicating that lack of general family cohesiveness and supervision, rather than father absence in itself, is the most significant factor associated with juvenile delinquency. Many familial and nonfamilial factors must be considered, and in only some cases is father-absence directly linked to delinquent behavior. For example, children in father-absent families who have a positive relationship with highly competent mothers seem less likely to become delinquent than boys in father-present families who have inadequate and maltreating fathers (Biller, 1974c).

Psychopathology

Garbower (1959), studying children from Navy families, found that those who were seen for psychiatric problems had more frequent and lengthy periods of father-absence than did a nondisturbed comparison group. The fathers of the disturbed children also seemed less sensitive to the effects of their absence on their families. In studying military families, Pedersen (1966) found a similar amount of father-absence among eleven- to fifteen-year-old boys, regardless of whether they had been referred for psychiatric help. He did find, however, that the degree of their psychopathology was highly associated with the amount of father-absence they had experienced.

Trunnell (1968) studied children seen at an outpatient clinic and found that severity of psychopathology varied with the length of father-absence and the age of onset of the father's absence. The longer the absence and the younger the child at the onset of his absence, the more serious the psychopathology. Oltman and Friedman (1967) found particularly high rates of childhood father-absence among adults who had chronically disturbed personalities and inadequate moral development. In addition, there were above-average rates of father-absence among neurotics and drug addicts. Rosenberg (1969) also reported extremely high rates of frequent childhood father-absence among young alcoholics and drug addicts. Maternal dominance combined with father-absence or inadequacy is common in the histories of drug addicts (Chein, Gerrard, Lee, & Rosenfield, 1964; Wood & Duffy, 1966).

Rubenstein (1980) described data that are relevant to the consideration of the long-term effects of father-absence due to divorce. She focused on the adjustment of adults who as children had experienced parental divorce. Her survey research, in collaboration with Phillip Shaver, suggested that feelings of loneliness and low self-esteem were more common among adults who had grown up in one-parent families than among those whose families had remained intact. The earlier the divorce in the individual's life, the more likely he or she was to have low self-esteem and experience profound loneliness as an adult. Worry, despair, feelings of worthlessness, fearfulness, and general separation anxiety seemed especially common among those who as children grew up in families where the parent had divorced. Berlinsky and Biller (1982) have reviewed considerable data suggesting a link between father-loss in childhood and depression and suicidal behavior in adulthood. They emphasize, however, that the total context of parental death must be carefully analyzed (reason for death, developmental characteristics of the child at the time of the loss, reaction of the remaining parent to the loss, and so on).

Brill and Liston (1966) reported that loss of father due to death in childhood was not unusually high among mental patients. However, the frequency of loss of father due to divorce or separation in childhood was much higher for individuals suffering from neurosis, psychosis, or personality disorders than for a number of different comparison groups. Consistent with Brill and Liston's data, father-absence due to divorce, separation, or desertion (as compared to father-absence due to death of the father) has also been found to be more highly associated with delinquency (Goode, 1961); maladjustment (Baggett, 1967);

low self-esteem and sexual acting out (Hetherington, 1972); and cognitive deficits (Santrock, 1972). In a study of children who were referred for school adjustment problems, Felner, Stolberg, and Cowen (1975) found that those whose parents were divorced were likely to display aggressive and acting-out behavior, whereas those from homes where the father had died were likely to display anxiety, depression, and moody withdrawal. Other researchers who have reported that rates of childhood father-absence are higher among patients classified as neurotic or schizophrenic than among the general population have not done systematic analyses with respect to the reason for father-absence (e.g., DaSilva, 1963; Madow & Hardy, 1947; Oltman, McGarry, & Friedman, 1952; Wahl, 1954, 1956).

Gregory (1958, 1965b) critically evaluated many studies and emphasized some of the methodological pitfalls in comparisons involving the relative incidence of mental illness among father-present and father-absent individuals. Lack of consideration of the possible effects of socioeconomic status is a major shortcoming of most of the studies. Cobliner (1963) reported some provocative findings suggesting that father-absence is more likely to be related to serious psychological disturbance in lower-class than in middle-class individuals. Middle-class families, particularly with respect to the mother-child relationship, may have more psychological as well as economic resources with which to cope with paternal deprivation (Biller, 1971a, 1974c, 1981a).

Types of Paternal Deprivation

There are data suggesting that boys from father-absent homes are in many cases less retarded in their personality development than are boys from intact maternally dominant homes (Biller, 1968a; Reuter & Biller, 1973). In Nye's (1957) study, children from broken homes were found to have better family adjustments, and to have lower rates of antisocial behavior and psychosomatic illness than were children from unhappy unbroken homes. Other research has also suggested that a child may function more adequately in a father-absent home than in one in which there is a severely dysfunctional husband-wife relationship (e.g., Benson, 1968; Hetherington, Cox, & Cox, 1978, 1982; Landis, 1962).

Father-absent children may be more influenced by factors outside the home than are children from intact but unhappy and/or maternally dominanted homes. Some children may be particularly affected by attention from an adult male because of their intense feelings of paternal deprivation. Children with inadequate fathers often become resigned to their situation. For example, the father-present but maternally dominated child is likely to develop a view of men as ineffectual, especially if his father is continually being controlled by his mother. In contrast, the father-absent child may evolve a much more flexible view of adult male behavior (Biller, 1974c, 1982a.)

Research that is described in this section and in other parts of this book indicates that maltreatment by the father and/or father-absence predisposes children toward certain developmental deficits. Many paternally deprived children, however, are generally well adjusted. Such children should be studied more carefully to determine why they differ from less well adjusted paternally deprived children. Investigators should consider both type of child maladjustment and type of family inadequacy.

Berlinsky and Biller (1982) found much research linking death of a parent during childhood and psychopathology in adulthood. There was consistent evidence that paternal loss was associated with adjustment difficulties in children that continued into adulthood. Berlinsky and Biller emphasized the importance of examining the total context of parental death, including the child's individual characteristics (age, cognitive level, temperament); the reason for parental death; relationship with the parent prior to the loss; the quality of the family system (reaction of the remaining parent to the loss; siblings and extended family support network); and sociocultural and socioeconomic factors.

Father-loss was at least as predictive of later developmental problems as was mother-loss, and death of the father before age seven was especially associated with self-concept and social adjustment difficulties. Daughters seemed to be affected as much as sons by death of the father. Especially interesting was the discovery that the father's death was related to an inhibited, dependent, restricted, nonassertive, conforming personality style for both males and females, as well as to greater risk for depression. Paternal deprivation as a result of divorce was more likely to be associated with acting-out impulse control problems and with cognitive deficits. Though at risk to suffer from self-doubt, insecurity, withdrawal, anxiety, depressive tendencies, and passivity, father-bereaved individuals were more often viewed as having made a socially appropriate adjustment than were those who suffered from father-loss due to divorce.

Researchers have investigated the extent to which problems or deficiencies are associated with the loss of a parent. The notion that losing a parent during childhood may be related to positive consequences is not a popular one. Such a possibility would seem to run counter to much of what is now known about child development. Research into family relationships, however, might well produce data showing that a child may benefit from the loss of a physically or sexually abusive parent.

A broader-based conceptualization would allow for the possibilty that a parent's absence or death could have either favorable or adverse consequences (Berlinsky & Biller, 1982). A parent's death could, for example, lead a child to feel deprived and to search continually for someone to take responsibility for him. Others' reactions toward the child could well encourage self-defeating behaviors that, in their most serious form, would be associated with chronic depression. Yet another child who has lost a parent may have the same feelings of affective deprivation but still have the resources to channel them differently. Such a child may come to feel more need for self-reliance and become an energetic achiever whose attitudes and behaviors differ markedly from those of the person who becomes chronically depressed after a parent's death. Some data, for example, suggest that, under certain circumstances, some individuals may react to the early death of the father with unusual creative achievements (Albert, 1971; Cox, 1926; Eisenstadt, 1978; Martindale, 1972).

Longitudinal Perspective

The most important studies dealing with the effects of divorce on children's personal and social adjustment have been done by Hetherington, Cox, and Cox (1982) and Wallerstein and Kelly (1980b). These studies highlight the importance of the developmental and family–social system context in evaluating the influence on children of divorce and father-absence. The developmental stage of the child *and* the length of time that has elapsed since the initial family breakup must be considered in attempting to understand how boys and girls cope with the divorce process.

Hetherington, Cox, and Cox (1978a, 1982) have carried out an interesting, exhaustive, and methodologically complex longitudinal research project on the effects of divorce on young children. Because this study is so provocative and also much better controlled than other research endeavors relating to father-absence, it deserves special consideration. Hetherington, Cox, and Cox focused on the effects of divorce on families with preschool-age children. They analyzed a vast array of findings garnered from several types of procedures, including measures of social interaction at home and at school as well as observer, teacher, and peer ratings. Their longitudinal analyses included assessments of individual and family functioning at various points during the first two years after the divorce.

Hetherington, Cox, and Cox (1978a, 1982) presented evidence clearly indicating that both father-absence due to divorce and high family conflict in intact families are associated with difficulties in the personal and social adjustment of young children. On a variety of social interaction measures, children in father-absent homes and those from homes with a high degree of father-mother conflict were generally less mature and independent in their social interactions than were children from families in which there was little or only moderate father-mother conflict. Interestingly, the relative standing of the father-absent children compared to children in higher-conflict families changed during the aftermath of divorce. At one year after the divorce, the father-absent children generally were experiencing more interpersonal conflict at school and at home than were children from high-conflict, intact families. Two years after the divorce, however, the father-absent children seemed to be faring better than were the children from high-conflict families. The girls seemed to be less affected by both marital discord and father-absence than were the boys.

As has been previously mentioned, data from the Hetherington, Cox, and Cox (1978a, 1982) study revealed that father-absence, or the decreased availability of the father due to divorce, is associated with a lowered level of cognitive and sex-role functioning in boys two years after the divorce. Girls at the same age did not appear to be similarly affected. However, individual differences in the quality of mother-child interactions in the father-absent home had a strong association for both the boys' and girls' cognitive functioning, and personal and social adjustment two years after the divorce.

Wallerstein and Kelly (1974, 1976, 1980a, 1980b) have reported much interesting longitudinal data from their long-term project studying the effects of divorce on children. Their findings are based on extensive interviews with family members and the children's teachers at three intervals: just after the separation, one year later, and after five years. The parents in the 60 families involved in the study had initially participated in a six-week counseling program aimed at helping them to cope with divorce-related issues. The families from Marin County, California, were generally white, middle-class, and well educated. At the five-year follow-up, the investigators were still able to locate and interview 58 of the 60 families and 101 of the 131 children, who at that point ranged in age from seven to twenty-three. Initially after the divorce, almost all the children experienced some degree of father-absence in the sense of not living with the fathers. Over 90 percent lived with their mothers at the start of the study; at the five-year follow-up, 77 percent remained with their mothers, 11 percent (many of the older adolescents) were now living in separate residences, 8 percent lived with their fathers, and 3 percent spent a significant period of time shuffling back and forth between their parents' homes.

The wealth of findings from the Wallerstein and Kelly research is very provocative, but unfortunately no intact family comparison group was used in this study. Such a comparison (or control group) could give a much clearer frame of reference concerning the relative severity of difficulties associated with divorce. Questions could also be raised about the representativeness of the families in this study, who were predominantly middle-class and were involved in an initial six-week counseling program. Nevertheless, since the Wallerstein and Kelly study appears to have been the most extensive in terms of number and variety of children at different ages and the span of years covered, the findings should be important in stimulating more focused and controlled research efforts. For this reason we are summarizing many of the major findings.

Different Stages

In order to assess the effects of divorce on children at different developmental levels, Wallerstein and Kelly (1974, 1975, 1976) divided the children into several different groups on the basis of age at the time of the initial separation. They divided the children into six different age groups: two- to three-year-olds; three- to four-year-olds; five- and six-year-olds; seven- and eight-year-olds; nine- and ten-year-olds; and those from thirteen through eighteen. The youngest children (two- and three-year-olds) were particularly prone to regress and express bewilderment, anger, and a clinging and indiscriminate neediness toward adults in reaction to parental divorce. Regression seemed to be rather brief if children received adequate and consistent emotional involvement from adult family members. But those children who experienced continuously intense parental conflict and whose mothers were devastated by the divorce appeared very depressed and developmentally delayed a year after the divorce (Wallerstein & Kelly, 1975).

Among the three- and four-year-olds, a poor self-image and loss of self-esteem were frequent concomitants of parental divorce. A feeling of responsiblity for the parents' divorce was common among these children. More of the five- and six-year-olds, in contrast to the younger children, seemed able to weather the divorce without manifesting clear-cut developmental setbacks. Such data are, of course, very consistent with other findings indicating that children are particularly vulnerable to early father-absence beginning before the age of five (Biller, 1971a, 1974c).

Children who were seven to eight years old seemed intensely sad in response to parental divorce (Kelly & Wallerstein, 1976). They were more likely to show regressive behaviors than were the nine- and ten-year-olds but were more directly communicative about the reason for their feelings than were the younger children. The seven- and eight-year-olds appeared to be quite frightened about the consequences of the divorce and all seemed desperately to want their parents back together again, even those exposed to particularly intense and abusive parental conflict. Frequent expressions of sadness about not being with their fathers was especially prevalent for most of the seven- and eight-year-olds. A year after the divorce, the modal response seemed to be more a placid resignation than an energetic striving to make the family intact again.

As might be expected from the more mature cognitive development of nine- and ten-year-olds, they often seemed able to deal with divorce in a more controlled and realistic fashion (Wallerstein & Kelly, 1976). They were more likely to use a variety of defensive and coping patterns so that their everyday lives seemed less disrupted than those of the younger children. However, loneliness, physical symptoms, feelings of shame, and especially an intense conscious anger toward the parents was quite common among the nine- and ten-year-olds. About half of the nine- and ten-year-olds appeared to be coping adequately a year after the divorce, although they were still dealing with feelings of sadness and bitterness. In contrast, the rest of the children in this age group were severely handicapped by feelings of low self-esteem and depression, which often interferred with their peer relationships and academic functioning. Approximately one-quarter of the children were clearly more psychologically disabled one year after the divorce.

For adolescents, the divorce was characterized by much pain, anger, sadness, and often conflicts concerning their parents' sexual behavior (Wallerstein & Kelly, 1974). Those adolescents who were relatively mature at the time of the divorce and were able to maintain some distance from their parents' conflicts (by not taking sides) seemed to be doing better by the end of the first year after the divorce; they had developed a strikingly realistic perception of their parents. In contrast, those child adolescents who had emotional and social problems before the divorce tended to manifest even more serious difficulties afterward.

At the five-year follow-up, many different patterns of adaptation were evident from Wallerstein and Kelly's data (1980a, 1980b). In general, about one-third (34 percent) of the children appeared to be doing especially well personally, socially, and educationally. They had very positive self-concepts and showed generally high levels of competence, which included coping well with experiences related to the divorce. A slightly greater proportion (37 percent) expressed rather severe adjustment problems, including personal and social difficulties, with many having particularly strong feelings of loneliness, alienation, and depression. They were extremely dissatisfied with their lives, though even among this group about half were able to do adequately in some areas, such as school. The remaining children (29 percent) made what could be termed mixed adjustments, showing typical ups and downs in coping with their life situations. Although these children appeared to be making what might be called an average adaptation to school and social demands, there was some evidence that feelings about the divorce sometimes had negative effects on their self-esteem and overall competence.

Although they noted that other factors seemed to be operating for some children who made successful adjustments to the divorce, Wallerstein and Kelly (1980a, 1980b) emphasized that in the majority of cases the most important variable was the positive involvement of both the father and the mother. At the five-year postdivorce assessment, almost one-third (30 percent) of the children had an emotionally meaningful *and* warm relationship with their father. This type of positive relationship with the father was strongly associated with a healthy adjustment for both boys and girls. The investigators pointed out the importance of frequent but flexible father-child visiting patterns. Again, such findings suggest that even when divorce results in the child not living with the father, it does not mean that he or she must be "father-absent" in a general way. It is clear that many of the children who resided with their mothers still enjoyed much better relationships with their fathers than do many children from intact families.

Wallerstein and Kelly underscored the importance of the child's relationships with both parents, the support that the mother gives to the father's visitation (or that the father gives to the mother's visitation), and the ability of the divorced parents to develop ways to cooperate in dealing with the needs of their children even though they were no longer married. Only in instances where a father was seriously disturbed, or abusive, did it seem that the child was better off having no contact with him. Although there was often much initial conflict, a relationship with an interested stepfather generally appeared to have positive benefits for most children. Those over the age of eight often had particular difficulties in accepting a stepfather, but at least most of the younger children seemed to be able to enlarge their view of their family constuctively to allow for positive feelings toward both their fathers and their stepfathers (Wallerstein & Kelly, 1980a, 1980b).

Preliminary results from the ten-year follow-up of the Wallerstein and Kelly research are very provocative. Interview data suggest that children who were the youngest at the time of the divorce were doing better a decade later than their older siblings, at least with respect to dealing with memories of family conflict and being relatively optimistic about their own futures. The eleven- to seventeen-year-olds were not as negatively preoccupied with troubled memories of family life as were the nineteen- to twenty-eight-year-olds. Wallerstein (1984) emphasized that younger siblings typically had emotional and social difficulties in their initial adjustment to the divorce but now, as a group, seemed to have more psychological equilibrium than their older counterparts.

Although the younger siblings seemed to be doing surprisingly well (in comparison both to their earlier problems and to the current functioning of their older siblings), many were still quite obsessed with the persistence of parent reconciliation fantasies and with holding on to small details of very fragmented and unsatisfactory relationships with elusive fathers (Wallerstein, 1984). Some of the adolescent females, in particular, were making energetic attempts to interact with neglectful fathers with whom they essentially had had no contact since their preschool years. As the younger siblings approach and attain adulthood, they may experience some of the same divorce-related conflicts as their older siblings. When they have to deal with their own potential and new marriages and parenting responsibilities, for many of them there may be a resurgence of conflicts that were relatively quiescent during middle childhood and early adolescence.

The Mother-Child Relationship

Many factors can affect the way the child is influenced by divorce and father-absence. The quality of mothering a child receives is crucial and can become even more important when the child is paternally deprived. This section emphasizes the way in which variations in mothering may be related to individual differences in the father-absent child's behavior. The major topics considered include the influence of the mother's evaluation of the absent father, matrifocal families, and dimensions of effective mothering.

Maternal attitudes are of critical significance when a boy is father-absent. In his study of children separated from their fathers during wartime, Bach (1946,

p. 75) described "curiously ambivalent aggressive affectionate father fantasies in some cases where maternal father-typing tended to be depreciative." Wylie and Delgado (1959) analyzed the family backgrounds of aggressive fatherless boys referred to a child guidance clinic. With few exceptions, the mothers described their ex-husbands and their sons in highly similar and negative terms, emphasizing the dangerously aggressive quality of their behavior. Kopf (1970) found that poor school adjustment among father-absent boys was associated with their mothers' negative attitude toward their absent husbands. Clinical cases dramatically illustrate how the mother's consistently derogatory comments about the absent father can contribute to the development of a poor self-concept and maladaptive behavior in the child (Neubauer, 1960). As might be expected, maternal attitudes concerning the absent father influence the child's reaction if the father returns home (Biller, 1978; Stolz et al., 1954).

The mother's evaluation of the absent father is related to the reason for his absence. Feelings of resentment and loneliness can be associated with many different reasons for husband absence, but it is usually easier for a mother to talk positively about a husband who has died than about one who has divorced or deserted her (Benson, 1968; Hetherington, 1972). Discussing the absent father with her children may be very frustrating for the mother; when the father is absent because of divorce of desertion, such discussion may be even more painful. It is very difficult to maintain a positive image of the father in the face of the conflict and competition concerning children that often takes place before, during, and after a divorce. Sociocultural factors can also influence the family's reaction to father absence. For example, divorce seems to be less acceptable and more disruptive for Catholic and Jewish families than for Protestant families (Rosenberg, 1965).

The death of a father may lead to more acute behavioral reactions in children than the loss of a father through other factors, but father-absence may have general effects on personality regardless of the reason for father-absence (Biller, 1971c). If the reason for father-absence has an impact on the child's personality development, much of the effect is mediated through the mother-child relationship. Researchers should also examine why certain women whose husbands are absent remain unmarried or without consistent male companionship. Long-term father- or father-surrogate absence, as well as onset of father-absence is, in some cases, largely a function of the mother's attitudes toward men (Biller, 1974c).

The father-child relationship prior to father-absence and the child's age at the onset of the absence are also very important factors in determining the extent of the influence of maternal attitudes toward the absent father. For example, the father-absent boy who has had a positive relationship with his father up until ten years of age is less likely to be influenced by negative maternal views about the father than is the boy who was paternally deprived even before his father's absence. Unfortuantely, there have been no systematic investigations of how the reasons for father-absence at different developmental periods influence the mother-child relationship.

Matrifocal Families

Negative evaluation of the father often occurs in matrifocal families. (The female-centered family is sometimes referred to as *matriarchial,* but the term *matrifocal* seems a more accurate label.) This type of family is very common in socioeconomically poor neighborhoods and appears to be particularly prevalent among lower-class blacks (Pettigrew, 1964). There are many poor black families in which the father is a respected and integral member, but there seem to be even more in which he is absent or a relatively peripheral member (Dai, 1953; Frazier, 1939; McAdoo, 1978; Moynihan, 1965).

Sociocultural factors lessen the probability of long-term marriage relationships among lower-class blacks (Pettigrew, 1964). The instability of marriage relationships among lower-class blacks may be related to the fact that individuals with certain personality patterns are predisposed to become divorced and/or to seek out very tangential marriage relationships (Grønseth, 1957; Loeb, 1966). Their inability to tolerate close relationships with men leads some women to marry individuals who, because of their own personality functioning and/or occupational commitments, cannot get very deeply involved in family life. The wife's negative attitudes toward men can be a central factor in the husband's decision to desert her and his children.

The mother who has a positive attitude concerning masculinity, however, can facilitate her father-absent child's personality development. For instance, by praising the absent father's competence she may be able to help her son learn to value his own maleness. On the other hand, maternal depreciation of the father's masculinity can lead the young boy to avoid acting masculine, at least until he comes into contact with his peer culture.

Maternal attitudes concerning masculinity and men form a significant part of the mother-son relationship, and a mother is apt to view her husband and her son in a similar manner. Nevertheless, maternal reactions are not independent from individual differences in children. The degree to which a mother perceives her son or daughter as similar to the father is often related to the child's behavioral and physical characteristics. For example, if a boy very much resembles his father in appearance, it is more likely that the mother will expect her son's behavior to approximate his father's than if there is little father-son resemblance (Biller, 1974c).

Overprotection

Maternal overprotection is a frequent concomitant of paternal deprivation. In maternally overprotective families, the father generally plays a very submissive and ineffectual role (Levy, 1943). Fathers who are actively involved with their families are usually very critical of their children being overprotected and also serve as models for independent behavior. If the father is absent, the likelihood of maternal overprotectiveness is increased. The child's age at the onset of father-absence is an important variable. The boy who becomes father-absent during infancy or during his preschool years is more likely to be overprotected by his mother; if father-absence begins when the boy is older, however, he may be expected to take over many of his father's responsibilities.

Stendler (1952) described two critical periods in the development of over-dependency: (1) at around age nine months, when the child first begins to test whether his mother will meet his dependency needs, and (2) from two to three years of age, when the child must give up his perceived control of his mother and learn to act independently in culturally approved ways. Paternal depriva-tion during these periods can make the child particularly prone to overdepen-dence. Studying first-grade children, Stendler (1954) found that many of those who were rated as overdependent by their teachers came from families with high rates of father-absence. Among the twenty overdependent children, thir-teen lacked the consistent presence of the father in the home during the first three years of life, compared to only six of twenty in the control group. Moreover, the six relatively father-absent children in the control group had generally been without their fathers for a much shorter time than the overdependent children. The actively involved father discourages the mother's overprotective tendencies and encourages independent activity, especially in boys. Unfortunately, Stendler did not provide separate data analyses for boys and girls.

Retrospective maternal reports compiled by Stolz et al. (1954) suggested that mothers whose husbands were away in military service tended to restrict their infants' locomotor activities to a greater extent than did mothers whose husbands were present. These findings might be more meaningful, however, if the researchers had presented separate analyses in terms of the child's sex. Similar results were reported by Tiller (1958) in his study with mothers of eight- and nine-year-old Norwegian children. Compared to the mothers of the con-trol group, mothers whose husbands were seldom home (naval officers) were more overprotective, as judged by maternal interview data and by the children's responses to a structured doll play test.

The Stolz et al. (1954) and Tiller (1958) investigations suggested that pater-nally deprived and maternally overprotected boys are particularly likely to suffer in their masculine development. In a study of five-year-old children, Biller (1969a) found that mothers of father-absent boys were less encouraging of independent and aggressive behavior than were mothers of father-present boys. Many of the informal responses of the husband-absent mothers indicated that they were especially fearful of their children being physically injured (Biller, 1974c).

An intense relationship with the mother and little opportunity to observe appropriate male-female interactions are more common when the child is father-absent. A close-binding mother-son relationship in the context of paternal deprivation is a frequent factor contributing to difficulties in heterosexual relationships and to the etiology of homosexuality (Biller, 1974c, 1981a).

Sociocultural Context

Adams, Milner, and Schrepf (1984) cogently marshalled data concerning the economic and social difficulties typically encountered by the mother in the fatherless family. In a provocative article, Kriesberg (1967, p. 288) poignantly described the plight of the mother whose husband is absent:

> His absence is likely to mean that his former wife is poor, lives in poor neighborhoods, and lacks social, emotional, and physical assistance in childrearing. Furthermore, how husbandless mothers accommodate themselves to these circumstances can have important consequences for their children.

The degree to which social and economic resources are available to the husbandless mother can influence the child's interpersonal and educational opportunities. Kellam, Ensminger, and Turner's (1977) research indicates that a major difficulty in the economically disadvantaged father-absent home is that the mother is flooded with responsibilities but often has no other adult to help her. Single-mother families were much more likely to be related to children's social and personal maladjustment among poor, black children than were father-present families. Families in which there was both a mother and grandmother, however, were associated with less developmental risk for children than were families where the mother had all the child-rearing responsibility.

Paternal absence or inadequacy adds to the generally debilitating effects already experienced by the economically disadvantaged members of our society. Paternal absence or inadequacy is often associated with a lack of material resources. Economic deprivation can make it much more difficult for the father-absent child to take advantage of experiences that might positively affect his or her development. Consistent economic deprivation makes it easy to develop a defeatist attitude about one's potential impact on the environment. As Herzog and Sudia (1973) cogently pointed out, many researchers uncritically assume that a child's personality difficulties are due simply to father-absence, without also considering the impact of economic deprivation.

The mother's attitudes are related to her social and economic opportunities and are readily transmitted to the child. Maternal views about the value of education are linked to sociocultural background. As a function of differing maternal values and reinforcement patterns, middle-class, father-absent children are generally less handicapped in intellectual pursuits than are lower-class, father-absent children. Middle-class, father-absent boys appear to receive more maternal encouragement for school achievement than do lower-class, father-absent boys (Biller, 1974a, 1974b). (The interacting effect of social class and maternal behavior on the cognitive functioning of paternally deprived children was discussed in an earlier section of this chapter.)

Maternal Employment

Many effective mothers are employed and have demanding extrafamilial responsiblities. Nye (1959) reported a tendency among father-absent children whose mothers were employed to be better adjusted than those whose mothers were not employed. Kriesberg (1967, 1970) also presented evidence indicating that maternal employment among father-absent, lower-class families can be a positive factor in children's adjustment. Among low-income families, father-absent children whose mothers were employed achieved higher school grades than those whose mothers did not work. However, there was no relationship between maternal employment and school grades for children from intact families. Kriesberg's findings are very provocative, but unfortunately his comparison groups were not carefully matched and there was no analysis concerning sex of child.

In a post hoc analysis of data from her study of lower-class adolescents, Barbara Miller (1960) found that maternal employment was negatively related to masculinity of interests among father-present boys, but positively related to masculinity of interests among father-absent boys. She speculated that in the lower-class, father-absent family the mother who works may present her son with a model of competence and independence, whereas maternal employment in the lower-class, father-present family may imply to the child that the father is inadequate and an economic failure. Consistent with Miller's supposition, some studies have indicated that lower-class, father-present boys perceive their fathers less positively when their mothers work full-time than when their mothers do not work (Etaugh, 1974; Hoffman, 1974; McCord, McCord & Thurber, 1962).

The mother's having a more prestigious and well-paying job than the father has may be a disruptive factor in the boy's sex-role development, particularly if he is from a lower-class background. There does not appear to be any systematic research concerning how such factors might influence the child's personality functioning, but frequent marital conflicts are reported in families in which the wife has a job with higher status and better pay than does the husband (Hoffman, 1974). Such findings are interesting, but unfortunately there is a paucity of research dealing with the possible differential effects of various types of maternal employment on father-absent and father-present children as a function of social-class level (Biller, 1974c).

The middle-class father generally seems less threatened by his wife's employment than does the lower-class father, and is more likely to facilitate her working. King, McIntyre, and Axelson (1968) found that children's acceptance of maternal employment increased as a function of how much their fathers participated in household tasks. The father's attitude toward the mother's working and his willingness to share domestic responsibilities can be a major factor in the way maternal employment affects the child. For example, in some cases maternal employment actually helps the father become more involved with his children, while in others the child may suffer the joint effects of paternal and maternal deprivation (Biller & Meredith, 1974; Hoffman, 1983; Pleck, 1979).

Middle-class mothers are more likely to feel good about their jobs, which if full-time are usually more prestigious and well-paying than those of lower-class mothers. When a mother is happy about her job, she is more apt to have effective interactions with her family than if she considers her job unfulfilling or demeaning (Hoffman, 1974). For example, Coopersmith (1967) presented some data suggesting that regular maternal employment is related to high self-esteem in sons when mothers view their jobs positively. If a mother feels satisfied with her career, there is also much less chance of her becoming overly focused on her children. Maternal employment may be especially beneficial in allowing the mother to successfully accept the child's growing needs for independence and autonomy (Biller & Meredith, 1974).

Maternal employment, in itself, does not seem to have a clear-cut effect on the child's personality development (Hoffman, 1974, 1983). What is important is how the mother feels about being a woman, how secure she is in her basic femininity, and how this affects the way she relates to her children. The quality of the mothering or fathering that a child receives is of much more significance than whether or not the mother is employed (Biller & Meredith, 1974).

Effective Mothering

The mother-child relationship can either stimulate or hinder adequate personality development. When the child is paternally deprived, his or her relationship with the mother is particularly influential. McCord, McCord, and Thurber (1962) analyzed social workers' observations of ten- to fifteen-year-old lower-class boys. The presence of a rejecting and/or disturbed mother was related to various behavior problems (sexual anxiety, regressive behavior, and criminal acts) in father-absent boys; father-absent boys with apparently well-adjusted mothers were much less likely to have such problems.

Pedersen (1966) compared a group of emotionally disturbed boys with a group of nondisturbed boys. The boys all came from military families and ranged in age from eleven to fifteen. Relatively long periods of father-absence were common for both the emotionally disturbed and the nondisturbed children. Only in the disturbed group, however, was degree of father absence related to level of emotional disturbance (measured by the Rogers Test of Personality Adjustment). Pedersen also found that the mothers of the emotionally disturbed children were themselves more disturbed (in terms of MMPI responses) than were the mothers of the nondisturbed children. An implication of these findings is that psychologically healthy mothers may be able to counteract some of the effects of paternal deprivation.

Using a retrospective interview technique, Hilgard, Neuman, and Fisk (1960) studied adults whose fathers had died when they were children. These investigators concluded that the mother's ego strength was an important determinant of her child's adjustment as an adult. Mothers who could use both their own and outside resources and could assume some of the dual functions of mother and father with little conflict appeared to be able to deal constructively with the problems of raising a fatherless family. Such women were described as relatively feminine while their husbands were alive but as secure enough in their basic sex-role identifications to perform some of the traditional functions of the father after his death. It is important to emphasize that the mother's ego strength, rather than her warmth or tenderness, seemed to be the essential variable in her child's adjustment. For a child who is paternally deprived, excessive maternal warmth and affection may be particularly detrimental to personality development. A close-binding, overprotective relationship can severely hamper his or her opportunities for interpersonal growth.

A mother who is generally competent in interpersonal and environmental interactions, may be an important model for her child. A child's personality development, however, seems to be facilitated only if the parent allows him or her sufficient freedom and responsibility to imitate effective parental behaviors (Biller, 1969b, 1971a). Maternal encouragement of masculine behavior seems particularly important for the father-absent boy. In a study of kindergarten boys, Biller (1969a) assessed maternal encouragement of masculine behavior with a multiple-choice questionnaire. The measure of maternal encouragement of masculine behavior was significantly related to the father-absent boys' masculinity, as assessed by a game preference measure and a multidimensional rating scale filled out by teachers. Father-absent boys whose mothers accepted and reinforced assertive, aggressive, and independent behavior were more masculine than father-absent boys whose mothers discouraged such behavior. The degree of maternal encouragement for masculine behavior was not significantly related to the father-present boy's masculine development.

When the father is present, the father-son relationship is more crucial than is the mother-son relationship. It can be predicted that maternal encouragement and expectations concerning sex-role behavior are less important when the father is present than when he is absent. For instance, a warm relationship with a masculine and salient father can outweigh the effects of a mildly overprotective mother. Maternal behavior, however, is an especially significant variable in facilitating or inhibiting masculine development in the young father-absent boy. By reinforcing specific responses and expecting masculine behavior, the mother can increase the father-absent boy's perception of the incentive value of the masculine role. Such maternal behavior may, in turn, promote a positive view of males as salient and powerful, and thus motivate the boy to imitate their behavior.

Father-absence generally has more of a retarding impact on the boy's sex-role orientation than it does on his sex-role preference or his sex-role adoption. Sex-role preference and sex-role adoption seem more easily influenced by maternal behavior. If a father-absent boy receives both consistent maternal and peer group reinforcement, however, he is likely to view himself and his masculinity positively and develop a masculine sex-role orientation at least by his middle school years.

Father-absence before the child is five years old has more effect on a boy's masculine development than does father-absence after that age, and the mother-child relationship is particularly crucial when a boy becomes father-absent early in life. Biller and Bahm (1971) found that degree of perceived maternal encouragement for masculine behavior was highly related to the masculinity of junior high school boys who had been father-absent since before the age of five. (Encouragement for aggressive behavior was assessed by the subjects' responses to a Q-sort procedure, and masculinity by their self-descriptions on an adjective checklist.) Among the boys who became father-absent before the age of five, those who perceived their mothers as encouraging their assertive and aggressive behavior had much more masculine self-concepts than did those who perceived their mothers as discouraging such behavior.

Boss's (1977) work also underscores the crucial role of the mother in the father-absent family. She cogently stressed the dysfunctionality of a family that focuses on the psychological presence of a father who is actually physically absent. The absent father can be treated as if he has just left the home temporarily when in reality he is not coming back. Boss, like many others who have studied families of fathers who are missing-in-action, was impressed by the tenacity and rigidity with which some of the families support the notion of pervasive father-presence even though several years have passed since there has been any indication that the father is still alive.

It is very important for the family to resolve the ambiguity of the loss situation by redistributing various role functions and realistically acknowledging that the father is not coming back. Boss found that the emotional health of the family was highly related to the wife's ability to accept the reality that her husband was no longer an active part of the family, except in the sense that the family was still receiving a military allotment. The mother's ability to go on with her own life, strive for personal growth, have close relations with others, seek further education, and develop plans to remarry all were strongly related to her children's emotional adjustment. Of course, such data should not be seen as inconsistent with the mother supporting positive memories of the father: letters, photographs, home movies, and possessions of the father, as well as the mother's descriptions of his accomplishments, can play a very constructive role in helping children develop a concrete and positive image of a father they may have never even known (Biller, 1974c; 1978). A major implication of Boss's work is that the mother should not encourage unrealistic expectations concerning the continuing or future role of a father who is not going to return.

Hetherington, Cox, and Cox's (1978b, 1982) research revealed a wealth of data highlighting the importance of individual differences in the mother-child relationship in the father-absent home. In their study assessing the impact of divorce on young children, they found that a positive relationship with the mother was likely to be associated with healthy social and emotional adjustment in the child. Even where mother and father were in conflict, a good mother-child relationship seemed capable of serving as a buffer for the child in the father-absent home. The quality of the mother-child relationship in the father-absent home had much impact on the cognitive, sex-role, and social functioning of the young children. Mothers who were authoritative and helped present a structured and orderly environment seemed to facilitate the father-absent child's cognitive functioning and ability to develop self-control. Mothers who reinforced sex-typed behavior, encouraged independent and exploratory behavior, were low in anxiety, and had a positive view of the child's father seemed particularly likely to facilitate the father-absent boy's masculine development. On the other hand, a combination of maternal fearfulness and inhibition, maternal discouragement of independence, and maternal disapproval of the father were found to be associated with anxious dependency and a feminine pattern of behavior in some of the father-absent boys.

Research Implications

At this juncture we briefly highlight *some* of the major research avenues that are worthy of further exploration in the attempt to understand the complex impact of father-absence and divorce on development. A developmental, longitudinal, and multivariate perspective is necessary in order to grasp the complex influences of father-absence. Obviously, carefully selected comparison groups are needed, and any approach should take into account process variables and consider possible advantages as well as deficits that the father-absent child may encounter. Researchers need to consider the potential interactions of biological-constitutional, family, and sociocultural variables.

A longitudinal-developmental approach may help give more attention to both genetic and prenatal environmental factors. Further scientific advances could lead to a clearer indication of the father's genetic contribution, even if he no longer plays a direct behavioral role in the child's life. For instance, how are positive and negative temperamental patterns in the child influenced by the father's genetic contribution? There is some evidence that father-absence may be at least indirectly associated with maternal stress factors during the prenatal period, which may in turn have negative effects on fetal development. For example, among poor expectant mothers, those without husbands seem particularly unlikely to receive adequate prenatal care. Even among unwed couples, the expectant father can give the expectant mother an emotional source of support and, in a practical way, may be a factor in her going to a doctor (Biller & Salter, 1982). Some research evidence has indicated that the expectant father's death during the prenatal period is associated with a greater probability of behavior disorders in the child (Huttunen & Niskanen, 1978). It is possible that in some cases a highly negative maternal stress reaction may damage the fetus and/or that the mother who lacks the father's support during the birth process is less likely to nurture the newborn infant adequately. These "explanations," though speculative, could provoke some exciting research projects.

It is important to consider the child's characteristics if we are to understand the impact of father-absence. We need more research that will assess carefully how sex and temperament differences and level of intellectual and social functioning may influence children's adaptation to father-absence. Research by Biller (1974c), for example, suggested that young children who are highly physically and intellectually competent at the onset of father-absence are not as handicapped as are children who are average or below in their developmental level. We need more data on so-called invulnerable children. The child's temperament and behavior certainly can have a big impact on the quality of the mother-child relationship and other adult-child relationships. Researchers need to be aware of various family-structure and social system variables, including the sibling composition of the family and the availability of surrogate models. The child's characteristics and the parents' difficulty in dealing with them may actually be a factor contributing to the father's unavailability and/or parental divorce.

The reason for the father's absence is another important variable. Divorce seems to have very different consequences for the child than the father's death or his absence because of employment. As has been emphasized in this chapter, the mother's reaction to her husband's absence can be very influential. There needs to be more research focusing on how the reasons for divorce, and the perceptions of these reasons, may relate to the child's adaptation. How much difference does it make if the same-sex noncustodial parent is perceived by the child as the parent who initiated the divorce? Such variables need to be considered in a social systems context.

Family Patterns

Researchers comparing father-absent families and intact families can more carefully analyze individual differences in family functioning among different types (and subtypes) of family patterns. Although studying the father-absent family may be of heuristic value in suggesting certain functions of fathers that may not be fulfilled, such research is no substitute for direct analysis of the father's complex role in the intact family. We can profit from much more research on family dynamics in both father-present and father-absent homes, with particular emphasis on parent-child-sibling interactions. Other sources of interpersonal influence, including extended family and peers, should also be considered.

An approach that takes into account the developmental stages of various family members, as well as the quality of family functioning, could be very revealing in understanding the impact of divorce on the child. For example, the reaction of different individuals (and sets of individuals) in the family at various times, pre- and postdivorce, may greatly influence the child's short- and/or long-term adaptation. A longitudinal perspective will help differentiate short-term setbacks or spurts in development from longer-term deficits or gains in later functioning. Certainly a more limited cross-sectional approach can at least consider the impact of divorce and father-absence on children at specific developmental periods (Wallerstein, 1984).

It is very clear from data reviewed in this and the previous chapter that divorce does not necessarily mean that a child will be "father-absent." Many fathers visit and remain involved with their children; still others have shared, joint, or full custody of their children. An analysis of different types of custody patterns can help us learn more about how the father's availability and quality of functioning (along with the interaction of other factors) influences the child whose parents are divorced (Santrock & Warshak, 1979).

Research on father-absence should also consider potential benefits of what is usually viewed as an unfortunate family situation. In some families, the loss of a father may actually have favorable effects on the child's development. A parent involved in an unhappy marriage who is released through a spouse's death may consequently have more time, energy, and resources to devote to his or her child. The loss of a parent who has been sexually or physically abusive, rejecting, or merely uninterested, may have positive ramifications for the child's self-concept and emotional adjustment (Berlinsky & Biller, 1982).

Even if the parent's absence actually represents a loss of constructive influence, a child's development could still be enhanced under certain circumstances. Of necessity, the child could become more independent, could develop superior problem-solving skills, and could be prompted to strive for higher achievement in order to cope with the loss. The few studies that have attempted to link parental bereavement with achievement indicate the potential for this line of research (Eisenstadt, 1978).

Most needed in order to understand more fully how a child is affected by father-loss are longitudinal inquiries. Research following a child, ideally from before a father's absence through adulthood, would indicate whether immediate effects endure, whether they change in nature, and how environmental factors interact with the outcomes. For example, Bendicksen and Fulton's (1975) work suggests that the intensity of effects of parental death may lessen with age.

Following a number of groups of children who have experienced different types of father-loss at different ages would provide even more complete data, possibly indicating critical periods of loss relative to different areas of functioning (Biller, 1971a, 1974c, 1981a).

Longitudinal research could be designed to follow the development of large groups of father-absent children, as well as children with various qualities of father involvement. Ideally, subjects would be diverse with respect to ethnicity, religion, socioeconomic status, age, temperament, and intellectual level. Such a selection process would ensure inclusion of subjects from various backgrounds, so that family and other situational variables could be studied extensively. Assessment, prior and subsequent to father loss, using standardized instruments, could be conducted with respect to a wide range of abilities, interests, affective tendencies, adjustment, and social and sexual patterns. Long- and short-term effects of father-loss could be assessed by following children of different ages through different stages of adulthood. There could be an analysis of individual, family, and situational factors that mediate the potential negative effects of father-loss. Information about children who are particularly vulnerable or resilient following father-loss would also become available.

Future research should lead to a much clearer delineation of the kinds of maternal behaviors, and the dimensions of the mother-child relationship, that are relevant to the father-absent child's personality development. It is important for investigators studying the impact of father-absence to examine systematically the possible differential effects of the mother-child relationship as a function of the child's sex, temperament, and developmental level. Data from such studies can be useful for programs designed to maximize the interpersonal and intellectual potential of father-absent children, and to help mothers in father-absent families to become more effective parents.

11
Intervention and Prevention

T here is a great need to develop a comprehensive, coordinated set of guidelines to help families that have suffered from child maltreatment and, moreover, to take a preventative and educational approach in reaching out to families at risk. A major thrust in dealing with child maltreatment must involve addressing the rampant pattern of paternal deprivation in our society. More support needs to be given to single-parent families, to children and adults affected by divorce, and to expectant and potential parents (Biller & Meredith, 1974; Biller & Salter, 1985). In particular, we are advocating a focus on prevention, especially for educating potential fathers, expectant fathers, and new fathers.

We are concerned not only with obvious forms of paternal deprivation, child maltreatment, and individual and family pathology, but also with optimizing parenting skills and giving adults and children the opportunity to grow and reach their full potential. We are encouraging didactic-experiential programs that provide opportunities to discuss feelings and experiences in a supportive group context and also include factual information about parenthood and child and adult development (Gershon & Biller, 1977). Such programs can begin in the context of family life education in our schools for adolescents (and even for much younger children), who may relatively soon be assuming parental responsibilities.

We are not suggesting any decrease in efforts to set up programs for females, but we are emphasizing that males should be included. Moreover, we are arguing that child-rearing education opportunities that can attract men are vital if we are to reduce child maltreatment and paternal deprivation. Both fathers and prospective fathers must be dealt with directly in prevention programs. We cannot continue to focus treatment, rehabilitation, and prevention efforts on mothers alone.

The first part of this chapter is devoted to a critique of intervention programs that are specifically targeted at reducing the incidence of child maltreatment. There is a general analysis of intervention strategies, and different treatment modalities (such as individual, parent-group, child, family, and milieu therapy) are reviewed with respect to therapeutic change processes. Unfortunately, most of the programs discussed in the first part of this chapter are directed only at parents who abuse their children physically and are not aimed at the broader dimensions of child maltreatment, including various types of paternal deprivation.

The later sections of this chapter are focused on education, treatment, and prevention efforts that can help to alleviate problems associated with the link between child maltreatment and paternal deprivation. It is our contention that a major effort needs to be made to make men as well as women responsible and accountable for rearing children. There must be greater cooperation between the social system and the family system, and between fathers and mothers, in order to decrease the incidence of child maltreatment associated with inadequate fathering. This chapter contains some guidelines for effective fathering that are particularly relevant to a parent-education perspective.

Alleviating Maltreatment

Efforts at intervention have not kept pace with the dramatic increase in reported incidents of child maltreatment (Green, 1978). Intervention programs have been constrained by two related factors. First, most social service agencies are limited to coordinating the provision of services rather than delivering direct treatment because of exhaustive caseloads (U.S. Department of Health, Education and Welfare, 1977). Second, the technology of psychotherapeutic interventions for maltreatment situations is in its early stages of development (Williams, 1980a). In general, there has been the delivery of inadequate treatment programs, which have remained relatively ineffective in ameliorating most abusive situations (Starr, 1979).

The ineffectiveness of most intervention programs appears to be related to their theoretical shortcomings, more specifically to the unitary perspectives of child maltreatment that have been discussed in previous chapters. An interactionist perspective suggests that child maltreatment does not reflect simple medical or social pathology (Frodi & Lamb, 1980a). With the realization that the maltreatment situation comprises a complex network of interactive factors, intervention programs must be constructed that address the broad etiological structure of this phenomenon. Most professionals agree about the need for interdisciplinary and interagency cooperation in developing effective remediative programs (Newberger, 1975). But most clinicians are hampered by excessive caseloads, poor community resources, and a limited technology that potentially detracts from treatment efforts (Starr, 1979; Williams, 1980b).

An example of the deleterious effects that current theoretical shortcomings may exert on intervention is reflected in the treatment model focusing on changing maternal personality. Such a perspective is articulated by Polansky, DeSaix, and Sharlin (1972) in their guide for child welfare workers. This treatment strategy focuses on just the individual therapy of the mother. It is derived from personality profiles that they suggest as characteristic of maltreating mothers. According to Polansky, DeSaix, and Sharlin, most maltreating mothers represent one of the following typologies: the apathetic-futile mother, the impulse-ridden mother, the mentally retarded mother, the reactive depressive mother, or the psychotic mother. Their guidelines for protective workers fail to consider characteristics of the child, the father, and the family structure; community variables; economic factors; and other relevant factors that may be involved in the maltreatment environment.

Helfer (1975) emphasized that it would be extremely difficult to find enough therapists to address child maltreatment on a one-to-one basis. The economic aspects of such a service delivery system are also impractical on a large scale (Parke & Collmer, 1975). A therapeutic orientation directed toward the treatment of individual parents cannot adequately address the complex etiological structure of most maltreatment incidents.

Fontana and Besharov (1977, p. 53), in a discussion of treatment approaches, offer the following guidelines for clinicians:

1. Eliminate or diminish the social or environmental stresses.

2. Lessen the adverse psychological impact of the social factors on the parent.

3. Reduce the demands on the mother to a level which is within her capacity.

4. Provide emotional support . . . instruction in maternal care and aid in learning to plan for, assess and meet the needs of the infant.

5. Resolve or diminish the inner psychic world.

This intervention framework at least includes several potential causal variables in the maltreatment situation and encourages the worker to investigate beyond the intrapsychic world of the abuser.

Several potentially important factors are still ignored within Fontana and Besharov's guidelines—most notably child, sibling, and paternal factors. Nevertheless, their approach does attempt to intervene in the maltreatment environment from a multidisciplinary base and represents an initial effort to integrate characterological and sociological factors. These researchers developed their intervention model through their work at the New York Foundling Hospital Center for Parent and Child Development. Their program offers a residential facility for both parent and child in order to avoid separation, as well as intensive individual and group treatment components. This program is noteworthy because of a broad theoretical base that draws on the implications of various research perspectives.

Most intervention studies do not use any empirical system of measuring treatment effectiveness and fail to gather follow-up data to assess recidivism rates (Parke & Collmer, 1975). The methodological shortcomings of most treatment programs include a lack of systematic data collection, unrepresentative sampling techniques, and descriptive summaries that fail to detail the program's criteria for success (Starr, 1979; Williams, 1980a).

Therapy for Maltreating Parents

Most parent therapy programs have been derived from the psychiatric model of maltreatment (Belsky, 1978b). This perspective focuses primarily on characterological deficits within abusive parents and attempts modifications of their character structure (see chapter 4). For example, Green (1978) emphasized the need to address and remediate characterological factors such as masochism, poor self-esteem, infantile needs, hostility, and withdrawal. Therapy is delivered either through outpatient services or in residential programs. Most individual therapeutic models require a minimum of one session per week, with the duration of treatment varying from several months to three to five years.

Steele and Pollock (1968) described a long-term psychiatric treatment study of abusive parents. Their theoretical model of maltreatment is derived from a psychodynamic framework. Their treatment program focuses on psychoanalytic therapy and adopts what could be considered a consciousness-raising perspective (Prochaska, 1984). There is no empirical documentation of therapeutic effectiveness beyond the level of subjective description. Several patients moved away or lived too far away to maintain continuous treatment, although Steele and Pollock generally asserted that the great majority of therapy interventions with parents were quite successful.

The intensive individual therapy model is one of the least cost-effective means of clinical service delivery. Another difficulty is the absence of reliable outcome studies, which subsequently limits the conclusions that may be generated concerning the effectiveness of treatment programs (Justice & Justice, 1976). This model remains popular, however, mandating the completion of comparative evaluations that investigate the relative impact of different intervention strategies.

Several parent intervention programs have applied cognitive-behavioral principles to the specific problems of child maltreatment (e.g., Denicola, 1980; Gilbert, 1976). These programs are generally of shorter duration than those based on insight-oriented models, and they specifically target abusive behavior rather than addressing broader and more generalized dependent measures. For example, Sandler, Van Dercor, and Milhoan (1978) developed and evaluated an intervention program that included contingent reinforcement for positive parent-child interactions and a parental training component designed to shape more appropriate child-rearing behaviors. The program was carried out over a two-month period with two physically abusive single mothers. In both instances, graphic data were presented documenting the success of the program. More important, these approaches represent a reformulation of theoretical bases for intervention programs (Jensen, 1976). The focus on behavioral and cognitive processes shifts the theoretical orientation into a concrete model that emphasizes environmental determinants and skill training, as opposed to the restructuring of hypothetical personality characteristics.

Additional research is necessary in order to explore the impact of different change processes with different populations within varying settings. The nonbehavioral programs may add behavioral observations, attitude change measures, self-monitoring charts, or other relevant means of assessment. The important point is that intervention programs employing verbal change processes can still develop relevant and valid indexes of change (Solomon, 1982).

Parent Groups

Parent self-help groups have become a popular form of intervention through the efforts of the Parents Anonymous organization (Collins, 1978). Parents Anonymous originated in California in 1969 and has since expanded into a national organization with more than five hundred chapters. The program involves weekly group sessions where parents can: "talk about their behavior toward their children, their values, anger, hurt feelings, experiences growing up, and any other issue that may result from a parent abusing or neglecting a child" (Seals, 1980, p. 39). The groups usually maintain two leaders: an outside sponsor who is familiar with issues surrounding child maltreatment, and a parent who has successfully completed participation in a Parents Anonymous group.

Justice and Justice (1976) argued that child maltreatment is most effectively dealt with through a group treatment model. Although these researchers offer no empirical evidence for the supremacy of the group model over other treatment modalities, they suggest that child maltreatment is a social and psychological problem. Therefore, group treatment offers parents the opportunity to "acquire the social skills and the sense of belonging and acceptance they so badly need" (Justice & Justice, 1976, p. 216). Others, such as Feinstein, Paul, and Esmial (1964), have noted that parent groups provide the opportunity for meaningful social experience for otherwise isolated parents.

Parent self-help groups focus on consciousness raising as a change process. Paulson and Chaleff (1973) stated that their role as group leaders is to represent "surrogate parents" because of their age difference in relation to the participating parents (the therapists were in their fifties; the parents' average age was twenty-six). Their clinical focus was on increasing "intimacy, empathy, trust and 'mothering' " (p. 512). Collins (1978) also described a stage model of consciousness-raising activities for participants in Parents Anonymous:

1. Being different and feeling guilty.
2. Moral identification.
3. Apprenticeship and moral frustration.
4. Becoming a self-acknowledged child abuser.
5. Being different and feeling competent.
6. Moral self-acceptance and becoming a recruiter.

Paulson and Chaleff's (1973) emphasis is upon cathartic processes while Collins (1978) stresses utilization of a social learning model to account for behavior change. Paulson and Chaleff encouraged parents to "cry out the agony of their emotional pain" (p. 39); Collins stated that the "real accomplishment is exposing the apprentice to a normative pattern of response to stimulus" (p. 90). The stimulus (that is, the child) remains the same but the parents learn new response patterns as "the sponsor . . . and often the chairpersons serve as models for the member" (p. 90).

Neither Paulson and Chaleff (1973) or Collins (1978) offered empirical data concerning outcome variables. The emphasis on consciousness-raising processes, as opposed to observable behavior change, may have discouraged them from gathering quantifiable indexes of therapeutic progress. There are severe limitations concerning the conclusions that can be drawn from either investigation, and there is no presentation of follow-up data. Sound evaluation programs are required that would include a longitudinal analysis of treatment effects.

Therapy for Maltreated Children

Most theories of child maltreatment have placed primary emphasis on parent psychopathology (Friedrich & Boriskin, 1976). Other researchers, however, have investigated the role of the child in the maltreatment environment (Steele, 1980). Indeed, a multitude of child characteristics have been correlated with child maltreatment, as discussed in chapter 3. Prematurity, mental retardation, and physical and emotional handicaps are among the characteristics associated with greater risk for child maltreatment (Klein & Stern, 1971; Elmer & Gregg, 1967).

Steele (1980) has noted that an unfortunate by-product of investigations into relevant child characteristics has been the subtle implication that maltreatment of such children can almost be forgiven "in as much as the infant's fault explains the parent action" (p. 67). The potential certainly exists for intervention programs to target the exceptional child without fully evaluating the total family system and other determinants such as situational characteristics and community variables. The emphasis on the exceptional nature of the child may offer subtle condonement of the maltreatment situation and can detract from a more valid framework of multiple causation. In practice, this attitude toward child maltreatment has remained infrequent simply because there have been few programs employing child therapy as a primary treatment modality. (We are very skeptical about treating the child in isolation of intervention with the family system.)

Although Steele's (1980) concern about using the child as a cause and subsequent excuse for maltreatment is important, a positive outcome has been the recognition that the child may gain from therapeutic intervention (Beezley,

Martin, & Kempe, 1976). This intervention strategy encourges the delivery of services that do not terminate after the physical environment has been deemed safe for the child since the earlier maltreatment may continue to inferfere with various aspects of the child's functioning (Barahal, Waterman, & Martin, 1981). As detailed in chapters 7 through 10, there are long-term developmental implications for the child who has suffered from maltreatment and paternal deprivation. The justification for direct clinical intervention is that therapy may assist the child in overcoming the deleterious effects of maltreatment through the establishment of a physically secure and emotionally supportive environment.

The preeminence of the psychiatric model has influenced child intervention programs in a way similar to its effect on those dealing with abusive parents. Most intervention literature dealing with children emphasizes such concepts as ego development, self-concept, and other characerological structures. A noticeable difference is that cognitive-behavioral strategies have rarely been applied to child intervention programs, whereas the recent adult literature reflects a variety of therapeutic change processes. The same array of methodological difficulties that exist with treatment modalities for adults also exist in the child intervention literature. Most studies offer subjective assessment of treatment outcomes, fail to use comparison groups, and do not control for confounding variables such as unrepresentative sampling and observer bias (Solomon, 1982).

Most studies involving maltreated children include analyses of demographic variables and epidemiological data rather than the potential treatment effects of clinical intervention: "By and large, children are seen in passing and are excluded from the therapeutic process" (U.S. Department of Health, Education and Welfare, 1977, p. 169). Even less seems to be understood about the intervention processes with maltreated children than with other treatment populations. Although there are several intervention programs described in the literature that target the abused child as the primary recipient of services, few of these offer an empirical analysis of treatment effects. Most publications dealing with these intervention programs are descriptive summaries based on the investigators' clinical impressions of the abused child.

Programs that focus on the resolution of emotional difficulties typically encourage the maltreated child to express his or her anger and offer a supportive environment in which the child can resolve intrapsychic conflicts arising from the maltreatment (Flanzraich & Steiner, 1980; In & McDermott, 1978). The primary difficulty with studies evaluating these programs is the absence of quantifiable indexes of change. Levitt (1971) has emphasized that methodological shortcomings generally characterize therapy outcome studies on children. The absence of conceptual models of behavior and attitude change, inadequate or absent comparison groups, and inappropriate nosological systems are among the methodological difficulties encountered in attempts to evaluate the impact of child therapy programs. These difficulties are generally applicable to investigations relating to child maltreatment.

An interest in child intervention studies is a relatively recent development. Historically, most clinicians have addressed child maltreatment by doing therapy or counseling with the parent (Herzberger, Potts, & Dillon, 1981). The more recent focus on the child's environment and potential dfficulties in development is a significant achievement. More attention in future investigations needs to be directed toward such factors as the developmental stage and sex of the child, home environment and neighborhood characteristics, and the manner in which these variables interact with different treatment programs.

Milieu and Family Approaches

Milieu and family therapy programs are combined in this discussion because the latter is usually a treatment component of the former. Beezley, Martin, and Alexander (1976) noted that clinical intervention with abusive families usually requires more outreach and service availability than other forms of treatment. The involvement of more than one family member necessitates that the treatment plan incorporate the needs of several participants. In order to meet these needs, a significant amount of clinical time and resources must be committed to the family. Family therapy usually becomes one component of a treatment package that involves other intervention procedures. Home visitors, day care, vocational counseling, and lay therapy are among the program components that are frequently intergrated into a comprehensive milieu model.

A difficulty inherent in evaluating milieu and family programs is the absence of outcome data. This limitation, which has been noted in the discussions of each of the previous treatment models, becomes even more apparent in light of the rapid increase in the number of milieu therapy programs, each offering a different array of clinical services. Initially it may be helpful for evaluators to investigate the contribution of each component (such as day care) before offering general statements about the overall effectiveness of the program.

During 1978 and 1979, the Blosser Home Program served thirty families, twenty-three of which consisted of single parents and their children (Wood, 1980). Parents participated in a comprehensive program including counseling, recreation, housekeeping, and child care. There was no time limit to the treatment. Participants could remain in the program until the family and staff felt certain that major problems have been resolved. Wood (1980) indicated that one-half of those accepted failed to complete the program. This may not be unexpected given the level of commitment required and the intense supervision that a family received while in residence.

The theoretical premise behind the Blosser Home Program is that maltreatment arises from disturbances in the bonding process. Consequently, the program's objectives are twofold. First, it attempts to foster an emotional connection between parent and child. Second, it assumes an educative function in instructing the parent in more effective parent-child interactions. Consciousness-raising processes, and expanding parental choices through modeling techniques, appear to be the program's major intervention strategies. The program's comprehensive treatment model may also permit the potential incorporation of behavioral techniques. Such strategies as self-monitoring procedures and positive reinforcement of the child's behavior can increase parental effectiveness (Solomon, 1982).

Outpatient Programs

There are several examples of outpatient milieu therapy programs in the literature. We review two programs that have been relatively well documented: Galdston's (1975) Parents' Center Project in Boston, and the Bowen Center in Chicago (Holmes & Kagle, 1977). The Parents' Center Project uses two separate but related intervention procedures; a therapeutic day care unit for children and a weekly parents group. The purpose of the project is to offer concurrent treatment to children and parents while maintaining the integrity of the family unit. This procedure affords the opportunity to monitor the abused children closely and involve parents in a regular schedule of group therapy.

The theoretical premise for this program is psychodynamic. Weekly group meetings encourage the parents to verbalize difficulties in their marriage, relational problems, early childhood issues, and other personally relevant concerns. A clinical objective of this program is to resolve the parents' ambivalence about their parental role. More specifically, clinical content focuses on intraindividual dynamic issues and underlying conflict that disturbs the parenting process. Consciousness-raising at the experiential level (feedback) is the primary change process encouraged by this program.

Galdston (1975) offers a comprehensive description of his program's organizational structure, but his discussion of the program's effectiveness does not include a systematic framework for assessing outcome variables, nor is the need for follow-up data suggested or offered. Another potential limitation is the lack of integration between parents and children within the project's treatment program. Indeed, Galdston observed: "There was no demonstrable correlation between the progress made by the child and that made by his parents" (p. 380). This conclusion is limited to observations completed within the project's facilities. It would seem that any progress attained by either the child or the parent will likely be nullified should the other party maintain maladaptive behavior patterns at home. Consequently, it would appear that the integration of the parents' and children's treatment components is essential in order to facilitate concurrent improvement and reinforce mutual gains.

Another outstanding example of an outpatient milieu program was the Bowen Center Project in Chicago (Holmes & Kagle, 1977). Six program objectives were cited:

1. Provide treatment to parents.
2. Provide therapeutic and supplemental parenting services to children.
3. Develop a model of service integration within a single multipurpose center.
4. Develop a treatment model to promote ego development and functioning for children and families.
5. Provide training and consultation to the Department of Children and Family Services.
6. Provide consultation to other agencies seeking to develop services for abusive and neglectful families.

Of the ninety-eight families served by the Bowen Center from 1971 to 1974, half were led by single mothers. Most of the families were on welfare and had more than four children. From the perspective of Prochaska's (1984) model of therapeutic change processes, the program emphasizes consciousness-raising interventions. The program encourages intraindividual dynamic change, such as addressing difficulties in object relations, impulse control, and other aspects of ego functioning.

The broad range of service components in the Bowen Center Project represented an ambitious effort to respond to child maltreatment. The center also attempted to fulfill an important resource role for the training of personnel from other agencies, but the Department of Children and Family Services criticized the center because of the extensive cost and relatively few families that were served. Another potentially serious limitation was the active encouragement of a dependency relationship between the center and the parent (Holmes & Kagle, 1977). The explicit avoidance of expectations for behavior change may encourage parents to remain dependent and reduce the number of families potentially served. The use of consciousness-raising techniques may be effectively augmented by other time-limited approaches emphasizing personal responsiblity.

Interactional Perspective

The theoretical shortcomings that exist in the field of child maltreatment hinder the development of effective preventive and remediative programs (Zigler, 1980). Researchers are not certain which treatment variables are most effectively targeted under particular conditions. Nevertheless, in light of the high rate of child maltreatment, it is imperative that intervention and prevention efforts continue despite current theoretical and research limitations.

The interactive model presented in chapter 4 (figure 4–1) offers a perspective concerning the levels of intervention that must be targeted. Using an interactive approach, Gil (1979) and Alvy (1975) suggested that researchers investigate abusive conditions at three levels: home abuse, institutional abuse (such as that in schools and juvenile courts), and societal abuse. This latter variable refers to the collective attitudes held by our society that deny children an optimum environment in which to mature and to protect their civil rights adequately. Examples of societal abuse are racial and social class discrimination and the existence of substandard child-rearing conditions in improverished neighborhoods. Paternal deprivation is a major interacting factor contributing to such conditions (Biller & Meredith, 1974).

Studies that have been discussed in this book may be useful in guiding the planning of intervention strategies. For example, at the family level, Burgess and Conger (1978) found that maltreating parents demonstrate lower rates of interaction and tend to emphasize negative issues in their relationships with children (see chapter 4). Wolfe, Sandler, and Kaufman (1981) have constructed a successful training program for maltreating parents that is based on the premise that maltreatment may reflect inadequate parenting skills (poor knowledge of child development, unrealistic expectations, ineffective coping and disciplinary techniques). Potential fathers, expectant fathers, and new fathers have especially strong needs for parent education programs (Biller & Meredith, 1974; Biller & Salter, 1985).

On an exosystem (community) level, Garbarino (1980) has investigaged the role of neighborhood variables in child maltreatment (see chapter 4). Neighborhoods that are weak in interpersonal and social support resources are more likely to manifest higher rates of child maltreatment and are more likely to exacerbate the isolating effects of economic impoverishment (that is, low-income families are less able to draw on other resources than high-income families). An especially profound lack in such neighborhoods is the dearth of effective fathers and other competent adult male role models (Biller, 1971a, 1974c). Large families in such circumstances have fewer financial and coping resources and are also less likley to respond successfully to clinical interventions. Garbarino's (1980) data contain implications for mental health professionals concerning the need for social support services in low-resource neighborhoods. Examples are day care programs, community groups, baby-sitting, transportation, and recreational programs. Educating maltreating families concerning the existence of neighborhood support services may be an important intervention strategy in reducing the risk of future maltreatment. It is crucial that men as well as women begin to take more responsibility at both the community and family levels for the welfare of children (Biller, 1974c; Biller & Meredith, 1974).

Social Change

At this point it may be valuable to offer the "ideal" intervention model based on the data and concepts reviewed in this book. This broad-based program would focus on the multiple intervention strategies necessary for the elimination of child maltreatment. Altering society's response to children involves the modification of several long-standing notions about childhood, especially those concerning stereotypes about fathers as well as the reformulation of social priorities. Widespread cultural change is required concerning the nature of social, community, and parental interactions with children. Children and families must be accepted as the most important social priority, with generous funding for the development of educational and recreational resources. Such a cultural shift in appraising children, and the relationships between fathers and children, may require extensive government and public support that encourages media attention, program development, and child advocacy legislation. It is important, however, for families not to feel that their value systems and right to rear their children are being infringed on or somehow programmed by government intrusion (Biller & Meredith, 1974; Lamb & Sagi, 1983).

While government and public support for attending to the needs of children is being strengthened, concurrent efforts must be directed to community structure. As noted previously, the structure of a community must be evaluated in terms of its ability to provide for the needs of children and ways in which fathers and other men can become more active participants.

Garbarino's (1980) extensive investigations of community variables emphasized the importance of social support systems in reducing child maltreatment. Mental health programs whose staff consult to other agencies, conduct parenting programs, and attend to the specific needs of neighborhoods may help parents develop more effective means of interacting with children. Intervention with maltreating parents may also be more adequately accomplished within this "community perspective," especially if there is a greater focus on the total family system and the quality of father-mother-child interactions. Schools have also been identified by several researchers as key components of the community intervention and prevention process (e.g., Biller, 1971a, 1974c; Garbarino & Gilliam, 1980; Gershon & Biller, 1977; O'Block, Billimoria, & Behan, 1981; Volpe, 1980).

The educational setting may have more potential for exerting a successful impact on child-rearing practices than any other social institution (Kline, Cole, & Fox, 1981). Professionals in a school setting can help to identify maltreated children, establish a referral network, and organize prevention programs. Parent preparation classes for both male and female students and direct counseling and referral of abusive families can be organized successfully within the school. Kline, Cole, and Fox (1981) emphasized that child maltreatment is a school problem as well as a family problem.

An all-encompassing definition of child maltreatment is very difficult to articulate. A more meaningful approach is the generation of a continuum perspective that encourages researchers to attend to the maltreatment environment and its attendant complexities (see especially chapters 2 through 6).

Maltreatment is most meaningfully conceptualized as the result of potential interactions among sociocultural values, legal frameworks, family systems, and community environments. The continuum model discourages researchers from regarding maltreatment as an all-or-none phenomenon and extends the responsibility for maltreatment from the parent to include the community and social contexts. We certainly feel that parents should be held accountable, and strongly argue that more responsibility should be placed on fathers, but we also recognize the significance of extrafamilial variables.

An interactional model of child maltreatment focuses on multiple levels of causation and, most important, on the interactions among these variables. This theoretical perspective is consistent with the continuum definition in its emphasis on multiple determinants.

The time has arrived for researchers to follow through on multivariate models when investigating and intervening in child maltreatment. Maltreatment does not reflect a unitary pathology, isolated within one component of the child's environment. Factors pertaining to both fathers and mothers and their relationship to each other, community variables, child characteristics, and social values are components of the interactional model (see figure 4–1). These factors exist within a dynamic, constantly changing framework that can potentially elicit maltreatment.

It is crucial to remember that maltreatment may be influenced by the child's characteristics and biologically related problems. Public health preventative programs may help to alleviate the incidence of negative prenatal factors and early childhood medical difficulties. For example, educating potential and expectant fathers and mothers to the risks of poor prenatal care and the importance of the quality of the prebirth husband-wife relationship can do much to make infants and young children more rewarding for their parents and can help to strengthen the family system (Biller, 1974a; Biller & Meredith, 1974; Biller & Salter, 1985, 1986).

An important implication of the interactional model is that intervention for child maltreatment must be targeted at different levels. The bases for maltreatment are interwoven into the total fabric of our society. Biological, cultural, parental, and community factors, each of which reinforces maltreatment must be addressed and reformulated in terms of their relationship to both fathers' and mothers' roles in child rearing. Recognition of the basic rights of all children to a supportive, nonthreatening, and nurturing environment, including the presence of a positively involved father as well as a mother, is a crucial step.

Dealing with Paternal Deprivation

Since paternally deprived individuals are overrepresented among those who are maltreated and who have psychological problems, it is not surprising that they are found in abundance in the case reports of psychotherapists. Despite the lack of controlled research, there are many illuminating descriptions of how clinicians have attempted to help father-absent or inadequately fathered children (e.g., Cath, Gurwitt, & Ross, 1982; Forrest, 1966, 1967; Green, 1974; Meerloo, 1956; Neubauer, 1960; Wylie & Delgado, 1959).

Glueck & Glueck (1950) reported that many delinquent boys who form a close relationship with a father-surrogate resolve their antisocial tendencies. Similarly, Trenaman (1952) found that young men who had been chronically delinquent while serving in the British army improved as a function of their relationships with father surrogates. A young father-absent child may be particularly responsive to a male therapist or role model because of his motivation for male companionship. Rexford (1964), in describing the treatment of young antisocial children, noted that therapists are more likely to be successful with father-absent boys than with boys who have strongly identified with an emotionally disturbed, criminal, or generally inadequate father.

There are many organizations, including Big Brothers, YMCA, Boy Scouts, athletic teams, camps, churches, and settlement houses, which provide paternally deprived children with meaningful father-surrogates. Additional professional consultation and more community support (especially more father-surrogates), would allow these organizations to be of even greater benefit to many more children (Biller, 1974c; Jenkins, 1979).

Even in the first few years of life, the child's personality development can be very much influenced by the degree and type of involvement of a father or father-surrogate. Group settings such as day care centers can be used as vehicles to provide father-surrogates for many more children (*both boys and girls*). The facilities of such organizations as Big Brothers and the YMCA could also be used to help younger children come into contact with effective father-surrogates.

Children confined to institutions are especially in need of warm relationships with competent father-surrogates. Institutionalized children, including those who are orphaned or emotionally disturbed, can benefit from a larger proportion of interaction with competent and positively involved adult males. For example, Nash's (1965) data suggest that having institutionalized children live in a situation in which they are cared for and supervised by a husband-wife team is beneficial for their personality development. Keller and Alper (1970) have contributed many useful guidelines for adults working with delinquent children in institutional settings, group homes, and halfway houses. Many of the same variables that are involved in children's social learning and imitation within the family setting are important to consider in an analysis of the impact of child care workers in residential settings (Portnoy, Biller, & Davids, 1972).

Family Intervention

The father should be encouraged to participate in the assessment and treatment of the child's problem. In many cases, the father's participation can be made a condition for helping the family. The importance of the father to the family and his potential for positively affecting his child should be stressed in making such demands. Even if the child's problems do not stem from inadequate fathering, the father's active involvement may do much to improve the situation. If a child has been paternally deprived, a family difficulty may provide the opportunity for getting the father better integrated into the family (Biller & Meredith, 1974). It is striking how many well-meaning fathers are relatively peripheral members of their families. Many difficulties that children and mothers experience can be quickly remedied or mitigated if ways in which the father can become a more active and positive participant are clearly communicated to the family. Much of the success of family therapy is due to the inclusion of the father (e.g., Forrest, 1969; Grebstein 1986; Green, 1974; Gurman & Kniskeon, 1981).

A child's problems, even if not directly a result of family interactions, are exacerbated by the family's reaction to them. Treating the father, mother, child, and other relevant family members as a group allows the therapist to observe both strengths and difficulties in family interactions. Valuable time can be saved and a more accurate understanding can be achieved by observing family behavior directly rather than trying to infer how the family interacts from comments made separately by the child or the parents.

The application of modeling and related behavior modification techniques is a particularly meaningful course to explore in individual, group, and family therapy with paternally deprived children (Biller, 1974c). The probability of successful treatment can be greatly increased if knowledge concerning positive fathering is integrated into the psychotherapy process. For example, the therapist can demonstrate appropriate paternal behaviors in his interactions with the family; however, the therapist must be careful to support the father's strengths and not undermine his effectiveness by unwittingly competing with him.

The therapist can explicitly model ways in which a father can communicate to his wife and to his children. Having both a male and a female therapist provides even more concrete examples of appropriate male-female interactions for the family to observe. Role-playing procedures for family members are very helpful in teaching and reinforcing effective behavior patterns. Of course, any attempt to modify the family's functioning should take into account their previous modes of interaction and their sociocultural background. It is important that the family's environment be considered in treatment. Observing and modifying the family's behavior is often more meaningful when it is done in their own home rather than in the therapist's office (Biller, 1974c).

Green (1974) presented some particularly helpful therapeutic suggestions that are relevant for working with paternally deprived children who have severe sex-role conflicts. He gave a detailed description of a promising multifaceted therapy program that includes individual and group sessions for mothers and fathers as well as for children. His depth interview protocols are especially impressive. He has developed a very creative integration of a number of different methods for increasing the incentive value of masculine behavior and male models for extremely feminine boys.

A book edited by Cath, Gurwitt, and Ross (1982) provides some excellent guidelines for professionals dealing with father and family issues; the authors of various chapters are very bullish on strengthening the bonds of *both* parents to their children. There is much for the practitioner to gain from a careful reading of the more theoretical and data-oriented chapters as well as those in the last section devoted more directly to issues in prevention and individual and family therapy (e.g., Ferholt, & Gurwitt, 1982; Samaraweera & Cath, 1982). The importance of dealing with the father's feelings, even during the expectant-parent period, is emphasized (e.g., Gurwitt, 1982; Herzog, 1982). There are many useful suggestions for health-care professionals in supporting the father's involvement during infancy and early childhood, and for mental health professionals engaged in evaluation and treatment (e.g., Ferholt & Gurwitt, 1982; Samaraweera & Cath, 1982).

A theme running through much of Cath, Gurwitt, and Ross (1982) is the role of the analyst (or therapist) as a potential father figure who, through transference, will allow the individual to develop or reexperience healthy fathering. Some of the most fascinating examples in the book deal with the working through of intergenerational fathering issues. It is striking how the analytic process may provide positive fathering for the child while also allowing the adult, in working through childhood experiences, to be free to become a more effective parent (e.g., Gurwitt, 1982; Herzog, 1982). Of course, as we have already emphasized, there is a great need to develop programs that are more generally available and cost-effective than individual therapy approaches.

Social Intervention

Prospective fathers and father-surrogates should be made more aware of the significance of the father in child development through education and the mass media. (Biller & Meredith, 1972, 1974; Biller & Salter, 1985). Such exposure, along with other programs, has the potential to lessen the number of families that become father-absent, and paternally deprived. Explicit advantages such as financial and other support for fathers remaining with their families, in contrast to the current rewarding of father-absence by many welfare departments, might do much to keep some families intact and to reconstitute other families.

Preventative programs can focus on families that seem to have a high risk of becoming father-absent. Systematic techniques can be developed to determine the potential consequences of father-absence for a family where separation or divorce is being contemplated. During the divorce process, more consideration should be given to whether all or some of the children might benefit from remaining with the father (Biller & Meredith, 1974). Data collected by Santrock and Warshak (1979) suggest that it may be advantageous for children whose parents divorce to live with the same-sex parent, if a joint or shared custody arrangement is not possible (Thompson, 1983).

It is usually easier to find mother-surrogates (such as grandmothers or housekeepers) than to find father-surrogates. It is also relevant to consider potential paternal effectiveness in placing children with adoptive or foster parents. There is much evidence that fathers can be just as effective parents as can mothers, whether in a typical nuclear family or as single parents (Biller & Meredith, 1974a; Greif, 1985; Lamb, 1981d; Rosenthal & Keshet, 1981; Walters, 1976).

Much more needs to be done to support continued father-child interactions in families in which the parents are divorced or in the process of becoming divorced (Abarbanel, 1979; Wallerstein & Kelly, 1980b). Furthermore, there is increasing evidence of the advantages for children and parents of a joint custody and/or shared parenting arrangement (Abarbanel, 1979; Biller & Meredith, 1974; Greif, 1979; Hetherington, Cox, & Cox, 1982; Roman & Haddad, 1978; Thompson, 1983; Wallerstein & Kelly, 1980a, 1980b).

Much of the recent research on the impact of divorce (see chapters 9 and 10) on various family members has emphasized that parents' difficulties in coping with their own needs may interfere with their adequacy in dealing with their children's distress (Hetherington, Cox, & Cox, 1978a, 1982; Wallerstein & Kelly, 1980b). Parents in the one-parent family must not be neglected. For example, the mother's reaction to husband-absence may greatly influence the extent to which father-absence or lack of father availability affects her children. She often needs psychological as well as social and economic support. Mental health professionals have outlined many useful techniques for helping mothers and children in fatherless families (e.g., Baker et al., 1968; Jenkins, 1979; Klein, 1973; Mitchell & Hudson, 1985; Weiss, 1975).

In a pilot project, one of the central goals of a welfare mothers' group was to help husbandless mothers deal constructively with their social and familial problems (Biller & Smith, 1972). In a discussion of the common interpersonal and sexual problems of parents without partners, Pollak (1970) offered some excellent suggestions for helping such individuals cope with their concerns. Educational and therapeutic groups such as Parents without Partners can be very meaningful for the wifeless father as well as the husbandless mother (e.g., Egelson & Frank, 1961; Gershon & Biller, 1977; Jenkins, 1979; Schlesinger, 1966; Wallerstein & Kelly, 1980b; Weiss, 1975).

A significant dimension of community mental health efforts, in terms of both prevention and treatment, should be in supporting fathers to be more effective parents and in locating father-surrogates for paternally deprived children. Far-reaching community, state, and government programs are needed. A vast number of children have no consistent, meaningful contact with adult males. This serious situation must be remedied if all our children are to take full advantage of their growing social and educational opportunities.

Educational Implications

Our educational system could do much to mitigate the effects of paternal deprivation if more male teachers were available, particulary in nursery school, kindergarten, and the early elementary-school grades. Competent and interpersonally able male teachers could facilitate the cognitive development of many children as well as contribute to their general social functioning (Biller, 1974a, 1974b, 1974c).

There is much need for greater incentives to encourage more males to become teachers of young children. There must be more freedom and autonomy to innovate, as well as greater financial rewards. We must make both men and women aware of the impact that males can have in the early years of the child's development. Just having more male teachers is not going to be a significant factor. The feminized school atmosphere must become more *humanized*. Teachers should be selected on the basis of interpersonal ability *and* overall competency, and must receive adequate training with respect to issues in human development. If a man is basically feminized or allows himself to be dominated by a restrictive atmosphere, he may be a particularly poor model for children (Biller, 1974a; Biller & Meredith, 1974).

The remedy for the feminized classroom is not just having more male teachers in itself, but giving men and women a more equal distribution of the responsibilities and decisions related to education. As Sexton (1969) suggested, both boys and girls might be better off if there were more women in top administrative positions *and* more men in the classroom. As in the family situation, children can profit from opportunities to see males and females interact in a cooperative, creative manner. Men and women together in the classroom could help each other better understand the different socialization experiences of males and females.

Even if significantly more male teachers are not immediately available, our school systems could better use existing personnel. Many of the males who teach in the upper elementary-school grades, junior high, and high school could also be very effective with younger children. Again, we need to emphasize the importance of males interacting with young children as well as with older children. Programs could be planned so that male teachers could spend some of their time with a wider range of children, particularly in tasks where they had a lot of skill and enthusiasm. Perhaps their responsibilities could be concentrated on father-deprived children. Other males, such as older students or retired men, may also be encouraged to participate in the education of young children.

There is a general need to make our schools more a part of the community and to invite greater participation, especially from fathers (Biller & Meredith, 1974). Men in the community could be invited to talk about and demonstrate their work. Participants could include members of various professions, skilled craftsmen and technicians, politicians, and athletes. Of course, it is also important to have women in various occupations come to the school and describe their activities. Both boys and girls need to become aware that women can be successful in traditionally masculine fields.

An atmosphere in which older children help younger children, or children help less able peers of the same age, could go a long way toward encouraging males to gain the skills and experiences that are important in being competent fathers. Men from the community could come in during lunch breaks and eat with the children. They could also interact with children on the playground and ride with them on school buses. It is hoped that businesses and industries would cooperate regularly in giving men the opportunities and incentives to make such contributions. Another possible function of business and industry would be to set up regular visits for children to various settings in their community. Such visits can be educational and can provide children with more experiences in interacting with competent adults of both sexes. These and other suggestions have also been made by a number of observers who have criticized the lack of male influence in our educational system (e.g., Biller, 1974c; Garai & Scheinfeld, 1968; Grambs & Waetjen, 1966; Ostrovsky, 1959; Sexton, 1969).

In a variety of different educational and treatment contexts, Biller (1974b) observed some dramatic responses of paternally deprived children to the attention of an interested male adult. In practicing and supervising psychotherapy with young boys, Biller often found an improvement in schoolwork associated with explicit reinforcement from adult males. Some particularly interesting results were achieved by having books about sports and sports heroes available during therapy. In these cases, reading and talking about sports became a major focus of therapy. These boys needed to become aware that there was no incompatibility between intellectual endeavors such as reading and their conception of masculine behavior. It seemed particularly helpful to the boys when the therapist clearly exhibited athletic as well as reading skill and, that equally important, obviously enjoyed both types of activities. In therapy the emphasis was on modeling and joint participation in concretely reinforcing activities. Through the process of family therapy, positive involvement of the father (or father-surrogate) has often been associated with a marked improvement in the child's academic functioning (Biller, 1974a, 1974b).

Some Guidelines for Effective Fathering

A crucial dimension in the battle against child maltreatment and paternal deprivation should be in terms of educational and training programs for parents and prospective parents. Gordon's (1970) *Parent Effectiveness Training* is probably the best-known example of a program designed to improve parent-child relationships, but there have been no systematic programs designed especially for fathers. Unfortunately, parent and family education programs focus on mothers (Florin & Dokecki, 1983), and relatively few fathers participate. Biller and Meredith (1974) wrote *Father Power* in the hope it would stimulate parent education programs focusing on issues relating to the father-child and father-mother relationships. The following are some general guidelines for effective fathering (Biller, 1973a, 1974c; Biller & Meredith, 1974; Biller & Salter, 1985, 1986).

Where to Begin

Learning how to be an effective father begins in childhood. Perhaps the best way to develop the ability to be a good father is the experience of having had one. A realistic evaluation by a man of the strengths and weaknesses of his relationship with his own father can be a helpful ingredient in developing his ability to become an effective father. Some men (and women) are unthinkingly trapped in patterns of behavior evolving out of inadequate and maltreating interactions with their own fathers.

Boys seldom get many opportunities to interact with young children in a positive, supportive manner. They usually perceive caring for young children more as a restriction than as a gratifying experience. If we can remedy this situation creatively by allowing older boys to demonstrate their skills, knowledge, and experiences to younger children, we may do much to promote a basic foundation for fatherhood. Setting up nursery schools as a part of a high school's family life education curriculum may be one way to give adolescent males more opportunity to interact constructively with the young.

The New Father

Having a child should be a well-thought-out decision for both father and mother. Even before the child is conceived, the prospective parents should feel a mutual commitment to their future family. The positive influence of the father is greatly increased when it exists in a context of father-mother mutuality. Moreover, the expectant father should not be ignored. Often all the attention is focused on the expectant mother, while the expectant father is left out in the cold. Many expectant fathers feel alienated, with adverse effects on their psychological and physical health. Husbands can be involved in visits to the obstetrician and can be with their wives during labor and in the delivery room. The new father should be encouraged to spend considerable time with his wife and infant, and to apply for a paternity leave. The earlier the father can feel involved with the infant, the more likely will a strong father-child attachment develop.

A father can be very important even in his infant's first few months. The father's involvement in various activities with the infant can build a strong foundation for a growing relationship. Whether or not a father changes diapers or dresses or feeds the infant is not the key factor. What is important is that the father and infant find some mutually satisfying activities, and also that the father and mother can develop the view that they both have definite day-to-day responsibilities for the infant's welfare. Many fathers enjoy holding and snuggling their babies, watching their reactions to new objects and situations, and tossing and crawling with them as they get older. Infants and fathers can provide each other with much mutual stimulation. Babies can be fascinating when fathers feel comfortable and relaxed with them. New fathers are often anxious about holding infants—some have never held an infant before—and the wife's support and encouragement can be very helpful.

It is never too early for the father to get involved, and sharing responsibilities for the child can also do a lot to strengthen the husband-wife bond and overall family cohesiveness. The father who gets a good start with his first child can play a significant role with the arrival of additional children. For example, a young child who can spend much time with an involved father is less likely to feel depressed or jealous when his mother is out of the home giving birth to his new brother or sister, or to express severe sibling rivalry when the mother and infant return home.

Father and Work

A common problem that interferes with father-child interaction is the father's work schedule. In some cases, modifications in the father's work schedule are possible to ensure his fuller participation in the family. Some fathers spend great amounts of time at work as a means of avoiding family responsibilities, not because of economic necessity. Many fathers are very competent and active at work but feel inexperienced and ineffectual at home with their children. Of course, each family must assess its priorities, but it is important that both the husband and wife share in such decisions about how much money is necessary, the degree to which each contributes, and the amount of time they spend with their children. Many fathers, because of long-term goals, sacrifice time with their families only to find that they have lost their children, at least psychologically, in the process. They may end up with financial security but with a very empty family life.

In some cases the father often must be away from home. Whether this is a temporary or a relatively permanent situation, adjustments in family schedules can be made to maximize the father's involvement. For example, if the father works until late in the evening, the child can take naps and then spend time with him when he comes home, or they can regularly have a special time in the mornings. In many cases, children may be able to accompany their fathers to work, or the mother and child can visit the father at work during the lunch hour. Business and industry should also become sensitive to such problems. Each family may have a unique situation, but there are ways to schedule maximal opportunity for father-child interaction.

Learning with Father

Father-child interaction, even for the young child, does not have to be limited to the home and the neighborhood. Many fathers enjoy taking their children on errands (to the local garage, flower shop, or grocery store) and including them in various recreational activities. For the young child, activities that may seem beyond his comprehension to the adult may in fact be intriguing. Seeing new faces, new buildings, new machinery can be engrossing, especially when the child is with someone he loves and respects. The one-year-old may not comprehend the meaning of a movie or sporting event, but he may be stimulated, engrossed in the action, and happy to be sharing something with his father (provided it doesn't last too long). On the other hand, a father may get added enjoyment from seeing his child's reaction to an experience that is rather mundane solely from an adult perspective. Similarly, although a child may not fully understand the intricacies of his father's job, he may be very excited by seeing where his father works and by meeting his father's co-workers.

Doing things with his father offers the child many new learning experiences and stimulates his curiosity. A father does not have to be a scholar to whet his child's appetite for new knowledge. A child may enjoy hearing about jobs his father has had, places he's visited, and people he's known. Answering the child's questions can be a learning experience for both the father and child. A child's academic success and, more important, the degree to which he manifests his creative potential may have much to do with his interactions with his father, especially if they have a close relationship. For example, a father who enjoys reading and who reads to his child (and, when his child is ready, encourages the child to read to him) can have a much more positive impact than a father who continually tells his child that school is important but does not participate in an intellectual activity in a way that his child can observe.

The specific activities that father and child engage in are not the key. The quality of their interaction is what is crucial. Open communication and the sharing of mutually gratifying experiences are important. Young children learn best by observing and imitating their parents. The best way for a father to instill positive qualities in a child is by demonstrating these qualities in his relationship with the child. A father may be skillful in understanding people and in solving problems, but if a child sees his father only occasionally he will not learn much from him. Similarly, a child will not learn respect and tolerance from a father who constantly criticizes and verbally abuses him, even if fellow workers and friends consider the father a wonderful person.

Special Times

Respect and understanding work both ways. A father must give if he expects to receive. A good father-child relationship may be particularly fostered when the father and child can have some special times alone together. Such occasions are very important for focusing on each other's needs and interests. It is usually much easier to listen to a child when you are alone with him or her, and such attention is an essential quality of being a good parent. We usually attend very carefully to our children's material needs, while sometimes neglecting their needs for individual expression. Our children's attitudes and feelings frequently get less consideration than those of our friends or, often, even strangers.

Attention to special times can be especially crucial in families with many children, where it may be very difficult for family members to know each other as individuals. The ability of parents to relate to each of their children is at least as important as their ability to provide for them economically. This consideration should be taken into account in family planning.

The father and child should be able to develop many mutual interests and awareness of each other's activities. Often the father can take the initiative by paying attention to what the child is doing. There is nothing immature about a father getting down on the floor and playing with his child, building with blocks, moving dolls and toy animals around. Such activities can be fun for both participants. Some fathers do not have much patience for traditional children's games but may be able to teach their children activities that they enjoy such as chess or various card games. The child can participate happily with his father in many typical adult activities, including washing the car, fixing furniture, or working in the garden, if the father takes into account the child's developmental level. Such activities may also provide the beginnings of his sharing responsibilities at home. A child needs to feel that his father values him as an individual and appreciates his skills. It is easy for a father to be critical of the way his child plays a game or hammers a nail, but the father's capacity to remember, or imagine, his own level of performance when he was a young child can be helpful. A child will usually respond positively to his father's comment that the child is doing as well as or better than the father did at a similar age.

Fathers can enjoy frolicking and wrestling with their children. Physical contact between father and child can be a very good experience, particularly when love and tender feelings are expressed. Hugging, tickling, cuddling, and tossing are meaningful expressions of caring and closeness between father and child. The child can sense his father's strength and power and yet feel secure rather than being frightened. It is important for both father and child to feel comfortable in expressing warmth and tenderness toward each other. Too many fathers and, consequently, too many children become inhibited in expressing positive emotions.

The disadvantages of paternal deprivation affect fathers as well as children. The uninvolved father does not experience the gratification of actively facilitating the successful development of his children. He misses an important opportunity to learn to deal sensitively with many interpersonal situations. Widespread paternal inadequacy helps create large numbers of interpersonally insensitive men. Many of these men are in positions of authority, and their alienation as fathers has limited their ability to interact with young people. Inadequate paternal involvement is a factor in the problems of communication between individuals of different ages, thereby contributing to the generation gap.

Discipline and Responsibility

Discipline is a chronic problem in many families. Traditionally, this was often the scope of the father's role; "Wait till your father gets home" is still a frequent cry of many frustrated mothers. But making the father's role center on discipline can lead to a very unsatisfactory father-child relationship. If the mother is alone with the child, she should take the responsibility, as should the father when he is alone with the child. The child should feel that both mother and father generally are supportive of each other's actions. If the parents are together with the child, setting limits should be a joint responsibility. Again, the best way to teach a child appropriate behavior is by exposing him to effective models; the parents' own behavior is significant. If parents are continually yelling at each other, if they don't listen to or trust each other, it is difficult to expect their child to develop respect for the feelings of others.

The child can learn a lot from resolving disagreements with his parents. The father is wise to have clear-cut standards, but he should be responsive to his child's rational arguments and needs to express himself. Children must learn constructive ways of influencing others and asserting their rights. Inattention to a child's reasoning is no better than giving in to immature temper tantrums. The father does not always have to have the last word. The father who must always win an argument does not allow his child to develop independence and assertiveness. A child should be encouraged to respect his father but should not be burdened with the image of "perfect" father. If he is to learn to assess his own capabilities objectively, a child must become aware that his father also has his limtiations and can make mistakes. The father who can occasionally admit that he is wrong and his child is right may do much to facilitate his child's sense of competence. A father who "never" makes a mistake can be too frustrating to emulate.

Father-Mother Relationship

The opportunities the child has to spend with both his mother and father together are important. A child forms much of his attitude toward male-female relationships by watching his mother and father interact. The effective father values his wife's competencies and respects her opinions. The child's sex-role adjustment is greatly influenced by the quality of the father-mother relationship. A father who feels confident about his basic masculinity is more likely to accept his wife positively than is one who rejects his masculinity or must constantly prove his manliness. The effective father encourages his daughter to feel positively about being a female and his son about being a male. He communicates his pride in their developing bodies and biological potentialities. However, this does not mean that he expects his children to rigidly adhere to cultural stereotypes. For example, he fosters the development of assertiveness and independence in his daughters as well as his sons, and the development of nurturance and sensitivity in his sons as well as his daughters.

The parents' respect for one another and their ability to communicate openly and honestly foster the child's development. Parental consistency and agreement give the child a feeling of security. It is helpful to the child to know that his parents have discussed issues concerning his welfare and that they are in general agreement. Of course, parents will not always agree, the child is fortunate if he can observe parental disagreements as long as they usually result in mutually satisfactory outcomes. Father-mother interactions can provide important lessons in how to resolve conflicts.

The purpose of this book has not been to argue that the father is more important than the mother. The child who experiences *both* positive fathering *and* positive mothering is more likely to achieve effective personality functioning than is the child who has only one adequate parent. Child rearing can be a very demanding process but can be much more rewarding when the father and mother function as a cooperative team. Together, parents often react in a more creative and responsible manner. They can be more secure in allowing their children autonomy and freedom, as well as maintaining firmness in setting necessary limits. Supportive cooperation between fathers and mothers can go a long way to alleviating the tremendous problems of paternal deprivation and child maltreatment.

Training Fathers

Biller and Meredith (1974) emphasized the importance of fathers as well as mothers being involved in educational experiences that could foster their knowledge about development and their competence in child rearing. Opportunities for expectant fathers and new fathers to practice caretaking activities and to learn about various processes in infant and child development are particularly important. As both Biller and Meredith (1974) and Parke and Collmer (1975) have stressed, training for parenthood including information about individual and family development should be part of the educational curriculum even during the elementary-school years, or at least pre–high school. Such exposure should help prevent child maltreatment and paternal deprivation.

Ferrante and Biller (1986) evaluated a program geared to help children deal with family issues and the impact of divorce. It is interesting to note that their findings suggest that younger children may profit more from such interventions than do older children. In their research, fourth-graders seemed to change more as a function of group experiences than did fifth-graders. There was some evidence of better problem-solving skills and a more internalized sense of control after children attended six group sessions, conducted by a male psychologist, during which family issues and communication problems were discussed. Parents and teachers also reported that they perceived positive benefits for the children who attended these groups. Ferrante and Biller (1986) reviewed other research supporting the potential of school-based interventions for helping children deal more effectively with divorce-related problems. A major issue in such interventions can be to help children cope better with paternal deprivation and, if possible, to give them specific guidelines for taking initiative to improve the quality of their interactions with their fathers as well as their mothers.

A strong case can be made for the importance of programs involving fathers in the childbirth education process, even if postbirth parenting issues are not discussed. When husbands are supportive of their wives during labor, there is evidence that wives are less anxious and distressed (Anderson & Standley, 1976; Henneborn & Cogan, 1975). Mothers are less likely to need medication, and both mothers and fathers are more satisfied about the overall birth process, when fathers are present during labor and delivery (Henneborn & Cogan, 1975). Even more significant for their potential impact on fathering are findings by Peterson, Mehl, and Leiderman (1979). In a longitudinal investigation, these researchers found that the father's positive descriptions of the birth-related events were highly associated with the quality of father- infant attachment during the infant's first six months of life. Fathers who were pleased about their involvement in the birth process were strongly attached to their infants, according to both observational and self-report data.

Parke and Tinsley (1981) and Lamb (1981c) have reviewed much evidence indicating that fathers *can be* just as competent caretakers of infants as can mothers, although mothers typically assume the primary role for direct physical care. Parke and Tinsley (1981) summarize studies indicating that in certain situations, such as subsequent to a caesarean delivery or when an infant is born prematurely, fathers may very successfully assume a greater role in direct day-to-day physical care.

As part of a highly sophisticated research effort, Parke, Hymel, Power, and Tinsley (1980) designed a hospital-based intervention program for fathers. In the initial phase, during their wives' postdelivery hospitalization, fathers were shown an educational videotape focusing on father-infant interactions, specific care taking activities, and infants' cognitive and social capacities. There was an emphasis on fathers becoming active participants in the care and stimulation of even very young infants. Parke et al. reported a clear-cut impact of the intervention on the behavior and attitudes of fathers, especially those who had sons.

Fathers who viewed the videotape, compared to those who did not, were more willing to take care of their infants and to stimulate them actively. Viewing the videotape was also correlated with fathers' diary reports of frequency of feeding and changing diapers of their three-month-old sons. According to observational data, those fathers who viewed the videotape engaged in more feeding-related caretaking behavior with newborns and when their infants were three months old. Perhaps most significant was the fact that fathers who viewed the videotape were more likely than those who did not to connect their stimulating and affectionate behavior with their infants' overtures. Fathers who were exposed to the videotape seemed more sensitive and attuned to their infants' needs.

In chapter 6 we briefly noted other intervention studies directed at improving the father-infant relationship. In their pioneering intervention effort, Zelazo et al. (1977) trained low-interacting fathers to play at home with their infants on a regular basis for thirty minutes a day over a four-week period (Kotelchuck, 1976). They provided observational modeling of play activities as well as direct coaching to the fathers. Their laboratory-based assessment indicated that the trained fathers became more active with their infants than did the untrained fathers and, moreover, that their infant sons took more social initiative with them than did the sons of untrained fathers. In another intervention study, Dickie and Carnahan (1979) trained parents to become more responsvie and effective in interacting with their four- to twelve-month-old infants. Over a two-month period, parents received eight two-hour sessions, including information on individual differences in infants and ways in which parents and infants stimulated one another. Consistent with Zelazo et al. (1977), they reported that infants of fathers who participated in the training sessions initiated more social interaction with their fathers than did those whose fathers were in the control group.

Levant (1983) described a promising experimental parent education program for married fathers of school-aged children (six to twelve years). The client-centered procedure focused on developing better communication skills during eight three-hour sessions. The didactic-experiential format included an emphasis on helping the men pay more attention to their own and others' feelings, as well as including homework exercises involving father-child interactions. Self-report paper-and-pencil measures indicated a significant positive gain in the participants' overall sensitivity to children and a trend toward increased acceptance of their children's feelings. Perhaps most important, as reflected both in structured interviews and in kinetic family drawings, their children themselves perceived more improvement in their relationships with their fathers than did children in the control group, whose fathers did not participate in this program.

Fortunately, more teaching tools that can raise the awareness of children and adults about the potential influence of fathers are now available. There are many books written for the general public with an emphasis on fathering (e.g., Biller & Meredith, 1974; Bittman & Zalk, 1978) as well as educational films (e.g., Biller, 1980a; Biller et al. 1977). The program designed by Parke et al. (1980) appears particularly promising for use with prospective and expectant parents as well as those who already have infants.

Policies and Values

An important volume, *Fatherhood and Family Policy*, edited by Lamb and Sagi (1983), brings together a vast amount of relevant interdisciplinary literature dealing with factors which may influence paternal involvement in child rearing. The contributors presented in a cross-cultural context lots of provocative data concerning how interrelationships between economic, historical, legal, political, and social factors affect perspectives on the father's role in the family and often undermine active male participation with children. They made excellent recommendations about how public policy can strengthen the father's role in general. Although they were highly supportive of greater participation of fathers in the lives of their children, they also emphasized the complexity of issues associated with such changes, the value judgments that are involved, and some of the possible disadvantages (as well as advantages) that may occur with respect to various family members when there is an increase in paternal involvement. They pointed out that there are many significant gaps in knowledge about family development, and that it is crucial not to impose any rigid paradigms for father participation. There were many specific recommendations designed to strengthen the father's role in the family and cogent discussions of employment, legal practices, health care delivery, education, social services, and overall public policy.

We enthusiastically endorse most of the recommendations put forth in the Lamb and Sagi (1983) volume. We also respect the positions of the contributors who expressed some caution with regard to value judgments, unrealistic expectations of increased father involvement, and the possible negative repercussions from too much pressure on men *and* women who are not ready for more active paternal participation in the family. We realize the need to keep a holistic perspective on the complex and reciprocal interrelationships between the family system and other social institutions. Furthermore, we readily acknowledge the resistance to change that is presented by basic cultural sex-role patterns. However, society can support increased male participation in child rearing without necessarily expecting men to somehow individually change their basic views of themselves as masculine. We insist that there does not have to be an incompatibility between active masculinity and active parenting; in fact, men can indeed gain a greater sense of security with respect to their sex-role adequacy by being involved and successful fathers (Biller, 1971a, 1974c; Biller & Meredith, 1974; Heath, 1978; Levinson, 1978; Vaillant, 1977).

Most fathers retain a relatively distinctive "masculine style" in interacting with their children, even when there is a marked increase in their level of child-rearing involvement. Just because a father becomes more involved in traditionally female child-rearing tasks does not mean that he adopts a nonmasculine style of interacting with his son or daughter. The reasons a father may be perceived as nonmasculine or feminized by his children have much more to do with his basic personality structure than with the kinds of caretaking responsibilities he assumes in the family. Even active fathers in so-called nontraditional two-parent families, as well as those who are full-time or part-time postdivorce single parents, typically have a distinctly masculine pattern of interacting with their children and are readily perceived by them as quite different from mothers (Biller & Meredith, 1974; Field, 1978; Lamb, 1982; Radin & Russell, 1983).

We agree with the Lamb and Sagi (1983) position that choice is very important and that arbitrary and rigid structures of parenting should not be imposed by public and social policy. As we have emphasized, there are many different ways in which men can contribute to the successful development of children whether it be in a nuclear family or another social structure. However, we take a stronger stance in advocating change than is expressed in the Lamb and Sagi volume. When men become parents, they should be expected to share responsibility with women. They should be held accountable for their level of commitment and quality of involvement. If we are truly concerned about children's rights and prevention of maltreatment, men must be expected to cooperate actively with mothers in child-rearing endeavors. The form and style of father-mother cooperation and the specific types of parent-child interaction leave room for tremendous cultural variation and individual choice as long as there is the clear expectation of both positive paternal and positive maternal involvement.

We have put much emphasis on issues relating to both the traditional two-parent family and the single-parent, female-headed family. However, it is relevant to underscore our position that constructive participation by males *and* females is important in child rearing irrespective of family structure. Given a choice, most adults would opt for a nuclear family, yet this family form is no longer the model pattern. Adult male influence can be important whatever the family context. For example, if men are positively involved, they can be successful in facilitating the development of children as divorced noncustodial parents, as single custodial parents, as married househusbands, or as foster or stepparents. We are not advocating that men strive to be more influential in child rearing than are women but that they actively and cooperatively share such responsibilities in the individualized manner that benefits all members of their family. The specific activities that men perform when with children are not as crucial as is the overall quality and commitment that is evidenced in their parenting (Biller & Meredith, 1974; Russell, 1983).

Current and Future Directions

Florin and Dokecki (1983) provided an excellent and systematic review of the history and evaluation of parent and family education programs. However, they did not mention a single program that even has an explicit subfocus on the inclusion of fathers (Biller & Salter, 1986). It is striking that despite the growing concern for parent and family education during the 1960s and 1970s, there were no widespread programs that included special components for fathers (Gershon & Biller, 1977).

The 1980s have witnessed a burgeoning interest in the role of the father in child development, as well as the recognition of the family problems often associated with paternal deprivation. *Paternal Absence and Fathers' Roles*, a Hearing before the Select Committee on Children, Youth and Families, House of Representatives, took place in November 1983 (Miller et al., 1984). During this hearing a variety of scientists, professionals, military personnel, and community and political leaders shared their data and experiences. A major emphasis of the hearing was to provide information on concrete ways to support the father's participation in intact families, as well as to help father-absent families. The presentations were varied and enlightening.

In the context of prevention and of training men to take more responsibility for children, two of the presentations appear especially noteworthy. David Bahlmann, executive vice-president of Big Brothers/Big Sisters of America, talked about the tremendous growth of his organization in providing Big Brothers for children in father-absent families (Bahlmann, 1984). His organization now includes more than 450 agencies serving more than 100,000 children across the country. Further, in his role as chair, National Collaboration for Youth, Bahlmann described several other major organizations (including the Boys' and Girls' Clubs of America, the Boy Scouts of America, the Girl Scouts of America, Camp Fire Inc., and the United Neighborhood Center of America) that are becoming increasingly sensitive to the needs of children in father-absent families. Bahlmann's efforts to facilitate communication and collaboration among such organizations and other community resources certainly appear to us to be a very important component in dealing constructively with paternal deprivation and child maltreatment.

James Levine, director, and Debra Klinman, project manager, outlined the relatively recent and exceedingly important work of The Fatherhood Project, which was based at the Bank Street College of Education (Levine & Klinman, 1984). The Fatherhood Project, initiated in September 1981 and no longer in operation, was an exciting and innovative attempt to coordinate, on a national level, research and demonstration programs concerning the paternal role. The project had many and varied functions, including providing a countrywide clearinghouse for information, weekend group programs for fathers and their preschool-age children, courses for both male and female preadolescents on infant care, and a national series of Fatherhood Forums. To increase their impact, the staff prepared valuable resource materials, including a comprehensive guide to programs and services across the country, and manuals relating to *How to Start a Father-Child Group* and *How to Start a Babycare Program for Boys and Girls*. Co-directors of this extremely promising project were Michael Lamb of the University of Utah and Joseph Pleck of Wellesley College (Klinman & Kohl, 1984; Levine, Pleck, & Lamb, 1983).

In our view, The Fatherhood Project had great potential to contribute in powerful ways to raising the consciousness of men *and* women about the importance of the father-child relationship and to help parents, families, and communities work together to alleviate the devastating impact of child maltreatment and paternal deprivation.

12
Summary and Overview

The purpose of this chapter is to summarize briefly and integrate some of the major points discussed in earlier parts of the book. Our goal is to provide an overview that underscores the need for research, intervention, and prevention in confronting child maltreatment and paternal deprivation. This is not an attempt to summarize completely the vast amount of material covered in the book but, rather, to list and highlight some relatively provocative statements that we hope will stimulate action from researchers and clinicians, as well as many other individuals and groups, interested in the welfare of children and families.

Basic Perspectives

1. The interrelated problems of child maltreatment and paternal deprivation pose a great threat to the healthy development of our children and the future of our society. Directly or indirectly, paternal deprivation is a factor in the great majority of incidents of child maltreatment, both within and outside the family. (See figure 4–1.)

2. A holistic, transactional view is necessary to understanding the impact of child maltreatment and paternal deprivation on human development. The complex and variegated interactions of biological, familial, and social system factors must be considered in a longitudinal and interdisciplinary context. For example, constitutional and prenatal factors relating to individual differences in children reciprocally interact with cultural and socioeconomic variables, as well as with the quality of parenting in the family context. Too little emphasis has been given to the father's role in child maltreatment, but paternal behavior cannot be viewed as an isolated variable and must be analyzed within a framework of biological and individual differences, marital and family relationships, and historical and sociocultural factors.

3. The concepts of child maltreatment and paternal deprivation should be viewed in a multidimensional context, including continua relating to optimal through adequate to very inadequate parenting. Child maltreatment involves more than severe neglect or physical and sexual abuse; various forms of inappropriate verbal and emotional insensitivity, rejection of individuality, and overrestrictiveness must also be considered. With respect to the behavior of fathers and mothers, child maltreatment pertains to those *patterns* of parental involvement (verbal abuse, physical abuse, sexual abuse, infantilization,

overrestrictiveness, and so on) or uninvolvement (disinterest, nonresponsivity, neglect, abandonment) that may potentially undermine adequate affective, social, sexual, intellectual, and/or physical development. Men and women who maltreat their children do not fit neatly into the psychiatric nomenclature. Their pathology may be most manifested in their relationships with their children even though many of them may be functioning adequately in their extrafamilial endeavors and careers. Their inadequacy in parenting is in part a reflection of their deficient relationships with their own parents, which they may be able to defend against except when having to deal with the emotional demands of their children. In addition, complex social factors which discourage paternal involvement must be taken into account.

4. Child maltreatment and paternal deprivation are present, to some extent, at all socioeconomic levels and in all subcultures. However, children in economically disadvantaged situations, and those with particular developmental handicaps, are especially prone to suffer from both child maltreatment and paternal deprivation. Inadequate parenting is only one of several possible sources of child maltreatment, and there has also not been enough support of children's rights in settings outside the family. In particular, men in positions of authority have not been sensitive enough to the needs of children. Paternal deprivation extends beyond the family; it permeates our society. Paternally deprived children, in their hunger for male attention, are especially vulnerable to maltreatment by adults outside the family.

5. The degree to which the father as well as the mother is nurturant, caring, and accepting is highly related to the successful development of the child. The father's constructive support of the child's sexuality and individuality is especially crucial to early self-concept development. Children in two-parent families who are deprived of positive interaction with their fathers, either through some form of father-absence or in the context of paternal neglect (or other forms of paternal maltreatment), are more at risk for later psychological and emotional difficulties. Both men and women have something special to offer children. For various important cognitive, emotional, and social learning experiences, the presence of two parents is advantageous for the child. Boys and girls need to learn how to interact adequately with both males and females, and the two-parent family situation can provide the possibility of an effective model of male-female communication. Many factors need to be assessed to determine whether paternal deprivation in itself will have a damaging impact on the child's development, or if the child may have the personal and social resources to overcome such potentially negative consequences. The lack of adequate fathering does not necessarily lead to psychopathology, but it can certainly impede the actualization of the child's talents.

6. Children develop best when given the opportunity to form a basic relationship with both a positively involved father and a positively involved mother. Fathers are as important as mothers in the overall development of children. This

is not to say that, with sufficient resources, children may not develop relatively well in families with one competent parent, especially with respect to those from less-than-adequate two-parent families. For example, a major consideration is the type of father-absent and father-present groups we are comparing. There needs to be a clear description of the quality and quantity of paternal contact among the father-present children in order to establish a meaningful frame of reference. Analyzing the impact of paternal deprivation with respect to the father-absence/father-availability continuum requires consideration of the interaction of a myriad of factors. If we focus on father-absence, we must examine the type and reason for the absence (divorce, death, employment); the child's age, developmental stage, and adequacy of functioning at the time of the absence; the preabsence father-child and mother-father relationships; the quality of the mother-child relationship and the mother's adjustment and attitude toward the father's absence; sibling relationships and the availability of surrogate models; sociocultural and socioeconomic factors, including the family's financial resources and social support system; and the amount of other family changes related to the absence (moving to another residence, changing schools, and the like).

7. If we are to gain a fuller understanding of child maltreatment, more attention needs to be given to sex differences in both effective and ineffective parenting. There are both similarities and differences in the ways in which fathers and mothers maltreat their children. In two-parent families, fathers are much more likely to be chronically neglectful and also to have a higher rate of being reported for physical abuse, especially severe battering, and incestuous behavior. Because of the large number of single-parent female-headed families, mothers do outnumber fathers in committing many types of maltreatment, including physical abuse. In two-parent families, mothers are more likely to overprotect, overrestrict, and infantilize their children, whereas fathers are more apt to reject or withdraw from their children. In many families both parents are abusive and/or are involved in multiple forms of maltreatment. Again, it is crucial to examine the total family and social system as well as child-specific variables if we are to understand the short and long-term consequences of specific forms of maltreatment.

8. Father neglect is the most prevalent form of child maltreatment in our society. Paternal deprivation in its many forms (including emotional uninterest, aloofness, rejection, and verbal derogation, as well as physical unavailability) has a particularly negative impact on child and family development. There has been a double standard concerning parenting, with paternal uninterest being accepted or even expected, especially if the father is very achievement- and work-oriented. Fathers as well as mothers must be held accountable for providing adequate parenting to their children. Children need the opportunity to interact in a positive, stimulating manner with both parents. In terms of the number of children affected, paternal deprivation is more of a problem for our society

than is maternal deprivation. Inadequately fathered children, particularly if they are young, are relatively unlikely to receive compensatory male influence, whereas most children, even if their mother is somewhat inadequate, are exposed to a variety of caring females, including other female relatives and teachers.

9. Children who are paternally deprived and maltreated are at risk for a variety of developmental problems, but this is not the same as assuming that they all will be victims of severe personality deficits or psychopathology. The child's personal resources and other compensatory factors in the social environent must be considered. There are a wide variety of possible outcomes, some of which can be viewed as temporary while others will not become manifest until later in the individual's development. Some children may have very limited and specific difficulties, whereas others may appear psychologically and socially incapacitated in a longer-term, more general way. Constitutional predispositions have much to do with the way in which individual children are influenced by inadequate parenting. Whereas most children suffer some deficits, some constitutionally gifted children may actually develop special competence out of the experience of constructively coping with deprivation and/or abuse. It is important to examine thoroughly the quality of the child's other family and nonfamily relationships as well as focusing on the experience with the maltreating parent(s).

Parenting and Family-System Factors

10. Mothers are more likely to maltreat their children when fathers are uninvolved in child rearing. Father neglect in both two-parent and one-parent families is often associated with a high incidence of maternal stress. The acting out of the overburdened mother's frustration can be expressed in a variety of inappropriate ways, including overdominance, overprotection, and sometimes direct physical abuse and neglect of her children. Many fathers in two-parent families are uninvolved or are involved in only a very narrow way in disciplining their children, often in an inappropriate or maltreating fashion. The high level of maltreatment of children by single mothers can also be viewed, at least in part, as being related to a set of social values that tends to put too much pressure on the mother's acountability and not enough on the father's participation in child rearing.

11. Even during pregnancy, the cooperative involvement of the expectant father is important. The health and well-being of the fetus can be affected if the pregnant mother does not get adequate prenatal care. Economic and subcultural factors certainly are involved in the availability of high-quality prenatal care, but expectant mothers with supportive husbands or committed boyfriends are more likely than those without a partner to be accepting of their pregnancy, to go for regularly scheduled obstetrical visits, and to be appropriately concerned about the effects of their own well-being and health on the fetus. Partner

support can be crucial for the expectant mother's self-esteem and positive concern for her health. Inadequate concern for the fetus can be construed as a particularly serious form of child abuse, with potentially irreversible and devastating consequences for later development.

12. Given the chance to interact with them, fathers as a group have just as great a capacity to be sensitive to their infant's needs and to be responsive to them as mothers do. Although men do not appear as generally interested in children who are not their own as women do (which is also a factor in the widespread extrafamilial paternal deprivation in our society), they are fully capable of being involved with their own children, even with their neonates, if they have the opportunity. There are similarities and differences between the ways in which involved fathers and mothers interact with their infants. Although their styles of stimulating and caring may differ, however, fathers can parent even young infants adequately. The infant who has both an involved father and an involved mother receives some special stimulation from each.

13. The degree to which the father and mother are supportive of each other's participation with the infant also influences the quality of parenting the child receives. Fathers and infants are fully capable of forming reciprocal attachments with one another. Even in the first few months of life, the infant can have a very special relationship with the father. Attachment to the father and paternal social play and stimulation have been found to facilitate the infant's sensory-motor and cognitive development, and comfort and confidence in exploring the physical and interpersonal environment. More and more evidence is accumulating of the long-term developmental benefits for children who had positive relationships with their fathers during infancy and early childhood.

14. The failure of a father to form an early bonding or attachment with the child is one factor that may increase the likelihood not only of early paternal neglect but also, given other family-system factors, of probable emotional, physical, and/or sexual abuse later in the child's development. It is crucial for the father to develop a feeling of responsibility and protectiveness toward the child. Such a commitment-attachment can do much to facilitate the father's capacity for positive nurturance and stimulation, as well as helping him not to act out inappropriate impulses toward the child. The formation of an early and reciprocal attachment also increases the probability that the infant will be responsive in a way that the father perceives as positive.

15. Attachment is a two-way process, and there is a need to consider the characteristics of the child as well as the parent. Some parents have difficulty in bonding sufficiently with a child because of that child's constitutional predispositions, behavior, and/or appearance. At one extreme are infants who remain so totally unresponsive or atypical in their response patterns to others that few if any parents would have the capacity to develop a strong attachment to them. Fathers are more likely than mothers to have a problem in developing an attachment to a handicapped child or a child whom they perceive as

permanently defective. Many parents also have difficulty in bonding with a child when they are separated from the child for a significant period of time while the child is an infant. The parent who is most likely to be separated from the infant is the father. When an infant has special problems, it is particularly important that a strong bonding develops with both parents. On the other hand, some children either are less likely to be targets of maltreatment or are more resilient in the face of negative family experiences. Even as infants and toddlers, some children are very adaptable and have the capacity to relate quickly in a positive way to nonfamily members. Such children, because they are especially attractive, sociable, bright, and/or perceptive may be able to decrease their susceptibility to abuse within their own family, and, even when they are subjected to very inadequate parenting, may still have the personal resources somehow to make a relatively positive personality adaptation.

16. All types of maltreatment do not pose the same risk for children. Generally speaking, severe consistent physical and/or sexual abuse has a more negative impact than does overprotection or restrictiveness. For example, the child who is fatherless, though at risk, may at least attempt to search for some sort of father-surrogate, whereas the child with a grossly inappropriate and/or abusive father may be rigidly trapped with a view of all male adults as destructive. Similarly, a very negative relationship with a family member with whom a child lives on a day-to-day basis may be much more insidious than intermittent contact with a maltreating extended family member. The child who is occasionally physically abused but has at least one generally adequate parent and some family warmth is not as much at risk for a severe psychological handicap as is the child who consistently receives hostile verbal abuse and emotional rejection from both parents. There are many family-system variables in addition to parental behavior that influence the child's development. For example, the quality of sibling interactions; individual differences among siblings (including age, sex, and spacing); and the way in which siblings view each other are important to consider in an attempt to understand the impact of various forms of parenting on a particular child in the family.

17. Family-system factors beyond the individual parent-child relationship must be examined. The quality of the father-mother relationship and the husband-wife relationship is extremely crucial. A severe imbalance in the family system, typically with the mother being overinvolved and the father underinvolved, can result in problems for the parents as well as the children. Parents who feel supported by their partners in their child-rearing efforts are more effective in dealing with their children and less likely to maltreat them. On the other hand, a parent who is frustrated in the marital relationship, or spouseless, is more apt to deal with the child in an inappropriate manner, including possible physical or sexual abuse. Stress factors are more predictive with respect to whether a parent will maltreat the child in some way than in identifying the particular form of abuse. Taking into account the personal characteristics and

background of the parents along with the stress factors and the individual behavior of the child can promote a clearer view of the probability of occurrence of a specific type of maltreatment. For example, a parent with poor impulse control and low frustration tolerance is likely to abuse the highly active child physically.

18. Support from other family members in addition to the spouse can be crucial when a particular parent, typically the mother, feels totally responsible for child rearing. Factors such as economic pressures, the presence of several children close in age or of a handicapped child, and lack of neighborhood and peer resources can all add to parental stress and increase the likelihood of child maltreatment. It is important to emphasize, however, that two parents cooperating together have a much better chance to deal with such obstacles.

Developmental Outcomes

19. Sex-role functioning in *young* children is viewed as very important because of its initial influence on the child's identity and self-concept. A positive father-child relationship helps give the child a healthy start in the development of self-esteem, whereas paternal maltreatment makes the child especially vulnerable in later life to many different types of sex-role-related difficulties. With respect to overall psychological adjustment, it is a positive sex-role orientation, a happy acceptance of one's sexuality, and not the extent of superficial masculinity or femininity that is most important. For example, the fact that young father-absent boys tend to score lower in masculinity than their father-present counterparts is not in itself a sign of a psychological deficit (abnormality or pathology) but may indicate a lack of a positive sex-role orientation, which in turn increases the risk of later developmental problems. Although the degree to which an older child, adolescent, or adult conforms to sex-role expectations may reveal little about paternal adequacy and overall personality integration, the younger child's positive acceptance of basic sex-role expectations is quite likely to be a function of having constructive relationships with both parents. Even before the age of one, and certainly by three, the active modeling of the same-sex parent and other same-sex adults, and the choosing of same-sex toys and activities, is usually much related to a healthy initial sex-role development. Sex-role preferences typically become more flexible at later stages of development, but it is important that the young child achieves a foundation of sex-role security.

20. Children who are both well fathered *and* well mothered are likely to have positive self-concepts and security about their biological sexuality. They feel good about being male or female and have a pride in their basic sex-role orientation. They are comfortable with themselves and their sexuality yet are able to be relatively flexible as they get older in their interests and responsivity to

others. They are able to deal confidently and in an individualized manner with respect to socially prescribed sex-role expectations. Security in sex-role orientation gives the individual more of an opportunity to develop in an actualized way. On the other hand, children who are paternally deprived or otherwise inadequately fathered are more likely to take either a defensive posture of rigid adherence to cultural sex-role standards or, ambivalently, to attempt to avoid expected gender-related behaviors. Inadequate parenting can undermine the developing child's comfortable acceptance of his or her biological sexuality and sex-role functioning. A noninvolved, rejecting, or manipulative father can make it much more difficult for the child to achieve a positive sex-role orientation. Such parental behavior as verbal derogation of the child's body adequacy and sexuality, as well as direct erotic-genital abuse, can be considered as part of a broad definition of sexual maltreatment. Children who are inadequately fathered and sexually maltreated are at risk for developing severe sex-role conflicts and serious deficits in interpersonal competence.

21. In two-parent families there are generally very different developmental outcomes for children who are maltreated by their fathers than for those who have experienced positive, nurturant fathering. Paternal maltreatment tends to be associated with deficits in self-concept and personal adjustment as well as with lessened competence in cognitive, academic, social, emotional, and heterosexual functioning. The maltreating father is an especially poor model for his child. Fathers who are very controlling, punitive, authoritarian, and nonnurturant are likely to have children who are relatively timid, passive, anxious, and low in self-esteem and interpersonal competence. Fathers who demonstrate poor impulse control and are abusive and rejecting are likely to have children who have serious identity and relationship problems and who may engage in antisocial and/or delinquent behavior. Maltreatment by fathers is a major factor in the development of insecure children, especially vulnerable to negative peer influence and to alcohol- and other drug-related difficulties. In contrast, fathers who are nurturant, accepting, and relatively rational and calm in dealing with their children are likely to have confident, socially and academically successful sons and daughters. Well-fathered individuals typically have an advantage in intellectual and academic achievement, social skills, and sexual adjustment and have high rates of self-esteem and overall mental health. The degree to which the father provides an appropriate model of social behavior and problem solving and the quality of his relationship with the mother are very important, but the most basic ingredient is his nurturance and acceptance of the child's individuality.

22. Both males and females are greatly influenced by the quality of fathering they receive, but variations relating to the sex and developmental stage of the child must be considered. In general, in early development (including infancy) boys, compared to girls, appear to be both more positively influenced by active fathering and more handicapped by paternal deprivation. At least

superficially, young boys are more consistently affected in self-concept and in cognitive and social functioning by the quality of fathering they receive. However, the quality of the early father-daughter relationship has much to do with the female's psychological and social competence with respect to interactions with males in adolescence and adulthood, ability to function as a wife and mother, and competence in dealing with various aspects of career development. Early paternal influence is important for girls but tends to manifest itself less dramatically in preadolescence than it does for boys. For boys as well as girls there are so-called sleeper effects: the influence of a particular form of fathering does not have to have a visible and immediate impact on the child's behavior, but its ramifications may become clearer at a later developmental stage. Some of the consequences of early paternal deprivation do not seem to become apparent until later in development or even in adulthood, when the individual confronts certain family and vocational responsibilities.

23. Although paternal deprivation, particularly if it occurs early and chronically in the child's development, is likely to have a deleterious impact, there are a vast number of factors to consider and tremendous variations in outcome. A major factor is the specific etiology of paternal deprivation, which may greatly influence the quality of parenting the child receives from the mother. The reason the mother is husband-absent may have much to do with whether or not she abuses her child and, if so, with the type of maltreatment. For example, children who lose their fathers because of death seem to be influenced in different ways than children whose fathers are absent because of divorce. *In general,* mothers in families in which the father has died are less likely to act out toward their children and are also more apt to present a positive view (perhaps too positive and unrealistic) of the absent parent, whereas mothers who are divorced are more likely to express frustration toward their children, particularly sons, and to have much unresolved bitterness toward their ex-husbands. The mother's financial resources, interactions with other family members, and social network are likely to vary greatly as a function of whether she is a widow or a divorcée, which in turn can grealty affect the way she deals with her children.

24. The child who has an involved and competent mother *and* father is more likely to have generally adequate psychological functioning and is less likely to suffer from developmental deficits and psychopathology than is the child who is reared in a female-headed single-parent family. However, this generalization is not the same as assuming that all father-absent children will have more difficulties in their development than all father-present children. For example, children with competent mothers are less likely to have certain types of developmental deficits than are children who have a dominating mother and a passive-ineffectual father. Also, individuals whose fathers are highly available in terms of physical presence but very uninvolved with them emotionally may have serious difficulties in interpersonal adjustment. The father-absent child

may develop a more flexible image of adult men and at least may seek out some type of father-surrogate, whereas the child with a passive-ineffectual and/or rejecting father may have a very negative and ambivalent image of adult males and have great difficulty interacting with them.

25. The psychological adjustment of the mother in the father-absent family is a crucial factor; a mother who is emotionally disturbed and/or interpersonally handicapped can have a very negative effect on the child's self-concept and ability to relate to others. On the other hand, mothers who are self-accepting, have high ego strength, are interpersonally mature, and can effectively set limits can do much to facilitate positive personality development among their paternally deprived children. The mother's attitudes are related to her social and economic opportunities and are readily transmitted to the child. Maternal views concerning the worth of education are often linked to sociocultural background. As a function of differing maternal values and reinforcement patterns, middle-class father-absent children are generally less handicapped in intellectual and academic pursuits than are father-absent children of low socioeconomic status. Middle-class father-absent children appear to receive more maternal encouragement for developing language, reading, and other academic skills, as well as for school achievement, than do economically deprived father-absent children.

Potential Solutions

26. Children living with their mothers subsequent to a divorce or separation may be labeled father-absent, but there is tremendous variation in the amount and quality of contact they have with their fathers. In some families, children whose parents are divorced may never see their fathers again; in other families they may have contact with their fathers on a daily basis and may even spend more time with them than they did before the divorce. Many children whose fathers do not live with them spend more time with their fathers than do children in so-called father-present families. There are clear advantages of a high level of positive father-child interaction, even when the parents are divorced or separated. In most cases, joint or shared custody arrangements are more beneficial to the development of the child and of the parents than are traditional custody arrangements, which tend to limit father-child contact and to overburden single mothers. Many fathers in two-parent families could learn much from those divorced fathers who constructively share parenting responsibilities with their ex-wives; it is ironic that some fathers make *more* of a commitment to child rearing postdivorce. A major impetus in divorce prevention and in family therapy should be to strengthen the cooperation of fathers and mothers in parenting.

27. A very important developmental implication of paternal deprivation and child maltreatment is that children who are inadequately parented are likely

to show deficiencies in their abilities to deal constructively with their own children. A dramatic illustration of this is the difficulty that many men and women who were physically or sexually abused as children have in interacting with their own sons and daughters. Intergenerational patterns of child maltreatment and paternal deprivation all too often appear to be like family heirlooms. The most effective way to alleviate the incidence and cost of child maltreatment is to involve males as well as females directly in various types of parenting preparation and parent training programs aimed at decreasing paternal deprivation in the family and other social institutions.

28. Males as well as females can improve their parenting skills. Expectant and new fathers who are given information about early child development and opportunities to talk about issues in fathering, including experiences with their own fathers, are more effective with their infants than are those who lack such exposure. Fathers can be taught through modeling techniques and special "homework assignments" how to relate more positively to their children. Such learning experiences have a constructive impact on both the men and their children. Intervention procedures in which father-child interactions are targeted directly have demonstrated improvement in both father and child behavior. Certainly, men need to be motivated to take advantage of such endeavors: expectant and new fathers, or those who are experiencing frustrations with their children, may be particularly interested in developing better fathering skills. More family life education programs for children and adolescents also need to be mounted within our school systems.

29. It is crucial to strengthen societal attitudes and values supporting the importance of men in the lives of children. Our business, educational, and political leaders need to acknowledge, through their own behaviors and with respect to their leadership of organizations that fathers should be more involved and accessible to their children and should share more child-rearing responsibilities with mothers. Men and women in leadership positions should give more attention to advocating social policy and legislation supportive of a stronger paternal role in child and family development. Educational leaders should more fully address the needs of children and families in their communities. As they become more aware of various problems associated with paternal deprivation and child maltreatment, they can incorporate prevention and intervention efforts into school and community programming. The segregation of men from children must be greatly decreased in order to fight paternal deprivation at the broad social level. Major corporations need to allow more paternity leaves, more opportunity to bring children to work, more flexible scheduling, and more outreach to children in sharing their resources. Incentives should also be provided to involve more men in careers relating to child care and early childhood education. Creative solutions are necessary for helping men as well as women balance career and child-rearing responsibilities.

30. A fundamental thrust in dealing with child maltreatment must be addressing the rampant paternal deprivation in our society. More support needs to be given to single-parent families, to childen and adults affected by divorce, and to unwed, expectant and potential parents. A major focus should be on reaching out especially to potential fathers, expectant fathers, and new fathers. The concern should be not only with obvious forms of paternal deprivation, child maltreatment, and individual and family pathology, but also with optimizing parenting skills and giving adults and children the opportunity to grow and reach their full potential. There should be programs that provide opportunities to discuss feelings and experiences in a supportive group context as well as dispensing factual information about parenting and prenatal, child, and adult development. Such programs can begin in the context of family life education in our schools for children who may relatively soon themselves be assuming parenting responsibilities. We are not suggesting any lessened effort in setting up programs for females, but we are emphasizing that males must be included. Child-rearing education opportunities that can attract men are vitally necessary if we are to reduce maltreatment and paternal deprivation. Both fathers and prospective fathers need to be involved directly in prevention as well as intervention efforts.

Bibliography

Abarbanel, A. 1979. Shared parenting after separation and divorce: A study of joint custody. *American Journal of Orthopsychiatry, 49,* 320–329.

Abelin, E.L. 1975. Some further observations and comments on the earliest role of the father. *International Journal of Psychoanalysis, 56,* 293–302.

Aberle, D.F., & Naegele, F.D. 1952. Middle-class fathers' occupational role and attitude toward children. *American Journal of Orthopsychiatry, 22,* 366–378.

Adams, P.L.; Milner, J.R.; & Schrepf, N.A. 1984. *Fatherless children.* New York: Wiley.

Aichorn, A. 1935. *Wayward youth.* New York: Viking.

Ainsworth, M.D.S. 1973. The development of infant-mother attachment. In B.M. Caldwell & G.H.N. Ricciuti (Eds.), *Review of child development research* (Vol. 3). Chicago: University of Chicago Press.

Ainsworth, M.D.S. 1980. Attachment and child abuse. In G. Gerbner, C.J. Ross, & E. Zigler (Eds.), *Child abuse: An agenda for action.* New York: Oxford University Press.

Albee, G.W. 1980. Primary prevention and social problems. In G. Gerbner, C.J. Ross, & E. Zigler (Eds.), *Child abuse: An agenda for action.* New York: Oxford University Press.

Albert, R. 1971. Cognitive development and parent loss among the gifted, the exceptionally gifted, and the creative. *Psychological Reports, 29,* 19–26.

Alexander, H.; McQuiston, M.; & Rodeheffon, M. 1976. Residential family therapy. In H.P. Martin (Ed.), *A multi-disciplinary approach to developmental issues and treatment.* Cambridge, Mass.: Ballinger.

Alkire, A.A. 1969. Social power and communication within families of disturbed and nondisturbed preadolescents. *Journal of Personality and Social Psychology, 13,* 335–349.

Allport, G. 1937. *Personality: A psychological interpretation.* New York: Henry Holt.

Allport, G. 1965. *Letters from Jenny.* New York: Harcourt Brace Jovanovich.

Altucher, N. 1957. Conflict in sex identification in boys. Ph.D. dissertation, University of Michigan.

Altus, W.D. 1958. The broken home and factors of adjustment. *Psychological Reports, 4,* 477.

Alvy, K. 1975. Preventing child abuse. *American Psychologist, 30,* 921–928.

American Humane Association. 1978. *National analysis of official child neglect and abuse reporting*. Denver: American Humane Association.

American Humane Association. 1979. *Annual statistical analysis of child neglect and abuse reporting, 1978*. Denver: American Humane Association with the Denver Research Institute, 1979.

American Humane Association. 1985. *National analysis of official child neglect and abuse reporting*. Denver: American Humane Association.

Ancona, L.; Cesa-Bianchi, M.; & Bocquet, C. 1964. Identification with the father in the absence of the paternal model: Research applied to children of Navy officers. *Archivo di Psicologia Neurologia e Psichiatria, 24*, 339–361.

Andersand, P.B. 1968. Parental rejection and adolescent academic advancement. *Dissertation Abstracts, 28* (11-B), 4751.

Anderson, B.J., & Standley, K. 1976. A methodology for observation of the child-birth environment. Paper presented at the meetings of the American Psychological Association, Washington, D.C., September.

Anderson, L.M., & Shafer, G. 1979. The character-disordered family: A treatment model for family sexual abuse. *American Journal of Orthopsychiatry, 49*, 436–445.

Anderson, R.E. 1968. Where's Dad? Paternal deprivation and delinquency. *Archives of General Psychiatry, 18*, 641–649.

Andrews, R.O., & Christensen, H.T. 1951. Relationship of absence of parent to courtship status: A repeat study. *American Sociological Review, 16*, 541–544.

Andry, R.G. 1962. Paternal and maternal roles in delinquency. In *Deprivation of maternal care*, Public Health Paper No. 14. Geneva: World Health Organization, pp. 31–43.

Anthony, E.J. 1982. Afterword. In S.H. Cath, A.R. Gurwitt, & J.M. Ross (Eds.), *Father and child: Developmental and clinical perspectives*. Boston: Little, Brown, pp. 579–586.

Apperson, L.B., & McAdoo, W.G., Jr. 1968. Parental factors in the childhood of homosexuals. *Journal of Abnormal Psychology, 73*, 201–206.

Archibald, H.; Bell, D.; Miller, C.; & Tuddenham, P. 1962. Bereavement in childhood and adult psychiatric disturbance. *Psychosomatic Medicine, 4*, 343–351.

Aries, P. 1962. *Centuries of childhood: A social history of family life*. New York: Random House.

Arney, W.R.; Nagy, J.N.; & Little, G. 1978. Caring for parents of sick newborns. *Clinical Pediatrics, 17*, 35–39.

Arnstein, H. 1972. The crisis of becoming a father. *Sexual Behavior, 2*, 42–48.

Avery, J.C. 1973. The battered child: A shocking problem. *Mental Hygiene, 57*, 40–43.

Bach, G.R. 1946. Father-fantasies and father typing in father-separated children. *Child Development, 17*, 63–80.

Bach, G.R., & Bremer, G. 1947. Projective father fantasies of preadolescent, delinquent children. *Journal of Psychology, 24*, 3–17.

Bacon, M.K.; Child, I.L.; & Barry, H. 1963. A cross-cultural study of correlates of crime. *Journal of Abnormal and Social Psychology, 66*, 291–300.

Baggett, A.T. 1967. The effect of early loss of father upon the personality of boys and girls in late adolescence. *Dissertation Abstracts, 28* (1-B), 356–357.

Bahlmann, D. 1984. Prepared statement concerning Big Brothers/Big Sisters. In G. Miller, et al., *Paternal absence and fathers' roles*. Hearing before the Select Committee on Children, Youth and Families. House of Representatives, 98th Congress, 1st Session. Washington, D.C.: U.S. Government Printing Office.

Bakan, D. 1971. *Slaughter of the innocents*. San Francisco: Jossey-Bass.

Baker, J.W., & Holzworth, A. 1961. Social histories of successful and unsuccessful children. *Child Development, 32*, 135–149.

Baker, S.L.; Cove, L.A.; Fagen, S.A.; Fischer, E.G.; & Janda, E.J. 1968. Impact of father-absence: III. Problems of family reintegration following prolonged father-absence. Paper presented at the meeting of the American Orthopsychiatric Association, Washington, D.C., March.

Ban, P.L., & Lewis, M. 1971. Mothers and fathers, girls and boys: Attachment behavior in the one-year-old. Paper presented at the meeting of the Eastern Psychological Association, New York, April.

Ban, P.L., & Lewis, M. 1974. Mothers and fathers, girls and boys: Attachment behavior in the one-year-old. *Merrill-Palmer Quarterly, 20*, 195–204.

Bandura, A. 1969. *Principles of behavior modification*. New York: Holt, Rinehart and Winston.

Bandura, A. 1973. *Aggression: A social learning analysis*. Englewood Cliffs, N.J.: Prentice-Hall.

Bandura, A. 1977. *Social learning theory*. Englewood Cliffs, N.J.: Prentice-Hall.

Bandura, A., & Walters, R.A. 1958. Dependency conflicts in aggressive delinquents. *Journal of Social Issues, 14*, 52–65.

Bandura, A., & Walters, R.H. 1959. *Adolescent aggression: A study of the influence of child-rearing practices and family interrelationships*. New York: Ronald Press.

Bank, S., & Kahn, M. 1982. In M.E. Lamb & B. Sutton-Smith (Eds.), *Sibling relationships: Their nature and significance across the lifespan*. Hillsdale, N.J.: Lawrence Erlbaum Associates.

Barahal, R.M.; Waterman, J.; & Martin, H.P. 1981. The social cognitive development of abused children. *Journal of Consulting and Clinical Psychology, 49*, 508–516.

Barclay, A.G., & Cusumano, D. 1967. Father-absence, cross-sex identity, and field dependent behavior in male adolescents. *Child Development, 38*, 243–250.

Barclay, J.R.; Stilwell, W.E.; and Barclay, L.K. 1972. The influence of parental occupation on social interaction measures of elementary school children. *Journal of Vocational Behavior, 2*, 433–446.

Barnard, K.E. 1980. Maternal involvement and responsiveness: Definition and developmental course. Paper presented at the Second International Conference on Infant Studies, New Haven, Conn.

Barnes, G.B.; Chabon, R.S.; & Hertzberg, L.J. 1974. Team treatment for abusive families. *Social Casework, 55*, 600–611.

Barnett, R.C., & Baruch, G.K. 1978. *The competent woman: Perspectives on development*. New York: Irvington.

Barry, W.A. 1970. Marriage research and conflict: An integrative review. *Psychological Bulletin, 73*, 41–55.

Baumrind, D. 1967. Child rearing practices anteceding three patterns of preschool behavior. *Genetic Psychology Monographs, 78*, 43–88.

Baumrind, D. 1971. Current patterns of parental authority. *Developmental Psychology Monographs, 4*, 1–103.

Baumrind, D., & Black, A.E. 1967. Socialization practices associated with dimensions of competence in preschool boys and girls. *Child Development, 38,* 291–327.

Baxter, J.C.; Horton, D.L.; & Wiley, R.E. 1964. Father identification as a function of the mother-father relationship. *Journal of Individual Psychology, 20,* 167–171.

Beck, A.T.; Sehti, B.B.; & Tuthill, R.W. 1963. Childhood bereavement and adult depression. *Archives of General Psychiatry, 9,* 295–302.

Becker, W.C. 1964. Consequences of different types of parental discipline. In M.L. Hoffman & L.W. Hoffman (Eds.), *Review of child development research, Vol. 1.* New York: Russell Sage Foundation.

Becker, W.C.; Peterson, D.R.; Hellmer, L.A.; Shoemaker, D.J.; & Quay, H.C. 1959. Factors in parental behavior and personality as related to problem behavior in children. *Journal of Consulting Psychology, 23,* 107–118.

Becker, W.C.; Peterson, D.R.; Luria, Z.; Shoemaker, D.S.; & Hellmer, L.A. 1962. Relations of factors derived from parent interview ratings to behavior problems of five-year-olds. *Child Development, 33,* 509–535.

Beezley, P.; Martin, H.; & Alexander, H. 1976. Comprehensive family oriented therapy. In R.E. Helper & C.H. Kempe (Eds.), *Child abuse and neglect: The family and the community.* Cambridge, Mass.: Ballinger.

Beezley, P.; Martin, H.P.; & Kempe, R. 1976. Psychotherapy. In H.P. Martin (Ed.), *A multidisciplinary approach to developmental issues and treatment.* Cambridge, Mass.: Ballinger.

Bell, R.Q. 1968. A reinterpretation of the direction of effects in studies of socialization. *Psychological Review, 75,* 81–95.

Beller, E.K. 1967. Maternal behaviors in lower-class Negro mothers. Paper presented at the meeting of the Eastern Psychological Association, Boston, April.

Belsky, J. 1978a. A theoretical analysis of child abuse remediation strategies. *Journal of Clinical Child Psychology, 8,* 113–117.

Belsky, J. 1978b. Three theoretical models of child abuse. *Child Abuse and Neglect: The International Journal, 3,* 37–49.

Belsky, J. 1979a. The interrelation of parental and spousal behavior in traditional nuclear families: An exploratory analysis. *Journal of Marriage and the Family, 41,* 749–755.

Belsky, J. 1979b. Mother-father-infant interaction: A naturalistic observational study. *Developmental Psychology, 15,* 601–607.

Belsky, J. 1980a. Child abuse: An ecological integration. *American Psychologist, 35,* 320–335.

Belsky, J. 1980b. A family analysis of parental influence on infant exploratory competence. In F.A. Pedersen (Ed.), *The father-child relationship: Observational studies in the family system.* New York: Praeger.

Belsky, J. 1981. Early human experience: A family perspective. *Developmental Psychology, 17,* 3–23.

Belsky, J.; Gilstrap, B.; & Ravine, M. 1984. The Pennsylvania Infant and Family Development Project: Stability and change in mother-infant and father-infant interactions in a family setting at one, three and nine months. *Child Development, 55,* 692–705.

Belsky, J., & Steinberg, L.D. 1978. The effects of day care: A critical review. *Child Development, 49,* 929–949.

Bem, S.L. 1979. Theory and measurement of androgeny: A reply to the Pelahuzur-Tetenbaum and Locksley-Collon critiques. *Journal of Personality and Social Psychology, 37,* 1047–1054.

Bem, D., & Allen, A. 1974. On predicting some of the people some of the time: The search for cross-situational consistencies in behavior. *Psychological Review, 81,* 506–520.

Bendicksen, R., & Fulton, R. 1975. Death and the child: An anteriospective test of the childhood bereavement and later behavior disorder hypothesis. *Omega: Journal of Death and Dying, 6,* 45–49.

Bené, E. 1965. On the genesis of female homosexuality. *British Journal of Psychiatry, 3,* 815–821.

Bennett, I. 1959. *Delinquent and neurotic children: A comparative study.* New York: Basic Books.

Benson, L. 1968. *Fatherhood: A sociological perspective.* New York: Random House.

Benward, J., & Denson-Gerber, J. 1975. Incest as a causative factor in antisocial behavior: An exploratory study. *Contemporary Drug Problems, 4,* 322–340.

Berkeley Planning Associates. 1977. *Evaluation of child abuse and neglect demonstration projects 1974–1977,* Vols. I–XII. Final Report, Berkeley, Calif. NTIS No. PB-278 439.

Berkeley Planning Associates. 1981. *Client impact report: Evaluation of the Plaza Family Support Center,* Berkeley, Calif.

Berliner, L., & Stevens, D. 1982. Clinical issues in child sexual behavior. *Journal of Social Work and Human Sexuality, 132,* 93–109.

Berlinsky, E.B., & Biller, H.B. 1982. *Parental death and psychological development.* Lexington, Mass.: Lexington Books, D.C. Heath.

Berman, A., & Siegal, A. 1976a. Adaptive and learning skills in juvenile delinquents: A neuropsychological analysis. *Journal of Learning Disabilities, 9,* 583–590.

Berman, A., & Siegal, A. 1976b. A neuropsychological approach to the etiology, prevention and treatment of juvenile delinquency. In A. Davids (Ed.), *Child personality and psychopathology, current topics,* Vol. III. New York: Wiley.

Berman, D.B. 1978. The facilitation of mourning: A preventative mental health approach. *Dissertation Abstracts International, 78,* 10684.

Bible, C., & French, A.P. 1979. Depression in the child abuse syndrome. In A.P. French (Ed.). *Depression in children and adolescents.* New York: Human Sciences Press.

Bieber, I., et al. 1962. *Homosexuality: A psychoanalytic study.* New York: Basic Books.

Bieri, J. 1960. Parental identification, acceptability, and authority, and within-sex differences in cognitive behavior. *Journal of Abnormal and Social Psychology, 60,* 76–79.

Biller, H.B. 1968a. A multiaspect investigation of masculine development in kindergarten-age boys. *Genetic Psychology Monographs, 76,* 89–139.

Biller, H.B. 1968b. A note on father-absence and masculine development in young lower-class Negro and white boys. *Child Development, 39,* 1003–1006.

Biller, H.B. 1969a. Father-absence, maternal encouragement, and sex-role development in kindergarten-age boys. *Child Development, 40,* 539–546. Reprinted in R.C. Smart & M.S. Smart (Eds.), *Readings in child development and relationships* (New York: Macmillan, 1972).

Biller, H.B. 1969b. Father dominance and sex-role development in kindergarten-age boys. *Developmental Psychology, 1,* 87–94. Reprinted in slightly abridged form in D.R. Heise (Ed.), *Personality and socialization* (New York: Rand McNally, 1972).

Biller, H.B. 1969c. Maternal salience and feminine development in young girls. *Proceedings of the Seventy-seventh Annual Convention of the American Psychological Association, 4,* 259–260.

Biller, H.B. 1970. Father-absence and the personality development of the male child. *Developmental Psychology, 2,* 181–201. Reprinted in S. Chess & A. Thomas (Eds.), *Annual progress in child psychology and child development* (New York: Brunner/Mazel, 1971). Reprinted in slightly abridged form in D.R. Heise (Ed.), *Personality and socialization* (New York: Rand McNally, 1972).

Biller, H.B. 1971a. *Father, child, and sex role,* Lexington, Mass.: Lexington Books, D.C. Heath and Company.

Biller, H.B. 1971b. Fathering and female sexual development. *Medical Aspects of Human Sexuality, 5,* 116–138.

Biller, H.B. 1971c. The mother-child relationship and the father-absent boy's personality development. *Merrill-Palmer Quarterly, 17,* 227–241. Reprinted in slightly abridged form in U. Bronfenbrenner (Ed.), *Influences on human development* (Hinsdale, Ill.: Dryden Press, 1972).

Biller, H.B. 1971d. Sexual attitudes of one-parent children (Invited commentary). *Medical Aspects of Human Sexuality* 5(9), 214. Reprinted in L. Gross (Ed.), *Medical aspects of human sexuality* (New York: Williams and Williams, 1975).

Biller, H.B. 1972. Include the father in pregnancy (Invited commentary). *Medical Aspects of Human Sexuality,* 2(4), 47. Reprinted in L. Gross (Ed.), *Sexual issues in marriage* (New York: Spectrum, 1975).

Biller, H.B. 1973a. The father's role. *London Sunday Times Magazine,* February 25, 48–50.

Biller, H.B. 1973b. Sex-role uncertainty and psychopathology. *Journal of Individual Psychology, 29,* 24–25.

Biller, H.B. 1974a. Paternal and sex-role factors in cognitive and academic functioning. In J.K. Cole & R. Dienstbier (Eds.), *Nebraska Symposium on Motivation, 1973.* Lincoln: University of Nebraska Press, pp. 83–123.

Biller, H.B. 1974b. Paternal deprivation, cognitive functioning and the feminized classroom. In A. Davids (Ed.), *Child personality and psychopathology: Current topics.* New York: Wiley, pp. 11–52.

Biller, H.B. 1974c. *Paternal deprivation: Family, school, sexuality and society.* Lexington, Mass.: Lexington Books, D.C. Heath and Company.

Biller, H.B. 1974d. Syndromes of paternal deprivation in man. In J.H. Cullen (Ed.), *Experimental behavior: A basis for the study of mental disturbance.* Dublin: Irish University Press.

Biller, H.B. 1975a. The effects of intermittent but prolonged absence of the father. *Medical Aspects of Human Sexuality, 9,* 179.

Biller, H.B. 1975b. Review of Richard Green's *Sexual identity conflicts in children and adults. Archives of Sexual Behavior, 4,* 105–106.

Biller, H.B. 1976a. The father and personality development: Paternal deprivation and sex-role development. In M.E. Lamb (Ed.), *The role of the father in child development.* New York: Wiley, pp. 89–156.

Biller, H.B. 1976b. The father-child relationship: Some crucial issues. In V. Vaughn & B. Brazelton (Eds.), *The family—Can it be saved?* Chicago: Year Book Medical Publishers, pp. 69–76.

Biller, H.B. 1977a. Father absence and paternal deprivation. In B. Wolman (Ed.), *International encyclopedia of neurology, psychiatry, psychoanalysis and psychology.* New York: Van Nostrand Reinhold.

Biller, H.B. 1977b. Fathers and children. In B. Wolman (Ed.), *International encyclopedia of neurology, psychiatry, psychoanalysis and psychology.* New York: Van Nostrand Reinhold.

Biller, H.B. 1977c. Sex-role learning: Some comments and complexities from a multidimensional perspective. In S. Cohen & T.J. Comiskey (Eds.), *Child development: A study of growth processes.* Ithaca, Ill.: Peacock, pp. 201–207.

Biller, H.B. 1978. Father absence and military families. In E.J. Hunter (Ed.), *A report on the military family research conference.* San Diego: Family Studies Branch, Naval Health Research Center, pp. 45–48.

Biller, H.B. (featured commentator/consultant). 1980a. *Fathers.* Washington, D.C. Durrin Films/ASPO/Lamaze.

Biller, H.B. 1980b. Methodologic problems in research on psychosexual differentiation. In R. Green & J. Weiner (Eds.), *Methodology of sex research.* Rockville, Md.: National Institutes of Mental Health.

Biller, H.B. 1981a. Father absence, divorce, and personality development. In M.E. Lamb (Ed.), *The role of the father in child development* (2nd Ed.). New York: Wiley.

Biller, H.B. 1981b. The father and sex role development. In M.E. Lamb (Ed.), *The role of the father in child development* (2nd Ed.). New York: Wiley.

Biller, H.B. 1982a. Fatherhood: Implications for child and adult development. In B.B. Wolman (Ed.), *Handbook of developmental psychology.* Englewood Cliffs, N.J.: Prentice-Hall, pp. 702–725.

Biller, H.B. 1982b. The father-infant relationship. Unpublished manuscript, University of Rhode Island.

Biller, H.B. 1982c. Review of M.S. Rosenthal and H. Keshet, *Fathers without partners. Contemporary Psychology, 27,* 25–26.

Biller, H.B. 1983a. The effect on the boy of a passive father. In L. Gross (Ed.), *The parents' guide to teenagers.* New York: Macmillan, pp. 225–226.

Biller, H.B. 1983b. Fatherhood: Doing it right. *USA Today,* June 17, Section D, p. 1.

Biller, H.B. 1984a. Oral testimony concerning father absence and paternal deprivation. In G. Miller et al., *Paternal absence and fathers' roles.* Hearing before the Select Committee on Children, Youth and Families. House of Representatives, 98th Congress, 1st Session. Washington, D.C.: U.S. Government Printing Office, pp. 78–82.

Biller, H.B. 1984b. Prepared statement concerning father absence and paternal deprivation. In G. Miller et al., *Paternal absence and fathers' roles.* Hearing before the Select Committee on Children, Youth and Families. House of Representatives, 98th Congress, 1st Session. Washington, D.C.: U.S. Government Printing Office, pp. 82–85.

Biller, H.B. 1984c. Prepared statement concerning paternal deprivation, therapy and prevention. In G. Miller et al., *Paternal absence and fathers' roles.* Hearing before the Select Committee on Children, Youth and Families. House of Representatives, 98th Congress, 1st Session. Washington, D.C.: U.S. Government Printing Office, pp. 128–129.

Biller, H.B., & Bahm, R.M. 1971. Father-absence, perceived maternal behavior and masculinity of self-concept among junior high school boys. *Developmental Psychology, 4*, 178–181.

Biller, H.B., & Barry, W. 1971. Sex-role patterns, paternal similarity, and personality adjustment in college males. *Developmental Psychology, 4*, 107.

Biller, H.B., & Borstelmann, L.J. 1965. Intellectual level and sex-role development in mentally retarded children. *American Journal of Mental Deficiency, 70*, 443–447.

Biller, H.B., & Borstelmann, L.J. 1967. Masculine development: An integrative review. *Merrill-Palmer Quarterly, 13*, 253–294.

Biller, H.B.; Costello, I.; Dill, J.R.; Hetherington, E.M.; Hoffman, L.W.; Laosa, L.M.; McAdoo, H.P.; Pedersen, F.A.; Sprung, B.; Stein, P.J.; & Sullivan, J. (Board of Consultants). 1977. *Mothers and fathers*. New York: Parents' Magazine Films.

Biller, H.B., & Davids, T. 1973. Parent-child relations, personality development and psychopathology. In T. Davids (Ed.), *Issues in abnormal child psychology*. Belmont, Calif.: Brooks/Cole.

Biller, H.B., & Liebman, D.A. 1971. Body build, sex-role preference, and sex-role adoption in junior high school boys. *Journal of Genetic Psychology, 118*, 81–86.

Biller, H.B., & Meredith, D.L. 1972. The invisible American father. *Sexual Behavior, 2*(7), 16–22. Reprinted in slightly abridged form in L. Gross (Ed.), *Sexual issues in marriage* (New York: Spectrum, 1975).

Biller, H.B., & Meredith, D.L. 1974. *Father power*. New York: David McKay, 1974; Reprinted, New York: Doubleday Anchor Books, 1975.

Biller, H.B., & Meredith, D.L. 1982. Father power, mother power. In S. Cahill (Ed.), *Motherhood: A reader for men and women*. New York: Avon Books, pp. 170–176.

Biller, H.B., & Poey, K. 1969. An exploratory comparison of sex-role related behavior in schizophrenics and nonschizophrenics. *Developmental Psychology, 1*, 629.

Biller, H.B., & Salter, M. 1982. Adolescent unwed fathers. Unpublished manuscript, University of Rhode Island.

Biller, H.B., & Salter, M. 1985. Fathers, mothers and infants growing together. *Lamaze Parents Magazine*. Arlington, Va.: ASPO/Lamaze, pp. 56–64.

Biller, H.B., & Salter, M. 1986. *Fathers, mothers and children growing together: A lifespan perspective*. In preparation.

Biller, H.B.; Singer, D.L.; & Fullerton, M. 1969. Sex role development and creative potential among kindergarten-age boys. *Developmental Psychology, 1*, 291–296.

Biller, H.B., & Smith, A.E. 1972. An AFDC mothers' group: An exploratory effort in community mental health. *Family Coordinator, 21*, 287–290.

Biller, H.B., & Weiss, S. 1970. The father-daughter relationship and the personality development of the female. *Journal of Genetic Psychology, 114*, 79–93. Reprinted in D. Rogers (Ed.), *Issues in adolescent psychology* (New York: Appleton-Century-Crofts, 1970).

Biller, H.B., & Zung, B. 1972. Perceived maternal control, anxiety, and opposite sex role preference among elementary school girls. *Journal of Psychology, 81*, 85–88.

Billingsley, A. 1968. *Black families in white America.* Englewood Cliffs, N.J.: Prentice-Hall.

Birtchnell, J. 1970. Early parent death and mental illness. *British Journal of Psychiatry, 116*, 281–287.

Birtchnell, J. 1975. The personality characteristics of early bereaved psychiatric patients, *Social Psychiatry, 10*, 97–103.

Bittman, S., & Zalk, S.R. 1978. *Expectant fathers.* New York: Ballantine Books.

Black, R., & Mayer, J. 1980. Parents with special problems: Alcoholism and opiate addiction. In C.H. Kempe & R.E. Helfer, *The battered child* (3rd Ed.). Chicago: University of Chicago Press.

Blanchard, R.W., & Biller, H.B. 1971. Father availability and academic performance among third grade boys. *Developmental Psychology, 4*, 301–305.

Block, J. 1969. Parents of schizophrenic, neurotic, asthmatic, and congenitally ill children: A comparative study. *Archives of General Psychiatry, 20*, 654–674.

Block, J. 1971. *Lives through-time.* Berkeley, Calif.: Bancroft Books.

Block, J.H. 1974. Another look at sex differentiation in the socialization behaviors of mothers and fathers. In F. Denmark (Ed.), *Psychology of women: Future directions of research.* New York: Psychological Dimensions.

Block, J.; von der Lippe, A.; & Block, J.H. 1973. Sex role and socialization: Some personality concomitants and environmental antecedents. *Journal of Consulting and Clinical Psychology, 41*, 321–341.

Bloom-Feshbach, J. 1981. Historical perspectives on the father's role. In M.E. Lamb (Ed.), *The role of the father in child development* (2nd Ed.). New York: Wiley, pp. 71–112.

Blumberg, M.L. 1974. Psychopathology of the abusing parent. *American Journal of Psychotherapy, 28*, 21–29.

Bolton, F.G.; Laner, R.H.; & Kane, S.P. 1980. Child maltreatment risk among adolescent mothers: A study of reported cases. *American Journal of Orthopsychiatry, 50*, 489–504.

Boss, P.G. 1977. A clarification of the concept of psychological father presence in families experiencing ambiguity of boundary. *Journal of Marriage and the Family, 39*, 141–151.

Boss, P.G.; McCubbin, H.I.; & Lester, G. 1979. The corporate executive wife's coping patterns in response to routine husband-father absence. *Family Process, 18*, 79–86.

Bourdin, C.M., & Henggeler, S.W. 1982. Psychosocial development of father-absent children: A systems perspective. In S.W. Henggeler (Ed.), *Delinquency and adolescent psychopathology: A family-ecological systems approach.* Littleton, Mass.: PSG-Wright.

Bourne, R. 1979. Child abuse and neglect: An overview. In R. Bourne & E.H. Newberger (Eds.), *Critical perspectives on child abuse.* Lexington, Mass.: Lexington Books, D.C. Heath and Company, 1979.

Bowerman, C.E., & Irish, D. 1962. Some relationships of stepchildren to their parents. *Marriage and Family Living, 24*, 113–121.

Bowlby, J. 1958. The nature of the child's tie to his mother. *International Journal of Psychoanalysis, 39*, 350–375.

Bowlby, J. 1969. *Attachment and loss* (Vol. 1). *Attachment*. New York: Basic Books.

Bowlby, J. 1973. *Attachment and loss* (Vol. 2). *Separation, anxiety and anger*. New York: Basic Books.

Brady, S. 1978. Daddy's gone to Colorado: Male staffed child care for father-absent boys. *Counseling Psychologist, 7*, 33–36.

Brandwein, H. 1973. The battered child: A definite and significant factor in mental retardation. *Mental Retardation, 11*, 50–51.

Brandwein, R.A.; Brown, C.A.; & Fox, E.M. 1974. Women and children last: The social situation of divorced mothers and their children. *Journal of Marriage and the Family, 36*, 498–514.

Brazelton, T.B.; Yogman, M.W.; Als, H.; & Tronick, E. 1979. The infant as a focus for family reciprocity. In M. Lewis & L.A. Rosenblum (Eds.), *The child and its family*. New York: Plenum.

Bremmer, R.H. 1976. *Children and youth in America: A documentary history* (Vol. II). Cambridge, Mass.: Harvard University Press.

Bretherton, I., & Waters, E. (Eds.). 1985. Growing points of attachment theory and research. *Monographs of the Society for Research in Child Development, 50* (1–2, Serial No. 209).

Breton, M. 1980. The school's role in the coordination of child-protection efforts. In R. Volpe, M. Breton, & J. Mitton (Eds.), *The maltreatment of the school-aged child*. Lexington, Mass.: Lexington Books, D.C. Heath and Company.

Brill, N.Q., & Liston, E.H. 1966. Parental loss in adults with emotional disorders. *Archives of General Psychiatry, 14*, 307–314.

Broderick, G.B. 1977. Fathers. *Family Coordinator, 26*, 269–275.

Brody, S., & Axelrad, S. 1978. *Mothers, fathers, and children*. New York: International Universities Press.

Bronfenbrenner, U. 1958. The study of identification through interpersonal perception. In R. Taguiri & L. Petrullo (Eds.), *Person perception and interpersonal behavior*. Stanford: Stanford University Press, pp. 110–130.

Bronfenbrenner, U. 1960. Freudian theories of identification and their derivatives. *Child Development, 31*, 15–40.

Bronfenbrenner, U. 1961. Some familial antecedents of responsibility and leadership in adolescents. In L. Petrullo & B.M. Bass (Eds.), *Leadership and interpersonal behavior*. New York: Holt, Rinehart and Winston, pp. 239–272.

Bronfenbrenner, U. 1967. The psychological costs of quality and equality in education. *Child Development, 38*, 909–925.

Bronfenbrenner, U. 1972. The roots of alienation. In U. Bronfenbrenner (Ed.), *Influences on human development*, Hinsdale, Ill.: Dryden Press.

Bronfenbrenner, U. 1973. Who cares for America's children? In F. Rebelsky & Z. Dorman (Eds.), *Child development and behavior* (2nd Ed.). New York: Knopf.

Bronfenbrenner, U. 1975. The origins of alienation. In U. Bronfenbrenner & M.A. Mahoney (Eds.), *Influences on human development*. Hinsdale, Ill.: Dryden Press.

Bronfenbrenner, U. 1977. Toward an experimental ecology of human development. *American Psychologist, 32*, 513–532.

Bronson, W.C. 1959. Dimensions of ego and infantile identification. *Journal of Personality, 27*, 532–545.

Brooks-Gunn, J., & Lewis, M. 1979. Why mama and papa? The development of social labels. *Child Development, 50*, 1203–1206.

Brown, F. 1961. Depression and childhood bereavement. *Journal of Mental Science, 107*, 754–777.

Brown, F., & Eppos, P. 1966. Childhood bereavement and subsequent psychiatric disorder. *British Journal of Psychiatry, 112*, 1035–1042.

Buchanan, A., & Oliver, J.E. 1977. Abuse and neglect as a cause of mental retardation: A study of 140 children admitted to subnormality hospitals in Wiltshire. *British Journal of Psychiatry, 131*, 458–467.

Burgess, A.W., & Holmstrom, L.L. 1975. Sexual trauma of children and adolescents: Pressure, sex and secrecy. *Nursing Clinics of North America, 10*, 551–563.

Burgess, D.S. 1979. An international perspective on children's rights. In P.A. Verdin & I.N. Brody (Eds.), *Children's rights: Contemporary perspectives*. New York: Teacher's College Press.

Burgess, R. 1978. Child abuse. A behavioral analysis. In B.B. Lahey & A.E. Kazdin (Eds.), *Advances in clinical psychology*. New York: Plenum.

Burgess, R., & Conger, R. 1978. Family interaction in abusive, neglected and normal families. *Child Development, 49*, 1163–1173.

Burlingham, D. 1973. The pre-oedipal infant-father relationship. *The Psychoanalytic Study of the Child, 29*, 23–47.

Burton, R.V. 1972. Cross-sex identity in Barbados. *Developmental Psychology, 6*, 365–374.

Burton, R.V., & Whiting, J.W.M. 1961. The absent father and cross-sex identity. *Merrill-Palmer Quarterly, 7*, 85–95.

Caffey, J. 1946. Multiple fractures in the long bones of infants suffering from chronic subdural hematoma. *American Journal of Roentgenology, 56*, 163–173.

Cain, A.C., & Fast, I. 1965. Children's disturbed reactions to parent suicide. *American Journal of Orthopsychiatry, 36*, 873–880.

Cantoni, L. 1981. Clinical issues in domestic violence. *Social Casework, 62*, 3–12.

Cantwell, H.B. 1981. Sexual abuse of children in Denver, 1979: Reviewed with implications for pediatric intervention and possible prevention. *Child Abuse and Neglect, 5*, 75–85.

Carlsmith, L. 1964. Effect of early father-absence on scholastic aptitude. *Harvard Educational Review, 34*, 3–21.

Cath, S.H.; & Gurwitt, A.R.; & Ross, J.M. (Eds.). 1982. *Father and child: Developmental and clinical perspectives*. Boston: Little, Brown.

Cath, S.H., & Herzog, J.M. 1982. The dying and death of a father. In S.H. Cath, A.R. Gurwitt, & J.M. Ross (Eds.), *Father and child: Developmental and clinical perspectives*. Boston: Little, Brown, pp. 339–356.

Chandler, S.M. 1982. Knowns and unknowns in sexual abuse of children. *Journal of Social Work and Human Sexuality, 1–2*, 51–68.

Chang, J., & Block, J. 1960. A study of identification in male homosexuals. *Journal of Consulting Psychology, 24*, 307–310.

Chapman, M. 1977. Father absence, stepfathers, and the cognitive performance of college students. *Child Development, 48*, 1155–1158.

Chase, N.F. 1976. *A child is being beaten*. New York: McGraw-Hill.

Chein, I.; Gerrard, D.L.; Lee, B.S.; & Rosenfield, E. 1964. *The road to H*. New York: Basic Books.

Chesler, P. 1986. *Mothers on trial: The battle for children and custody*. New York: McGraw-Hill.

Chibucos, T. 1980. A perspective on the mistreatment of children. *Infant Mental Health Journal, 1*, 212–223.

Chilman, C. 1979. *Adolescent sexuality in a changing society: Social and psychological perspectives.* Washington, D.C.: U.S. Department of Health, Education and Welfare.

Cicchetti, C., & Rizley, R. 1981. Developmental perspectives on the etiology, intergenerational transmission, and sequelae of child maltreatment, *New Directions in Child Development, 11*, 31–55.

Clarke, P.A. 1961. A study of the effect upon boys of father absence in the home. Ph.D. dissertation, University of Maryland.

Clarke-Stewart, K.A. 1973. Interactions between mothers and their young children: Characteristics and consequences. *Monographs of the Society for Research in Child Development, 38*, No. 153.

Clarke-Stewart, K.A. 1978. And daddy makes three: The father's impact on mother and young child. *Child Development, 49*, 466–478.

Clarke-Stewart, K.A. 1980. The father's contribution to children's cognitive and social development in early childhood. In F.A. Pedersen (Ed.), *The father-infant relationship: Observational studies in a family setting.* New York: Praeger.

Cobliner, W.G. 1963. Social factors in mental disorders: A contribution to the etiology of mental illness. *Genetic Psychology Monographs, 67*, 151–215.

Cohen, L.J., & Campos, J.J. 1974. Father, mother and stranger as elicitors of attachment behaviors in infancy. *Developmental Psychology, 10*, 146–154.

Cohen, M.; Raphling, D.; & Green, P. 1966. Psychological aspects of the maltreatment syndrome of childhood. *Journal of Pediatrics, 69*, 279–284.

Cohen, S.; Gray, E.; & Wald, M. 1984. *Preventing child maltreatment: A review of what we know.* Chicago: National Committee for Prevention of Child Abuse.

Cohen, S., & Sussman, A. 1975. Incidence of child abuse in the United States. *Child Welfare, 54*, 432–443.

Cohen, T. 1983. The incestuous family revisited. *Social Casework, 69*, 159–161.

Cohn, A.H.; Ridge, S.S.; & Collignon, F.C. 1975. Evaluating innovative treatment programs in child abuse and neglect. *Children Today, 4*, 10–12.

Coleman, J.S., et al. 1966. *Equality of educational opportunity.* Washington, D.C.: National Center for Educational Statistics, Office of Education.

Collins, M.C. 1978. *Child abuser: A study of child abusers in self-help group therapy.* Littleton, Mass.: PSG Publishing Company.

Conte, J. 1982. Sexual abuse of children: Enduring issues for social work. *Journal of Social Work and Human Sexuality, 1–2*, 119.

Conte, J. 1984. Progress in treating the sexual abuse of children. *Social Work, 84*, 258–263.

Conte, J.R., & Berliner, L. 1984. Sexual abuse of children: Implications for practice. *Social Casework, 62*, 601–606.

Cooper, I., & Cormier, B.M. 1982. Inter-generational transmission of incest. *Canadian Journal of Psychiatry, 27*, 231–235.

Coopersmith, S. 1967. *The antecedents of self-esteem.* San Francisco: W.H. Freeman.

Cortés, C.F., & Fleming, E. 1968. The effects of father absence on the adjustment of culturally disadvantaged boys. *Journal of Special Education, 2*, 413–420.

Cowan, L.P.; Cowan, P.A.; Coie, L.; & Coie, J.D. 1978. Becoming a family: The impact of a first child's birth on the couple's relationship. In W.B. Miller & L.F. Newman (Eds.), *The first child and family formation.* Chapel Hill, N.C.: Carolina Population Center.

Cox, C. 1926. Genetic studies of genius: The early mental traits of 300 geniuses. Stanford, Calif.: Stanford University Press.

Crandall, V.J.; Dewey, R.; Katkovsky, W.; & Preston, A. 1964. Parents' attitudes and behaviors and grade-school children's academic achievements. *Journal of Genetic Psychology, 104,* 53–66.

Crockenberg, S.B. 1981. Infant irritability, mother response and social support influences on sensitivity of infant-mother attachment. *Child Development, 52,* 857–865.

Cronenwett, L.R., & Newmark, L.L. 1974. Fathers' responses to child birth. *Nursing Research, 23,* 210–217.

Crook, T., & Eliot, J. 1980. Parental death during childhood and adult depression: A critical review of the literature. *Psychological Bulletin, 87,* 252–259.

Crumley, F.E., & Blumenthal, D.S. 1973. Children's reactions to temporary loss of the father. *American Journal of Psychiatry, 130,* 778–782.

Dai, B. 1953. Some problems of personality development among Negro children. In L. Kluckhohn, H.A. Murray, & D.M. Schneider (Eds.), *Personality in nature, society and culture.* New York: Knopf, pp. 545–566.

Daley, E. 1978. *Father feelings.* New York: William Morrow.

D'Andrade, R.G. 1962. Father absence and cross-sex identification. Ph.D. dissertation, Harvard University.

Daniel, J.; Newberger, E.; Reed, R.; & Kotelchuck, M. 1978. Child abuse screening: Implications of the limited predictive power of abuse discriminants from a controlled family study of pediatric social illness. *Child Abuse and Neglect: The International Journal, 2,* 247–260.

DaSilva, G. 1963. The role of the father with chronic schizophrenic patients. *Journal of the Canadian Psychiatric Association, 8,* 190–203.

DeFrancis, V. 1969. *Protecting the child victims of sex crimes committed by adults.* Denver: American Humane Association.

DeLozier, P. 1979. An application of attachment theory to the study of child abuse. Ph.D. dissertation, California School of Professional Psychology.

deMause, L. 1973. The history of childhood: The basis for psychohistory. *History of Childhood Quarterly, 1,* 1–3.

deMause, L. 1974. The evolution of childhood. *History of Childhood Quarterly, 1,* 503–575.

deMause, L. 1980. Our forebears made childhood a nightmare. In G.J. Williams & J. Money (Eds.), *Traumatic abuse and neglect of children at home.* Baltimore, Md.: The Johns Hopkins University Press.

Demos, J. 1974. The American family in past time. *American Scholar, 43,* 422–446.

Denicola, J. 1980. Training abusive parents in child management. *Journal of Behavior Therapy, 11,* 263–270.

Dennehey, C. 1966. Childhood bereavement and psychiatric illness. *British Journal of Psychiatry, 112,* 1049–1069.

Despert, I.J. 1957. The fatherless family. *Child Study, 34,* 22–28.

Deutsch, H. 1944. *The Psychology of Women, Vol. I.* New York: Grune & Stratton.

Deutsch, M. 1960. Minority group and class status as related to social and personality factors in scholastic achievement. *Monograph of the Society for Applied Anthropology, 2,* 1–32.

Deutsch, M., & Brown, B. 1964. Social influences in Negro-white intelligence differences. *Journal of Social Issues, 20,* 24–35.

Devereux, E.C.; Bronfenbrenner, U.; & Suci, G. 1962. Patterns of parent behavior in the United States of America and the Federal Republic of Germany: A cross-cultural comparison. *International Social Science Journal, 14,* 408–506.

deYoung, M. 1982. Self-injurious behavior in incest victims: A research note. *Child Welfare, 61,* 577–584.

Dickens, C. 1980. Speech on behalf of the Hospital for Sick Children. In G.J. Williams & J. Money (Eds.), *Traumatic abuse and neglect of children at home.* Baltimore, Md.: The Johns Hopkins University Press.

Dickie, J., & Carnahan, S. 1979. Training in social competence: The effect on mothers, fathers, and infants. Paper presented at the biennial meeting of the Society for Research in Child Development, San Francisco.

Dietrick, D.R. 1979. Psychopathology and death fear. *Dissertation Abstracts International, 79,* 18593.

Distler, L.S. 1964. Patterns of parental identification: An examination of three theories. Ph.D. dissertation, University of California, Berkeley.

Divoky, D. 1976. Child abuse: Mandate for teacher intervention? *Learning, 5,* 4–22.

Dodson, F. 1974. *How to father.* Los Angeles: Nash.

Donini, G.P. 1967. An evaluation of sex-role identification among father-absent and father-present boys. *Psychology, 4,* 13–16.

Dorpat, T. 1972. Psychological effects of parental suicide on surviving children. In A. Cain (Ed.), *Survivors of suicide.* Springfield, Ill.: Charles Thomas.

Douvan, E., & Adelson, J. 1966. *The adolescent experience.* New York: Wiley.

Downey, K.J. 1963. Parental interest in institutionalized severely retarded children. *Social Problems, 11,* 186–193.

Drake, C.T., & McDougall, D. 1977. Effects of the absence of father and other male models on the development of boys' sex roles. *Developmental Psychology, 13,* 537–538.

Dreyfus-Brisac, C. 1974. Organization of sleep in prematures: Implications for caregiving. In M. Lewis & L. Rosenblum (Eds.), *The effect of the infant on its caregiver,* New York: Wiley.

DuHamel, T.R., & Biller, H.B. 1969. Parental imitation and nonimitation in young children. *Developmental Psychology, 1,* 772.

Dyk, R.B., & Witkin, H.A. 1965. Family experiences related to the development of differentiation in children. *Child Development, 36,* 21–55.

Dyl, A.S., & Biller, H.B. 1973. Paternal absence, social class and reading achievement. Unpublished study, University of Rhode Island.

Easterbrooks, M.A., & Goldberg, W.A. 1984. Toddler development in the family: Impact of father involvement and parenting characteristics. *Child Development, 55,* 740–752.

Easterbrooks, M.A., & Goldberg, W.A. 1985. Effects of early maternal employment on toddlers, mothers, and fathers. *Developmental Psychology, 21,* 774–783.

Ebeling, N.B., & Hill, D.A. (Eds.). 1975. *Child abuse: Intervention and treatment.* Acton, Mass.: Publishing Sciences Group.

Egeland, B., & Sroufe, E. 1981. Developmental sequelae of maltreatment in infancy. In R. Rizley & D. Cicchetti (Eds.), *Developmental perspectives in child maltreatment.* San Francisco: Jossey-Bass.

Egeland, B., & Vaughn, B. 1981. Failure of bond formation as a cause of abuse, neglect and maltreatment. *American Journal of Orthopsychiatry, 51,* 78–84.

Egelson, J., & Frank, J.F. 1961. *Parents without partners*. New York: Dutton.

Eisenstadt, J.M. 1978. Parental loss and genius. *American Psychologist, 33,* 211–223.

Eisikovits, R. 1983. Paternal childcare as a policy relevant social phenomenon and research topic: The question of values. In M.E. Lamb and A. Sagi (Eds.), *Fatherhood and family policy*. Hillsdale, N.J.: Lawrence Erlbaum Associates.

Elder, G.H. 1974. *Children of the Great Depression*. Chicago: University of Chicago Press.

Elder, G.H., Jr., & Bowerman, C.C. 1963. Family structure and child-rearing patterns: The effect of family size and sex composition. *American Sociological Review, 28,* 891–905.

Elkind, D. 1981. *The hurried child: Growing up too fast too soon*, Reading, Mass.: Addison-Wesley.

Elmer, E. 1963. Identification of abused children. *Children, 10,* 180–184.

Elmer, E. 1967. *Children in jeopardy: A study of abused minors and their families*. Pittsburgh: University of Pittsburgh Press.

Elmer, E. 1981. Traumatized children, chronic illness and poverty. In L.H. Pelton (Ed.), *The social context of child abuse and neglect*. New York: Human Sciences Press.

Elmer, E., & Gregg, G. 1967. Developmental characteristics of abused children. *Pediatrics, 40,* 596–602.

Emmerich, W. 1969. The parental role: A functional cognitive approach. *Monographs of the Society for Research in Child Development, 34,* No. 132.

Entuisle, D.R., & Dooring, S.G. 1980. *The first birth*. Baltimore, Md.: The Johns Hopkins University Press.

Erikson, E.H. 1950. *Childhood and society*. New York: Norton.

Eron, L.D.; Walder, L.O.; Toigo, R.; & Lefkowitz, M.M. 1963. Social class, parental punishment for aggression, and child aggression. *Child Development, 34,* 849–867.

Escalona, S.K. 1968. *The roots of individuality*. Chicago: Aldine.

Etaugh, C. 1974. Effects of maternal employment on children: A review of recent research. *Merrill-Palmer Quarterly, 20,* 71–98.

Evans, R.B. 1969. Childhood parental relationships of homosexual men. *Journal of Consulting and Clinical Psychology, 33,* 129–135.

Fagot, B.I. 1978. The influence of sex of child on parental reactions to toddler children. *Child Development, 49,* 459–465.

Faller, K.C. 1981. Sexual abuse. In K.C. Faller (Ed.), *Social work with abused and neglected children*. New York: Free Press.

Farber, B. 1962a. Effects of a severely mentally retarded child on the family. In E.P. Trapp & P. Himelstein (Eds.), *Readings on the exceptional child*. New York: Appleton-Century Crofts.

Farber, B. 1962b. Marital integration as a factor in parent-child relations. *Child Development, 33,* 1–14.

Farber, B., & McHale, J.L. 1959. Marital integration and parent's agreement on satisfaction with their child's behavior. *Marriage and Family Living, 21,* 65–69.

Faretra, G. 1981. A profile of aggression from adolescence to adulthood: An 18 year follow-up of psychiatrically disturbed and violent adolescents. *American Journal of Orthopsychiatry, 51,* 439–453.

Fein, R.A. 1976. Men's entrance to parenthood. *Family Coordinator, 25,* 341–348.

Feinstein, H.M.; Paul, N.; & Esmial, P. 1964. Group therapy for mothers with infanticidal impulses. *American Journal of Psychiatry, 120,* 882–886.

Feldman, S.S., & Nash, S.C. 1972. The effect of family formation on sex-stereotypic behavior: A study of responsiveness to babies. In W. Miller & L. Newman (Eds.), *The first child and family formation.* Chapel Hill: University of North Carolina Press.

Feldman, S.S., & Nash, S.C. 1978. Interest in babies during young adulthood. *Child Development, 49,* 617–622.

Felner, R.; Stolberg, A.; and Cowen, E. 1975. Crisis events and school mental health referral patterns of young children. *Journal of Consulting and Clinical Psychology, 43,* 305–310.

Fenichel, O. 1945. *The psychoanalytic theory of neurosis.* New York: Norton.

Ferholt, J.B., & Gurwitt, A.R. 1982. Involving fathers in treatment. In S.H. Cath, A.R. Gurwitt, & J.M. Ross (Eds.), *Father and child: Developmental and clinical perspectives.* Boston: Little, Brown, pp. 547–568.

Ferracuti, F. 1972. Incest between father and daughter. In H.L.P. Resnick & M. Wolfgang (Eds.), *Sexual Behavior.* Boston: Little, Brown.

Ferrante, R.J., & Biller, H.B. 1986. School-based counseling for children of divorce. Unpublished manuscript, University of Rhode Island.

Ferreira, A.J.; Winter, W.D.; & Poindexter, E.J. 1966. Some interactional variables in normal and abnormal families. *Family Process, 5,* 60–75.

Ferri, E. 1973. Characteristics of motherless families. *British Journal of Social Work, 3,* 91–100.

Ferri, E. 1976. *Growing up in a one-parent family: A long-term study of child development.* London: National Foundation for Education Research.

Feshbach, N.D. 1973. The effects of violence in childhood. *Journal of Clinical Psychology, 11,* 28–31.

Field, T.M. 1978. Interaction behaviors of primary versus secondary caretaker fathers. *Developmental Psychology, 14,* 183–184.

Field, T.M., & Widmayer, S.M. 1982. Motherhood. In B.B. Wolman (Ed.), *Handbook of developmental psychology.* Englewood Cliffs, N.J.: Prentice-Hall.

Finkelhor, D. 1978. Psychological, cultural and family factors in incest and family sexual abuse. *Journal of Marriage and Family Counseling, 4,* 41–99.

Finkelhor, D. 1979. *Sexuality victimized children.* New York: Free Press.

Finkelhor, D. 1984. *Child sexual abuse.* New York: Free Press.

Finkelhor, D., & Browne, A. 1985. The traumatic impact of child sexual abuse: A conceptualization. *American Journal of Orthopsychiatry, 55,* 530–541.

Fish, K.D. 1969. Paternal availability, family role-structure, maternal employment and personality development in late adolescent females. Ph.D. dissertation, University of Massachusetts.

Fish, K.D., & Biller, H.B. 1973. Perceived childhood paternal relationships and college females' personal adjustment. *Adolescence, 8,* 415–420.

Fisher, S.F. 1973. *The female organism: Psychology, physiology, fantasy.* New York: Basic Books.

Flanzraich, M., & Steiner, G.L. 1980. Therapeutic interventions that foster ego development in abused/neglected children. In G.J. Williams & J. Money (Eds.), *Traumatic abuse and neglect of children at home.* Baltimore, Md.: The Johns Hopkins University Press.

Flavell, J.H. 1963. *The developmental psychology of Jean Piaget.* Princeton, N.J.: D. Van Nostrand.

Fleck, J.R.; Fuller, C.C.; Malin, S.Z.; Miller, D.H.; & Acheson, K.R. 1980. Father psychological absence and heterosexual behavior, personal adjustment and sex-typing in adolescent girls. *Adolescence, 15,* 847–860.

Florin, P.R., & Dokecki, P.R. 1983. Changing families through parent and family education: Review and analysis. In I.E. Sigel & L.M. Laosa (Eds.), *Changing families.* New York: Plenum Press.

Fontana, V.J. 1974. *The maltreated child.* Springfield, Ill.: Charles C Thomas.

Fontana, V.J. 1976. *Somewhere a child is crying.* New York: Mentor Books.

Fontana, V.J., & Besharov, F.J. 1977. *The maltreated child.* Springfield, Ill.: Charles C Thomas.

Fontana, V.J., & Schneider, C. 1978. Help for abusing parents. In L.E. Arnold (Ed.), *Helping parents help their children.* New York: Brunner-Mazel.

Forrest, T. 1966. Paternal roots of female character development. *Contemporary Psychoanalyst, 3,* 21–28.

Forrest, T. 1967. The paternal roots of male character development. *The Psycho-analytic Review, 54,* 81–99.

Forrest, T. 1969. Treatment of the father in family therapy. *Family Process, 8,* 106–117.

Forward, S., & Buck, C. 1978. *Betrayal of innocence: Incest and its devastation.* New York: Penguin Books.

Frazier, E.F. 1939. *The Negro family in the United States.* Chicago: University of Chicago Press.

Freeberg, N.E., & Payne, D.T. 1967. Parental influence on cognitive development in early childhood: A review. *Child Development, 38,* 65–87.

Freedheim, D.K., & Borstelmann, L.J. 1963. An investigation of masculinity and parental role-patterns. *American Psychologist, 18,* 339 (Abstract).

Freud, A., & Burlingham, D.T. 1944. *Infants without families.* New York: International University Press.

Freud, S. 1950a. Mourning and melancholia. In J. Rivers (Ed.), *Collected papers of Sigmund Freud.* London: Hogarth Press.

Freud, S. 1950b. Some psychological consequences of the anatomical distinction between the sexes (1939). In J. Rivers (Ed.), *Collected papers of Sigmund Freud* (Vol. 5). London: Hogarth Press.

Freud, S. 1957. On narcissism. In *The complete psychological works of Sigmund Freud.* London: Hogarth Press.

Freud, S. 1961. *The ego and the id.* London: Hogarth Press.

Freud, S. 1962. *Three essays on the theory of sexuality* (1905). New York: Avon.

Freudenthal, K. 1959. Problems of the one-parent family. *Social Work, 4,* 44–48.

Friedrich, W.N., & Boriskin, J.A. 1976. The role of the child in abuse: A review of the literature. *American Journal of Orthopsychiatry, 49,* 580–590.

Frodi, A.M., & Lamb, M.E. 1978. Sex differences in responsiveness to infants: A developmental study of psychophysiological and behavioral responses. *Child Development, 49,* 1182–1188.

Frodi, A.M., & Lamb, M.E. 1980a. Child abuser's responses to infant smiles and cries. *Child Development, 51,* 239–241.

Frodi, A.M., & Lamb, M.E. 1980b. Infants at risk for child abuse. *Infant Mental Health Journal, 1,* 240–247.

Frodi, A.M.; Lamb, M.E.; Leavitt, L.A.; & Donovan, W.L. 1978. Fathers' and mothers' responses to infant smiles and cries. *Infant Behavior and Development, 1,* 187–198.

Frodi, A.M.; Lamb, M.E.; Leavitt, L.A.; Donovan, W.L.; Neff, C.; & Sherry, D. 1978. Fathers' and mothers' responses to faces and cries of normal and premature infants. *Developmental Psychology, 14,* 490–498.

Gaensbauer, T.J., & Harmon, R.J. 1982. Attachment behavior in abused/neglected and premature infants. In D.N. Ende & R.J. Harman (Eds.), *Attachment and affiliative systems.* New York: Plenum.

Galdston, R. 1971. Violence begins at home. *Journal of the American Academy of Child Psychiatry, 10,* 336–350.

Galdston, R. 1975. Preventing the abuse of little children: The Parents' Center project for the Study and Prevention of Child Abuse. *American Journal of Orthopsychiatry, 45,* 372–382.

Galinsky, E. 1982. *Between generations: The stages of parenthood.* New York: Berkeley Books.

Garai, J.E., & Scheinfeld, A. 1968. Sex differences in mental and behavioral traits. *Genetic Psychology Monographs, 77,* 169–299.

Garbarino, J. 1976. A preliminary study of some ecological correlates of child abuse: The impact of socioeconomic stress on mothers. *Child Development, 47,* 178–185.

Garbarino, J. 1977. The human ecology of child maltreatment: A conceptual model for child abuse. *Journal of Marriage and the Family, 39,* 721–735.

Garbarino, J. 1980. What kind of society permits child abuse? *Infant Mental Health Journal, 1,* 270–281.

Garbarino, J. 1981. An ecological approach to child maltreatment. In L.H. Pelton (Ed.), *The social context of child abuse and neglect.* New York: Human Sciences Press.

Garbarino, J., & Gilliam, G. 1980. *Understanding abusive families.* Lexington, Mass.: Lexington Books, D.C. Heath and Company.

Garbarino, J., & Sherman, D. 1979. High-risk neighborhoods and high-risk families: The human ecology of child maltreatment. Unpublished paper, Center for the Study of Youth Development, Boys Town, Nebraska.

Garbarino, J., & Sherman, D. 1980. Identifying high-risk neighborhoods. In J. Garbarino & S.H. Stocking (Eds.), *Protecting children from abuse and neglect.* San Francisco: Jossey-Bass.

Garbarino, J., & Stocking, S.H. 1980. *Protecting children from abuse and neglect.* San Francisco: Jossey-Bass.

Garbower, G. 1959. *Behavior problems of children in Navy officer's families: As related to social conditions of Navy family life.* Washington, D.C.: Catholic University Press.

Gardiner, L.P. 1959. Separation of the parents and the emotional life of the parents. In S. Glueck (Ed.), *The problems of delinquency.* Boston: Houghton-Mifflin.

Gassner, S., & Murray, E.J. 1969. Dominance and conflict in the interactions between parents of normal and neurotic children. *Journal of Abnormal Psychology, 74,* 33–41.

Gavron, H. 1966. *The captive wife: Conflicts of housebound mothers.* London: Routledge & Kegan Paul.

Gay, M.J., & Tonge, W.L. 1967. The late effects of loss of parents in childhood. *British Journal of Psychiatry, 113*, 753–759.

Gelles, R.J. 1972. *The violent home.* Beverly Hills, Calif.: Russell Sage.

Gelles, R.J. 1973. Child abuse and psychopathology: A sociological critique and reformulation. *American Journal of Orthopsychiatry, 43*, 611–612.

Gelles, R.J. 1975. The social construction of child abuse. *American Journal of Orthopsychiatry, 45*, 363–371.

Gelles, R. 1976. Demythologizing child abuse. *The Family Coordinator, 25*, 135–141.

Gelles, R. 1980. A profile of violence toward children in the United States. In G. Gerbner, C.J. Ross, & E. Zigler (Eds.), *Child abuse: An agenda for action.* New York: Oxford University Press.

Gelles, R.J., & Cornell, C.P. (Eds.). 1983. *International perspectives on family violence.* Lexington, Mass.: Lexington Books, D.C. Heath and Company.

Gelles, R., & Strauss, M. 1985. The second national family violence survey. Paper presented at the Seventh National Conference on Child Abuse and Neglect, Chicago, November.

George, G.E., & Main, M. 1979. Social interaction of young abused children: Approach, avoidance and aggression. *Child Development, 50*, 306–318.

Gerbner, G.; Rose, C.J.; & Zigler, E. (Eds.). 1980. *Child abuse: An agenda for action.* New York: Oxford University Press.

Gershon, M., & Biller, H.B. 1977. *The other helpers: Paraprofessionals and nonprofessionals in mental health.* Lexington, Mass.: Lexington Books, D.C. Heath and Company.

Gewirtz, H.B., & Gewirtz, J.L. 1968. Visiting and caretaking patterns for kibbutz infants: Age and sex trends. *American Journal of Orthopsychiatry, 38*, 427–447.

Giaretto, H. 1976a. Humanistic treatment of father-daughter incest. In R.E. Helfer & C.E. Kempe (Eds.), *Child abuse and neglect: The family and the community.* Cambridge, Mass.: Ballinger.

Gairetto, H. 1976b. The treatment of father/daughter incest: A psychosocial approach. *Children Today, 5*, 2–5.

Giaretto, H. 1982. A comprehensive child sexual abuse treatment program. *Child Abuse and Neglect, 6*, 263–278.

Gil, D.G. 1970. *Violence against children.* Cambridge, Mass.: Harvard University Press.

Gil, D.G. 1979. Unraveling child abuse. In R. Bourne & E.H. Newberger (Eds.), *Critical perspectives on child abuse.* Lexington, Mass.: Lexington Books, D.C. Heath and Company.

Gil, D.G. 1981. The United States versus child abuse. In L.A. Pelton (Ed.), *The social context of child abuse and neglect.* New York: Human Sciences Press.

Gilbert, M.T. 1976. Behavioral approach to the treatment of child abuse. *Nursing Times, 72*, 140–143.

Ginsburg, H. 1972. *The myth of the deprived child.* Englewood Cliffs, N.J.: Prentice-Hall.

Giovanni, J.M. 1971. Parental mistreatment: Perpetrators and victims. *Journal of Marriage and the Family, 33*, 649–657.

Giovanni, J.M., & Becerra, R.M. 1979. *Defining child abuse.* New York: Free Press.

Giovanni, J.M., & Billingsley, A. 1970. Child neglect among the poor: A study of parental adequacy in three ethnic groups. *Child Welfare, 49*, 196–204.

Glass, G.V. 1978. Integrating findings: The meta-analysis of research. *Review of Research in Education, 6*, 351–379.

Glasser, P., & Navarre, E. 1965. Structural problems of the one-parent family. *Journal of Social Issues, 21*, 98–109.

Glazier, A.E. (Ed.). 1971. *Child abuse: A community challenge.* Buffalo, N.Y.: H. Steward.

Glick, P.G., & Norton, A.J. 1978. Marrying, divorcing and living together in the U.S. today. *Population Bulletin, 32*, 3–38.

Glueck, S., & Glueck, E. 1950. *Unravelling juvenile delinquency.* Cambridge, Mass.: Harvard University Press.

Gold, D., & Andres, D. 1978a. Comparisons of adolescent children with employed and unemployed mothers. *Merrill-Palmer Quarterly, 24*, 243–259.

Gold, D., & Andres, D. 1978b. Relations between maternal employment and development of nursery school children. *Canadian Journal of Behavioral Science, 10*, 116–129.

Goldberg, S. 1973. Family tasks and reactions in the crisis of death. *Social casework, 54*, 398–405.

Goldberg, S., & Lewis, M. 1969. Play behavior in the year-old infant: Early sex differences. *Child Development, 40*, 21–31.

Goldberg, W.A., & Easterbrooks, M.A. 1984. Role of marital quality in toddler development. *Developmental Psychology, 20*, 504–514.

Goode, W.J. 1961. Family disorganization. In R.K. Merton & R.A. Nisbet (Eds.), *Contemporary social problems.* New York: Harcourt, Brace and World.

Goode, W.J. 1971. Force and violence in the family. *Journal of Marriage and the Family, 33*, 624–636.

Goodenough, E.W. 1957. Interest in persons as an aspect of sex differences in the early years. *Genetic Psychology Monographs, 55*, 287–323.

Gordon, R.S., & Gordon, K. 1959. Social factors in the prediction and treatment of emotional disorders of pregnancy. *American Journal of Obstetrics and Gynecology, 77*, 1074–1083.

Gordon, T. 1970. *Parent effectiveness training.* New York: Peter Wyden.

Grambs, J.D., & Waetjen, W.B. 1966. Being equally different: A new right for boys and girls. *National Elementary School Principal, 46*, 59–67.

Gray, J.; Cutler, C.; Dean, J.; & Kempe, C.H. 1977. Prediction and prevention of child abuse and neglect. *Child Abuse and Neglect: The International Journal, 1*, 45–48.

Gray, S.W. 1957. Masculinity-femininity in relation to anxiety and social acceptance. *Child Development, 28*, 203–214.

Gray, S.W. 1959. Perceived similarity to parents and adjustment. *Child Development, 30*, 91–107.

Gray, S.W., & Klaus, R. 1956. The assessment of parental identification. *Genetic Psychology Monographs, 54*, 81–114.

Grebstein, L.C. 1986. An eclectic family therapy. In J. Norcross (Ed.), *Handbook of eclectic therapy.* New York: Brunner/Mazel.

Green, A.H. 1978. Child abuse. In B.B. Wolman, J. Egan, & A. Ross (Eds.), *Handbook of treatment of mental disorders in children and adolescents.* Englewood Cliffs, N.J.: Prentice-Hall.

Green, A.H. 1979. Child-abusing fathers. *Journal of The American Academy of Child Psychiatry, 18*, 270–282.

Green, A.H.; Gaines, R.; & Sandgrund, A. 1974. Child abuse: Pathological syndrome of family interaction. *American Journal of Psychiatry, 8*, 882–886.

Green, R. 1974. *Sexual identity conflict in children and adults.* New York: Basic Books.

Green, R. 1976. One hundred ten feminine and masculine boys: Behavioral contrasts and demographic similarities. *Archives of Sexual Behavior, 5*, 425–446.

Green, R. 1978. Sexual identity of 37 children raised by homosexual or transsexual parents. *American Journal of Psychiatry, 6*, 692–697.

Green, R.; Williams, K.; & Goodman, M. 1985. Masculine or feminine gender identity in boys: Developmental differences between two diverse groups. *Sex Roles, 12*, 1155–1171.

Greenberg, M., & Morris, N. 1974. Engrossment: The newborn's impact upon the father. *American Journal of Orthopsychiatry, 44*, 520–531.

Greene, M. 1979. An overview of children's rights: A moral and ethical perspective. In P.A. Vardin & I.N. Brady (Eds.), *Children's rights.* New York: Teachers College Press.

Greenstein, J.F. 1966. Father characteristics and sex-typing. *Journal of Personality and Social Psychology, 3*, 271–277.

Greer, S. 1966. Parental loss and attempted suicide: A further report. *British Journal of Psychiatry, 112*, 465–470.

Gregory, I. 1958. Studies of parental deprivation in psychiatric patients. *American Journal of Psychiatry, 115*, 432–442.

Gregory, I. 1965a. Anterospective data following childhood loss of a parent; I. Delinquency and high school dropout. *Archives of General Psychiatry, 13*, 99–109.

Gregory, I. 1965b. Anterospective data following childhood loss of a parent: II. Pathology, performance, and potential among college students. *Archives of General Psychiatry, 13*, 110–120.

Greif, J.B. 1979. Fathers, children and joint custody. *American Journal of Orthopsychiatry, 49*, 311–319.

Greif, J.B. 1985. *Single fathers.* Lexington, Mass.: Lexington Books, D.C. Heath and Company.

Grønseth, E. 1957. The impact of father absence in sailor families upon the personality structure and social adjustment of adult sailor sons, part 1. In N. Anderson (Ed.), *Studies of the family, Vol. 2.* Gottingen: Vandenhoeck and Ruprecht.

Groth, A.N., with Birnbaum, H.J. 1979. *Men who rape: The psychology of the offender.* New York: Plenum Press.

Groth, A.N.; Hobson, W.F.; & Gary, T.S. 1982. The child molester: Clinical observations. *Journal of Social Work and Human Sexuality, 1–2*, 129–144.

Grunnebaum, M.G.; Hurwitz, I.; Prentice, N.M.; & Sperry, B.M. 1962. Fathers of sons with primary neurotic learning inhibition. *American Journal of Orthopsychiatry, 32*, 462–473.

Guidubaldi, J. 1983. The impact of parental divorce on children: Report of the nationwide NASP study. *School Psychology Review, 12*, 300–323.

Guidubaldi, J., & Perry, J.D. 1984. Divorce, socioeconomic status, and children's cognitive-social competence at school entry. *American Journal of Orthopsychiatry, 54*, 459–468.

Gundlach, R.H. 1969. Childhood parental relationships and the establishment of gender roles of homosexuals. *Journal of Consulting and Clinical Psychology, 33,* 136–139.

Gundlach, R.H., & Reiss, B.F. 1968. Self and sexual identity in the female: A study of female homosexuals. In B.F. Reiss (Ed.), *New directions in mental health.* New York: Grune and Stratton.

Gunsburg, L. 1982. Selected critical review of psychological investigations of the early father-infant relationship. In S.H. Cath, A.R. Gurwitt, & J.M. Ross (Eds.), *Father and child: Developmental and clinical perspectives.* Boston: Little, Brown, pp. 65–86.

Gurman, A.S., & Kniskeon, D.P. (Eds.). 1981. *Handbook of family therapy.* New York: Brunner Mazel.

Gurwitt, A.R. 1976. Aspects of prospective fatherhood. *Psychoanalytic Study of the Child, 31,* 237–271.

Gurwitt, A.R. 1982. Aspects of prospective fatherhood. In S.H. Cath, A.R. Gurwitt, & J.M. Ross (Eds.), *Father and child: Developmental and clinical perspectives.* Boston: Little, Brown.

Haan, N.; Langer, J.; & Kohlberg, L. 1976. Family patterns of moral reasoning. *Child Development, 47,* 1204–1206.

Hainline, L., & Feig, E. 1978. The correlates of childhood father absence in college-aged women. *Child Development, 49,* 37–42.

Hall, P., & Tonge, W.L. 1963. Long standing continuous unemployment in male patients with psychiatric symptoms. *British Journal of Preventative and Social Medicine, 17,* 191–196.

Hamilton, C.V. 1929. *A research in marriage.* New York: Boni.

Hamilton, D.M., & Wahl, J.G. 1948. The hospital treatment of dementia praecox. *American Journal of Psychiatry, 104,* 346–352.

Handel, G. 1965. Psychological study of whole families. *Psychological Bulletin, 63,* 19–41.

Hanson, R., McCulloch, U., & Hartley, S. 1978. Key characteristics of child abuse. In A.W. Franklin (Ed.), *The challenge of child abuse.* New York: Grune and Stratton.

Harper, L.W. 1971. The young as a source of stimuli controlling caretaking behavior. *Developmental Psychology, 4,* 73–85.

Harrington, D.M.; Block, J.H.; & Block, J. 1978. Intolerance of ambiguity in preschool children: Psychometric considerations, behavioral manifestations and parental correlates. *Developmental Psychology, 14,* 242–256.

Hartley, R.E., & Klein, A. 1959. Sex role concepts among elementary school-age girls. *Marriage and Family Living, 21,* 59–64.

Haworth, M.R. 1964. Parental loss in children as reflected in projective responses. *Journal of Projective Techniques, 28,* 31–35.

Heath, D.H. 1976. Competent fathers: Their personalities and marriages. *Human Development, 19,* 26–39.

Heath, D.H. 1978. What meaning and what effects does fatherhood have on the maturing of professional men? *Merrill-Palmer Quarterly, 24,* 265–278.

Heckel, R.V. 1963. The effects of fatherlessness on the pre-adolescent female. *Mental Hygiene, 47,* 69–73.

Hecksher, B.J. 1967. Household structure and achievement orientation in lower-class Barbadian families. *Journal of Marriage and the Family, 29,* 521–526.

Heilbrun, A.B., Jr. 1962. Parental identification and college adjustment. *Psychological Reports, 10,* 853–854.

Heilbrun, A.B., Jr. 1965a. An empirical test of the modeling theory of sex-role learning. *Child Development, 36,* 789–799.

Heilbrun, A.B., Jr. 1965b. The measurement of identification. *Child Development, 36,* 111–127.

Heilbrun, A.B., Jr. 1973. *Aversive maternal control.* New York: Wiley.

Heilbrun, A.B., Jr. 1974. Parent identification and filial sex-role behavior: The importance of biological context. In J.C. Cole & R. Dienstbier (Eds.), *Nebraska Symposium on Motivation, 1973.* Lincoln: University of Nebraska Press, pp. 125–194.

Heilbrun, A.B., Jr. 1976. Identification with the father and sex-role development of the daughter. *Family Coordinator, 25,* 411–416.

Heilbrun, A.B., Jr., & Fromme, D.K. 1965. Parental identification of late adolescents and level of adjustment: The importance of parent-model attributes, ordinal position, and sex of child. *Journal of Genetic Psychology, 107,* 45–49.

Heilbrun, A.B., Jr.; Harrell, S.N.; & Gillard, B.J. 1965. Perceived identification of late adolescents and level of adjustment: The importance of parent model attributes, ordinal position and sex of child. *Journal of Genetic Psychology, 107,* 49–59.

Heilbrun, A.B., Jr.; Harrell, S.N.; & Gillard, B.J. 1967. Perceived childrearing attitudes of fathers, and cognitive control of daughters. *Journal of Genetic Psychology, 111,* 29–40.

Helfer, R.E. 1975. Why physicians won't get involved in child abuse cases and what to do about it. *Children Today, 4,* 28–32.

Helfer, R.E. 1976. Basic issues concerning prediction. In R.E. Helfer & C.H. Kempe (Eds.), *Child abuse and neglect: The family and the community.* Cambridge, Mass.: Ballinger Publishing Company.

Helfer, R.E., & Kempe, C.H. (Eds.). 1974. *The battered child.* Chicago: University of Chicago Press, 1974.

Helper, M.M. 1955. Learning theory and the self-concept. *Journal of Abnormal and Social Psychology, 51,* 184–194.

Henneborn, W.J., & Cogan, R. 1975. The effect of husband participation on reported pain and probability of medication during labor and birth. *Journal of Psychosomatic Research, 19,* 215–222.

Herman, J.L. 1981. *Father-daughter incest.* Cambridge, Mass.: Harvard University Press.

Herzberger, S.D.; Potts, D.A.; & Dillon, M. 1981. Abusive and nonabusive parental treatment from the child's perspective. *Journal of Consulting and Clinical Psychology, 49,* 81–90.

Herzog, E., & Sudia, C.E. 1973. Children in fatherless families. In B.M. Caldwell & H.N. Ricciuti (Eds.), *Review of child development research* (Vol. 3). Chicago: University of Chicago Press.

Herzog, J.M. 1982. On father hunger: The father's role in the modulation of aggressive drive and fantasy. In S. Cath, A.R. Gurwitt, & J.M. Ross (Eds.), *Father and child: Developmental and clinical perspectives.* Boston: Little, Brown, pp. 163–174.

Hess, R.D.; Shipman, V.C.; Brophy, J.E.; Bear, R.M.; & Adelberger, A.B. 1969. *The cognitive environments of urban preschool children: Follow-up phase.* Chicago: Graduate School of Education, University of Chicago.

Hetherington, E.M. 1965. A developmental study of the effects of sex of the dominant parent on sex-role preference, identification, and imitation in children. *Journal of Personality and Social Psychology, 2,* 188–194.

Hetherington, E.M. 1966. Effects of paternal absence on sex-typed behaviors in Negro and white preadolescent males. *Journal of Personality and Social Psychology, 4,* 87–91.

Hetherington, E.M. 1972. Effects of father-absence on personality development in adolescent daughters. *Developmental Psychology, 7,* 313–326.

Hetherington, E.M. 1979a. Divorce: A child's perspective. *American Psychologist, 34,* 851–858.

Hetherington, E.M. 1979b. Play and social interaction in children following divorce. *Journal of Social Issues, 35,* 26–39.

Hetherington, E.M., & Brackbill, Y. 1963. Etiology and covariation of obstinacy, orderliness, and parsimony in young children. *Child Development, 34,* 919–943.

Hetherington, E.M.; Cox, M.; & Cox, R. 1976. Divorced fathers. *Family Coordinator, 25,* 417–428.

Hetherington, E.M.; Cox, M.; & Cox, R. 1978a. The aftermath of divorce. In J.H. Stevens & M. Mathews (Eds.), *Motherchild, fatherchild relationships.* Washington, D.C.: National Association for the Education of Young Children.

Hetherington, E.M.; Cox, M.; & Cox, R. 1978b. Family interaction and the social, emotional and cognitive development of children following divorce. Paper presented at the Johnson and Johnson Conference on the Family, Washington, D.C., May.

Hetherington, E.M.; Cox, M.; & Cox, R. 1979a. Family interaction and the social, emotional, and cognitive development of children following divorce. In V. Vaughn & B. Brazelton (Eds.), *The family: Setting priorities.* New York: Science and Medicine Publishing Company.

Hetherington, E.M.; Cox, M.; & Cox, R. 1982. Effects of divorce on parents and children. In M.E. Lamb (Ed.), *Nontraditional families.* Hillsdale, N.J.: Lawrence Erlbaum Associates.

Hetherington, E.M., & Deur, J. 1971. The effects of father absence on child development. *Young Children, 26,* 233–248.

Hetherington, E.M., & Frankie, G. 1967. Effects of parental dominance, warmth, and conflict on imitation in children. *Journal of Personality and Social Psychology, 6,* 119–125.

Hetherington, E.M., & Martin, B. 1979. Family interaction. In H.C. Quay & J.S. Werry (Eds.), *Psychopathological disorders of childhood.* New York: Wiley.

Hetherington, E.M., & Parke, R.D. 1986. *Child psychology: A contemporary viewpoint* (3rd Ed.). New York: McGraw-Hill.

Hett, E.J., & Fish, J.E. 1979. Some descriptive characteristics of abusive families evaluated at Kansas University Medical Center. *Journal of Clinical Child Psychology, 8,* 7–9.

Hilgard, J.R.; Neuman, M.F.; & Fisk, F. 1960. Strength of adult ego following bereavement, *American Journal of Orthopsychiatry, 30,* 788–798.

Hill, J.P. 1967. Similarity and accordance between parents and sons in attitudes towards mathematics. *Child Development, 38 ,777–791.*

Hill, O.W., & Price, J.S. 1967. Childhood bereavement and adult depression *British Journal of Psychiatry, 113,* 743–751.

Hill, R. 1949. *Families under stress.* New York: Harper.

Hillenbrand, E.D. 1976. Father absence in military families. *Family Coordinator, 25,* 451–458.

Hoffman, L.W. 1961. The father's role in the family and the child's peer-group adjustment. *Merrill-Palmer Quarterly, 7,* 91–105.

Hoffman, L.W. 1974. Effects of maternal employment on the child: A review of the research. *Developmental Psychology, 10,* 204–228.

Hoffman, L.W. 1977. Changes in family roles, socialization and sex differences. *American Psychologist, 32,* 644–657.

Hoffman, L.W. 1983. Increased fathering: Effects on the mother. In M.E. Lamb & A. Sagi (Eds.), *Fatherhood and family policy.* Hillsdale, N.J.: Lawrence Erlbaum Associates.

Hoffman, L.W., & Nye, F.I. 1974. *Working mothers.* San Francisco: Jossey-Bass.

Hoffman, M.L. 1960. Power assertion by the parent and its impact on the child. *Child Development, 31, 129–143.*

Hoffman, M.L. 1970. Conscience, personality, and socialization technique. *Human Development, 13,* 90–126.

Hoffman, M.L. 1971a. Father-absence and conscience development. *Child Development, 4,* 400–406.

Hoffman, M.L. 1971b. Identification and conscience development. *Child Development, 42,* 1071–1082.

Hoffman, M.L. 1975. Altruistic behavior and the parent-child relationship. *Journal of Personality and Social Psychology, 31,* 937–943.

Hoffman, M.L. 1981. The role of the father in moral internalization. In M.E. Lamb (Ed.), *The role of the father in child development* (2nd Ed.). New York: Wiley, pp. 359–378.

Hoffman, M.L., & Saltzstein, H.D. 1967. Parent discipline and the child's moral development. *Journal of Personality and Social Psychology, 5,* 45–57.

Holman, P. 1959. The etiology of maladjustment in children, *Journal of Mental Science, 99,* 654–688.

Holmes, D.L.; Reich, J.N.; & Pasternak, J.A. 1983. *The psychological development of infants born at risk.* Hillsdale, N.J.: Lawrence Erlbaum Associates.

Holmes, M., & Kagle, A. 1977. Bowen Center, Chicago, Illinois. In U.S. Department of Health, Education and Welfare, *Child abuse and neglect programs: Practice and theory.* Washington, D.C.: U.S. Government Printing Office.

Holstein, C.E. 1972. The relation of children's moral judgment level to that of their parents and to communication patterns in the family. In R.C. Smart & M.S. Smart (Eds.), *Readings in child development and relationships.* New York: Macmillan.

Honzik, M.P. 1963. A sex difference in the age of onset of the parent-child resemblance in intelligence. *Journal of Educational Psychology, 54,* 231–237.

Honzik, M.P. 1967. Environmental correlates of mental growth: Prediction from the family setting at 21 months. *Child Development, 38,* 338–364.

Horney, K. 1933. The denial of the vagina. *International Journal of Psychoanalysis,* 14, 57–70.

Huckel, L.H. 1984. Personality correlates of parental maltreatment. (Ph.D. dissertation, University of Rhode Island). *Dissertation Abstracts International, 44,* 3592B.

Hughes, R.C. 1974. A clinic's parent-performance training program for child abusers. *Hospital and Community Psychiatry, 25,* 779–784.

Hunt, D. 1970. *Parents and children in history: The psychology of family life in early modern France.* New York: Basic Books.

Hunt, L.L., & Hunt, J.B. 1975. Race and the father-son connection. *Social Problems, 23,* 35–51.

Hurley, J.R. 1967. Parental malevolence and children's intelligence. *Journal of Consulting Psychology, 31,* 199–204.

Huttunen, M.O., & Niskanen, P. 1978. Prenatal loss of father and psychiatric disorders. *Archives of General Psychiatry, 35,* 429–436.

Illsley, R., & Thompson, B. 1961. Women from broken homes. *Sociological Review.* 9, 27–54.

In, P.A., & McDermott, J.F. 1978. The treatment of child abuse: Play therapy with a four-year-old child. *Journal of American Academy of Child Psychiatry, 15,* 430–440.

Ingham, H.V. 1949. A statistical study of family relationships in psychoneurosis. *American Journal of Orthopsychiatry, 106,* 91–98.

Jacklin, C.W.; Maccoby, E.E.; & Doering, C. 1983. Neonatal sex-steroid hormones and timidity in 6–18 month old boys and girls. *Developmental Psychology, 16,* 163–168.

Jacob, T. 1974. Patterns of family conflict and dominance as a function of child age and social class. *Developmental Psychology, 10,* 1–12.

Jacobson, G., & Ryder, R.G. 1969. Parental loss and some characteristics of the early marriage relationship. *American Journal of Orthopsychiatry, 39,* 779–787.

Jaffe, E.D. 1983. Fathers and child welfare services: The forgotten client? In M.E. Lamb & A. Sagi (Eds.), *Fatherhood and family policy.* Hillsdale, N.J.: Lawrence Erlbaum Associates.

James, J., & Meyerding, T. 1977. Early sexual experience and prostitution. *American Journal of Psychiatry, 134,* 1381–1388.

Jayaratne, S. 1977. Child abusers as parents and children: A review. *Social Work, 22,* 5–9.

Jeffery, M. 1976. Practical ways to change parent-child interaction in families of children at risk. In R.E. Helfer & C.H. Kempe (Eds.), *Child abuse and neglect: The family and the community.* Cambridge, Mass.: Ballinger.

Jenkins, R.L. 1969. The varieties of children's behavioral problems and family dynamics. *American Journal of Psychiatry, 124,* 1440–1445.

Jenkins, S. 1979. Children of divorce. In S. Chess & A. Thomas (Eds.), *Annual progress in child psychiatry and child development.* New York: Brunner/Mazel, pp. 283–292.

Jensen, R.E. 1976. A behavior modification program to remediate child abuse. *Journal of Clinical Child Psychology, 5,* 30–32.

Johnson, B., & Morse, H.A. 1968. Injured children and their parents. *Children, 15,* 147–152.

Johnson, M.M. 1963. Sex-role learning in the nuclear family. *Child Development, 34*, 319–333.

Jones, E. 1963. *Raising your child in a fatherless home.* New York: Macmillan.

Jordan, B.E.; Radin, N.; & Epstein, A. 1975. Paternal behavior and intellectual functioning in preschool boys and girls. *Developmental Psychology, 11*, 407–408.

Justice, B., & Justice, B. 1976. *The abusing family.* New York: Human Sciences Press.

Justice, B., & Justice, R. 1979. *The broken taboo: Sex in the family.* New York: The Free Press.

Kadushin, A., & Martin, J.A. 1981. *Child abuse: An interactional event.* New York: Columbia University Press.

Kagan, J. 1958a. The concept of identification. *Psychological Review, 65*, 295–305.

Kagan, J. 1958b. Socialization of aggression and the perception of parents in fantasy, *Child Development, 29*, 311–320.

Kagan, J. 1964. Acquisition and significance of sex-typing and sex-role identity. In M.L. Hoffman & L.W. Hoffman (Eds.), *Review of child development research* (Vol. 1). Beverly Hills, Calif.: Russell Sage Foundation.

Kagan, J.; Hosken, B.; & Watson, S. 1961. Children's symbolic conceptualization of parents. *Child Development, 32*, 625–636.

Kagan, J.; Kearsley, P.; & Zelazo, P. 1978. *Infancy: Its place in human development.* Cambridge, Mass.: Harvard University Press.

Kagan, J., & Moss, H. 1962. *Birth to Maturity.* New York: Wiley.

Kaliski, J., & Biller, H.B. 1985. The sex role development of children with liberated parents. Unpublished manuscript, University of Rhode Island.

Kamerman, S.B. 1975. Eight countries: Cross-national perspectives on child abuse and neglect. *Children Today, 4*, 34–37.

Kamerman, S.B. 1983. Fatherhood and social policy: Some insights from a comparative perspective. In M.E. Lamb & A. Sagi (Eds.), *Fatherhood and family policy.* Hillsdale, N.J.: Lawrence Erlbaum Associates.

Kane, B. 1979. Children's concepts of death. *Journal of Genetic Psychology, 130*, 141–153.

Katz, I. 1967. Socialization of academic motivation in minority group children. In D. Levine (Ed.), *Nebraska Symposium on Motivation, 1966.* Lincoln: University of Nebraska Press.

Katz, M.N., & Konner, M.J. 1981. The role of the father: An anthropological perspective. In M.E. Lamb (Ed.), *The role of the father in child development* (2nd Ed.), pp. 155–186.

Kaufman, I. 1982. Father-daughter incest. In S.H. Cath, A.R. Gurwitt, & J.M. Ross (Eds.), *Father and child: Developmental and clinical perspectives.* Boston: Little, Brown, pp. 491–518.

Kaufman, I.; Peck, A.L.; & Tagiuri, C.K. 1954. The family constellation and overt incestuous relations between father and daughter. *American Journal of Clinical Psychiatry, 24*, 266–279.

Kaye, H.E., et al. 1967. Homosexuality in women. *Archives of General Psychiatry, 17*, 626–634.

Kayton, R., & Biller, H.B. 1971. Perception of parental sex-role behavior and psychopathology in adult males. *Journal of Consulting and Clinical Psychology, 36*, 235–237.

Kayton, R., & Biller, H.B. 1972. Sex-role development and psychopathology in adult males. *Journal of Consulting and Clinical Psychology, 36*, 235–257.

Kazdin, A.E. 1975. *Behavior modification in applied settings.* Homewood, Ill.: Dorsey Press.

Kellam, S.G.; Ensminger, M.E.; & Turner, R.J. 1977. Family structure and the mental health of children. *Archives of General Psychiatry, 34*, 1012–1022.

Keller, O.J., Jr., & Alper, B.S. 1970. *Halfway houses: Community-centered correction and treatment.* Lexington, Mass.: Lexington Books, D.C. Heath and Company.

Kelly, F.J., & Baer, D.J. 1969. Age of male delinquents when father left home and recidivism. *Psychological Reports, 25*, 1010.

Kelly, J.A., & Worrell, J. 1977. New formulations of sex roles and androgyny: A critical review. *Journal of Consulting and Clinical Psychology 45*, 1101–1115.

Kelly, J.B, & Wallerstein, J.S. 1976. The effects of parental divorce. Experiences of the child in early latency. *American Journal of Orthopsychiatry, 46*, 20–32.

Kempe, C.H. 1973. A practical approach to the protection of the abused child and rehabilitation of the abusing parent. *Pediatrics, 51*, 804–812.

Kempe, C.H. 1980. Incest and other forms of sexual abuse. In C.H. Kempe & R.E. Helfer (Eds.), *The battered child.* Chicago: University of Chicago Press.

Kempe, C.H., & Helfer, R.E. (Eds.). 1972. *Helping the battered child and his family.* Philadelphia: Lippincott Press.

Kempe, C.H., & Helfer, R.E. (Eds.). 1980. *The battered child.* Chicago: University of Chicago Press.

Kempe, C.H.; Silverman, F.N.; Steele, B.F.; Droegemueller, W.; & Silver, H.K. 1962. The battered child syndrome. *Journal of the American Medical Association, 181*, 17–24.

Kempe, R.S., & Kempe, C.H. 1978. *Child abuse.* Cambridge, Mass.: Harvard University Press.

Kempe, R.S., & Kempe, C.H. 1984. *The common secret: Sexual abuse of children and adolescents.* New York: W.H. Freeman.

Kemper, T.D., & Reichler, M.L. 1976. Father's work integration and types and frequencies of rewards and punishments administered by fathers and mothers to adolescent sons and daughters. *Journal of Genetic Psychology, 129*, 207–214.

Kennell, J.; Voos, D.; & Klaus, M. 1976. Parent-infant bonding. In R.E. Helfer, & C.H. Kempe (Eds.), *Child abuse and neglect: The family and the community.* Cambridge, Mass.: Ballinger.

Kent, J. 1976. A follow-up study of abused children. *Journal of Pediatric Psychology, 1*, 25–31.

Keshet, J., & Rosenthal, R. 1978. Fathering after marital separation. *Social Work, 25*, 14–18.

Kestenberg, J. 1968. Outside and inside, male and female. *Journal of the American Psychoanalytic Association, 16*, 459–520.

Kestenberg, J. 1975. *Children and parents.* New York: Aronson.

Kestenberg, J.S.; Marcus, H.; Sossin, K.M.; & Stevenson, R. 1982. The development of parental attitudes. In S.H. Cath, A.R. Gurwitt, & J.M. Ross (Eds.), *Father and child: Developmental and clinical perspectives.* Boston: Little, Brown, pp. 209–218.

Kimball, B. 1952. The sentence completion technique in a study of scholastic under-achievement. *Journal of Consulting Psychology, 16,* 353–358.

Kinard, E.M. 1980. Emotional development in physically abused children. *American Journal of Orthopsychiatry, 50,* 686–696.

Kinard, E.M., & Klerman, L.V. 1980. Teenage parenting and child abuse. Are they related? *American Journal of Orthopsychiatry, 50,* 481–488.

King, K.; McIntyre, J.A.; & Axelson, L.J. 1968. Adolescents' views of maternal employment as a threat to the marital relationship. *Journal of Marriage and the Family, 30,* 633–637.

Kiresuk, T.J., & Sherman, R.E. 1968. Goal attainment scaling: A general method for evaluating comprehensive mental health programs. *Community Mental Health Journal, 4,* 443–453.

Kirkpatrick, J.; Samuels, S.; Jones, H.; & Zweibelson, I. 1965. Bereavement and child adjustment. *Journal of School Psychology, 3,* 58–63.

Klaus, M.H., & Kennell, J.H. 1970. Mothers separated from their newborn infants. *Pediatric Clinics of North America, 17,* 1015–1037.

Kleeman, J. 1971a. The establishment of core gender identity in normal girls, I. *Archives of Sexual Behavior, 1,* 103–116.

Kleeman, J. 1971b. The establishment of core gender identity in normal girls, II. *Archives of Sexual Behavior, 1,* 117–129.

Klein, C. 1973. *The single parent experience.* New York: Avon.

Klein, M., & Stern, L. 1971. Low birth weight and the battered child syndrome. *American Journal of Diseases of Children, 122,* 15–18.

Kline, D.F.; Cole, P.; & Fox, P. 1981. Child abuse and neglect: The school psychologist's role. *School Psychology Review, 10,* 65–71.

Klinman, D.C., & Kohl, R. 1984. *Fatherhood U.S.A.: The first national guide to programs, services, and resources for and about fathers.* New York: Garland Publishing.

Koch, H.L. 1956. Sissiness and tomboyishness in relation to sibling characteristics. *Journal of Genetic Psychology, 88,* 231–244.

Koch, M.B. 1961. Anxiety in preschool children from broken homes. *Merrill-Palmer Quarterly, 1,* 225–231.

Kohlberg, L. 1966. A cognitive-developmental analysis of children's sex-role concepts and attitudes. In E.E. Maccoby (Ed.), *The development of sex differences.* Stanford, Calif.: Stanford University Press, pp. 81–173.

Kohlberg, L. 1969. Stage and sequence: The cognitive-developmental approach to socialization. In D.A. Goslin (Ed.), *Handbook of socalization theory and research.* Chicago: Rand McNally.

Kohn, M.L. 1959. Social class and parental values. *American Journal of Sociology, 64,* 337–351.

Kohn, M.L. 1979. The effects of social class on parental value and practices. In D. Reiss & H.A. Hoffman (Eds.), *The American family: Dying or developing?* New York: Plenum Press.

Kohn, M.L., & Carroll, E.E. 1960. Social class and the allocation of parental responsibilities. *Sociometry, 23,* 372–392.

Kohn, M.L., & Rosman, B.L. 1973. Cognitive functioning in five-year-old boys as related to social-emotional and background-demographic variables. *Developmental Psychology, 8,* 277–294.

Koller, K. 1970. Parental deprivation, family background, and female delinquency. *British Journal of Psychiatry, 116*, 319–327.

Kopf, K.E. 1970. Family variables and school adjustment of eighth grade father-absent boys. *Family Coordinator, 19*, 145–150.

Korbin, J. 1978. Very few cases: Child abuse in the People's Republic of China. Paper presented at the Annual Meeting of the American Anthropological Association, Los Angeles, November.

Kotelchuck, M. 1976. The infant's relationship to his father: Experimental evidence. In M.E. Lamb (Ed.), *The role of the father in child development*. New York: Wiley.

Kotelchuck, M.; Zelazo, P.; Kagan, J.; & Spelke, E. 1975. Infant reaction to parental separations when left with familiar and unfamiliar adults. *Journal of Genetic Psychology, 126*, 255–262.

Kriesberg, L. 1967. Rearing children for educational achievement in fatherless families. *Journal of Marriage and the Family, 29*, 288–301.

Kriesberg, L. 1970. *Mothers in poverty: A study of fatherless families*. Chicago, Aldine.

Krupp, G. 1972. Maladaptive reactions to the death of a family member. *Social Casework, 53*, 425–434.

Lamb, M.E. 1976a. Effects of stress and cohort on mother- and father-infant interaction. *Developmental Psychology, 12*, 435–443.

Lamb, M.E. 1976b. Interactions between eight-month-old children and their fathers and mothers. In M.E. Lamb (Ed.), *The role of the father in child development*. New York: Wiley.

Lamb, M.E. (Ed.). 1976c. *The role of the father in child development*. New York: Wiley.

Lamb, M.E. 1977a. The development of mother-infant and father-infant attachments in the second year of life. *Developmental Psychology, 13*, 637–648.

Lamb, M.E. 1977b. Father-infant and mother-infant interaction in the first year of life. *Child Development, 48*, 167–181.

Lamb, M.E. 1978. Qualitative aspects of mother- and father-infant attachments. *Infant Behavior and Development, 1*, 265–275.

Lamb, M.E. 1979. Paternal influence and the father's role: A personal perspective. *American Psychologist, 34*, 938–943.

Lamb, M.E. 1981a. The development of father-infant relationships. In M.E. Lamb (Ed.), *The role of the father in child development* (2nd Ed.). New York: Wiley, pp. 459–478.

Lamb, M.E. 1981b. The development of social expectations in the first year of life. In M.E. Lamb & L.R. Sherrod (Eds.), *Infant social cognition: Empirical and theoretical considerations*. Hillsdale, N.J.: Lawrence Erlbaum Associates.

Lamb, M.E. 1981c. Fathers and child development: An integrative overview. In M.E. Lamb (Ed.), *The role of the father in child development* (2nd Ed.). New York: Wiley, pp. 11–70.

Lamb, M.E. (Ed.). 1981d. *The role of the father in child development* (2nd Ed.). New York: Wiley.

Lamb, M.E. (Ed.). 1982. *Nontraditional families: Parenting and child development*. Hillsdale, N.J.: Lawrence Erlbaum Associates.

Lamb, M.E. 1983. Fatherhood and social policy in international perspective. In M.E. Lamb & A. Sagi (Eds.), *Fatherhood and family policy*. Hillsdale, N.J.: Lawrence Erlbaum Associates.

Lamb, M.E. 1984. Prepared statement concerning the father-child relationship. In G. Miller et al., (Eds.), *Paternal absence and fathers' roles*. Hearing before the Select Committee on Children, Youth and Families, House of Representatives, 98th Congress, 1st Session. Washington, D.C.: U.S. Government Printing Office.

Lamb, M.E., & Bronson, S.K. 1980. Fathers in the context of family influences: Past, present, and future. *School Psychology Review, 9*, 336–353.

Lamb, M.E., & Elster, A.B. 1985. Adolescent mother-father relationships. *Developmental Psychology, 21*, 768–773.

Lamb, M.E.; Frodi, A.M.; Hwang, C.P.; & Frodi, M. 1982. Varying degrees of paternal involvement in infant care: Attitudinal and behavioral correlates. In M.E. Lamb (Ed.), *Non-traditional families: Parenting and child development*. Hillsdale, N.J.: Lawrence Erlbaum Associates.

Lamb, M.E., & J.E. Lamb. 1976. The nature and importance of the father-child relationship. *Family Coordinator, 25*, 370–386.

Lamb, M.E., & Levine, J. 1983. The Swedish parental insurance policy: An experiment in social engineering. In M.E. Lamb & A. Sagi (Eds.), *Fatherhood and family policy*. Hillsdale, N.J.: Lawrence Erlbaum Associates.

Lamb, M.E.; Owen, M.; & Chase-Lansdale, L. 1979. The father-daughter relationship: Past, present and future. In C.B. Kopp (Ed.), *Becoming female: Perspectives on development*. New York: Plenum Press.

Lamb, M.E.; Russell, G.; & Sagi, A. 1983. Summary and recommendations for public policy. In M.E. Lamb & A. Sagi (Eds.), *Fatherhood and family policy*. Hillsdale, N.J.: Lawrence Erlbaum Associates.

Lamb, M.E., & Sagi, A. (Eds.). 1983. *Fatherhood and family policy*. Hillsdale, N.J.: Lawrence Erlbaum Associates.

Lamb, M.E., & Sutton-Smith, B. (Eds.). 1982. *Sibling relationships: Their nature and significance across the lifespan*. Hillsdale, N.J.: Lawrence Erlbaum Associates.

Landis, J.T. 1956. Experiences of 500 children with adult sexual deviation. *Psychiatric Quarterly Supplement, 30*, 91–109.

Landis, J.T. 1962. A re-examination of the role of the father as an index of family integration. *Marriage and Family Living, 24*, 122–128.

Landis, P.H. 1965. *Making the most of marriage*. New York: Appleton-Century-Crofts.

Landy, F.; Rosenberg, B.G.; & Sutton-Smith, B. 1967. The effect of limited father absence on the cognitive and emotional development of children. Paper presented at the meeting of the Midwestern Psychological Association, Chicago, May.

Landy, F.; Rosenberg, B.G.; and Sutton-Smith, B. 1969. The effect of limited father-absence on cognitive development. *Child Development, 40*, 941–944.

Langer, W.L. 1974. Infanticide: A historical survey. *History of Childhood Quarterly, 1*, 353–365.

Langlois, J.H., & Downs, A.C. 1980. Mothers, fathers, and peers as socialization agents of sex-typed play behaviors in young children. *Child Development, 51*, 1237–1247.

Langner, T.S., & Michael, S.T. 1963. *Life stress and mental health*. New York: The Free Press.

Lansky, L.M. 1956. Patterns of defense against conflict. Ph.D. dissertation, University of Michigan.

Lansky, L.M. 1964. The family structure also affects the model: Sex-role identification in parents of preschool children. *Merrill-Palmer Quarterly, 10,* 39–40.

Lansky, L.M. 1967. The family structure also affects the model: Sex-role attitudes in parents of preschool children. *Merrill-Palmer Quarterly, 13,* 139–150.

Lauer, B.; Broed, E.J.; & Grossman, M. 1974. Battered child syndrome: Review of 130 patients with controls. *Pediatrics, 54,* 67–72.

Laughlin, J., & Weiss, M. 1981. An outpatient milieu therapy approach to treatment of child abuse and neglect problems. *Social Casework, 621,* 106–109.

Lawton, M.J., & Sechrest, L. 1962. Figure drawings by young boys from father-absent and father-present homes. *Journal of Clinical Psychology, 18,* 304–305.

Lazowick, L.M. 1955. On the nature of identification. *Journal of Abnormal and Social Psychology, 51,* 175–183.

LeCorgne, L.D., & Laosa, L.M. 1976. Father absence in low-income Mexican-American families: Children's social adjustment and conceptual differentiation of sex-role attitudes. *Developmental Psychology, 12,* 439–448.

Lederer, W. 1964. Dragons, delinquents, and destiny. *Psychological Reports, 10,* 43–53.

Lee, P.C., & Wolinsky, A.L. 1973. Male teachers of young children: A preliminary empirical study. *Young Children, 28,* 342–352.

Lefkowitz, M. 1962. Some relationships between sex role preference of children and other parent and child variables. *Psychological Reports, 10,* 43–53.

Leichty, M.M. 1960. The effect of father-absence during early childhood upon the Oedipal situation as reflected in young adults. *Merrill-Palmer Quarterly, 6,* 212–217.

Leiderman, G.F. 1959. Effect of parental relationships and child-training practices on boys' interactions with peers. *Acta Psychologica, 15,* 469.

Leiderman, P. 1974. Mothers at risk: A potential consequence of the hospital care of the premature infant. In E. Anthony & C. Koupernik (Eds.), *The child in his family: Children at psychiatric risk.* New York: Wiley.

Leifer, A.D.; Leiderman, P.H.; Barnett, C.R.; & Williams, J.A. 1972. Effects of mother-infant separation on maternal attachment behavior. *Child Development, 43,* 1203–1218.

Leighton, L.A.; Stollak, G.E.; & Ferguson, L.R. 1971. Patterns of communication in normal and clinic families. *Journal of Consulting and Clinical Psychology, 36,* 252–256.

LeMasters, E.E. 1970. *Parents in modern America: A sociological perspective.* Homewood, Ill.: Dorsey.

Leonard, M.M. 1966. Fathers and daughters. *International Journal of Psychoanalysis, 47,* 325–333.

Lerner, S.H. 1954. Effect of desertion on family life. *Social Casework, 35,* 3–8.

Lessing, E.E.; Zagorin, S.W.; and Nelson, D. 1970. WISC subtest and IQ score correlates of father absence. *Journal of Genetic Psychology, 67,* 181–195.

Levant, R.F. 1983. Communication skills training for fathers of school-aged children. Paper presented at the meetings of the American Psychological Association, Anaheim. Calif.

Levin, H., & Sears, R.R. 1956. Identification with parents as a determinant of doll play aggression. *Child Development, 37,* 135–153.

Levin, R.B. 1966. An empirical test of the female castration complex. *Journal of Abnormal Psychology, 71,* 181–188.

Levine, J.A. 1976. *And who will raise the children? New options for fathers and mothers.* Philadelphia: Lippincott.

Levine, J.A., & Klinman, D. 1984. Prepared statement concerning The Fatherhood Project. In D. Miller et al., *Paternal absence and fathers' roles.* Hearing before the Select Committee on Children, Youth and Families, House of Representatives, 98th Congress, 1st Session. Washington, D.C.: U.S. Government Printing Office..

Levine, J.A.; Pleck, J.H.; & Lamb, M.E. 1983. The fatherhood project. In M.E. Lamb & A. Sagi (Eds.), *Fatherhood and family policy.* Hillsdale, N.J.: Lawrence Erlbaum Associates.

Levinson, D.J. 1978. *The seasons of a man's life.* New York: Ballantine.

Levitt, E.E. 1971. Research on psychotherapy with children. In A.E. Bergin & S.L. Garfield (Eds.), *Handbook of psychotherapy of behavior change.* New York: Wiley.

Levy, D.M. 1943. *Maternal overprotection.* New York: Columbia University Press.

Lewis, M. 1972. Parents and children: Sex role development. *School Review, 80,* 229–240.

Lewis, M., & Feiring, C. 1978. The child's social world. In R.M. Lerner & G.D. Spanier (Eds.), *Child influences on marital and family interaction: A life-span perspective.* New York: Academic Press.

Lewis, M.; Feiring, C.; & Weinraub, M. 1981. The father as a member of the child's social network. In M.E. Lamb (Ed.), *The role of the father in child development* (2nd Ed.). New York: Wiley, pp. 259–294.

Lewis, M., & Rosenblum, L.A. (Eds.). 1974. *The effect of the infant on its caregiver.* New York: Wiley.

Lewis, M., & Weinraub, M. 1976. The father's role in the infant's social network. In M.E. Lamb (Ed.), *The role of the father in child development.* New York: Wiley.

Lidz, T.; Parker, N.; & Cornelison, A.R. 1956. The role of the father in the family environment of the schizophrenic patient. *American Journal of Psychiatry, 12,* 126–132.

Liebenberg, B. 1967. Expectant fathers. *American Journal of Orthopsychiatry, 37,* 358–359.

Lifshitz, M. 1976. Long-range effects of father's loss: The cognitive complexity of bereaved children and their school adjustment. *British Journal of Medical Psychology, 49,* 189–197.

Lifshitz, M.; Berman, D.; Galili, A.; & Gilad, D. 1977. Bereaved children: The effect of mother's perception and social system organization on their short-range adjustment. *Journal of the American Academy of Child Psychiatry, 16,* 272–284.

Light, R.J. 1973. Abused and neglected children in America: A study of alternative policies. *Harvard Educational Review, 43,* 556–598.

Light, R.J., & Smith, P.V. 1971. Accumulating evidence: Procedures for resolving contradictions among different research studies. *Harvard Educational Review, 41,* 429–471.

Liverant, S. 1959. MMPI differences between parents of disturbed and nondisturbed children. *Journal of Consulting Psychology, 23,* 256–260.

Locksley, A., & Colten, M.E. 1979. Psychological androgyny: A case of mistaken identity? *Journal of Personality and Social Psychology, 37,* 1017–1031.

Loeb, J. 1966. The personality factor in divorce. *Journal of Consulting Psychology, 30,* 562.

Longabaugh, R. 1973. Mother behavior as a variable moderating the effects of father absence. *Ethos, 1,* 456–477.

Lott, B.E. *Becoming a woman: The socialization of gender.* Springfield, Ill.: C.C. Thomas.

Louden, K.H. 1973. Field dependence in college students as related to father absence during the latency period. Ph.D. dissertation, Graduate School of Psychology, Fuller Theological Seminary.

Lovens, M.D., & Rako, J. 1975. A community approach to the prevention of child abuse. *Child Welfare, 54,* 83–87.

Lozoff, M.M. 1974. Fathers and autonomy in women. In R.B. Kundsin (Ed.), *Women and Success.* New York: Morrow, pp. 103–109.

Luckey, E.B. 1960. Marital satisfaction and parental concept. *Journal of Consulting Psychology, 24,* 195–204.

Lukianowicz, W. 1972. Incest: I. Paternal incest; II. Other types of incest. *British Journal of Psychiatry, 120,* 301–313.

Lynch, M. 1976. Risk factors in the child: A study of abused children and their siblings. In H.P. Martin (Ed.), *The abused child: A multidisciplinary approach to developmental issues and treatment.* Cambridge, Mass.: Ballinger.

Lynn, D.B. 1969. *Parental and sex-role identification.* Berkeley, Calif.: McCutchan.

Lynn, D.B. 1974. *The father: His role in child development.* Belmont, Calif.: Brooks/Cole.

Lynn, D.B. 1979. *Daughters and parents: Past, present and future.* Belmont, Calif.: Brooks/Cole.

Lynn, D.B., & Cross, A.R. 1974. Parent preferences of preschool children. *Journal of Marriage and the Family, 36,* 555–559.

Lynn, D.B., & Sawrey, W.L. 1959. The effects of father-absence on Norwegian boys and girls. *Journal of Abnormal and Social Psychology, 59,* 258–262.

Lytton, H. 1976. The socialization of two-year-old boys: Ecological findings. *Journal of Child Psychology and Psychiatry, 17,* 287–304.

Lytton, H. 1979. Disciplinary encounters between young boys and their mothers and fathers: Is there a contingency system? *Developmental Psychology, 15,* 256–268.

McAdoo, H. 1978. Factors related to stability in upwardly mobile black families. *Journal of Marriage and the Family, 40,* 761–776.

McCall, R. 1977. Challenges to a science of developmental psychology. *Child Development, 48,* 333–344.

McClelland, D.C., & Watt, N.F. 1968. Sex-role alienation in schizophrenia. *Journal of Abnormal Psychology, 73,* 226–239.

Maccoby, E.E., & Jacklin, C.N. 1973. Stress activity and proximity seeking: Sex differences in the year-old child. *Child Development, 44,* 34–42.

Maccoby, E.E., & Jacklin, C.N. (Eds.). 1974. *The development of sex differences.* Stanford, Calif.: Stanford University Press.

Maccoby, E.E., & Rau, L. 1962. Differential cognitive abilities. Final report, U.S. Office of Education, Cooperative Research Project No. 1040.

McCord, J.; McCord, W.; & Howard, A. 1963. Family interaction as an antecedent to the direction of male aggressiveness. *Journal of Abnormal and Social Psychology, 66,* 239–224.

McCord, J.; McCord, W.; & Thurber, E. 1962. Some effects of paternal absence on male children. *Journal of Abnormal and Social Psychology, 64,* 361–369.

McCord, W.; McCord, J.; & Howard, A. 1961. Familial correlates of aggression in non-delinquent male children. *Journal of Abnormal and Social Psychology, 62,* 79–93.

McDermott, J.F. 1968. Parental divorce in early childhood. *American Journal of Psychiatry, 124,* 1424–1432.

Machtlinger, V. 1976. Psychoanalytic theory: Preoedipal and oedipal phases with special reference to the father. In M.E. Lamb (Ed.), *The role of the father in child development.* New York: Wiley, pp. 277–306.

Machtlinger, V.T. 1981. The father in psychoanalytic theory. In M.E. Lamb (Ed.), *The role of the father in child development* (2nd Ed.). New York: Wiley, pp. 113–153.

McPherson, S. 1970. Communication of intents among parents and their disturbed adolescent child. *Journal of Abnormal Psychology, 76,* 98–105.

McQuiston, M. 1976. Crisis nurseries. In H.P. Martin (Ed.), *The abused child: A multi-disciplinary approach to developmental issues and treatment.* Cambridge, Mass.: Ballinger.

Maden, M.F., & Wrench, D.F. 1977. Significant findings in child abuse research. *Victimology, 2,* 196–224.

Madow, L., & Hardy, S.E. 1947. Incidence and analysis of the broken family in the background of neurosis. *American Journal of Orthopsychiatry, 17,* 521–528.

Mahl, G.F. 1982. Father-son themes in Freud's self-analysis. In S.H. Cath, A.R. Gurwitt, & J.M. Ross (Eds.), *Father and child: Developmental and clinical perspectives.* Boston: Little, Brown, pp. 33–64.

Mahler, M.S. 1968. *On human symbiosis and the vicissitudes of individuation.* New York: International Universities Press.

Mahler, M.S.; Pine, F.; & Bergman, A. 1975. *The psychological birth of the human infant.* New York: Basic Books.

Main, M., & Weston, D.R. 1981. The quality of the toddler's relationship to mother and to father: Related to conflict behavior and the readiness to establish new relationships. *Child Development, 52,* 932–940.

Margolin, G., & Patterson, G. 1975. Differential consequences provided by mothers and fathers for their sons and daughters. *Developmental Psychology, 11,* 537–538.

Marjoribanks, K. 1972. Environment, social class, and mental abilities. *Journal of Educational Psychology, 63,* 103–107.

Marsella, A.J.; Dubanoski, R.A.; & Mohs, K. 1974. The effects of father presence and absence upon maternal attitudes. *Journal of Genetic Psychology, 125,* 257–263.

Martel, L.F., & Biller, H.B. Forthcoming. *Stature and stigma: Psychological development among short men.* Lexington, Mass.: Lexington Books.

Martin, H.P. 1972. The child and his development. In C.H. Kempe & R.E. Helfer (Eds.), *Helping the battered child and his family.* Philadelphia: J.B. Lippincott Company, 1972.

Martin, H.P. 1976. Which children get abused: High risk factors in the child. In H.P. Martin (Ed.), *The abused child: A multidisciplinary approach to developmental issues and treatment.* Cambridge, Mass.: Ballinger.

Martin, H.P. 1980. The consequences of being abused and neglected: How the child fares. In C.H. Kempe & R.E. Helfer (Eds.), *The battered child* (3rd Ed.). Chicago: University of Chicago Press.

Martin, H.P., & Beezeley, P. 1976a. Personality of abused children. In H.P. Martin (Ed.), *The abused child: A multidisciplinary approach to developmental issues and treatment*. Cambridge, Mass.: Ballinger.

Martin, H.P., & Beezeley, P. 1976b. Therapy for abusive parents: Its effect on the child. In H.P. Martin (Ed.), *The abused child: A multidisciplinary approach to developmental issues and treatment*. Cambridge, Mass.: Ballinger.

Martin, H.P., & Beezeley, P. 1977. Behavioral observations of abused children. *Developmental Medicine and Child Neurology, 19*, 373–387.

Martin, H.P.; Beezeley, P.; Conway, E.F.; & Kempe, C.H. 1974. The development of abused children—Part I: A review of the literature; Part II: Physical, neurologic, and intellectual outcomes. *Advanced Pediatrics, 21*, 25–73.

Martindale, C. 1972. Father's absence, psychopathology, and poetic eminence. *Psychological Reports, 31*, 813–847.

Maurer, A. 1974. Corporal punishment. *American Psychologist, 29*, 614–626.

Maxwell, A.E. 1961. Discrepancies between the pattern of abilities for normal and neurotic children. *Journal of Mental Science, 107*, 300–307.

Maxwell, J.W. 1976. The keeping fathers of America. *Family Coordinator, 25*, 387–392.

Medinnus, G.N. 1963. The relation between inter-parent agreement and several child measures. *Journal of Genetic Psychology, 102*, 139–144.

Medinnus, G.N. 1965a. Adolescents' self acceptance and perceptions of their parents. *Journal of Consulting Psychology, 29*, 150–154.

Medinnus, G.N. 1965b. Delinquents' perceptions of their parents. *Journal of Consulting Psychology, 29*, 592–593.

Medinnus, G.N., & Johnson, T.M. 1970. Parental perceptions of kindergarten children. *Journal of Educational Research, 63*, 370–381.

Meerloo, J.A.M. 1956. The father cuts the cord: The role of the father as initial transference figure. *American Journal of Psychotherapy, 10*, 471–480.

Meichenbaum, D. 1977. *Cognitive-behavior modification: An integrative approach*. New York: Plenum Press.

Meiselman, K.C. 1978. *Incest: A psychological study of causes and effects with treatment recommendations*. San Francisco: Jossey-Bass.

Melear, J. 1973. Children's conceptions of death. *Journal of Genetic Psychology, 123*, 359–360.

Melnick, B., & Hurley, J.R. 1969. Distinctive personality attribution of child-abusing mothers. *Journal of Consulting and Clinical Psychology, 33*, 746–749.

Merrill, E. 1962. Physical abuse of children: An agency study. In V. DeFrancis (Ed.), *Protecting the battered child*. Denver, Colo.: American Humane Association.

Messer, S.B., & Lewis, M. 1972. Social class and sex differences in the attachment and play behavior of the one-year-old infant. *Merrill-Palmer Quarterly, 18*, 295–306.

Miller, B.A. 1960. Effects of father-absence and mother's evaluation of father on the socialization of adolescent boys. Ph.D. dissertation, Columbia University.

Miller, D.R., & Swanson, G.E. 1958. *The changing American parent*. New York: Wiley.

Miller, D.S. 1959. Fractures among children. *Minnesota Medicine, 42*, 1209–1213.

Miller, G., et al. 1984. *Paternal absence and fathers' roles.* Hearing before the Select Committee on Children, Youth and Families. House of Representatives, 98th Congress, 1st Session. Washington, D.C.: U.S. Government Printing Office.

Miller, M.K., & Fay, M.J. 1969. Emergency child care service: The evaluation of a project. *Child Welfare, 48,* 496–499.

Miller, W.B. 1958. Lower-class culture as a generating milieu of gang delinquency. *Journal of Social Issues, 14,* 5–19.

Milowe, I., & Lourie, R. 1964. The child's role in the battered child syndrome, *Journal of Pediatrics, 65,* 1079–1081.

Milton, G.A. 1957. The effects of sex-role identification upon problem solving skills. *Journal of Abnormal and Social Psychology, 55,* 208–212.

Minuchin, S. 1974. *Families and family therapy.* Cambridge, Mass.: Harvard University Press.

Mirandy, J. 1976. Preschool for abused children. In H.P. Martin (Ed.), *The abused child: A multi-disciplinary approach to developmental issues and treatment.* Cambridge, Mass.: Ballinger.

Mischel, W. 1958. Preference for delayed reinforcement: An experimental study of cultural observation. *Journal of Abnormal and Social Psychology, 56,* 57–61.

Mischel, W. 1961a. Delay of gratification, need for achievement, and acquiescence in another culture. *Journal of Abnormal and Social Psychology, 62,* 543–552.

Mischel, W. 1961b. Father-absence and delay of gratification. *Journal of Abnormal and Social Psychology, 62,* 116–124.

Mischel, W. 1961c. Preference for delayed reward and social responsibility. *Journal of Abnormal and Social Psychology, 62,* 1–7.

Mischel, W. 1968. *Personality and assessment.* New York: Wiley.

Mischel, W. 1970. Sex typing and socialization. In P.H. Mussen (Ed.), *Carmichael's manual of child psychology* (3rd Ed.) (Vol. 2). New York: Wiley.

Mischel, W. 1973. Toward a cognitive social learning reconceptualization of personality. *Psychological Review, 80,* 252–283.

Mischel, W. 1979. On the interface of cognition and personality: Beyond the person-situation debate. *American Psychologist, 34,* 740–754.

Mishler, E.G., & Waxler, N.E. 1968. *Interaction in families.* New York: Wiley.

Mitchell, D., & Wilson, W. 1967. Relationship of father-absence to masculinity and popularity of delinquent boys. *Psychological Reports, 20,* 1173–1174.

Mitchell, R.E., & Hudson, L.A. 1985. Coping and social support among battered women: An ecological perspective. In S. Hobfoll (Ed.), *Stress, social support and women.* New York: Hemisphere Publications.

Molwar, G., & Gamaron, P. 1975. Incest syndromes: Observations in a general hospital psychiatric unit. *Canadian Psychiatric Association Journal, 20,* 373–377.

Monahan, T.P. 1957. Family status and the delinquent child. *Social Forces, 35,* 250–258.

Money, J. 1977. The syndrome of abuse dwarfism: Behavioral data and case report. *American Journal of Diseases of Children, 131,* 508–513.

Money, J., & Ehrhardt, A. 1972. *Man and woman: Boy and girl.* Baltimore, Md.: The Johns Hopkins University Press.

Money, J.; Hampson, J.G.; & Hampson, J.L. 1957. Imprinting and the establishment of gender role. *Archives of Neurology and Psychiatry, 77,* 333–336.

Money, J., & Needleman, A. 1976. Child abuse in the syndrome of reversible hypo-somatotropic dwarfism. *Pediatric Psychology, 1,* 20–23.

Money, J., & Tucker, P. 1975. *Sexual signatures.* Boston: Little, Brown.

Money, J., & Wolff, G. 1973. Relationship between sleep and growth in patients with reversible somatotropism deficiency (psychosocial dwarfism). *Psychological Medicine, 3,* 18–27.

Morgan, S.R. 1979. Psycho-educational profile of emotionally disturbed abused children. *Journal of Clinical Child Psychology, 8,* 3–6.

Morrison, H.L., & Brubakken, D.M. 1980. Social isolation and deprivation: An environment of rehabilitation. In G.J. Williams & J. Money (Eds.), *Traumatic abuse and neglect of children at home.* Baltimore, Md.: The Johns Hopkins University Press.

Moss, H.A. 1967. Sex, age, and state as determinants of mother-infant interaction. *Merrill-Palmer Quarterly, 13,* 19–36.

Moulton, P.W.; Burnstein, E.; Liberty, D.; & Altucher, N. 1966. The patterning of parental affection and dominance as a determinant of guilt and sex-typing, *Journal of Personality and Social Psychology, 4,* 363–365.

Mowrer, O.H. 1950. Identification: A link between learning theory and psychotherapy. In O.H. Mowrer (Ed.), *Learning theory and personality dynamics.* New York: Ronald Press, pp. 573–616.

Moynihan, D.P. 1965. *The Negro family: The case for national action.* Washington, D.C.: U.S. Department of Labor.

Mrazek, P.B., & Kempe, C.H. (Eds.). 1981. *Sexually abused children and their families.* New York: Pergamon Press.

Mullahy, G.A. 1973. Sex differences in patterns of self-disclosure among adolescents: A developmental perspective. *Journal of Youth and Adolescence, 2,* 343–356.

Murphy, L.B., & Moriarty, A.E. 1976. *Vulnerability, coping and growth.* New Haven: Yale University Press.

Mussen, P.H. 1961. Some antecedents and consequences of masculine sex-typing in adolescent boys. *Psychological Monographs, 75,* No. 2 (Whole No. 506).

Mussen, P.H.; Bouterline-Young, H.; Gaddini, R.; & Morante, L. 1963. The influences of father-son relationships on adolescent personality and attitudes. *Journal of Child Psychology and Psychiatry, 4,* 3–16.

Mussen, P.H.; Conger, J.J.; & Kagan, J. 1974. *Child development and personality.* New York: Harper and Row.

Mussen, P.H., & Distler, L. 1959. Masculinity, identification, and father-son relationships. *Journal of Abnormal and Social Psychology, 59,* 350–356.

Mussen, P.H., & Distler, L. 1960. Child-rearing antecedents of masculine identification in kindergarten boys. *Child Development, 31,* 89–100.

Mussen, P.H., & Parker, A.L. 1965. Mother nurturance and the girls' incidental imitative learning. *Journal of Personality and Social Psychology, 2,* 94–97.

Mussen, P.H., & Rutherford, E.E. 1963. Parent-child relationships and parental personality in relation to young children's sex role preferences. *Child Development, 34,* 589–607.

Mussen, P.H.; Rutherford, E.; Harris, S.; & Keasey, C.B. 1970. Honesty and altruism among preadolescents. *Developmental Psychology, 3,* 169–194.

Mutimer, E.; Loughlin, L.; & Powell, M. 1966. Some differences in the family relationships of achieving and underachieving readers. *Journal of Genetic Psychology, 109,* 67–74.

Nakamura, C.V., & Rogers, M.M. 1969. Parents' expectations of autonomous behavior and children's autonomy. *Developmental Psychology, 1,* 613–617.

Nash, J. 1965. The father in contemporary culture and current psychological literature. *Child Development, 36,* 261–297.

Nash, J. 1978. *Developmental psychology: A psychobiological approach* (2nd Ed.). Englewood Cliffs, N.J.: Prentice-Hall.

Nash, J., & Hayes, T. 1965. The parental relationships of male homosexuals: Some theoretical issues and a pilot study. *Australian Journal of Psychology, 17,* 35–43.

National Center on Child Abuse and Neglect. 1981. *Study findings: National study of the incidence and severity of child abuse and neglect.* U.S. Department of Health and Human Services, No. (OHDS) 81-30325. Washington, D.C.: U.S. Government Printing Office.

Nelsen, E.A., & Maccoby, E.E. 1966. The relationship between social development and differential abilities on the scholastic aptitude test. *Merrill-Palmer Quarterly, 12,* 269–289.

Nelsen, E.A., & Vangen, P.M. 1971. The impact of father absence upon heterosexual behaviors and social development of preadolescent girls in a ghetto environment. *Proceedings of the 79th Annual Convention of the Annual Convention of the American Psychological Association, 6,* 165–166.

Neubauer, P.N. 1960. The one-parent child and his oedipal development. *The Psychoanalytic Study of the Child, 15,* 286–309.

Newberger, E.H. 1975. A physician's perspective on the interdisciplinary management of child abuse. In N.B. Ebeling & D.A. Hill (Eds.), *Child abuse: Intervention and treatment.* Acton, Mass.: Publishing Sciences Group.

Newberger, E.H. 1979. The myth of the battered child syndrome. In R. Bourne & E.H. Newberger (Eds.), *Critical perspectives on child abuse.* Lexington, Mass.: Lexington Books, D.C. Heath and Company.

Newberger, E.H., & Daniel, J.H. 1979. Knowledge and epidemiology of child abuse: A critical review of concepts. In R. Bourne & E.H. Newburger (Eds.), *Critical perspectives on child abuse.* Lexington, Mass.: Lexington Books, D.C. Heath and Company.

Niachamin, S. 1973. Battered child syndrome and brain dysfunction. *Journal of the American Medical Association, 223,* 1390–1394.

Niem, T.C., & Collard, R. 1971. *Parental discipline of aggressive behaviors in four-year-old Chinese and American children.* Paper presented at the Annual Meeting of the American Psychological Association, Washington, D.C.

Noller, P. 1980. Gross gender effects in two-child families. *Developmental Psychology, 16,* 159–160.

Norman, C.D. 1966. The interpersonal values of parents of achieving and nonachieving gifted children. *Journal of Psychology, 64,* 49–57.

Norton, A. 1952. Incidence of neurosis related to maternal age and birth order. *British Journal of Social Medicine, 6,* 253–258.

Nye, F.I. 1957. Child adjustment in broken and unhappy homes. *Marriage and Family Living, 19,* 356–361.

Nye, F.I. 1959. Employment status of mothers and adjustment of adolescent children. *Marriage and Family Living 19,* 240–244.

O'Block, F.R.; Billimoria, A.; & Behan, M. 1981. National survey of involvement of school psychologists with child abuse. *School Psychology Review, 10,* 62–64.

Oltman, J.E., & Friedman, S. 1967. Parental deprivation in psychiatric conditions: III. In personality disorders and other conditions. *Diseases of the Nervous System, 28,* 298–303.

Oltman, J.E.; McGarry, J.J.; & Friedman, S. 1952. Parental deprivation and the broken home in dementia praecox and other mental disorders. *American Journal of Psychiatry, 108,* 685–694.

Oshman, H.P., & Manosevitz, N. 1976. Father absence: Effect of stepfathers upon psychosocial development in males. *Developmental Psychology, 12,* 479–480.

Osofsky, J.D., & O'Connell, E.J. 1972. Parent-child interaction: Daughters' effects upon mothers' and fathers' behaviors. *Developmental Psychology, 1,* 157–168.

Ostrovsky, E.S. 1959. *Father to the child: Case studies of the experiences of a male teacher.* New York: Putnam.

Ounsted, C.; Oppenheimer, R.; & Lindsay, J. 1974. Aspects of bonding failure: The psychopathology and psychotherapeutic treatment of families of battered children. *Developmental Medicine and Child Neurology, 16,* 447–456.

Pakizegi, B. 1978. The interaction of mothers and fathers with their sons. *Child Development, 49,* 479–482.

Parish, T., and Copeland, T. 1980. Locus of control and father loss. *Journal of Genetic Psychology, 136,* 147–148.

Parke, R.D. 1979. Perspectives on father-infant interaction. In J.D. Osofsky (Ed.), *The handbook of infant development.* New York: Wiley, pp. 549–590.

Parke, R.D. 1981. *Fathers.* Cambridge, Mass.: Harvard University Press.

Parke, R.D. 1982. Theoretical models of child abuse: Their implications for prediction, prevention and modification. In R. Starr (Ed.), *Prediction of abuse.* New York: Ballinger.

Parke, R.D. 1985. Fathers, families, and children: New perspectives. In M. Green (Ed.), *The psychosocial aspects of the family: The new pediatrics.* Lexington, Mass.: Lexington Books, D.C. Heath and Company.

Parke, R.D, & Collmer, C.W. 1975. Child abuse: An interdisciplinary analysis. In E.M. Hetherington (Ed.), *Review of Child Development Research* (Vol. 5). Chicago: University of Chicago Press.

Parke, R.D.; Grossman, K.; & Tinsley, B.R. 1981. Father-mother-infant interaction in the newborn period: A German-American comparison. In T. Field (Ed.), *Culture and early interactions.* Hillsdale, N.J.: Lawrence Erlbaum Associates.

Parke, R.D.; Hymel, S.; Power, T.A.; & Tinsley, B.R. 1980. Fathers and risk: Hospital-based model of intervention. In D.B. Sawin, R.C. Hawkins, L.O. Walker, & J.H. Penticuff (Eds.), *Psychosocial risks in infant-environment transactions.* New York: Brunner/Mazel.

Parke, R.D.; O'Leary, S.; & West, S. 1972. Mother-father-newborn interaction: Effects of maternal medication, labor, and sex of infant. *Proceedings of the 80th Annual Convention of the American Psychological Association, 17,* 85–86.

Parke, R.D., & Sawin, D.B. 1976. The father's role in infancy: A reevaluation. *Family Coordinator, 25*, 365–371.

Parke, R.D., & Sawin, D.B. 1980. The family in early infancy: Social interactional and attitudinal analyses. In F.A. Pedersen (Ed.), *The father-infant relationship: Observational studies in the family setting.* New York: Praeger.

Parke, R.D., & Suomi, S.J. 1981. Adult male-infant relationships: Human and non-human primate evidence. In K. Immelman, G. Barlow, M. Main, & L. Petrinovitch (Eds.), *Behavioral development: The Bielafeld Interdisciplinary Project.* New York: Cambridge University Press.

Parke, R.D., & Tinsley, B.R. 1981. The father's role in infancy: Determinants of involvement in caregiving and play. In M.E. Lamb (Ed.), *The role of the father in child development* (2nd Ed.). New York: Wiley, pp. 429–459.

Parker, S., & Kleiner, R.T. 1966. Characteristics of Negro mothers in single-headed households. *Journal of Marriage and the Family, 28*, 507–513.

Parsons, T. 1954. The father symbol: An appraisal in the light of psychoanalytic and sociological theory. In L. Bryson, L. Finkelstein, R.M. MacIver, & R. McKeon (Eds.), *Symbols and values.* New York: Harper and Row.

Parsons, T. 1955. Family structure and the socialization of the child. In T. Parsons and R.F. Bales (Eds.), *Family, socialization and interaction process.* Glencoe, Ill.: Free Press, pp. 25–131.

Paulson, M.J. 1975. Child trauma intervention: A community response to family violence. *Journal of Clinical Child Psychology, 4*, 26–29.

Paulson, M.J., & Blake, P. 1969. The physically abused child: A focus on prevention. *Child Welfare, 48*, 85–95.

Paulson, M.J., & Chaleff, A. 1973. Parent surrogate roles: A dynamic concept in understanding and training abusive parents. *Journal of Clinical Child Psychology, 2*, 38–40.

Payne, D.E., & Mussen, P.H. 1956. Parent-child relations and father-identification among adolescent boys. *Journal of Abnormal and Social Psychology, 52*, 358–362.

Pedersen, F.A. 1966. Relationships between father-absence and emotonal disturbance in male military dependents. *Merrill-Palmer Quarterly, 12*, 321–331.

Pedersen, F.A. 1975. Mother, father and infant as an interactive system. Paper presented at the annual convention of the American Psychological Association, Chicago.

Pedersen, F.A. 1976. Does research on children reared in father-absent homes yield information on father influences? *Family Coordinator, 25*, 458–646.

Pedersen, F.A. (Ed.). 1980. *The father-infant relationship: Observational studies in the family setting.* New York: Praeger.

Pedersen, F.A. 1981. Father influences viewed in family context. In M.E. Lamb (Ed.), *The role of the father in child development* (2nd Ed.). New York: Wiley, pp. 295–317.

Pedersen, F.A.; Anderson, B.J.; & Cain, R.L. 1980. Parent-infant and husband-wife interactions observed at age five months. In F. Pedersen (Ed.), *The father-infant relationship: Observational studies in the family setting.* New York: Praeger.

Pedersen, F.A., & Robson, K.S. 1969. Father participation in infancy. *American Journal of Orthopsychiatry, 39*, 466–472.

Pedersen, F.A.; Rubinstein, J.; & Yarrow, L.J. 1979. Infant development in father-absent families. *Journal of Genetic Psychology, 135*, 51–61.

Pelton, L. 1978. Child abuse and neglect: The myth of classlessness. *American Journal of Orthopsychiatry, 48*, 608–617.

Pelton, L. (Ed.). 1981. *The social context of child abuse and neglect.* New York: Human Sciences Press.

Peterman, P.J. 1981. Parenting and environmental considerations. *American Journal of Orthopsychiatry, 5*, 351–355.

Peters, J.J. 1976. Children who are victims of sexual assault and the psychology of offenders. *American Journal of Psychotherapy, 30*, 398–421.

Peterson, D.R.; Becker, W.C.; Hellmer, L.A.; Shoemaker, D.J.; & Quay, H.C. 1959. Parental attitudes and child adjustment. *Child Development, 30*, 119–130.

Peterson, D.R.; Becker, W.C.; Shoemaker, D.J.; Luria, Z.; & Hellmer, L.A. 1961. Child behavior problems and parental attitudes. *Child Development 32*, 131–162.

Peterson, G.H.; Mehl, L.E.; & Leiderman, P.H. 1979. The role of some birth-related variables in father attachment. *American Journal of Orthopsychiatry, 49*, 330–338.

Pettigrew, T.F. 1964. *A profile of the Negro American.* Princeton, N.J.: Van Nostrand, 1964.

Phelan, H.M. 1964. The incidence and possible significance of the drawing of female figures by sixth-grade boys in response to the Draw-a-Person Test. *Psychiatric Quarterly, 38*, 1–16.

Piaget, J. 1954. *The construction of reality in the child.* New York: Basic Books.

Piaget, J. 1958. *The growth of logical thinking from childhood to adolescence* (Trans. A. Parsons and S. Seagrin). New York: Basic Books.

Piers, M.W. 1978. *Infanticide.* New York: W.F. Norton.

Plank, E.H., & Plank, R. 1954. Emotional components in arithematic learning as seen through autobiographies. *Psychoanalytic Study of the Child, 9*, 274–293.

Pleck, J. 1977. The work-family role system. *Social Problems, 24*, 417–427.

Pleck, J.H. 1979. Men's family work: Three perspectives and some new data. *Family Coordinator, 28*, 481–488.

Pleck, J.H. 1981. *The myth of masculinity.* Cambridge, Mass.: MIT Press.

Poffenberger, T.A., & Norton, D. 1959. Factors in the formation of attitudes towards mathematics. *Journal of Educational Research 52*, 171–176.

Polansky, N.A.; Chalmers, M.A.; Butterwieser, E.; & Williams, D.P. 1979. The absent father in child neglect. *Social Service Review, 53*, 163–174.

Polansky, N.A.; Chalmers, M.A.; Butterwieser, E.; & Williams, D.P. 1981. *Damaged parents: An anatomy of child neglect.* Chicago: University of Chicago Press.

Polansky, N.A.; DeSaix, C.; & Sharlin, S.A. 1972. *Child neglect: Understanding and reaching the parent.* New York: Child Welfare League of America.

Pollak, G.K. 1970. Sexual dynamics of parents without partners. *Social Work, 15*, 79–85.

Pollock, C., & Steele, B.F. 1972. A therapeutic approach to the parents. In C.H. Kempe & R.E. Helfer (Eds.), *Helping the battered child and his family.* Philadelphia: J.B. Lippincott.

Pope, B. 1953. Socioeconomic contrasts in children's peer culture prestige values. *Genetic Psychology Monographs, 48*, 157–200.

Porter, G., & O'Leary, O.K. In press. Marital discord and childrearing practices. *Journal of Abnormal Child Psychology.*

Portnoy, S.M.; Biller, H.B.; & Davids, A. 1972. The influence of the child care worker in residential treatment. *American Journal of Orthopsychiatry, 42*, 719–722.

Power, M.J.; Ash, P.M.; Schoenberg, E.; & Sorey, E.C. 1974. Delinquency and the family. *British Journal of Social Work, 4,* 13–48.

Price-Bonham, S., & Addison, S. 1978. Families and mentally retarded children: Emphasis on the father. *The Family Coordinator, 27,* 221–230.

Prochaska, J.O. 1984. *Systems of psychotherapy: A transtheoretical analysis* (2nd Ed.). Homewood, Ill.: Dorsey Press.

Radbill, S. 1980. Children in a world of violence: A history of child abuse and infanticide. In C.H. Kempe & R.E. Helfer (Eds.), *The battered child.* Chicago: University of Chicago Press.

Radin, N. 1972. Father-child interaction and the intellectual functioning of four-year-old boys. *Developmental Psychology, 6,* 353–361.

Radin, N. 1973. Observed paternal behaviors as antecedents of intellectual functioning in young boys. *Developmental Psychology, 8,* 369–376.

Radin, N. 1974. Observed maternal behavior with four-year-old boys and girls in lower class families. *Child Development, 45,* 1126–1131.

Radin, N. 1976. The role of the father in cognitive, academic, and intellectual development. In M.E. Lamb (Ed.), *The role of the father in child development.* New York: Wiley, pp. 237–276.

Radin, N. 1981. The role of the father in cognitive, academic and intellectual development. In M.E. Lamb (Ed.), *The role of the father in child development* (2nd Ed.). New York: Wiley, pp. 379–427.

Radin, N. 1982. Primary caregiving and role sharing fathers of preschoolers. In M.E. Lamb (Ed.), *Nontraditional families: Parenting and child development.* Hillsdale, N.J.: Lawrence Erlbaum Associates.

Radin, N., & Russell, G. 1983. Increased father participation and child development outcomes. In M.E. Lamb & A. Sagi (Eds.), *Fatherhood and family policy.* Hillsdale, N.J.: Lawrence Erlbaum Associates.

Rains, P. 1971. *Becoming an unwed mother.* Chicago: Aldine.

Redican, W.K. 1976. Adult male-infant interactions in nonhuman primates. In M.E. Lamb (Ed.), *The role of the father in child development.* New York: Wiley.

Reid, J.B.; Taplin, P.S.; & Loeber, R. 1981. A social interactional approach to the treatment of abusive families. In R.B. Stuart (Ed.), *Violent behavior: Social learning approaches to prediction, management and treatment.* New York: Brunner/Mazel.

Reis, M., & Gold, D. 1977. Relation of paternal availability to problem solving and sex-role orientation in young boys. *Psychological Reports, 40,* 823–829.

Reiss, J., & Herzberger, S. 1980. Problem and program linkage: The early and periodic screening, diagnosis and treatment program as a means of preventing and detecting child abuse. *Infant Mental Health Journal, 1,* 262–269.

Rendina, I., & Dickerscheid, J.D. 1976. Father involvement with first-born infants. *Family Coordinator, 25,* 373–379.

Reuter, M.W., & Biller, H.B. 1973. Perceived paternal nurturance-availability and personality adjustment among college males. *Journal of Consulting and Clinical Psychology, 40,* 339–342.

Rexford, E.N. 1964. Antisocial young children and their families. In M.R. Haworth (Ed.), *Child psychotherapy.* New York: Basic Books, pp. 58–63.

Richards, M.P.M.; Dunn, J.F.; & Antonis, B. 1977. Caretaking in the first year of life: The role of fathers' and mothers' social isolation. *Child Care, Health and Development, 3,* 23–26.

Roberts, W.B., & Long, J.M. 1958. Male models and sexual identification: A case from the Out Island Bahamas. *Human Organization, 27,* 326–331.

Roe, A. 1953. *The making of a scientist.* New York: Dodd Mead.

Rogers, W.B., & Long, J.M. 1968. Male models and sexual identification: A case from the Out Island Bahamas. *Human Organization, 27,* 326–331.

Rohrer, H.H., & Edmonson, M.S. 1960. *The eighth generation.* New York: Harper.

Roman, M., & Haddad, W. 1978. *The disposable parent.* New York: Holt, Rinehart and Winston.

Rosenbaum, A., & O'Leary, K.D. 1981. Children: The unintended victims of marital violence. *American Journal of Orthopsychiatry, 51,* 692–699.

Rosenberg, B.G., & Sutton-Smith, B. 1964. Ordinal position and sex-role identification. *Genetic Psychology Monographs, 70,* 297–328.

Rosenberg, C.M. 1969. Determinants of psychiatric illness in young people. *British Journal of Psychiatry, 115,* 907–915.

Rosenberg, M. 1965. *Society and the adolescent self-image.* Princeton, N.J.: Princeton University Press.

Rosenfeld, A.A. 1979a. Endogamic incest and the victim perpetrator model. *American Journal of Disease in Children, 133,* 406–410.

Rosenfeld, A.A. 1979b. Incidence of a history of incest among 18 female psychiatric patients. *American Journal of Psychiatry, 136,* 791–796.

Rosenthal, K., & Keshet, H.F. 1981. *Fathers without partners: A study of fathers and the family after marital separation.* Totowa, N.J.: Rowman & Littlefield.

Rosenthal, M., & Louis, J.A. 1981. The law's evolving role in child abuse and neglect. In L. Pelton (Ed.), *The social context of child abuse and neglect.* New York: Human Sciences Press.

Rosenthal, M.S.; Ni, E.; Finkelstein, M.; & Berkwitz, G.K. 1962. Father-child relationships and children's problems. *Archives of General Psychiatry, 7,* 360–373.

Rosenthal, R. 1978. Combining results of independent studies. *Psychological Bulletin, 85,* 185–193.

Ross, C.J. 1980. The lessons of the past: Defining and controlling child abuse in the United States. In G. Gerbner, C.J. Ross, & E. Zigler (Eds.), *Child abuse: An agenda for action.* New York: Oxford University Press.

Ross, G.; Kagan, J.; Zelazo, P.; & Kotelchuck, M. 1975. Separation protest in infants in home and laboratory. *Developmental Psychology, 11,* 256–257.

Ross, J.M. 1975. The development of paternal identity: A critical review of the literature on nurturance and generativity in boys and men. *Journal of the American Psychoanalytic Association, 23,* 783–817.

Ross, J.M. 1977. Toward fatherhood: the epigenesis of paternal identity during a boy's first decade. *International Review of Psychoanalysis, 4,* 327–348.

Ross, J.M. 1979. Fathering: A review of some psychoanalytic contributions on paternity. *International Journal of Psychoanalysis, 60,* 317–327.

Ross, J.M. 1982a. From mother to father: The boys' search for a generative identity and the oedipal era. In S.H. Cath, A.R. Gurwitt, & J.M. Ross (Eds.), *Father and child: Developmental and clinical perspectives.* Boston: Little, Brown, pp. 189–204.

Ross, J.M. 1982b. In search of fathering: A review. In S.H. Cath, A.R. Gurwitt, J.M. Ross (Eds.), *Father and child: Developmental and clinical perspectives.* Boston: Little, Brown, pp. 21–33.

Roth, F. 1975. A practice regimen for diagnosis and treatment of child abuse. *Child Welfare, 54,* 268–273.

Rothbart, M.K., & Maccoby, E.E. 1966. Parents' differential reactions to sons and daughters. *Journal of Personality and Social Psychology, 4,* 237–243.

Rubenstein, C. 1980. The children of divorce as adults. *Psychology Today, 14,* 74–75.

Rush, F. 1980. *The best kept secret: Sexual abuse of children.* Englewood Cliffs, N.J.: Prentice-Hall.

Rushing, W.A. 1964. Adolescent-parent relationships and mobility aspirations. *Social Forces, 43,* 157–166.

Russell, D.E.H. 1983. The incidence and prevalence of intrafamilial and extrafamilial sexual abuse of female children. *Child Abuse & Neglect 7,* 133–146.

Russell, G. 1978. The father role and its relation to masculinity, femininity, and androgyny. *Child Development, 49,* 1174–1181.

Russell, G. 1983. *The changing role of fathers?* St. Lucia, Queensland, Australia/New York: University of Queensland Press.

Russell, G., & Radin, W. 1983. Increased paternal participation. The father's perspective. In M.E. Lamb & A. Sagi (Eds.), *Fatherhood and family policy.* Hillsdale, N.J.: Lawrence Erlbaum Associates.

Rutherford, E.E., & Mussen, P.H. 1968. Generosity in nursery school boys. *Child Development, 39,* 755–765.

Rutter, M. 1971. Parent-child separation: Psychological effects on children. *Journal of Child Psychology and Psychiatry, 12,* 233–260.

Rutter, M. 1974. Epidemiological strategies and psychiatric concepts in research on the vulnerable child. In E.J. Anthony & C. Koopernik (Eds.), *The child in his family: Children at psychiatric risk* (Vol. 3). New York: Wiley.

Rutter, M. 1979. Maternal deprivation, 1972–1978: New findings, new concepts, new approaches. *Child Development, 50,* 283–305.

Rutter, M., & Madge, N. 1976. *Cycles of disadvantage: A review of research.* London: Heinemann.

Rychlak, J., & Legerski, A. 1967. A sociocultural theory of appropriate sexual role identification and level of personality adjustment. *Journal of Personality, 35,* 31–49.

Saghir, M.T., & Robbins, F. 1973. *Male and female homosexuality.* Baltimore, Md.: Williams and Wilkins.

Sagi, A. 1982. Antecedents and consequences of various degrees of paternal involvement in child rearing: The Israeli project. In M.E. Lamb (Ed.), *Nontraditional families: Parenting and child development.* Hillsdale, N.J. Lawrence Erlbaum Associates.

Sagi, A., & Sharon, N. 1983. Costs and benefits of increased paternal involvement in childrearing: The societal perspective. In M.E. Lamb & A. Sagi (Eds.), *Fatherhood and family policy.* Hillsdale, N.J.: Lawrence Erlbaum Associates.

Samaraweera, S., & Cath, C. 1982. Fostering the consolidation of paternal identity: The Tufts Family Support Program. In S.H. Cath, A.R. Gurwitt, & J.M. Ross (Eds.), *Father and child: Developmental and clinical implications.* Boston: Little, Brown, pp. 543–556.

Sandler, J.; Van Dercor, C.; & Milhoan, M. 1978. Training child abusers in the use of positive reinforcement techniques. *Behavior Research and Therapy, 16,* 169–175.

Santrock, J.W. 1970a. Influence of onset and type of paternal absence on the first four Eriksonian developmental crises. *Developmental Psychology, 3,* 273–274.

Santrock, J.W. 1970b. Paternal absence, sex-typing, and identification. *Developmental Psychology, 2,* 264–272.

Santrock, J.W. 1972. Relation of type and onset of father-absence to cognitive development. *Child Development, 43,* 455–469.

Santrock, J.W. 1975. Father absence, perceived maternal behavior and moral development in boys. *Child Development, 46,* 753–757.

Santrock, J.W. 1977. Effects of father absence on sex-typed behaviors in male children: Reason for the absence and age of onset of the absence. *Journal of Genetic Psychology, 130,* 3–10.

Santrock, J.W., & Tracy, R.L. 1978. Effects of children's family structure status on the development of stereotypes by teachers. *Journal of Educational Psychology, 70,* 754–757.

Santrock, J.W., & Warshak, R.A. 1979. Father custody and social development in boys and girls. *Journal of Social Issues, 35,* 112–125.

Santrock, J.W., & Wohlford, P. 1970. Effects of father absence: Influences of, reasons for, and onset of absence. *Proceedings of the 78th Annual Convention of the American Psychological Association, 5,* 265–266.

Satler, J. 1974. *Assessment of children's intelligence.* Philadelphia: W.B. Saunders.

Schacter, F.F. 1982. Sibling deidentification and split-parent identification: A family tetrad. In M.E. Lamb & B. Sutton-Smith (Eds.), *Sibling relationships: Their nature and significance across the lifespan.* Hillsdale, N.J.: Lawrence Erlbaum Associates.

Schaefer, E.S. 1965. Children's reports of parental behavior: An inventory. *Child Development, 36,* 413–424.

Schaffer, H.R., & Emerson, P.E. 1964. The development of social attachments in infancy. *Monographs of the Society for Research in Child Development, 29,* no. 94.

Schechter, M.D., & Roberge, L. 1976. Sexual exploitation. In R.E. Helfer & C.H. Kempe (Eds.), *Child abuse and neglect: The family and the community.* Cambridge, Mass.: Ballinger.

Schlesinger, B. 1966. The one-parent family: An overview. *Family Life Coordinator, 15,* 133–137.

Schneider, C.W.; Hoffmeister, J.; & Helfer, R.E. 1976. A predictive screening questionnaire for potential problems in mother-child interaction. In R.E. Helfer & C.H. Kempe (Eds.), *Child abuse and neglect: The family and the community.* Cambridge, Mass.: Ballinger.

Schneider-Rosen, K.; Braunwald, K.G.; Carlson, V.; & Cicchetti, D. 1985. Current perspectives in Attachment Theory: Illustration from the study of maltreated infants. In I. Bretherton & W. Waters (Eds.), *Growing points of attachment theory and research. Monographs of the Society for Research in Child Development, 50* (1–2, Serial No. 209), 194–210.

Schneider-Rosen, K.; & Cicchetti, D. 1984. The relation between affect and cognition in maltreated infants: Quality of attachment and development of visual self-recognition. *Child Development, 55,* 648–658.

Schuham, A.I. 1970. Power relations in emotionally disturbed and normal family triads. *Journal of Abnormal Psychology, 75,* 30–37.

Schultz, L.G. 1982. Child sexual abuse in historical perspective. *Journal of Social Work and Human Sexuality 1*, 21–36.

Sciara, F.J. 1975. Effects of father absence on the educational achievement of urban black children. *Child Study Journal, 5*, 45–55.

Seals, M. 1980. Parents Anonymous works. In U.S. Department of Health, Education and Welfare (Ed.), *Child abuse and developmental disabilities: Essays*. Washington, D.C.: U.S. Government Printing Office.

Sears, D.W. 1980. Incidence of child abuse and neglect. *Region VIII News, 2*, Denver: National Center on Child Abuse and Neglect.

Sears, P.S. 1951. Doll-play aggression in normal young children: Influence of sex, age, sibling status, father's absence. *Psychological Monographs, 65* (Whole No. 6).

Sears, P.S. 1953. Child-rearing factors related to playing of sex-typed roles. *American Psychologist, 8*, 431 (Abstract).

Sears, R.R. 1957. Identification as a form of behavioral development. In D.R. Harris (Ed.), *The concept of development*. Minneapolis: University of Minnesota Press.

Sears, R.R. 1970. Relations of early socialization experiences to self-concepts and gender role in middle childhood. *Child Development, 41*, 267–289.

Sears, R.R.; Pintler, M.H.; & Sears, P.S. 1946. Effect of father-separation on preschool children's doll-play aggression. *Child Development, 17*, 219–243.

Sears, R.R.; Rau, L.; & Alpert, R. 1965. *Identification and child rearing*. Stanford, Calif.: Stanford University Press.

Seward, G.H. 1945. Cultural conflict and the feminine role: An experimental study. *Journal of Social Psychology, 22*, 177–194.

Sexton, P.C. 1969. *The feminized male: Classrooms, white collars, and the decline of manliness*. New York: Random House.

Sgroi, S.M. 1981. *Handbook of clinical intervention in child sexual abuse*. Lexington, Mass.: Lexington Books, D.C. Heath and Company.

Sgroi, S.M. 1982. Family treatment of child sexual abuse. *Journal of Social Work and Human Sexuality, 1–2*, 109–128.

Shamroy, J.A. 1980. A perspective on childhood sexual abuse. *Social Work, 25*, 128–131.

Shaw, M.C., & White, D.L. 1965. The relationship between child-parent identification and academic underachievement. *Journal of Clinical Psychology, 21*, 10–13.

Shelton, L.A. 1969. A comparative study of educational achievement in one-parent families and in two-parent families. *Dissertation Abstracts, 29* (8-A), 2535–2536.

Shelton, W.R. 1975. A study of incest. *International Journal of Offender Therapy and Comparative Criminology, 19*, 139–153.

Shepherd, D., and Barraclough, G. 1976. The aftermath of parental suicide for children. *British Journal of Psychiatry, 129*, 267–276.

Shinn, M. 1978. Father absence and children's cognitive development. *Psychological Bulletin, 85*, 295–324.

Shortell, J.R., & Biller, H.B. 1970. Aggression in children as a function of sex of subject and sex of opponent. *Developmental Psychology, 3*, 143–144.

Shultz, W.J. 1924. *The humane movement in the United States, 1910–1922*. New York: Columbia University Press.

Sidel, R. 1972. *Women and child care in China*. New York: Hill & Wang.

Siegman, A.W. 1966. Father-absence during childhood and antisocial behavior. *Journal of Abnormal Psychology, 71,* 71–74.

Silver, L.; Dublin, C.; & Lourie, R. 1971. Agency action and interaction in cases of child abuse. *Social Casework, 52,* 164–171.

Silverman, F.N. 1953. The roentgen manifestations of unrecognized skeletal trauma infants. *American Journal of Roentgenology, 69,* 413–427.

Silverman, P., & Englander, S. 1975. The widow's view of her dependent children. *Omega: Journal of Death and Dying, 6,* 3–20.

Slater, P.E. 1961. Parental role differentiation. *American Journal of Sociology, 67,* 296–311.

Slater, P.E. 1962. Parental behavior and the personality of the child. *Journal of Genetic Psychology, 101,* 53–68.

Smelser, W.T. 1963. Adolescent and adult occupational choice as a function of family socio-economic history. *Sociometry, 26,* 393–409.

Smith, M.L., & Glass, G.V. 1977. Meta-analysis of psychotherapy outcome studies. *American Psychologist, 32,* 752–760.

Smith, S.; Hanson, R.; & Hoble, S. 1975. Parents of battered children: A controlled study. In A. Franklin (Ed.), *Concerning child abuse.* Edinburgh: Churchill Livingstone.

Solomon, D. 1969. The generality of children's achievement related behavior. *Journal of Genetic Psychology, 114,* 109–125.

Solomon, F.; Houlihan, D.A.; Busse, T.C.; & Parelius, R.J. 1971. Parent behavior and child academic achievement, achievement striving and related personality characteristics. *Genetic Psychology Monographs, 83,* 175–273.

Solomon, R.S. 1982. Child maltreatment: A critical review of the literature and intervention programs (Ph.D. dissertation, University of Rhode Island). *Dissertation Abstracts International, 43,* 4132B.

Solomon, T. 1973. History and demography of child abuse. *Pediatrics, 51,* 775–780.

Sopchak, A.L. 1952. Parental identification and tendencies toward disorders as measured by the MMPI. *Journal of Abnormal and Social Psychology, 47,* 159–165.

Sopchak, A.L. 1958. Spearman correlations between MMPI scores of college students and their parents. *Journal of Consulting Psychology, 22,* 207–209.

Spelke, E.; Zelazo, P.; Kagan, J.; & Kotelchuck, M. 1973. Father interaction and separation protest. *Developmental Psychology, 9,* 83–90.

Spence, J., & Helmreich, R.L. 1979. The many faces of androgyny: A reply to Locksley and Colten. *Journal of Personality and Social Psychology, 37,* 1032–1046.

Spinetta, J.J., & Rigler, D. 1972. The child abusing parent: A psychological review. *Psychological Bulletin, 77,* 296–304.

Spitz, R.A. 1945. Hospitalism: An inquiry into the genesis of psychiatric conditions in early childhood. *Psychoanalytic Study of the Child, 1,* 53–74.

Stanfield, R.E. 1966. The interaction of family variables and gang variables in the aetiology of delinquency. *Social Problems, 13,* 411–417.

Starr, R. 1979. Child abuse. *American Psychologist, 34,* 872–878.

Steele, B.F. 1975. Working with abusive parents: A psychiatrist's view. *Children Today, 4,* 3–5.

Steele, B.F. 1976. Experience with an interdisciplinary concept. In R.E. Helfer & C.H. Kempe (Eds.), *Child abuse and neglect: The family and the community.* Cambridge, Mass.: Ballinger.

Steele, B.F. 1980. Psychodynamic factors in child abuse. In C.H. Kempe & R.E. Helfer (Eds.), *The battered child* (3rd Ed.). Chicago: University of Chicago Press.

Steele, B.F. 1982. Abusive fathers. In S.H. Cath, A.R. Gurwitt, & J.M. Ross (Eds.), *Father and child: Developmental and clinical perspectives*. Boston: Little, Brown, pp. 481–490.

Steele, B.F., & Pollock, C.G. 1968. A psychiatric study of parents who abuse infants and small children. In R.E. Helfer & C.H. Kempe (Eds.), *The battered child*. Chicago: University of Chicago Press.

Steinberg, L.D.; Catalano, R.; & Dooley, D. 1981. Economic antecedents of child abuse and neglect. *Child Development, 52, 975–985.*

Steinmetz, S.K. 1974. Intra-familial patterns of conflict resolution: United States and Canada. Paper presented to the Society for the Study of Social Problems, Montreal.

Stendler, C.B. 1952. Critical periods in socialization and overdependency. *Child Development, 23, 3–12.*

Stendler, C.B. 1954. Possible causes of overdependency in young children. *Child Development, 25, 125–146.*

Stephens, W.N. 1961. Judgments by social workers on boys and mothers in fatherless families. *Journal of Genetic Psychology, 99, 59–64.*

Stephens, W.N. 1962. *The Oedipus complex: Cross-cultural evidence*. Glencoe, Ill.: The Free Press.

Stern, M.; Northman, J.E.; & Van Slyk, M.R. 1984. Father absence and adolescent "problem behaviors": Alcohol consumption, drug use and social activity. *Adolescence, 19, 301–312.*

Stoke, S.M. 1954. An inquiry into the concept of identification. In W.E. Martin & C.B. Stendler (Ed.), *Readings in child development*. New York: Harcourt, Brace & World.

Stolk, M.V. 1972. *The battered child in Canada*. Toronto: McClelland-Stewart.

Stoller, R.J. 1968. *Sex and gender*. New York: Science House.

Stolz, L.M., et al. 1954. *Father relations of war-born children*. Stanford, Calif.: Stanford University Press.

Straus, M.A.; Gelles, R.J.; & Steinmetz, S.K. 1980. *Behind closed doors: Violence in the American family*. New York: Anchor Books.

Suedfield, P. 1967. Paternal absence and overseas success of Peace Corps volunteers. *Journal of Consulting Psychology, 31, 424–425.*

Sumner, W.G. 1940. *Folkways*. New York: New American Library.

Sutherland, H.E.G. 1930. The relationship between IQ and size of family in the case of fatherless children. *Journal of Genetic Psychology, 38, 161–170.*

Sutton-Smith, B.N., & Rosenberg, B.G. 1970. *The sibling*. New York: Holt, Rinehart and Winston.

Sutton-Smith, B.; Rosenberg, B.G.; & Landy, F. 1968. Father-absence effects in families of different sibling compositions. *Child Development, 38, 1213–1221.*

Switzky, L.T.; Vietze, P.; & Switzky, H. 1979. Attitudinal and demographic predictors of breast-feeding and bottle-feeding behavior in mothers of six-week-old infants. *Psychological Reports, 45, 3–14.*

Tanzer, C.F., & Block, J. 1972. *Why natural childbirth?* New York: Doubleday.

Tasch, R.J. 1952. The role of the father in the family. *Journal of Experimental Education, 20, 319–361.*

Tasch, R.J. 1955. Interpersonal perceptions of fathers and mothers. *Journal of Genetic Psychology, 87,* 59–65.

Teahan, J.E. 1963. Parental attitudes and college success. *Journal of Educational Psychology, 54,* 104–109.

Terr, L.C., & Watson, A.S. 1980. The battered child rebrutalized: Ten cases of medical-legal confusion. In G. Williams & J. Money (Eds.), *Traumatic abuse and neglect of children at home.* Baltimore: The Johns Hopkins University Press.

Thomas, A.; Chess, S.; & Birch, H.G. 1968. *Temperament and behavior disorders in children.* New York: New York University Press.

Thompson, N.L.; Schwartz, D.M.; McCandless, B.R.; & Edwards, D.A. 1973. Parent-child relationships and sexual identity in male and female homosexuals and heterosexuals. *Journal of Consulting and Clinical Psychology, 41,* 120–127.

Thompson, R.A. 1983. The father's case in child custody disputes: The contributions of psychological research. In M.E. Lamb & A. Sagi (Eds.), *Fatherhood and family policy.* Hillsdale, N.J.: Lawrence Erlbaum Associates.

Thomson, E.M. 1971. *Child abuse: A community challenge.* East Aurora, N.Y.: Henry Stewart.

Tietjen, A.M. 1980. Integrating formal and informal support systems: The Swedish experience. In J. Garbarino & S.H. Stocking (Eds.), *Protecting children from abuse and neglect.* San Francisco: Jossey-Bass.

Tiller, P.O. 1958. Father-absence and personality development of children in sailor families. *Nordisk Psyckologi's Monograph Series, 9,* 1–48.

Tiller, P.O. 1961. *Father separation and adolescence.* Oslo, Norway: Institute for Social Research.

Toby, J. 1957. The differential impact of family disorganization. *American Sociological Review, 22,* 505–512.

Torgoff, I., & Dreyer, A.S. 1961. Achievement inducing and independence granting synergistic parental role components: Relation to daughter's parental role orientation and level of aspiration. *American Psychologist, 16,* 345 (Abstract).

Tracy, J.J., & Clark, E.H. 1974. Treatment for child abusers. *Social Work, 19,* 338–342.

Travis, J. 1933. Precipitating factors in manic-depressive psychoses. *Psychiatric Quarterly, 8,* 411–418.

Trenaman, J. 1952. *Out of step.* London: Methuen.

Trunnell, T.L. 1968. The absent father's children's emotional disturbances. *Archives of General Psychiatry, 19,* 180–188.

Tuck, S. 1971. Working with black fathers. *American Journal of Orthopsychiatry, 41,* 465–472.

Tyson, P. 1982. The role of the father in gender identity, urethal eroticism, and phallic narcissism. In S.H. Cath, A.R. Gurwitt, & J.M. Ross (Eds.), *Father and child: Developmental and clinical perspectives.* Boston: Little, Brown.

U.S. Department of Health, Education and Welfare. 1977. *Child abuse and neglect programs: Practice and theory.* Washington, D.C.: U.S. Government Printing Office.

U.S. Department of Health, Education and Welfare. 1979a. *Bowen Center Project for abused and neglected children.* Washington, D.C.: U.S. Government Printing Office.

U.S. Department of Health, Education and Welfare. 1979b. *Child abuse and developmental disabilities: Essays.* Washington, D.C.: U.S. Government Printing Office.

U.S. Department of Health, Education and Welfare. 1979c. *Child abuse and neglect research: Projects and publications.* Washington, D.C.: U.S. Government Printing Office.

U.S. Department of Health, Education and Welfare. 1979d. *Child sexual abuse: Incest, assault and sexual exploitation.* Washington, D.C.: U.S. Government Printing Office.

U.S. Department of Health, Education and Welfare. 1979e. *Planning and implementing child abuse and neglect service programs: The experience of eleven demonstration projects.* Washington, D.C.: U.S. Government Printing Office.

U.S. Department of Health and Human Services. 1980. *Family violence: Intervention strategies.* Washington, D.C.: U.S. Government Printing Office.

U.S. Social Security Administration Statistics. 1979. In *Statistical Abstract of the United States* (100th Ed.). Washington, D.C.: U.S. Bureau of the Census.

Vaillant, G.E. 1977. *Adaptation to life.* Boston: Little, Brown.

Vietze, P.; Falsey, S.; Sandler, H.; O'Connor, S.; & Altemeier, W.A. 1980. Transactional approach to prediction of child maltreatment. *Infant Mental Health Journal, 1,* 248–261.

Volman, R.; Ganzert, A.; Picker, L.; and Williams, W. 1971. Reactions of family systems to sudden and unexpected death. *Omega, 2,* 101–106.

Volpe, R. 1980. Schools and the problem of child abuse: An introduction and overview. In R. Volpe, M. Breton, & J. Mitton (Eds.), *The maltreatment of the school-aged child.* Lexington, Mass.: Lexington Books, D.C. Heath and Company.

Volpe, R.; Breton, M.; & Mitton, J. (Eds.). 1980. *The maltreatment of the school-aged child.* Lexington, Mass.: Lexington Books, D.C. Heath and Company.

Wachs, T.; Uzgiris, I.; & Hunt, J. 1971. Cognitive development in infants of different age levels and from different environmental backgrounds. *Merrill-Palmer Quarterly, 17,* 283–317.

Wahl, C.W. 1954. Antecedent factors in family histories of 392 schizophrenics. *American Journal of Psychiatry, 110,* 668–676.

Wahl, C.W. 1956. Some antecedent factors in the family histories of 568 male schizophrenics of the U.S. Navy. *American Journal of Psychiatry, 113,* 201–210.

Wahl, G.; Johnson, S.M.; Johannson, S.; & Martin, S. 1974. An operant analysis of child-family interaction. *Behavior Therapy, 5,* 64–78.

Wallerstein, J.S. 1984. Children of divorce: Preliminary report of a two-year follow-up of young children. *American Journal of Orthopsychiatry, 54,* 449–458.

Wallerstein, J.S., & Kelly, J.B. 1974. The effects of parental divorce: The adolescent experience. In E.J. Anthony & C. Koupernick (Eds.), *The child in his family: Children at psychiatric risk.* New York: Wiley.

Wallerstein, J.S., & Kelly, J.B. 1975. The effects of parental divorce: Experiences of the preschool child. *Journal of the American Academy of Child Psychiatry, 14,* 600–616.

Wallerstein, J.S., & Kelly, J.B. 1976. The effects of parental divorce: Experiences of the child in later latency. *American Journal of Orthopsychiatry, 46,* 256–269.

Wallerstein, J.S., & Kelly, J.B. 1977. Divorce counseling: A community service for families in the midst of divorce. *American Journal of Orthopsychiatry, 47,* 4–22.

Wallerstein, J.S., & Kelly, J.B. 1980a. California's children of divorce. *Psychology Today, 14*, 67–76.

Wallerstein, J.S., & Kelly, J.B. 1980b. *Surviving the breakup: How children actually cope with divorce.* New York: Basic Books.

Wallerstein, J.S., & Kelly, J.B. 1982. The father-child relationship: Changes after divorce. In S.H. Cath, R.A. Gurwitt, & J.M. Ross (Eds.), *Father and child: Developmental and clinical perspectives.* Boston: Little, Brown.

Walters, J. (Ed.). 1976. Special issue: Fatherhood. *Family Coordinator, 25,* 335–520.

Warren, D.I. 1980. Support systems in different types of neighborhoods. In J. Garbarino & S.H. Stocking (Eds.), *Protecting children from abuse and neglect.* San Francisco: Jossey-Bass.

Warren, M. 1972. Some psychological sequalae of parental suicide in surviving children. In A. Cain (Ed.), *Survivors of suicide.* Springfield, Ill.: Charles Thomas.

Warshak, R.A., & Santrock, J.W. 1983. The impact of divorce in father-custody and mother-custody cases: The child's perspective. In A. Kurdek (Eds.), *Children and divorce: New directions for child development.* San Francisco: Jossey-Bass.

Washburn, W.C. 1962. The effects of physique and intrafamily tension on self-concept in adolescent males. *Journal of Consulting Psychology, 26,* 460–466.

Wasserman, S. 1967. The abused parent of the abused child. *Children, 14,* 175–179.

Weinraub, M., & Frankel, J. 1977. Sex differences in parent-infant interaction during free play, departure, and separation. *Child Development, 48,* 1240–1249.

Weisbroth, S.P. 1970. Moral judgment, sex, and parental identification in adults. *Developmental Psychology, 2,* 396–402.

Weiss, R.S. 1975. *Marital separation.* New York: Basic Books.

Weiss, R.S. 1979. Growing up a little faster: The experience of growing up in a single parent household. *Journal of Social Issues, 35,* 97–111.

Weissberg, M. 1983. *Dangerous secrets: Maladaptive responses to stress.* New York: W.W. Norton and Company.

Wells, D. 1980. *Child abuse: An annotated bibliography.* Metuchen, N.J.: The Scarecrow Press.

Wente, A.S., & Crockenberg, S.B. 1976. Transition to fatherhood: Lamaze preparation, adjustment difficulty and the husband-wife relationship. *Family Coordinator, 25,* 351–357.

Werts, C.E., & Watley, D.J. 1972. Paternal influence on talent development. *Journal of Counseling Psychology, 19,* 367–373.

West, D.J. 1959. Parental relationships in male homosexuality. *International Journal of Social Psychiatry, 5,* 85–97.

West, D.J. 1967. *Homosexuality.* Chicago: Aldine.

Westley, W.A., & Epstein, N.B. 1960. Paternal interaction as related to the emotional health of children. *Social Problems, 8,* 87–92.

Westley, W.A., & Epstein, N.B. 1970. *The silent majority.* San Francisco: Jossey-Bass.

White, B. 1959. The relationship of self-concept and parental identification to women's vocational interests. *Journal of Consulting Psychology, 6,* 202–206.

White, R.W. 1960. Competence and the psychosexual stages of development. In M.R. Jones (Ed.), *Nebraska symposium on motivation.* Lincoln: University of Nebraska Press, pp. 174–195.

Whiting, J.W.M. 1959. Sorcery, sin, and the superego: A cross-cultural study of some mechanisms of social control. In M.R. Jones (Ed.), *Nebraska Symposium on Motivation*. Lincoln: University of Nebraska Press.

Whiting, J.W.M.; Kluckhohn, R.; & Anthony, A. 1958. The function of male initiation ceremonies at puberty. In E.E. Maccoby, T.M. Newcomb, & E.L. Hartley (Eds.), *Readings in social psychology*. New York: Holt, pp. 359–370.

Whiting, L. 1976. Defining emotional neglect. *Children Today, 5*, 2–5.

Willemsen, E.; Flaherty, D.; Heaton, C.; & Ritchey, G. 1974. Attachment behavior of one-year-olds as a function of mother vs. father, sex of child, session, and toys. *Genetic Psychology Monographs, 90*, 305–324.

Williams, G.J. 1980a. Child abuse and neglect. Problems of definition and incidence. In G.J. Williams & J. Money (Eds.), *Traumatic abuse and neglect of children at home*. Baltimore, Md.: The Johns Hopkins University Press.

Williams, G.J. 1980b. Cruelty and kindness to children: Documentary of a century, 1874–1974. In G.J. Williams & J. Money (Eds.), *Trauamtic abuse and neglect of children at home*. Baltimore, Md.: The Johns Hopkins University Press.

Williams, G.J., & Money, J. (Eds.). 1980. *Traumatic abuse and neglect of children at home*. Baltimore, Md.: The Johns Hopkins University Press.

Willoughby, A. 1979. *The alcohol troubled person*. Chicago: Nelson Hall.

Wilson, K.L.; Zurcher, L.A.; McAdams, D.C.; & Curtis, R.L. 1975. Stepfathers and stepchildren: An exploratory analysis from two national surveys. *Journal of Marriage and the Family, 37*, 526–536.

Winch, R.F. 1949. The relation between loss of a parent and progress in courtship. *Journal of Social Psychology, 29*, 51–56.

Winch, R.F. 1950. Some data bearing on the Oedipus hypothesis. *Journal of Abnormal and Social Psychology, 45*, 481–489.

Wohlford, P., & Liberman, D. 1970. Effects of father absence on personal time, field independence, and anxiety. *Proceedings of the 78th Annual Convention of the American Psychological Association, 5*, 263–264.

Wohlford, P.; Santrock, J.W.; Berger, S.E.; & Liberman, D. 1971. Older brothers' influence on sex-typed, aggressive, and dependent behavior in father-absent children. *Developmental Psychology, 4*, 124–134.

Wolfe, D.A.; Sandler, J.; & Kaufman, K. 1981. A competency-based training program for child abusers. *Journal of Consulting and Clinical Psychology, 49*, 633–640.

Wolins, M. 1983. The gender dilemma in social welfare: Who cares for children? In M.E. Lamb and A. Sagi (Eds.). *Fatherhood and family policy*. Hillsdale, N.J.: Lawrence Erlbaum Associates.

Wolkenstein, A.S. 1976. Evolution of a program for the management of child abuse. *Social Casework, 57*, 309–316.

Wolock, I., & Horowitz, B. 1984. Child maltreatment as a social problem. *American Journal of Orthopsychiatry, 54*, 530–543.

Wood, H.P., & Duffy, E.L. 1966. Psychological factors in alcoholic women. *American Journal of Psychiatry, 123*, 341–345.

Wood, P. 1980. Home for abusive parents. *Practice Digest, 3*, 7–10.

Woolley, P.V., & Evans, W.A. 1955. Significance of skeletal lesions in infants resembling those of traumatic origin. *Journal of the American Medical Association, 158,* 539–543.

Wright, B., & Tuska, S. 1966. The nature and origin of feeling feminine. *British Journal of Social Psychology, 5,* 140–149.

Wusterbarth, N.J., & Strain, P.S. 1980. Effects of adult-mediated attention on the social behavior of physically abused and neglected preschool children. *Education and Treatment of Children, 3,* 91–99.

Wylie, H.L., & Delgado, R.A. 1959. A pattern of mother-son relationship involving the absence of the father. *American Journal of Orthopsychiatry, 29,* 644–649.

Wynn, M. 1969. *Fatherless families.* London: Michael Joseph.

Yarrow, M.R.; Waxler, C.Z.; & Scott, P.M. 1971. Child effects on adult behavior. *Developmental Psychology, 5,* 300–311.

Yates, A. 1981. Narcissistic traits in certain abused children. *American Journal of Orthopsychiatry, 51,* 55–62.

Yogman, M.W. 1981. Development of the father-infant relationship. In H. Fitzgerald, B. Lester, & M.W. Yogman (Eds.), *Theory and research in behavioral pediatrics* (Vol. 1). New York: Plenum Prses.

Yogman, M.W. 1982. Observations on the father-infant relationship. In S.H. Cath, A.R. Gurwitt, & J.M. Ross (Eds.), *Father and child: Developmental and clinical perspectives.* Boston: Little, Brown, pp. 101–122.

Yogman, M.W. 1984. Prepared statement concerning the father-child relationship. In G. Miller et al. (Eds.), *Paternal absence and fathers' roles.* Hearing before the Select Committee on Children, Youth and Families, House of Representatives, 98th Congress, 1st Session. Washington, D.C.: U.S. Government Printing Office.

Yogman, M.W.; Dixon, S.; Tronick, E.; Adamson, L.; Als, H.; & Brazelton, T.B. 1976. Development of infant social interaction with fathers. Paper presented to the Eastern Psychological Association, New York, April.

Yogman, M.W.; Dixon, S.; Tronick, E.; Als, H.; Adamson, L.; Lester, B.; & Brazelton, T.B. 1977. The goals and structure of face-to-face interaction between infants and fathers. Paper presented to the Society for Research in Child Development, New Orleans, March.

Young, L. 1964. *Wednesday's children: A study of child neglect and abuse.* Westport, Conn.: Greenwood Press.

Zalba, S.R. 1966. The abused child: A survey of the problem. *Social Work, 11,* 3–16.

Zaphiris, A.G. 1978. *Incest: The family with two known victims.* Englewood, Colo.: American Humane Association.

Zaslow, M.J.; Pedersen, F.A.; Kramer, E.; & Cain, R.L. 198—. Postpartum depression in new fathers. Paper presented at the meeting of the Society for Research in Child Development, Boston, April.

Zastrow, C. 1981. Self-talk: A rational approach to understanding and treating child abuse. *Social Casework, 62,* 182–185.

Zelazo, P.R.; Kotelchuck, M.; Barber, L.; & David, J. 1977. Fathers and sons: An experimental facilitation of attachment behaviors. Paper presented to the Society for Research in Child Development, New Orleans, March.

Zigler, E. 1980. Controlling child abuse: Do we have the knowledge and/or the will. In G. Gerbner, C.J. Ross, & E. Zigler (Eds.), *Child abuse: An agenda for action.* New York: Oxford University Press.

Zill, N. 1985. *Happy, healthy and insecure: A portrait of middle childhood in the United States.* New York: Cambridge University Press.

Zuckerman, K.; Anbuel, J.P.; & Bandman, R. 1972. Child neglect and abuse: A study of cases evaluated at Columbus Children's Hospital in 1968–69. *Ohio State Medical Journal, 68,* 629–632.

Author Index

Subject Index

About the Authors

Henry Biller is professor of psychology at the University of Rhode Island, where he has taught since 1970. He has previously been a faculty member at the University of Massachusetts and at George Peabody College, Vanderbilt University. He has been affiliated with a variety of human-service settings for children and families, including Emma Pendleton Bradley Hospital (1970–1980), where he was involved in the training of clinical psychology interns. He is currently a consultant for the group home programs at the John E. Fogarty Center, North Providence, Rhode Island. He received the B.A. in 1962 from Brown University and the Ph.D. in 1967 from Duke University. He is a Fellow of the American Psychological Association and is listed in *Who's Who in America*. He is a consulting editor to *Archives of Sexual Behavior* and *Sex Roles*. His numerous publications include chapters in *Annual Progress in Child Psychiatry and Child Development* (Brunner/Mazel, 1971); *The Nebraska Symposium on Motivation* (University of Nebraska Press, 1974); *The International Encyclopedia of Neurology, Psychiatry, Psychoanalysis, and Psychology* (Van Nostrand Reinhold, 1977); and *The Handbook of Developmental Psychology* (Prentice-Hall, 1982). His previous books include *Father, Child, and Sex Role* (Lexington Books, 1971); *Paternal Deprivation* (Lexington Books, 1974); *Father Power*, with Dennis Meredith (McKay, 1974; Doubleday, 1975); *The Other Helpers*, with Michael Gershon (Lexington Books, 1977); and *Parental Death and Psychological Development*, with Ellen Berlinsky (Lexington Books, 1982).

Richard Solomon teaches psychology courses in the Continuing Education Program at the University of Rhode Island, and is co-director of a multidisciplinary group practice, Delta Consultants. He provides consultation to a variety of schools and social service agencies in Rhode Island, Massachusetts, and Connecticut. He received the B.S. in 1975 from Hobart College and the Ph.D. in 1982 from the University of Rhode Island. He is very active in state and national organizations concerned with child abuse and has given numerous presentations and workshops at professional meetings. He is president of the Rhode Island chapter of the National Committee for the Prevention of Child Abuse and is on the Board of Directors of the Blackstone Valley Emergency Shelter for Abused Children. He is a member of the American Psychological Association and the American Orthopsychiatric Association.

DATE DUE

MAY 1 2 1988			
DEC 1 6 1988			
SEP 2 0 1989			
DEC 1 2 1989			
APR 1 7 1990			
APR 1 1991			
OCT 1 7 1991			
NOV 1 6 1991			
NOV 2 1 1991			
OCT 1 4 1994			
AUG 2 0 1997			